HISTORY OF THE JEWS

HISTORY OF THE JEWS

BY

HEINRICH GRAETZ

VOL. I

FROM THE EARLIEST PERIOD TO THE DEATH OF SIMON
THE MACCABEE (135 B. C. E.)

PHILADELPHIA

THE JEWISH PUBLICATION SOCIETY OF AMERICA

5707—1946

60

PRINTED IN THE UNITED STATES OF AMERICA
PRESS OF THE JEWISH PUBLICATION SOCIETY
PHILADELPHIA, PENNA.

PREFACE.

It is a matter of especial satisfaction to me that my work, " The History of the Jews, from the Earliest Times to the Present Day," should be rendered accessible to the English-reading public in a compact form and by means of an adequate translation; for in countries where English is spoken, books are not only bought, bound, and placed in libraries, but are also read, taken to heart, and acted upon. It is therefore to be expected that the English-speaking people, which has never disregarded but has at all times recognised and appreciated the peculiar character of the Jewish race, will feel an increased sympathy for it, on reading the alternations of its sublime and tragical history.

English readers, to whom the forefathers of the Jews of to-day—the patriarchs, heroes, and men of God—are familiar characters, will the better understand the miracle which is exhibited in the history of the Jews during three thousand years. The continuance of the Jewish race until the present day is a marvel not to be overlooked even by those who deny the existence of miracles, and who only see in the most astounding events, both natural and preternatural, the logical results of cause and effect. Here we observe a phenomenon, which has developed and asserted itself in spite of all laws of nature, and we behold a culture which, notwithstanding unspeakable hostility against its exponents, has nevertheless profoundly modified the organism of nations.

It is the heartfelt aspiration of the author that this historical work, in its English garb, may attain its object by putting an end to the hostile bearing against the Jewish race, so that it may no longer be begrudged the peculiar sphere whereto it has been predestined through the events and sorrows of thousands of years, and that it may be permitted to fulfil its appointed mission without molestation.

This translation, in five volumes, is not a mere excerpt of my " Geschichte der Juden " (like my " Volksthümliche Geschichte der Juden "), but a condensed reproduction of the entire eleven volumes. But the foot-notes have been omitted, so as to render the present work less voluminous for the general reader. Historical students are usually acquainted with the German language, and can read the notes in the original.

In this English edition the " History of the Present Day " is brought down to 1870, whilst the original only goes as far as the memorable events of 1848. The last volume will contain a survey of the entire history of the Jewish nation, together with a comprehensive index of names and events.

In conclusion, I cannot refrain from expressing my gratitude to one whose life-task it is to further with rare generosity all humane and intellectual interests, and who has caused this translation to be made and published. At the risk of wounding his modesty, I must mention, as the Mæcenas of this work, Mr. Frederick D. Mocatta, whose name is a household word in every Jewish circle.

H. GRAETZ.

BRESLAU, *January*, 1891.

———

To the foregoing words of the author I merely wish to add, that while the first volume, as far as the period of the Hasmonæans, has been translated by me, the other volumes have for the greater part " been done into English by various hands," and have afterwards been revised and edited by me.

My cordial thanks are due to Mr. Israel Abrahams, whose scholarly co-operation has enabled me to cope with the difficulties presented by Hebrew and Jewish names and technicalities.

BELLA LÖWY.

LONDON, *January*, 1891.

PREFACE TO THE SOCIETY'S EDITION.

———

Owing to necessary revision by the American editors, there has been a delay in the publication of this work beyond the time announced for its appearance.

It is hoped that in the future such delay may be avoided.

THE PUBLICATION COMMITTEE.

June, 1891.

CONTENTS.

CHAPTER I.

THE EARLIEST PERIOD.

CHAPTER II.

OCCUPATION OF THE LAND OF CANAAN.

CHAPTER III.

NEIGHBOURING NATIONS.

CHAPTER IV.

THE JUDGES.

CHAPTER V.

ELI AND SAMUEL.

1100 ?—1067 B. C. E.

CHAPTER VI.

THE APOGEE.

1067—1055 B. C. E.

CHAPTER VII.

DAVID AND ISHBOSHETH.

xii CONTENTS.

CHAPTER XIV.

THE END OF THE KINGDOM OF THE TEN TRIBES, AND THE HOUSE OF DAVID.

CHAPTER XV.

THE LAST KINGS OF JUDAH.

CHAPTER XVI.

END OF THE KINGDOM OF JUDAH.

CHAPTER XX.

THE SOPHERIC AGE.

CHAPTER XXI.

SIMON THE JUST AND HIS DESCENDANTS.

CHAPTER XXII.

THE TYRANNICAL CONVERSION TO HELLENISM AND THE ELEVATION OF THE MACCABEES.

CHAPTER XXIII

VICTORIES AND DEATH OF JUDAS MACCABÆUS; JONATHAN THE HASMONÆAN.

CHAPTER XXIV.

THE JUDÆANS IN ALEXANDRIA AND THE GOVERNMENT OF SIMON.

HISTORY OF THE JEWS

HISTORY OF THE JEWS.

CHAPTER I.

THE EARLIEST PERIOD.

The Original Inhabitants of Canaan—Gigantic Anakim and Rephaim
—The Phœnicians—Israel's Claim to Canaan—The Patriarchs—
Hereditary Law—Emigration to Egypt—Tribal Union—Bright
and Dark Sides of the Egyptians—Moses, Aaron and Miriam
—The Prophetic Sage—Call of Moses as Deliverer—Oppo-
sition—Exodus from Egypt—Passage of the Red Sea—Wan-
derings in the Desert—Revelation on Mount Sinai—The
Decalogue—Relapse—Concessions—Crisis—Circuitous Wander-
ings—Victories over Populations of Canaan, on Trans-Jordanic
Side—Commencements of Hebrew Poetry—Death of Moses.

IT was on a spring day that some pastoral tribes
passed across the Jordan into a strip of land which
can only be regarded as an extended coast-line of
the Mediterranean. This was the land of *Canaan*,
subsequently called *Palestine*. The crossing of the
Jordan and the entry into this territory were destined to become of the utmost importance to mankind. The land of which the shepherd tribes
possessed themselves became the arena of great
events, so enduring and important in their results,
that the country in which they took place became
known as the *Holy Land*. Distant nations had
no conception that the entry of the *Hebrew* or
Israelite tribes into the land of Canaan would
have such momentous consequences. Even the
inhabitants of Palestine were far from recognising
in this invasion an occurrence fraught with vital
significance to themselves.

At the time when the Hebrews occupied this territory it was inhabited by tribes and peoples dissimilar in descent and pursuits. The primary place was held by the aborigines, the *Anakim* and *Rephaim*, a powerful race of giants. Tradition represents them as the descendants of that unruly and overbearing race which, in primæval times, attempted to storm the heavens. For this rebellious attempt they had been doomed to ignominious destruction.

Their reputed descendants, the powerful natives of the country—who by some of the ancient nations were called *Enim*, "terrible men"—were unable to maintain themselves; notwithstanding their imposing figures, they were destroyed by races of inferior stature. The rest were obliged to migrate to the East-Jordanic lands, to the south, and also to the south-west of the West-Jordanic region. This remnant of the *Anakim* filled the Israelite spies with such abject terror that they made the entire nation despair of ever obtaining possession of the country. This gave rise to the proverb, "Who can stand before the children of Anak?" "We were," said the spies, "in our own eyes as grasshoppers, and so we appeared unto them." These giants were eventually overcome by the Israelite dwarfs.

Another group of inhabitants which had settled in the land between the Mediterranean and the Jordan was that of the *Canaanites*, whom the Greeks called Phœnicians. These Phœnicians appear to have pursued the same employment in their new country as they had followed on the banks of the Red Sea or the Persian Gulf. Their chief pursuits were navigation and commerce. The position which they had selected was eminently favourable to their daring expeditions. The great ocean, forming a strait at the Pillars of Hercules, and separating Europe from Africa, as the Mediterranean Sea, has here its extreme limit. At the foot of the snow-topped Lebanon and its spurs, commodious inlets formed natural harbours that required but little improvement at the hand of man. On this seaboard the Canaanites built the town of Sidon, situated on a prominent crag which overhangs the sea. They afterwards built, on a small rocky island, the port of Tyre (Tor, which subsequently became celebrated); they also built Aradus to the north of Sidon, and Akko (Acre) to the south of Tyre. The neighbouring forests of the Lebanon and the Anti-Lebanon supplied them with lofty cedars and strong cypresses for ships. The Canaanites, who became the first mercantile nation in the world, owed much of their success to the advantage of finding on their coast various species of the murex (*Tolaat shani*), from the fluid of which was obtained a most brilliant and widely celebrated purple dye. The beautiful white sand of the river Belus, near Acre, supplied fine glass, an article which was likewise in much request in the Old World. The wealth of the country lay in the sands of the sea-shore. The Canaanites, on account of their extensive trade, required and introduced at an early period a convenient form of writing, and their alphabet, the Phœnician, became the model for the alphabets of ancient and modern nations. In a word, the narrow belt of land between the Mediterranean and Mount Lebanon, with its spurs, became one of the most important points on the face of the globe. Through the peaceful pursuits of commerce the Canaanites were brought into contact with remote nations, who were gradually aroused from a state of inactivity. They became subdivided into the small nationalities of Amorites, Hittites, Hivites, and Perizzites. The Jebusites, who inhabited this district, were of minor importance ; they dwelt on the tract of land which afterwards became the site for the city of Jerusalem. Of still less account were the Girgashites, who had no fixed residence. All these names would have remained unknown had not the Israelites entered the land.

But this people had not taken a footing in the country with the mere object of finding pasture land for their flocks; their pretensions were far greater. Chief of all, they claimed as their patrimony the land where the graves of their forefathers were situated. The first patriarch, Abraham, who had emigrated from Aram, on the borders of the Euphrates, had, after many wanderings through the country, acquired in Hebron, as an hereditary burial-place, the Cave of Machpelah, or the " Double Cave," together with the adjoining field and trees. There his wife Sarah had been interred, then he himself, and after him his son, the patriarch Isaac.

The third patriarch, Jacob, after many vicissitudes and wanderings, had purchased a plot of land near Shechem, and had taken that important city " with his sword and with his bow." The city was in the very heart of the territory of the Hivites, and its capture had taken place in consequence of a breach of peace, through the abduction and dishonour of Jacob's daughter. The land was henceforth regarded as the property of the patriarch, and he only reluctantly quitted it at the outbreak of a famine, in order to proceed to Egypt, where corn was plentiful. On his death-bed, Jacob impressed upon his sons that they should deposit his remains in the family tomb of the " Double Cave." Not alone did Canaan contain the graves of the three patriarchs, but also the altars which they had erected and named in various places, in honour of the Deity whom they worshipped. The Israelites were therefore firmly convinced that they had a right to the exclusive possession of the land.

These claims derived further strength from the tradition left by the patriarchs to their descendants as a sacred bequest, that the Deity, whom they had been the first to recognise, had repeatedly and indubitably, though only in visions, promised them this land as their possession, not merely for the sake of showing them favour, but as the means of attaining to a higher degree of culture. This culture would pre-eminently consist in Abraham's doctrine of a purer belief in the *One God*, whose nature differed essentially from that of the gods whom the various nations represented in the shape of idols and by means of other senseless conceptions. The higher recognition of the Deity was designed to lead Abraham's posterity to the practice of justice towards all men, in contradistinction to the injustice universally prevailing in those days. It was affirmed that this higher culture was ordained by the Almighty as "the way of God," and that as such it should be transmitted by the patriarchs to their families as a bequest and as a subject of hereditary instruction. They also received the promise that through their posterity, as the faithful guardians of this teaching, all nations of the earth should be blessed, and should participate in this intellectual advancement of Israel; and that with this same object the land of Canaan had been allotted to Israel, as especially adapted for the purposes of the hereditary law. Hence it was that the Israelites, while in a foreign country, felt an irrepressible yearning for their ancestral land. Their forefathers had impressed them with the hope that, though some of their generations would sojourn in a land which was not their own, a time would surely come when Israel should return to that land which was the resting-place of their patriarchs, and where the patriarchal altars had been erected and consecrated. This promise became identified with all their positive expectations, and with their conviction that the acquisition of Canaan was secured to them on condition that they performed the duties of worshipping the God of their fathers, and observed the ways of justice and righteousness. The nature of this worship and "the way of justice" was not clearly defined, nor did they require such a definition. The lives of the patriarchs, as commemorated by posterity, served as a sufficient illustration of the family law. Abraham was especially held up as a model of human excellence. Differing from other nations who *worshipped* their primæval ancestors, his descendants did not revere him as a performer of marvellous deeds, nor as one exalted to the eminent degree of a god or a demi-god. Not as a warrior and a conqueror did he live in the memory of his descendants, but as a self-denying, God-fearing man, who joined true simplicity and faith to nobleness in thought and in action. According to their conception, Abraham the Hebrew, although born of idolatrous parents in Aram, on the other side of the Euphrates, and although brought up amidst idolatrous associations, had obeyed the voice which revealed to him a higher God, and had separated himself from those around him. When disputes arose, he did not obstinately insist upon his claims, but renounced his rights for the sake of living at peace with his fellow-men. So hospitable was he, that he would go forth to invite the passing wayfarers, and delighted in entertaining them. He interceded for the sinners of Sodom and the neighbouring cities, when their cruel and inhuman acts had brought on them the punishment of Heaven; and he prayed that they might be spared for the sake of any few righteous men amongst them.

These and other remembrances of his peace-loving and generous disposition, of his self-abnegation, and of his submission to God, were cherished by his descendants, together with the conviction that such a line of conduct was agreeable to the God of their fathers; that for the sake of these virtues God had protected Abraham, as well as his son and his grandson, because the two latter had followed the example of their predecessor. This belief that God especially protects the virtuous, the just, and the good, was fully confirmed in the life of the patriarch Jacob, to whom the additional name ISRAEL was given. His life had been short and toilsome, but the God of his fathers had delivered him from all his sorrows. Such remembrances of ancestral piety were retained by the sons of Israel, and such family traditions served to supplement and illustrate their hereditary law.

The growth of Israel as a distinct race commenced amidst extraordinary circumstances. The beginning of this people bore but very slight resemblance to the origin of other nations. Israel as a people arose amidst peculiar surroundings in the land of Goshen, a territory situated in the extreme north of Egypt, near the borders of Palestine. The Israelites were not at once moulded into a nation, but consisted of twelve loosely connected shepherd tribes.

These tribes led a simple life in the land of Goshen. The elders (*Zekenim*) of the families, who acted as their chiefs, were consulted on all important occasions. They had no supreme chieftain, nor did they owe allegiance to the Egyptian kings; and thus they habitually enjoyed the freedom of a republic, in which each tribal section was enabled to preserve its independence without falling into subjection or serfdom. Although they did not become inter-mixed with the ancient Egyptians, who in fact had an aversion to shepherds—perhaps on account of the oppression they had in former ages endured from such shepherds (the Hyksos)—yet opportunities for contact and mutual communication could not be wanting. Some families of Israel had abandoned their pastoral pursuits, and devoted themselves to agriculture or industrial occupations, and were therefore brought into connection with the inhabitants of towns. It seems that the members of the tribe of Ephraim stood in closer social contact with the original inhabitants. This intercourse had a favourable influence upon the Israelites.

The Egyptians had already gone through a history of a thousand years, and attained to a high degree of culture. Their kings, or Pharaohs, had already built populous cities, and erected colossal edifices, temples, pyramids and mausoleums. Their priests had acquired a certain degree of perfection in such arts and technical accomplishments as were suited to the requirements of the country, as for example, architecture and hydraulic constructions, the kindred science of geometry, the art of medicine, and the mystery of embalming for the perpetual preservation of the remains of the departed; also the artistic working of objects in gold, silver and precious stones, in order to satisfy the luxurious demands of the kings. They also knew the art of sculpture and the use of pigments. They studied chronology, together with astronomy, which was suggested by the periodical overflow of the Nile. The all-important art of writing had been invented and perfected by the Egyptian priests. They first used stones and metals to commemorate the renown of their monarchs; and they afterwards employed the fibre of the papyrus shrub, which was originally marked with clumsy figures and subsequently with ingeniously drawn symbols. Of these several attainments the Israelites seem to have acquired some notion. The members of the destitute tribe of Levi in particular, being unencumbered by pastoral service or by landed possessions, appear to have learnt from the Egyptian priests the art of writing. Owing to their superior knowledge, they were treated by the other tribes as the sacerdotal class, and hence they held, even in Egypt, the privileged distinction of their priestly position.

The residence of the Israelites in Egypt was of great advantage to them. It raised them, or at least a portion of them, from a rude state of nature to a higher grade of culture. But what they gained on the one hand, they lost on the other; and in spite of their arts and accomplishments, they would in time have fallen into a more abject condition. Amongst no people which had advanced beyond the first stage of Fetish worship, had idolatry assumed such a hideous development, or so mischievously tainted the habits, as was the case with the Egyptians. By combining and intermingling the gods of the various districts, they had established a complete system of polytheism. As a matter of course they worshipped goddesses as well as gods. What made the mythology of the Egyptians especially repulsive, was the fact that they placed the deified beings of their adoration, from whom they expected help, far below the level of human beings.

They endowed their gods with the shape of animals, and worshipped the inferior creatures as divine powers. Ammon, their chief god, was represented with ram's horns, the goddess Pecht (Pacht) with a cat's head, and Hathor (Athyr), the goddess of licentiousness, with a cow's head. Osiris, who was worshipped throughout Egypt, was represented in a most loathsome and revolting image, and the universally honoured Isis was often pictured with a cow's head. Animals being scarce in the Nile region, great value was attached to their preservation, and they received divine homage. Such honours were paid to the black bull *Apis* (*Abir*) in Memphis, to the white bull *Mnevis* in Heliopolis, to the lustful goats, to dogs, and especially to cats; also to birds, snakes, and even mice. The killing of a sacred bull or cat was more severely punished than the murder of a human being.

This abominable idolatry was daily witnessed by the Israelites. The consequences of such perversions were sufficiently deplorable. Men who invested their gods with the shape of animals sank down to the level of beasts, and were treated as such by the kings and by persons of the higher castes—the priests and soldiers. Humanity was contemned;

no regard was paid to the freedom of the subjects,
and still less to that of strangers. The Pharaohs
claimed to be descended from the gods, and were
worshipped as such even during their lifetime. The
entire land with its population was owned by them,
it was a mere act of grace on their part that they
granted a portion of the territory to cultivators of
the soil.

Egypt, in fact, was not peopled by an independent
nation, but by bondmen. Hundreds of thousands
were forced to take part in compulsory labour for
the erection of the colossal temples and pyramids.
The Egyptian priests were worthy of such kings and
gods. Cruelly as the Pharaohs harassed their
subjects with hard labour, the priests continued to
declare that the kings were demi-gods. Under the
weight of this oppression the people became devoid
of all human dignity, and submitted to the vilest
bondage without ever attempting to relieve themselves from the galling yoke. The repulsive idolatry
then prevailing in Egypt had yet further pernicious
consequences. The people lost the idea of chastity,
after they had placed the brute creation on an
equality with their deities. Unspeakable offences in
the use of animals had become of daily occurrence,
and entailed neither punishment nor disgrace. The
gods being depicted in unchaste positions, there
appeared to be no need for human beings to be
better than the gods. No example is more conta-
gious and seductive than folly and sin. The Israelites, especially those who were brought into closer
contact with the Egyptians, gradually adopted
idolatrous perversions, and abandoned themselves
to unbridled license. This state of things was
aggravated by a new system of persecution.
During a long period, the Israelites residing in the
Land of Goshen had been left unmolested, they
having been looked upon as roving shepherds who
would not permanently settle in Egypt. But when

decades and even a century had passed by, and they still remained in the land and continued to increase in numbers, the council of the king begrudged them the state of freedom which was denied to the Egyptians themselves. The court now feared that these shepherd tribes, which had become so numerous in Goshen, might assume a warlike attitude towards Egypt. To avoid this danger, the Israelites were declared to be bondmen, and were compelled to perform forced labour. To effect a rapid decrease in their numbers, the king commanded that the male infants of the Israelites should be drowned in the Nile or in some of the canals, and that only the female infants should be spared. The Israelites, formerly free in the land of Goshen, were now kept " in a house of bondage," " in an iron furnace "; here it was to be proved whether they would conform to their hereditary law, or follow strange gods.

The greater part of the tribes could not stand this trial. They had a dim knowledge that the God of their fathers was a being very different from the Egyptian idols; but even this knowledge seemed to decrease from day to day. Love of imitation, sore oppression, and daily misery made them obtuse, and obscured the faint light of their hereditary law. The enslaved labourers did not know what to think of an unseen God who only lived in their memories. Like their masters, the Egyptians, they now lifted their eyes to the visible gods who showed themselves so merciful and propitious to Israel's tormentors. They directed their prayers to the bovine god Apis, whom they called *Abir*,[1] and they also offered to the he-goats.[2] The daughter of Israel, growing up to womanhood, sacrificed her virtue,

---

[1] In Hebrew the word *Abir* means *bull*, *mighty*, and hence *God*. It is connected with the Egyptian *abr* (a bull), from which *Apis* is derived.   Conf. Jeremiah xlvi. 15.

[2] Levit. xvii. 7.   The sending of the scape-goat to Azazel marked the abomination in which this lascivious cult was held.

and abandoned herself to the Egyptians.[1] It was probably thought that, in the images of the grass-eating animal, honour was paid to the god of the patriarchs. When the intellect is on a wrong track, where are the limits for its imaginings? The Israelites would have succumbed to coarse sensual idolatry and to Egyptian vice, like many other nations who had come under the influence of the people of the land of Ham, had not two brothers and their sister— the instruments of a higher Spirit—aroused them and drawn them out of their lethargy. These were MOSES, AARON and MIRIAM.[2] In what did the greatness of this triad consist? What intellectual powers led them to undertake their work of redemption, the elevating and liberating effect of which was intended to extend far beyond their own times? Past ages have left but few characteristic traits of Moses, and barely any of his brother and sister, which could enable us to comprehend, from a human point of view, how their vision rose step by step from the faint dawn of primitive ideas to the bright sunlight of prophetic foresight, and by what means they rendered themselves worthy of their exalted mission. The prophetic trio belonged to that tribe which, through its superior knowledge, was regarded as the sacerdotal tribe, namely, the tribe of Levi. This tribe, or at least this one family, had doubtless preserved the memory of the patriarchs and the belief in the God of their fathers, and had accordingly kept itself aloof from Egyptian idolatry and its abominations.

Thus it was that Aaron, the elder brother, as also Moses and Miriam, had grown up in an atmosphere of greater moral and religious purity. Of Moses the historical records relate that after his birth his mother kept him concealed during three months, to evade the royal command, and protect

[1] Conf. Ezekiel xxiii, 7, 8.
[2] Micah vi. 4, mentions also Miriam, with her brothers, as a deliverer.

him from death in the waters of the Nile. There is no doubt that the youthful Moses was well acquainted with Pharaoh's court at Memphis or Tanis (Zoan). Gifted with an active intellect, he had an opportunity of acquiring the knowledge that was to be learnt in Egypt, and by his personal and intellectual qualities he won the affections of all hearts. But even more than by these qualities, he was distinguished by his gentleness and modesty. "Moses was the meekest of men," is the only praise which the historical records have bestowed upon him. He is not praised for heroism or warlike deeds, but for unselfishness and self-abnegation.

Influenced by the ancient teaching, that the God of Abraham loved righteousness, he must have been repelled by the baseless idolatry of animal worship and by the social and moral wrongs which then were rife. Shameless vice, the bondage of a whole people under kings and priests, the inequality of castes, the treatment of human beings as though they were beasts or inferior to beasts, the spirit of slavery,—all these evils he recognised in their full destructive force, and he perceived that the prevailing debasement had defiled his brethren. Moses was the open antagonist of injustice. It grieved him sorely that Israel's sons were subjected to slavery, and were daily exposed to ill-treatment by the lowest of the Egyptians. One day when he saw an Egyptian unjustly beating a Hebrew, his passion overcame his self-control, and he punished the offender. Fearing discovery, he fled from Egypt into the desert, and halted at an oasis in the neighbourhood of Mount Sinai, where the Kenites, an offshoot of the tribe of Midianites, were dwelling. Here, as in Egypt, he witnessed oppression and wrong-doing, and here also he opposed it with zeal. He gave his aid to feeble shepherdesses. By such action he came into contact with their grateful father, the priest or elder of the tribe of the Midianites, and he married Zipporah, the daughter of that priest.

His employment in Midian was that of a shepherd. He selected fertile grazing plots for the herds of Reuel, his father-in-law, between the Red Sea and the mountain lands. In this solitude the prophetic spirit came upon him.

What is the meaning of this prophetic spirit? Even those who have searched the secrets of the world, or the secrets of the soul in its grasp of the universe, can give only a faint notion and no distinct account of its nature. The inner life of man has depths which have remained inscrutable to the keenest investigator. It is, however, undeniable that the human mind can, without help from the senses, cast a far-seeing glance into the enigmatic concatenation of events and the complex play of forces. By means of an undisclosed faculty of the soul, man has discovered truths which are not within the reach of the senses. The organs of the senses can only confirm or rectify the truths already elicited. They cannot discover them. By means of the truths brought to light by that inexplicable power of the soul, man has learned to know nature and to make its forces subservient to his will. These facts attest that the power of the soul owns properties which go beyond the ken of the senses, and transcend the skilled faculties of human reason. Such properties lift the veil of the dim future, and lead to the discovery of higher truths concerning the moral conduct of man; they are even capable of beholding a something of that mysterious Being who has formed and who maintains the universe and the combined action of all its forces. A soul devoted to mundane matters and to selfishness can never attain to this degree of perfection. But should not a soul which is untouched by selfishness, undisturbed by low desires and passions, unsoiled by profanity and the stains of everyday life,—a soul which is completely merged in the

Deity and in a longing for moral superiority,—should not such a soul be capable of beholding a revelation of religious and moral truths?

During successive centuries of Israel's history there arose pure-minded men, who unquestionably could look far into the future, and who received and imparted revelations concerning God and the holiness of life.   This is an historical fact which will stand any test.   A succession of prophets predicted the future destiny of the Israelites and of other nations, and these predictions have been verified by fulfilment.   These prophets placed the son of Amram as first on the list of men to whom a revelation was vouchsafed, and high above themselves, because his predictions were clearer and more positive.   They recognized in Moses not only the first, but also the greatest of prophets; and they considered their own prophetic spirit as a mere reflection of his mind.   If ever the soul of a mortal was endowed with luminous prophetic foresight, this was the case with the pure, unselfish, and sublime soul of Moses.   In the desert of Sinai, says the ancient record, at the foot of Horeb, where the flock of his father-in-law was grazing, he received the first divine revelation, which agitated his whole being.   Moved and elated—humble, yet confident, Moses returned after this vision to his flock and his home.   He had been changed into another being; he felt himself impelled by the spirit of God to redeem his tribal brethren from bondage, and to educate them for a higher moral life.

Aaron, who had remained in Egypt, likewise had a revelation to meet his brother on Mount Horeb, and to prepare himself jointly with him for the work of redemption.   The task of imbuing the servile spirit of the people with a desire for liberty seemed to them far more difficult than that of inducing Pharaoh to relax his rigor.   Both brothers therefore expected to encounter obstacles and stubborn opposition.   Although both men were already advanced in years, they did not shrink from the magnitude of the undertaking, but armed themselves with prophetic courage, and relied on the support of the God of their fathers. First they turned to the representatives of families and tribes, to the elders of the people, and announced their message that God would take pity on Israel's misery, that He had promised them freedom, and that He would lead them back to the land of their fathers. The elders lent a willing ear to the joyful news; but the masses, who were accustomed to slavery, heard the words with cold indifference. Heavy labour had made them cowardly and distrustful. They did not even desire to abstain from worshipping the Egyptian idols. Every argument fell unheeded on their obtuse minds. " It is better for us to remain enthralled as bondmen to the Egyptians than to die in the desert." Such was the apparently rational answer of the people.

The brothers appeared courageously before the Egyptian king, and demanded, in the name of the God who had sent them, that their people should be released from slavery, for they had come into the country of their own free will, and had preserved their inalienable right to liberty. If the Israelites were at first unwilling to leave the country, and to struggle with the uncertainties of the future, Pharaoh was still less inclined to let them depart. The mere demand that he should liberate hundreds of thousands of slaves who worked in his fields and buildings, and that he should do so in the name of a God whom he knew not, or for the sake of a cause which he did not respect, induced him to double the labours of the Hebrew slaves, in order to deprive them of leisure for thoughts of freedom. Instead of meeting with a joyful reception, Moses and Aaron found themselves overwhelmed with reproaches that through their fault the misery of the unfortunate sufferers had been increased. The King only determined to

give way after he and his country had witnessed
many terrifying and extraordinary phenomena and
plagues, and when he could no longer free himself from the thought that the unknown God was
punishing him for his obstinacy.   In consequence of
successive calamities, the Egyptian king urged the
Israelites to hasten and depart, fearing lest any
delay might bring destruction upon him and his
country.   The Israelites had barely time to supply
themselves with the provisions necessary for their
long and wearisome journey.   Memorable was the
daybreak of the fifteenth of Nisan (March), on which
the enslaved people regained their liberty without
shedding a drop of blood.   They were the first to
whom the great value of liberty was made known,
and since then this priceless treasure, the foundation
of human dignity, has been guarded by them as the
apple of the eye.

Thousands of Israelites, their loins girded, their
staves in their hands, their little ones riding on asses,
and their herds following them, left their villages
and tents, and assembled near the town of Rameses.
Strange tribes who had lived by their side, shepherd
tribes akin to them in race and language, joined
them in their migration.   They all rallied round the
prophet Moses, obeying his words.   He was their
king, although he was free from ambition, and he may
well be called the first promulgator of the doctrine of
equality amongst men.   The duty devolving on him
during this exodus was more difficult to discharge
than his message to the king and to the people of
Israel.   Only few amongst these thousands of newly
liberated slaves could comprehend the great mission
assigned to them.   But the masses followed him
stolidly.   Out of this horde of savages he had to
form a nation; for them he had to conquer a home, and
establish a code of laws, which rendered them capable
of leading a life of rectitude.   In this difficult task,
he could reckon with certainty only on the tribe of

Levi, who shared his sentiments, and assisted him in his arduous duties as a teacher.

Whilst the Egyptians were burying the dead which the plague had suddenly stricken down, the Israelites, the fourth generation of the first immigrants, left Egypt, after a sojourn of several centuries. They journeyed towards the desert which divides Egypt from Canaan, on the same way by which the last patriarch had entered the Nile country. But Moses would not permit them to go by this short route, because he feared that the inhabitants of Canaan, on the coast of the Mediterranean, would oppose their entry with an armed force; he also apprehended that the tribes, whom their long bondage had made timorous, would take to flight on the first approach of danger.

Their first destination was Mount Sinai, where they were to receive those laws and precepts for the practice of which they had been set free. Pharaoh had, however, determined to recapture the slaves who had been snatched from his grasp, when, in a moment of weakness, he had allowed them to depart. When the Israelites saw the Egyptians approaching from afar, they gave way to despair, for they found themselves cut off from every means of escape. Before them was the sea, and behind them the enemy, who would soon overtake them, and undoubtedly reduce them again to bondage. Crying and lamenting, some of them asked Moses, "Are there no graves in Egypt that thou hast brought us out to die in the desert?" However, a means of escape unexpectedly presented itself, and could only be regarded by them as a miracle. A hurricane from the northeast had driven the water of the sea southwards during the night, so that the bed had for the greater part become dry. Their leader quickly seized on this means of escape, and urged the frightened people to hurry towards the opposite shore. His prophetic spirit showed him that they would never again see the Egyptians. They rapidly traversed the short distance across the dry bed of the sea, the deeper parts of the water, agitated by a storm, forming two walls on the right and the left. During this time, the Egyptians were in hot pursuit after the Israelites, in the hope of leading them back to slavery. At daybreak, they reached the west coast of the sea, and, perceiving the Israelites on the other side, they were hastening after them along the dry pathway, when the tempest suddenly ceased. The mountain-like waves, which had risen like walls on both sides, now poured down upon the dry land, and buried men, horses, and chariots in the watery deep. The sea washed some corpses to the coast where the Israelites were resting in safety. They here beheld a marvellous deliverance. The most callous became deeply impressed with this sight, and looked with confidence to the future. On that day they put their firm trust in God and in Moses, His messenger. With a loud voice they sang praises for their wonderful deliverance. In chorus they sang—

"I will praise the Lord,
For He is ever glorious.
The horse and his rider He cast into the sea."

The deliverance from Egypt, the passage through the sea, and the sudden destruction of their resentful enemy were three occurrences which the Israelites had witnessed, and which never passed from their memories. In times of the greatest danger and distress, the recollection of this scene inspired them with courage, and with the assurance that the God who had redeemed them from Egypt, who had turned the water into dry land, and had destroyed their cruel enemy, would never desert them, but would "ever reign over them." Although the multitude did not long retain this trustful and pious disposition, but fell into despondency at every new difficulty, the intelligent portion of the Israelites were, in subsequent trials, sustained by their experiences at the Red Sea.

The tribes, delivered from the bonds of slavery, and from the terrors of long oppression, could peaceably now pursue their way. They had yet many days' journey to Sinai, the temporary goal of their wanderings. Although the country through which they travelled was a sandy desert, it was not wanting in water, and in pasture land for the shepherds. This territory was not unknown to Moses, their leader, who had formerly pastured the flocks of his father-in-law here. In the high mountains of Sinai and its spurs, the water in the spring-time gushes forth copiously from the rocks, forms into rills, and rushes down the slopes towards the Red Sea. Nor did the Israelites suffer through want of bread, for in its stead they partook of manna. Finding this substance in large quantities, and living on it during a long time, they came to consider its presence as a miracle. It is only on this peninsula that drops sweet as honey exude from the high tamarisk trees, which abound in that region. These drops issue in the early morning, and take the globular size of peas or of coriander seeds; but in the heat of the sun they melt away. Elated by their wonderful experiences, the tribes now seemed prepared to receive their holiest treasure, for, the sake of which they had made the long circuitous journey through the desert of Sinai. From Rephidim, which lies on a considerable altitude, they were led upwards to the highest range of the mountain, the summit of which appears to touch the clouds.[1] To this spot Moses led the Israelites in the third month after the exodus from Egypt, and ap-

[1] The situation of Sinai is not to be sought in the so-called Sinaitic peninsula, but near the land of Edom, on the confines of which was the desert of Paran. Neither Jebel Musa, with the adjacent peaks of Jebel Catherine and Ras-es-Sutsafeh, nor Mount Jerbal, was the true Sinai. See "Monatsschrift," by Fränkel-Graetz, 1878, p. 337.

pointed their camping ground. He then prepared them for an astounding phenomenon, which appealed both to the eye and the ear. By prayer and abstinence they were bidden to render themselves fit for lofty impressions, and worthy of their exalted mission. With eager expectation and anxious hearts they awaited the third day. A wall round the nearest mountain summit prevented the people from approaching too close. On the morning of the third day a heavy cloud covered the mountain top; lightning flashed, and enveloped the mountain in a blaze of fire. Peals of thunder shook the surrounding mountains, and awakened the echoes. All nature was in uproar, and the world's end seemed to be at hand. With trembling and shaking, the old and the young beheld this terrifying spectacle. But its terror did not surpass the awfulness of the words heard by the affrighted people. The clouds of smoke, the lightning, the flames and the peals of thunder had only served as a prelude to these portentous words.

Mightily impressed by the sight of the flaming mountain, the people clearly heard the commandments which, simple in their import, and intelligible to every human being, form the elements of all culture. Ten words rang forth from the mountain top. The people became firmly convinced that the words were revealed by God. Theft and bearing false witness were stigmatised as crimes. The voice of Sinai condemned evil thoughts no less than evil acts; hence the prohibition, " Thou shalt not covet thy neighbour's wife . . . nor any possession of thy neighbour." The Indians, the Egyptians, and other nations famous for their colossal structures, had, during more than two thousand years, gone through many historical experiences, which shrink into utter insignificance, when compared with this one momentous event.

The work accomplished at Sinai by an instan-

taneous act remained applicable to all times by
asserting the supremacy of ethical life and the
dignity of man. This promulgation of the Law
marked the natal hour of the "distinct people,"
like unto which none had ever existed. The sublime
and eternal laws of Sinai—coming from a Deity
whom the senses cannot perceive, from a Redeemer
who releases the enthralled and the oppressed—
were revealed truths treating of filial duty, of spotless
chastity, of the inviolable safety of human life and
property, of social integrity, and of the purity of
sentiment.

The Israelites had been led to Mount Sinai as
trembling bondmen ; now they came back to their
tents as God's people of priests, as a righteous
nation (*Jeshurun*). By practically showing that the
Ten Commandments are applicable to all the con-
cerns of life, the Israelites were constituted the
teachers of the human race, and through them all
the families of the earth were to be blessed. None
of the others could then have surmised that even
for its own well-being an isolated and insignificantly
small nation had been charged with the arduous
task of the preceptive office.

The Sinaitic teachings were not of an ephemeral
nature, even in regard to their form. Being engraven on tables of stone, they could be easily
remembered by successive generations. During a
long period these inscribed slabs remained in the
custody of the Israelites, and were called "the
Tables of the Testimony," or "the Tables of the
Law." Being placed in an ark, which became a
rallying centre, round which Moses used to assemble
the elders of the families, these tables served as a
sign of the Sinaitic Covenant. They formed a link
between God and the people who had formerly been
trodden under foot, and who were now bidden to
own no other Lord save the One from whom the Law
had gone forth. It was for this reason that the ark,

as the repository of the tables, was designated " the
Ark of the Covenant." The ethical truths of Sinai
became henceforth the basis for a new system of
morality, and for the national constitution of the
Israelites. These truths were further developed in
special laws which had a practical bearing upon the
public and private affairs of the people. Slave-
holders and slaves were no longer to be found
amongst the Israelites. The selling of Israelites as
slaves, and perpetual servitude of an Israelite became
unlawful. A man who forfeited his liberty was liable
to be held in service during six years, but in the
seventh year he regained his freedom. Wilful murder
and disrespect to parents were punishable with death.
The sanctuary could give no protection to criminals
condemned to die. The murder of a non-Israelitish
slave involved condign punishment. A gentile slave
ill-treated by his master recovered his liberty. A man
committing an offence on the virtue of a maiden was
bound to make her his wife, and to pay a fine to the
father of the injured woman. Equitable and humane
treatment of the widow and the orphan was enforced; a similar provision was ordained for the
benefit of strangers who had joined one of the tribes.
The Israelites, in fact, were bidden remember their
former sojourn in a foreign land, and to refrain from
inflicting upon strangers the inhuman treatment
which they themselves had formerly endured.

This spirit of equity and brotherly love, pervading
the ancient code of laws, could not at once change the
habits of the people. The duties involved in these
laws were too spiritual and too elevated to have such
an effect. Moses having temporarily absented himself to make preparations for the reception of the
Sinaitic law, the dull-witted portion of the people
imagined that their God was abandoning them in
the desert, and they clamoured for the rule of a visible
Godhead. Aaron, who had taken the lead in the
absence of Moses, timorously yielded to this impe-

tuous demand, and countenanced the production of a golden idol. This image of Apis or Mnevis received divine homage from the senseless multitude who danced around it. Moses, on descending from Mount Sinai, ordered the Levites to put to death some thousands of the people. Nothing but the exercise of extreme rigour could have repressed this worship of idols.

With the object of protecting the people from a relapse into idolatry, and of supporting them during their state of transition from barbarism, they were allowed to form a conception of the Deity—though not by means of an image—through some material aid which would appeal to the senses. On Sinai they had beheld flashes of lightning with flames of fire, and from the midst of a burning cloud they had heard the Ten Commandments. An emblem of this phenomenon was now introduced to remind the people of the presence of the Deity as revealed at Sinai. It was ordained that a perpetual fire should be kept alight on a portable altar, and be carried before the tribes during their migrations. Not the Deity Himself, but the revelation of the Deity at Sinai, should thereby be made perceptible to the sense of vision. The performance of sacrificial rites was a further concession to the crude perceptions of the people.

The spiritual religion promulgated at Sinai did not intend sacrifices as the expression of divine adoration, but was meant to inculcate a moral and holy life; the people, however, had not yet risen to this conception, and could only be advanced by means of education and culture. The other ancient nations having found in sacrifices the means of propitiating their deities, the Israelites were permitted to retain the same mode of divine service; but its form was simplified. The altar became an integral part of the sanctuary, in which no image was tolerated. The only objects contained therein were a candelabrum, a table with twelve loaves, symbolising the twelve tribes; and there was also a recess for the Ark of the Covenant. Altar, sanctuary and sacrificial rites required a priesthood. This primæval institution, too, was retained. The Levites, as the most devoted and best informed tribe, were charged with sacerdotal functions, as during the sojourn in Egypt. The priests of Israel, unlike those of the Egyptians, were precluded from holding landed property, as such possessions might have tempted them to misuse their prerogatives and neglect their sacred duties. For this reason it was prescribed that their subsistence should be derived from the offerings made by the people. Collaterally there existed a custom, dating from remote patriarchal ages, which demanded that the first-born son of every family should attend to the performance of sacrificial rites. This prerogative could not be abruptly abolished, and continued for some time alongside of the Levitical priesthood, though both of them stood in the way of the pure Sinaitic teachings. The materialism of the age demanded indulgent concessions, combined with provisions tending to the refinement of popular habits. Only through the aid of the spiritually gifted could the understanding of the subordinate nature of sacrifices be preserved in the consciousness of the people.

During the forty years of their wandering in the desert, the Israelites sought pastures for their flocks within the mountain region and its neighborhood.

During these migrations Moses instructed the people. The older generation gradually passed away. Their descendants, obedient to the teachings of the lawgiver and his disciples, formed a docile, pious, and valiant community, and became proficient in the knowledge of their laws.

Moses now surrounded himself with councillors, who were the chiefs of seventy families. This system became a model for later forms of administration. The Council of Elders participated in important deliberations, and assisted in the management of public business. On the advice of Jethro, his father-in-law, Moses appointed inferior and higher judges, who respectively had under their jurisdiction ten, a hundred, and a thousand families. The people had the right of electing their own judges, whose appointment they then recommended to Moses. These judges were charged to maintain strict impartiality in cases of litigation between members of the tribes of Israel, or between Israelites and strangers. Nor was it within the discretion of the judges to make distinctions between persons of high and low degree. They were also commanded to keep their hands clean from bribes, and to give their verdicts according to the principles of equity, "for justice belongs unto God," and has its source in God himself. Brotherly love, community of interests, equality before the law, equity and mercy were the high ideals which he held before the generations which he had trained. The inculcation of these laws and teachings marked an eventful era in the nation's history. As such it was characterised by the prophets, who called it "the bridal time of the daughter of Israel," and the season of "her espousals, when she went after her God in the land which was not sown."

Israel's wanderings had nearly come to a conclusion and the younger generation was well fitted for the attainment of the object of its settlement. A further sojourn in the desert would have inured the people to habits of restlessness, and might have reduced them for ever to the nomadic condition of the Midianites and the Amalekites. They appear to have made an unsuccessful raid in a northern direction, along the old caravan roads. In a second defeat some of them were captured by their enemies. But this discomfiture was apparently avenged by combatants belonging to the tribe of Judah, who were aided by men of the tribe of Simeon, and by Kenites, with whose assistance they seized several cities.

The other tribes were prepared to effect an entrance into the country by following a circuitous route on the eastern side. This expedition might have been shortened if the Idumeans, who dwelt on the mountain ranges of Seir, had permitted the Israelites to pass through their territory. Apparently the Idumeans were afraid that the invading Israelites would dispossess them of the land, and they therefore sallied forth to obstruct the direct road. Their opposition forced the tribes of Israel to make a long detour round the country of Idumea, and to turn to the east of the mountain ranges of Seir in order to approach Canaan from the opposite side. Not being permitted to attack the Idumeans and the kindred tribes of the Ammonites, the Israelites had to traverse the border of the eastern desert in order to reach the inhabited regions at the source of the Arnon, which flows into the Dead Sea.

Moses now sent conciliatory messages to Sihon, to request that the people might pass through his territory on their way to the Jordan. Sihon refused his consent, and marched an army to the borders of the desert to oppose the advance of the invaders. The Israelites of the new generation, animated with youthful prowess, put themselves in battle array, and routed the hostile troops, whose king they slew at Jahaz.

This victory was of incalculable importance to the Israelites; it strengthened their position and inspired them with self-reliance. They at once took possession of the conquered district, and henceforth abandoned their nomadic life. Whilst the Israelites felt confident of success in conquering the Land of Promise, the Canaanites, on the other hand, were terror-stricken at the defeat of the mighty Sihon. The Israelites could now move about freely, being no longer incommoded by the narrow belt of the desert, nor by the suspicions of unfriendly tribes. Dangers having given way to a

state of security, this sudden change of circumstances aroused in their bosoms virtuous emotions,
together with ignoble passions.

The people of Moab now perceived that their
feeble existence was threatened by their new
neighbours. Balak, their king, felt that he could
not cope with the Israelites in the open field of battle,
and he preferred to employ the arts of Balaam, the
Idumean or Midianite magician, whose maledictions were supposed to have the power of calling
down distress and destruction on an entire people
or on a single individual. Balaam having been struck
with amazement at the sight of Israel's encampment, the intended maledictions were changed on
his lips into blessings. He averred that no " en-
chantment avails against Jacob, and no divination
against Israel," a glorious future having been assured
to that people. But he advised the king to have
recourse to a different charm, which might have a
pernicious effect upon the Israelites, namely, to
beguile them to the vice of profligacy by means
of depraved temple maidens.

Balak accepted this advice. The Israelites, during
their migrations, had lived on friendly terms with
the wandering Midianites, and entertained no suspicions when admitting the latter into their encamp-
ments and tents. Counselled by Balaam and instigated by Balak, many Midianites brought their
wives and daughters into the tents of the Israelites,
who were then invited to join the idolatrous festiv-
ities at the shrine of Baal-Peor. On such occasions
it was the custom for women to sacrifice their
virtue in the tents, and the guerdon of dishonour
was then presented as an oblation to the idols.
Many an Israelite was led into profligacy by these
allurements, and partook of the sacrificial feasts,
two sins which tended to sap the foundation of the
doctrine revealed on Sinai. Unhappily no one in
Israel seemed willing to obey the command of Moses

by checking this outbreak of vice. Phineas, Aaron's grandson, was the only man whose heart revolted against these excesses. Seeing that a Midianite woman entered a tent with a chief of the tribe of Simeon, he stabbed both of them to death; and thus was the raging plague turned away from the people.

On the other hand, there was now witnessed a significant change in Israel. The unexpected and eventful victories had aroused amongst them the melodious power of song, the first indication of that talent, without which no nation can attain to a superior degree of culture. The first songs of the Hebrew muse were those of war and victory. The authors (*môshĕlim*) of warlike hymns rose at once in public estimation, and their productions were preserved in special collections, as for example, in the Book of the Wars of God.

Hebrew poetry, in its early stages, was deficient in depth and elegance, but it had two characteristics which in the course of time were developed to the highest stage of refinement. With regard to form, it exhibited a symmetry in the component parts of each verse (*parallelismus membrorum*). The same train of thought was repeated with appropriate variations in two or even three divisions of the verse. In the treatment of a theme, the muse of early Hebrew poetry displayed a tendency to irony, this being the result of a twofold conception, namely, that of the ideal aspect by the side of antithetic reality.

The Israelites, seeking to arrive at the goal of their wishes and to gain possession of the Land of Promise, could not tarry in the fertile region between the Arnon and the Jabbok. They had to prepare for crossing the Jordan. But now the evil consequences of having triumphed over Sihon and Og became manifest. The tribes of Reuben and Gad announced that they wished to remain in the conquered land, because its verdant pastures were well adapted for their numerous flocks and their herds of cattle and camels. In making such a demand it appeared that these tribes desired to sever their lot from that of their brethren, and to live as independent nomads. Oppressed with this cause of anxiety, Moses reproached them bitterly for their defection, but felt constrained to grant them the conquered land under the condition that a contingent of their combatants should assist the warriors of the brother-tribes, and follow them across the Jordan. This allotment of land to the two tribes caused an unexpected territorial division. The land possessed by these tribes became known as the Trans-Jordanic territory (*Eber ha-Jarden* or *Peraea*). In the process of time this concession proved more injurious than beneficial.

The rest of the tribes were on the eve of crossing the Jordan, when their great leader Moses was removed by death. The thirty days which the Israelites spent in mourning were not an excessive sacrifice. His loss was irreparable, and they felt themselves utterly bereft. Amongst all lawgivers, founders of states, and teachers of mankind, none has equalled Moses. Not only did he, under the most inauspicious circumstances, transform a horde of slaves into a nation, but he imprinted on it the seal of everlasting existence: he breathed into the national body an immortal soul. He held before his people ideals, the acceptance of which was indispensable, since all their weal and woe depended upon the realisation or non-realisation of those ideals. Moses could well declare that he had carried the people as a father carries his child. His patience and his courage had rarely deserted him; his unselfishness, and his meekness of disposition were two prominent qualities, which, together with his clear prophetic vision, eminently fitted him to be the instrument of the Deity. Free from jealousy, he wished that all Israelites might be prophets like himself, and that

God would endue them with His spirit. Moses became at a subsequent epoch the unattainable ideal of a prophet. Succeeding generations were elated by the thought that this brilliant example of humanity had watched the infant state of the people of Israel. Even the death of Moses served as an enduring lesson. In the land of Moab, in the valley facing Mount Peor—which was held sacred by the population of that district—he was quietly entombed, and to this day no one has known the spot where he was buried. It was designed that the Israelites should not deify him, but should be kept from following the idolatrous practice of other nations, who deified their kings, and their men of real or presumed greatness, as also the founders of their religions.

Sad at heart on account of the death of their beloved leader, who was not permitted to conduct them into the Land of Promise, but comforted by the lofty recollections of the redemption from Egyptian bondage, the passage through the sea, and the revelation on Sinai, encouraged also by the victories over Sihon, Og, and the Midianites—the tribes of Israel crossed the Jordan, on a day in the bright spring-time, and were conducted on their journey by Joshua, the faithful disciple of Moses.

CHAPTER II.

OCCUPATION OF THE LAND OF CANAAN.

Joshua's Succession—Passage of the Jordan—Conquest of Jericho—
The Gibeonites—Coalition of Canaanite Cities against the Israelites
—Settlement in the Land—Isolation of the Tribes—Allotments—
The Tribe of Levi—The Ark of the Covenant at Shiloh—Condition
of Canaan at the time of the Conquest—Climate and Fertility—
Intellectual Activity—Poetry of Nature—Remnants of Canaanite
Populations—Death of Joshua.

ON crossing the Jordan and entering Canaan, the
Israelites met with no resistance. Terror had
paralysed the tribes and populations who then held
the land. Nor were they united by any tie which
might have enabled them to oppose the invaders.
Although mention is made of thirty-one kings,
besides those who ruled near the coast-line of the
Mediterranean, these rulers were petty chiefs, who
were independent of each other, and each of them
governed only a single township with the adjoining
district. They remained passive, whilst the Israelites
were encamping near Gilgal, between the Jordan
and Jericho. The fortress of Jericho, exposed
to the first brunt of an attack from the Israelites,
could expect no help from elsewhere, and was
left entirely to its own resources. The tribes of
Israel, on the other hand, were headed by a well-
tried leader; they were united, skilled in warfare,
and eager for conquest.

Joshua, the son of Nun, of the tribe of Ephraim,
was accepted as the rightful successor of the great
Prophet. Moses, having laid his hands upon the
disciple, had endowed him with his spirit. Yet
Joshua was far from being a prophet. Practical in
his aspirations, he was more concerned in affairs of
immediate necessity and utility, than in ideals of the

future. In his early years, when overthrowing the Amalekites near Rephidim, he had given proof of courage and good generalship. His connection with the tribe of Ephraim, the most distinguished amongst the tribes, was likewise of advantage to his position as a commander. The Ephraimites, with their pride and obstinacy, might otherwise have withheld their allegiance. This tribe having yielded obedience to him, the other tribes readily followed the example.

The first place to be attacked was Jericho. This city was situated in an exceedingly fertile mountain district. Here throve the lofty palm tree and the precious balsam shrub. Owing to the proximity of the Dead Sea, the climate of Jericho has, during the greater part of the year, a high temperature, and the fruits of the field ripen earlier there than in the interior of the country. The conquest of Jericho was, therefore, of primary importance; this city was strongly fortified, and its inhabitants, timid under open attack, felt secure only within the precincts of their defences. The walls of Jericho, according to the scriptural narrative, crumbled to pieces at the mighty and far-sounding shouts of Israel's warriors. They entered the city, and, meeting with little resistance, they slew the population, which was enfeebled by depraved habits. After this easy victory the warriors of Israel became impetuous, and they imagined that a small portion of their force was sufficient to reduce Ai, a scantily populated fortress, which lay at a distance of two or three hours' journey to the north. Joshua therefore sent a small detach ment of his men against Ai, but at the first onslaugh; they were repulsed, and many of them were slain on the field of battle. This defeat spread terror among the Israelites, who feared that they were forsaken by God, whilst it gave new courage to the Canaanites. It was only by the entire army's drawing up and employ-ing a stratagem that Joshua succeeded in taking Ai.

Bethel, situated in the vicinity, likewise fell by a ruse into the hands of the Ephraimites. These two mountain fastnesses having been captured, the inhabitants of the adjoining towns and villages became even more faint-hearted. Without awaiting an attack, they abandoned their homes, and fled to the north, the west and the south. The country, being more or less denuded of its inhabitants, was now occupied by the conquerors. The Gibeonites, or Hivites, in the tract of land called Gibeon, freely submitted to Joshua and his people. They agreed that the Israelites should share with them the possession of their territory on the condition that their lives should be spared. Joshua and the elders having agreed to these terms, the compact, according to the practice of that age, was ratified by an oath. In this way the Israelites acquired possession of the whole mountain district from the borders of the great plain to the vicinity of Jerusalem, the subsequent metropolis of Palestine. The borderland of the plain separated the original inhabitants of the north from those of the south, and neither of these populations was willing to render help to the other. The southern Canaanites now became more closely allied. The apprehension that their land might fall an easy prey to the invaders overcame their mutual jealousies and their love of feud; being thus brought into closer union with each other, they ventured to engage in aggressive warfare. Five kings, or rather chiefs of townships, those of Jebus (Jerusalem), Hebron, Jarmuth, Lachish and Eglon, joined together to punish the Gibeonites for submitting to the invaders, for whom they had opened the road, and whom they had helped to new conquests. The Gibeonites, in face of this danger, implored the protection of Joshua, who forthwith led his victorious warriors against the allied troops of the five towns, and inflicted on them a crushing defeat near Gibeon. The beaten army fled many miles towards the west

and the south, and in their flight they were struck
down by a hailstorm.   This day of battle appears to
have been regarded as one of signal triumph, its
achievements were remembered even five hundred
years later, and were commemorated in a martial
song :—

> "Joshua spake:
> 'O Sun, stand thou still near Gibeon,
> And thou, O Moon, near the valley of Ajalon !'
> And the sun stood stiil,
> And the moon remained at rest,
> Until the people had chastised the foes."[1]

The passage of the Jordan, auspicious beyond
expectation, and the rapid succession of victories
were new wonders which could fitly be associated
with those of former days.   They afforded rich
themes for praise, which was not dedicated to the
great deeds of the people, but to the marvellous
working of the Deity.

The victory at Gibeon opened access to the south,
and the Israelites could now freely move their forces
in that direction; but there were still some strongholds in the south which they were unable either to
capture or to keep in subjection.

The principal work—the subjection of the central portion of Canaan—being now accomplished,
the tribes of Israel ceased to form one combined
army, and in this severance they were probably
influenced by the example of the children of
Joseph.   The latter, who were divided into the
tribes of Ephraim and Manasseh, claimed to have
precedence in the ranks of Israel.   This claim may
be traced back, as has already been shown, to
their sojourn in Egypt, and also to the fact that
Joshua, the leader of the Israelites, was descended
from Ephraim.   Hence it was that the children of
Joseph sought to obtain possession of the central
mountain range, which abounded in springs and had

[1] Joshua x. 12, 13.

a very rich soil. Shechem, the ancient town of the Hivites, being situated between Mount Gerizim and Mount Ebal, had a good supply of water on every side, and became the principal city of the land. But the two divisions, Ephraim and Manasseh, were unwilling to content themselves with this desirable district (which was named " Mount Ephraim "). As Joshua was one of their own tribe, they expected from him the favours of a partisan, and that he would yield to all their demands. They alleged, therefore, that the territory allotted to them was insufficient for their numerous families. They desired to possess not only the fine and fertile plain which extended many miles to the north, but also the land, lying beyond, round Mount Tabor; but they did not find Joshua so yielding as they had anticipated. With a touch of irony he told them that, since they were so numerous, they ought to be able to conquer Mount Tabor, in the land of the Perizzites and the Rephaites, and clear away the forest. Disappointed by this reply, they withdrew from the expeditions of the combined tribes, and contented themselves with the extent of territory which had originally been allotted to them. Owing to this withdrawal from the common cause, the other tribes were induced to follow a similar course, and to acquire, independently of each other, the land necessary for their respective settlements. Four tribes fixed their attention upon the north, and four upon the south and the west. The expedition, from which the sons of Joseph had retired, was hazarded by the four tribes of Issachar, Zebulon, Asher, and Naphtali. They descended into the plain of Jezreel, where they left a portion of their settlers. Another portion pushed on to the northern hill regions, which touched the base of the lofty mountain range. These tribes were even less prepared than the children of Joseph for engaging in warfare with the inhabitants of the plain, to whose rapidly moving war-chariots they

could have offered no resistance. The children of
Issachar were satisfied with the pasture land in the
great plain, and they had no desire to throw themselves into fortified cities. The men of this tribe
appear to have placed themselves under the supremacy of the Canaanites, for they loved a peaceful
life, and, as they found the land fertile, they readily
bore the imposition of tribute. Zebulon, the twin
tribe of Issachar, was more active, and appears to
have conquered for itself a safe settlement in the
north of Mount Tabor. The remaining two tribes,
Asher and Naphtali, seem to have met with greater
difficulties in gaining a firm footing among the
neighbouring Canaanite population, who were more
combative and also more closely united. These
warriors concentrated themselves at Hazor, where
Jabin, the local king, ruled over several districts.
This king summoned the inhabitants of the allied
cities to take up arms and destroy the invading
Israelites. The tribes of Asher and Naphtali, unable
to cope with the enemy, hastened to invoke Joshua's
assistance. At that time mutual sympathy was still
keen among the tribes, and Joshua found them ready
to bring speedy relief to their brethren in the north.
With these auxiliaries, and with the men of Asher
and Naphtali, Joshua surprised the Canaanites, who
were allied under King Jabin, near Lake Merom,
defeated them, and put the remainder to flight.
This was the second great victory he gained over
the allied enemies. Through the battle of Merom,
the two tribes succeeded in firmly establishing themselves in the region situated on the west side of the
upper course of the Jordan and the east side of the
Mediterranean Sea. Asher and Naphtali, being
settled at the extreme north, occupied the position
of outposts, the former being placed at the west,
and the other at the east, of the plateau.

At the same time four other tribes acquired their
settiements in the south; and they relied upon their

own efforts unaided by the entire army of the people. The small tribe of Benjamin, more closely connected with the children of Joseph, was probably assisted by the latter in obtaining a narrow and not very fertile strip of land near the southern frontier line. This was the district of the Gibeonites, with some additions on the east and the west.

The Canaanites, who dwelt in the western plain towards the seaboard, also had iron chariots, on which account the Israelites did not venture to attack them soon after their invasion. Still there was no alternative for the rest of the tribes, but to seek their homes in the western region. Judah was the most numerous and the mightiest of these tribes, and was joined by the children of Simeon, who subordinated themselves like vassals to a ruling tribe.

At the southern extremity, near the desert, the Kenites, kinsmen and allies of the Israelites, had been domiciled since the days of Israel's wandering through the wilderness. By the friendly aid of this people the Judeans hoped to succeed more easily in gaining new dwelling-places. They avoided a war with the Jebusites, with whom possibly they had made a compact of peace, and spared the territory in which Jerusalem, the subsequent capital, was situated.

The first place they captured was the ancient town of Hebron, where Caleb distinguished himself by his bravery. Hebron became the chief city of the tribe of Judah. Kirjath-Sepher, or Debir, was taken by Othniel, Caleb's half-brother. Other leaders of this tribe continued the conquest of various other cities. In the earlier days, the tribe of Judah seems to have lived on friendly terms with the original inhabitants of the land and to have dwelt peaceably by their side. The extensive settlement of Judah was better suited for pasture than for agriculture. The new settlers and the old inhabitants had therefore no inducements for displacing each other, or for in-

dulging in a deadly strife.   The large tract of land
was parcelled out into small plots, and the Canaanites
and the Amalekites retained their homesteads.

The tribe of Simeon had no independent possessions, not even a single town which it could claim as
its own, and was altogether merged in the tribe of
Judah. The Simeonites dwelt in towns of Judah,
without, however, having a voice in the deliberations
of the tribe. The scantiest provision seems to have
been made for the tribe of Dan, the number of families belonging to this tribe being apparently very
small. Nor does it appear to have received such
aid from a brother tribe as was given to Issachar and
to Simeon. The Danites seem to have been followers of the tribe of Ephraim. This tribe selfishly
allowed the Danites to acquire an insecure portion
in the south-west of its own territory, or, rather, a
small portion in the land of the Benjamites. It now
devolved upon the Danites to conquer for themselves the land on the plain of Saron, which extends
towards the sea, and to establish themselves there.
The Amorites, however, prevented them from accomplishing this design, and forced them to retreat
into the mountains; but here the sons of Ephraim
and the Benjamites refused them the possession of
permanent dwelling-places. The Danites were
therefore during a long time compelled to lead a
camp-life, and at last one section of this tribe had to
go in search of a settlement far away to the north.

The conquest of Canaan had proceeded with such
rapidity as to impress the contemporaries and the
posterity of the people with the opinion that this
success was the work of a miracle. Not quite half
a century before the Israelites had been scared
away from the borders of Palestine, after the spies
had spread the report that the inhabitants of the
land were too strong to be vanquished. The same
inhabitants were now in such dread of the Israelites
as to abandon their possessions without attempting

to make any resistance, or if they did take up a defensive position they were easily routed. On this account the conviction gained ground amongst the Israelites that the Deity Himself had led the warriors, and had scattered their opponents in utter confusion. This great conquest became, therefore, the natural theme of spirited poetry.

Although insufficient portions had been allotted to a few of the tribes, such as the Simeonites and the Danites, they still owned some lands which might afford a partial subsistence, and become the nucleus for a further extension of property. The Levites alone had been left altogether unprovided with landed possessions. This was done in strict conformity with the injunctions of Moses, lest the tribe of priests, by misusing its rights of birth, should become affluent agriculturists, and be drawn away from their holy avocations by the desire of enriching themselves—like the Egyptian priests, who, under the pretext of defending the interest of religion, despoiled the people of its property, and formed a plutocratic caste.

The Levites were to remain poor and content themselves with the grants made to them by the owners of lands and herds, they being required to devote all their attention to the sanctuary and the divine law.

During Joshua's rule the camp of Gilgal, between the Jordan and Jericho, was the centre of divine worship and of the Levitical encampment; here also the tabernacle of the covenant had been erected, and sacrifices were offered up. But Gilgal could not permanently serve as the place for assembling the people, for it lay in an unproductive and unfrequented district. As soon as the affairs of the people were more consolidated, and after the Trans-Jordanic warriors had returned to their homes another locality had to be selected for the sanctuary. As a matter of course, it was expedient that the sacred place should be situated within the confines of Ephraim. Joshua likewise had his seat amongst the Ephraimites, namely at Timnath-Serah, a town which that tribe had gratefully allotted to him.

Shiloh (Salem) was chosen as the spot for the establishment of the sanctuary. When the ark of the covenant arrived there, an altar was, as a matter of course, erected by its side. Here the public assemblies were held, if not by all the tribes, certainly by those of Ephraim, Manasseh and Benjamin. Phineas, the high priest of the house of Aaron, and the priests who succeeded him in office, took up their abode in Shiloh. It is highly probable that many of the Levites resided in that town whilst others were dispersed throughout the towns of the several tribes; but on the whole they led a wandering life.

Through the immigration of the Israelites, the land of Canaan not only received a new name, but assumed a different character. It became a "Holy Land," "the Heritage of God," and was regarded as favourable to the people's destination of leading a holy life.

Foreign countries, contrasted with Palestine, appeared to them to be profane, and utterly unadapted for perpetuating the devout worship of the One Spiritual God, or for enforcing the observance of His law. The Holy Land was imagined to be sensible of the pious or of the wicked conduct of its inhabitants. There were three iniquities which the land was supposed to spurn as the most heinous. These were murder, licentiousness, and idolatry. The conviction was general that on account of such misdeeds the land had cast out its former inhabitants, and that it would not retain the Israelites if they indulged in similar crimes. These ideas took deep root amongst the people of Israel, and they regarded Palestine as surpassing, in its precious qualities,

every other country. It was, indeed, an undeniable
fact that the Land of Israel (so it was named from
the time when this people took possession of it)
had striking distinctions, which were unequalled
in any other portion of the globe. Within the small
expanse of territory, one hundred and fifty miles by
sixty, if the Trans-Jordanic region be included, contrasting peculiarities are crowded together, which
give a marvellous character to that country. The
perpetual snow-tops of Lebanon and Hermon in
the north overlook the ranges of mountains and
valleys far away to the sandy desert in the south,
where scorching heat, like that of tropical Africa,
burns up all vegetation. In close proximity to each
other, trees of various kinds are found to thrive,
which elsewhere are separated by great distances.
Here is the slender palm tree, which shoots up
only under a high temperature, and there grows
the oak tree, which cannot endure such heat.
If the heat of the south fires the blood, and fills
man with violent passions, the wind sweeping over
northern snow-fields, on the other hand, renders
him calm, thoughtful, and deliberate.

On two sides Palestine is bordered by water. The
Mediterranean Sea, extending along the western
margin of the land, forms inlets for ships. Along
the eastern boundary flows the Jordan, which takes
its rise in the slopes of Mount Hermon, and runs in
nearly a straight line from north to south. In the
north the Jordan flows through the "Lake of the
Harp" (*Kinnereth*, *Genesareth*, or Lake of Tiberias),
and in the south this river is lost in the wonderful
"Salt Sea."   These two basins form likewise a
strange contrast. The "Lake of the Harp" (also
"Lake of Galilee") contains sweet water. In its
depths fishes of various kinds disport themselves.
On its fertile banks, the vine, the palm, the fig-tree,
and other fruit-bearing trees are found to thrive.
In the high temperature of this region, fruits arrive

at their maturity a month earlier than on the mountain land. The Salt Sea or "The Sea of the Deep Basin" (*arabah*) produces a contrary effect, and has rightly been called the Dead Sea. In its waters no vertebrate animals can exist. The excessive quantities of salt, together with magnesia, and masses of asphalt contained in that sea, kill every living object. The atmosphere of this region is likewise impregnated with salt, and, as the adjacent land is covered with lime-pits, it forms a dreary desert. The oval-shaped border of the Dead Sea rises, in some parts, to a height of more than 1,300 feet above the water level, and being totally bare and barren, the entire district presents a most dismal aspect.

Between the water-line and the mountain walls there are, however, some oases in which the balsam shrub thrives, and which, in regard to fertility, are not inferior to any spot on earth. Being situated near the centre of the western seaboard, this strip of land is exceedingly fruitful. But luxuriant as the vegetation of this place is, it is even surpassed by that of the oasis on the south-east corner of the Dead Sea. Here stood at one time the town of Zoar, which was noted as the city of palm-trees (Tamarah). This locality likewise favoured in former ages the growth of the balsam shrub. At a distance of five miles to the north-east, near the town of Beth-Haran, the famous balm of Gilead was found; but by the side of the Dead Sea miasmatic salt-marshes extend for a length of several miles. The shores of this sea and also of the sea of Galilee send forth thermal springs impregnated with sulphur, and these serve to cure various maladies.

The essentially mountainous configuration of Palestine was of great benefit to the Israelites. Two long and imposing mountain ranges, separated by a deep valley, raise their heads in the north, like two snow-capped giants. One of them is Mount Lebanon, the tallest peak of which has a height of more than 10,000 feet, and is named *Dhor el-Khedib*. The other mountain is Hermon (the Anti-Lebanon), the highest point of which, *the Sheikh*, has an elevation of 9,300 feet. The Lebanon was never included in the land of Israel; it remained in the possession of the Phœnicians, the Aramæans, and the people who succeeded the latter. This mountain range was of practical utility to the Israelites, who derived from its celebrated cedar forests the material for their edifices. Besides this, its lofty and odoriferous crests formed a favourite theme in the imagery of the Hebrew poets. Mount Hermon, with its snow-covered head, touches the north side of the ancient territory of Israel. This mountain, if not hidden by intervening hills, forms a charming object of admiration even at a distance of a hundred miles.

The spurs of these two ranges were continued in the northern mountains of Israel (Mount Naphtali, subsequently named the mountains of Galilee), the highest peak of which rises to 4,000 feet. These heights have a gradual slope towards the great and fertile plain of Jezreel, which is only 500 feet above the level of the sea. Several mountain ranges intersect this plain and divide it into smaller plains. Mount Tabor (1,865 feet high) is not so much distinguished for its height as for its cupola shape. Mount Moreh (1,830 feet), now called *Ed-Duhy*, seems to lean against Mount Tabor. Not far from there, somewhat towards the east, run the hill-tops of Gilboa (2,000 feet). On the west side of the great plain lies the extensive tree-crested range of Carmel, which forms a wall close to the sea. The great plain of Jezreel has the shape of an irregular triangle, with a length of twenty miles from north to south, and a breadth of from six to fifteen miles from east to west, having the mountain border of Carmel on the one side and that of Gilboa on the other. This plain divides the land into two unequal parts. The northern half, which is the smaller, received at a later time the name of Galilee. On the south of this plain, the ground gradually rises, and, at one point, attains an elevation of 2,000 feet. This district was called Mount Ephraim. From Jerusalem, southwards to Hebron, the land again ascends to a height of 3,000 feet, forming the land of Judah. Here there is a gradual descent, and at the old frontier town of Beersheba the level does not rise above 700 feet. At this point begins the table-land of Mount Paran. This district was not included in the actual territory of Israel. Both Mount Ephraim and Mount Judah have a slope from east to west. Between the mountain-side and the Mediterranean Sea, from north to south, that is, from Carmel to the southern steppe, extends a plain of increasing breadth, which is called "the Plain of Sharon," or the "low country" (*shefelah*). In the east the mountain declines towards the Jordan. Some peaks of this mountain acquired a special significance. Such were the two hills by the side of Shechem, *Gerizim*, "the mountain of the blessing" (2,650 feet), and *Ebal*, "the mountain of the curse" (2,700 feet); *Bethel*, in the east (2,400 feet); *Mizpeh*, some hours' journey from the subsequent capital; *Mount Zion* (2,610 feet); and the *Mount of Olives* (2,700 feet). This peculiar and greatly varied configuration of the land had its effect not only upon the productions of the soil, but also upon the character of the people. From north to south, Palestine is divided into three belts. The broad mountainous tract occupies the centre; the low land (*shefelah*) extends from the west to the sea, and the meadows (*kikkar, araboth*) from the east to the Jordan. In the lowland the climate is mild; in the mountains, it is severe during the rainy season, but temperate in the summer. In the district of the Jordan the heat continues during the greater part of the year.

With the exception of the Jordan, the land has no rivers which retain their waters throughout the year; but even this river, owing to its precipitous course, is not navigable. The Jordan rises from three sources in the slopes of Hermon. At first it runs sluggishly, and before entering the Lake of Merom it divides into small streams. On emerging from the lake, its waters are united in a narrow basalt bed, and flow into the Lake of Galilee. On issuing thence, the Jordan widens, rushes over rocks, and, after forming many rapids in its swift course, empties itself and disappears in the Dead Sea. During spring-time, when the melting snow of Hermon swells the waters, this river fertilises the adjoining low-lying plains, especially those on its eastern bank.

The other streams, including the Jarmuk and Jabbok, become dry in the hot summer season. Such winter streams (*nechalim*), nevertheless, enhance the productiveness of the district through which they flow, and the cultivated lands are situated on the banks of these intermittent streams. The fertility of the soil is also favoured by the small springs which flow down the hills without being collected into rivulets. The districts devoid of springs are supplied with drinking-water by the rain, which is gathered in cisterns excavated in the rocks.

The greater portion of Palestine is blessed with an abundant yield of produce. This is due to the nature of the soil, and to the copious drainage from the highlands of Lebanon, Hermon (Anti-Lebanon), with their spurs, as well as to the rain which falls twice a year. The land flowed "with milk and honey," and has retained this characteristic even to the present day, wherever the industry of man is active. It is decidedly a beautiful land "of brooks of water, of fountains and depths that spring out of valleys and hills; a land of wheat, and barley, and vines, and fig-trees, and pomegranates; a land of the oil-olive, and

of honey; a land wherein thou shalt eat bread without
scarceness, thou shalt not want anything in it; a
land whose stones are iron, and out of whose hills
thou mayest dig brass."[1] The plains are especially
fruitful, and yield to the laborious cultivator two
crops a year. But also the land lying to the
north of the plain of Jezreel is by no means sterile.
In olden times it had such an abundance of olive
trees as to give rise to the saying that the husband-
man " dips his foot in oil."

The central district to the south of the great plain,
which belonged to Ephraim and Manasseh, rewarded
its toilers with rich harvests. On all sides springs
gush forth from the rocky fissures; and as their
waters gather together, they attain sufficient force to
drive the mills, besides supplying the soil with
ample moisture. The land of the sons of Joseph
was blessed,

> " With the fruit of the heavens above,
> And of the deep that coucheth beneath ;
> And with precious fruit brought forth by the sun,
> And with the precious things put forth by the moon."[2]

The hill-sides were adorned with blooming gardens,
and with vineyards exuberantly laden with grapes.
The mountains, overshadowed by forests of terebinths, oaks and yew trees, favoured the fertility of
the valleys.

In favourable situations the palm-tree produced a
superabundance of sweet fruit, the juicy contents of
which sometimes even trickled to the ground.
There was less fruitfulness in the southern tracts,
owing to the numerous chalk hills and the small
number of valleys. But even here good pastures
were found for the herds. Below Hebron the
extreme south, with its barren rocks and strips of
sand, presents a dreary aspect. The burning wind,
in its passage over the desert, dries the atmosphere,

[1] Deut. viii. 7–9.   [2] Deut. xxxiii. 13, 14.

and impoverishes the soil. This district was therefore rightly termed *Negeb*, " the arid land." A few oases, which are found here and there, owed their verdure to the presence of water, which counteracted the effect of the scorching heat. In such humid places the vegetation became exceedingly luxuriant under the care of diligent cultivators. To the idler this land yielded no produce.

The climate was made salubrious by the sea breezes and the free currents of mountain air, the inhabitants being, therefore, of a sturdy frame. Here were no miasmatic swamps to poison the atmosphere. Diseases and the ravages of plagues are to this day of rare occurrence, and only caused by infections imported from elsewhere. Compared with the vast dominions of the ancient world, Palestine is extremely small. From some lofty central points one can, at the same time, survey the eastern and the western frontiers, the waves of the Mediterranean and the surface of the Dead Sea, together with the Jordan, and the opposite mountains of Gilead. A view from Mount Hermon is still more commanding, and presents beautiful and extremely diversified landscapes. Throughout the greater part of the year the air is so exceedingly pure and transparent as to afford a delusive conception of the distance between the eye and the surrounding scenery. Even remote objects appear to be placed within close proximity.

Sensitive hearts and reflecting minds may well be said to perceive " the finger of God " in this region, where " Tabor and Hermon praise His name." Lofty peaks and undulating crests of mountains are seen in alternation with verdant plains, and their images are reflected upon the glittering surface of many waters. These towering heights, far from overburdening and depressing the mind, draw it away from the din of the noisy world, and call forth cheering and elevating emotions.

If the beholder be endowed with the slightest

spark of poetic sentiment, it is brought into life and action by the attractive sight of this panorama. From the varied charms of scenic beauty the most gifted men of this land drew their inspiration for their pensive poetry. Neither the Greeks nor the Romans had a conception of this species of poesy, which has its root in a deep consciousness of the greatness of the Creator. Nations of a later epoch became adepts in this poetry only by being the disciples of Israel. Whilst the eye surveyed, from a prominent standpoint, the objects encircled by an extensive horizon, the soul was impressed with the sublime idea of infinitude—an idea which, without such aid, could only be indirectly and artificially conveyed to the intellectual faculties. Single-hearted and single-minded men, in the midst of such surroundings, became imbued with a perception of the grandeur and infinity of the Godhead, whose guiding power the people of Israel acknowledged in the early stages of their history. They recognised the existence of the same power in the ceaseless agitation of the apparently boundless ocean; in the periodical return and withdrawal of fertilising showers; in the dew which descended from the heights into the valleys; in the daily wonders of nature hidden from human sight where the horizon is narrow, but inviting admiration and devotion where the range of view is wide and open.

> " He that formeth the mountains and createth the winds,
> He who turneth the morning into darkness,
> Who treadeth upon the high places of the earth,
> The Lord, the God of hosts is his name."[1]

At a later period the religious conviction gained ground that God's omnipotence is equally manifested in ordaining the events of history as in regulating the succession of physical phenomena; that the same God who ordained the unchanging laws of nature,

[1] Amos iv. 13.

reveals himself in the rise and fall of nations. This conviction is a specific product of the Israelitish mind. Historical vicissitudes and natural surroundings conspired to sharpen its faculties for everything extraordinary and marvellous within the sphere of existing things.

The land of Gilead had the same characteristics that appertained to the region on the other side of the Jordan. This district, originally owned by the Amorites, and by the kings of Sihon and Og, was now held by the sons of Reuben and Gad. From the summits of this territory also immense tracts of land were visible at a single view; but nothing beyond a mere blue streak could be seen of the distant ocean. This side of the Jordan was, therefore, less than the opposite side, endowed with poetic suggestiveness. The land of Gilead gave birth to no poet, it was the home of only one prophet, and his disposition was marked by a fierceness which accorded well with the rude and rough character of the territory in which he was born. The Jordan formed both a geographical and an intellectual landmark.

At the time of Israel's conquests, Canaan was dotted with cities and fortified places, in which the invaders found some rudiments of civic culture. Gilead, on the other hand, contained but few towns, and these lay far apart from each other.

The territories to the west of the Jordan had only partially been subjected and allotted. Large and important tracts of land were still in possession of the original inhabitants, but it can no longer be determined whether it was through the remissness of Joshua that the land of Canaan was not completely conquered. In his advanced years, Joshua did not display such vigour of action as was shown by his teacher, Moses. Gradually he appears to have lost the energy that is necessary in a commander. His followers of the tribes of Ephraim and

Manasseh had already obtained the most productive part of the land; they were now resting on their laurels, and damped the warlike impetus of their brethren. The excitements of the early warfare having subsided, each of the tribes, or groups of tribes was concerned only with its individual affairs. This isolation prevented the several tribes from rounding off their territories by conquests from the original inhabitants of Canaan.

The Canaanites had, even before the invasion by the Israelites, been in possession of sacrificial altars and places for pilgrimage, with which myths calculated to satisfy the uncultured mind were connected. The high mountains, bordered by pleasant valleys, had been invested with sacred attributes. Mount Carmel had long been looked upon as a holy spot, whence the heathen priests announced their oracles. Mount Tabor was likewise regarded as holy. At the foot of Hermon, in a fine fertile valley, there stood a sanctuary dedicated to Baal Gad or Baal Hermon. After the conquest, these shrines were probably, in the first instance, visited only by the strangers who had cast their lot with the Israelites; but their example was soon followed by the ignorant portion of their Hebrew companions. In the interior of the country, where the people could not discriminate between paganism and the divine law of Israel, and still remembered the Egyptian superstitions, they were prone to join in the sacrificial rites of the pagan idolaters. The north, beyond Mount Tabor, likewise contained groups of the Canaanite population. The Danites, whose neglected treatment has already been noticed, were stationed in the centre of the Amorites. Their tenure of land was insignificant in extent. The tribes of Judah and Simeon were completely cut off from the other tribes. They were placed among pagans, whose occupations were divided between those of the shepherd and the freebooter. The Jebusites formed a barrier between the two southern tribes and their northern brethren. This division between the tribes was only removed after the conquest of Jebus (the city subsequently named Jerusalem). If Joshua in his declining years beheld with satisfaction the realisation of the Patriarchal promises, this satisfaction was not without its alloy. As in the lives of individuals, so in the lives of nations, the practical turn of events is liable to disappoint all anticipations. It is true the land of Canaan now belonged to the Israelites; but their conquests were of a precarious nature, and might again be wrested from them by a combined attack on the part of the dispossessed natives. The closing days of Joshua's life were therefore troubled by the consideration of this dangerous contingency, and by the fact that he had no successor whom the several tribes, especially the tribe of Ephraim, might be willing to follow. His death left the people in a state of utter bereavement, but, it seems, it failed even to understand the gravity of the national loss. No such grief took hold of them as was evinced at the death of their first leader. Yet there remained one ideal which Joshua bequeathed to the people, the prospect and the expectation that at some future time the entire land would become their undivided property. Hopes, to which a people clings persistently, carry within themselves the chances of fulfilment. Severe trials continued, however, to await them before the ideal of an undivided possession of Canaan could be fully realised.

CHAPTER III.

NEIGHBOURING NATIONS.

The Phœnicians, Aramæans, Philistines, Idumæans—Their Customs
and Mythology—The Moabites and Ammonites—Intercourse of
the Israelites with their Neighbours and Adoption of their
Manners—Disintegration of the Tribes—Consequent Weakness—
Temporary Deliverers.

THE sons of Israel, who had been severely tried
in Egypt, seemed destined to undergo trials still
more severe. Their new scene of activity was surrounded by various nations, and they could have
escaped the influences of their surroundings only
by either destroying the homes of the bordering
populations, or by being proof against the strongest
temptations. The neighbouring Phœnicians, Canaanites, Aramæans, Philistines, Idumæans, Moabites,
Ammonites, Amalekites, Arabs and half-castes of
Arabs, had their own peculiar customs, manners,
and religious observances. The tribes came into
more or less close contact with their neighbours,
and were soon dominated by the same law of
attraction and assimilation that is felt even in
more cultured spheres. Hence arose the strange
phenomenon, during a prolonged period of Israel's
history, of a nation's forfeiting every species of self-
dependence, regaining it, again relapsing, and thus
passing from change to change.

But these changes eventually gave shape and tena-
city to the character of the people. In the interim,
however, Israel became intimately united with the
Phœnicians; the northern tribes of Asher, Zebulon
and Issachar stood in especially close connection
with them. This people had already, particularly in
Sidon, attained a high degree of culture, when the

Israelites entered Canaan. But, from an ethical and a religious point of view, they were as backward as the most uncultured races of men, with the exception, perhaps, of the Egyptians, than whom they were on a higher level.

The Canaanites worshipped the male and female divinities, Baal and Astarte, who, in some cities, were designated by the names of Adonis and Baaltis. Baal was intended to be a personification of the sun, and Astarte of the moon; they did not, however, figure as luminous beings within the celestial space, but as the procreative powers of nature. The Canaanites also worshipped the then known seven planets termed *Cabiri, i. e.* the Mighty; as an eighth god they adored Ashmun, the restorer of health, who was depicted as a serpent. The rites, by which men and women dedicated themselves to the male and female deities, were of a loathsome description. The degraded priestesses of the temple were termed "consecrated women" (*Kedeshoth*).

In honour of Astarte, half-frantic youths and men mutilated themselves, and wore female attire. They then wandered about as beggars, collecting aid for their sanctuary, or rather for their priests, and were called "holy men" (*Kedeshim*). Such proceedings formed a main part of the religious discipline among the Phœnicians, and their abominations were constantly displayed before the Israelites.

The southern tribes, on the other hand, maintained friendly relations with the Philistines. This people had emigrated from Caphtor (Cydonia), a town on the island of Crete, and their territory had three ports—Gaza in the south, Ashdod (Azotus) in the north, and Ascalon, midway between these two towns. In the interior, the Philistines occupied the cities of Gath and Ekron. This group of five cities (Pentapolis) formed a small district, extending as far as the Egyptian frontier, and its population acquired much power and influence.   On this account, the Greeks and the Egyptians designated the entire country by the name of Palestine (*i. e.*, land of the Philistines). Most probably the Philistines were seafarers and merchants like the Phœnicians.   With these occupations, however, they combined the lust of conquest, whilst the Phœnicians, on the contrary, confined themselves to peaceful pursuits.

The Philistines, having a narrow seaboard, were induced to seek territorial extension on the eastern side.   The religious system of this people was essentially similar to that of the other Canaanites, and agreed, in fact, with that of the different nations of antiquity.   They reverenced the procreative power of nature under the name of Dagon.   This deity was depicted in a form half human, half piscine.

The Philistines had numerous soothsayers, wizards, and cloud-seers (*Meonenim*), who predicted future events from various auguries.

With the Idumæans, the Israelites had less intercourse.   The territory of the former extended from Mount Seir to the Gulf of the Red Sea.   It is thought that at a remote time they navigated this sea, and traded with Arabia.   Their mountains contained metals, including gold.   The Idumæans had the reputation of being sagacious and practical.   In early ages they were governed by kings, who apparently were elective.   On the north side of the Idumæans, to the east of the Dead Sea, the Moabites and the Ammonites were neighbours of the tribes of Reuben and Gad.   Their lascivious idolatry was also dedicated to a Baal on Mount Peor. Among the Ammonites, Baal was called Milcom or Malcom.   Besides this deity, the god Chemosh was worshipped by these two nations.   Amidst such surroundings, the Israelites could not well preserve their own political independence, and much less their spiritual peculiarity;   nor could they keep midway between isolation and social intercourse among populations akin to them in language and descent.

From the first, the Israelites had as many antagonists as neighbours. These, it is true, had no conception that Israel's doctrines tended to effect the destruction of their gods, altars, and sacred groves —the abolition, in fact, of senseless idolatry. Nor were they able to discriminate between their own gross materialism and the lofty, hidden aims of the invading Israelites. The old inhabitants simply abhorred the new-comers, who had entered with drawn swords to deprive them of their territories. In dealing with overt or secret enemies, the Israelites had only the choice between resorting to exterminating warfare or making amicable concessions. Warfare on a large scale was not even practicable; since Joshua's death, they had no accredited leader, and no plan for concerted action. They certainly did not seem to desire more than to live on neighbourly terms with the adjoining populations. This temporary truce might easily satisfy the Canaanites and Phœnicians, who were mainly concerned in keeping the high-roads open for commercial dealings. The Idumæans, the Philistines, and the Moabites were the only nations who sought to do injury to the Israelites. Every recollection of the troubles endured in the desert made the Israelites more desirous of living in undisturbed tranquillity. For this reason they took but a slight interest in the affairs of their fellow-tribesmen, and they allowed their sons and daughters to intermarry with non-Israelites. These alliances were most frequent among the border tribes, who found a strong element of security in this intimate union with their neighbours, the more so as in the early days of their history such intermarriages were not yet placed under the ban of interdiction. The tribes in the interior—for instance, those of Ephraim, Manasseh and Benjamin—were less in favour of intermarriages; least of all did the exclusive Levites approve of a union with non-Israelites. From an intermarriage with the heathen to a participation in their idolatrous rites there was but one step.

In rural districts the Israelites could easily be led to join the pagan rites, as their memories were still attached to Egyptian superstitions, and they were unable to discriminate between pagan discipline and the divine doctrine of Sinai. By degrees this idolatrous worship gained ground among the majority of the Israelites, who were fascinated by the arts and accomplishments of the Phœnicians.

The Sanctuary at Shiloh, where the sons of Aaron, together with the Levites, conducted the sacerdotal rites, was not situated in a sufficiently central position for tribes settled at great distances, nor was it in high favour among those living within easier reach. The neighbouring tribes were displeased with the arrogance and the egotism of the sons of Ephraim. In the early stages of Israel's history, the performance of sacrifices was held to be an essential part of divine worship, and of communion with the Deity. Persons clinging to the observance of sacrificial rites either erected domestic altars, or connected themselves with a temple in their vicinity. This tendency remained unchecked, as there was no chief or leader to inculcate a proper adoration of the Godhead. The Levites, who were intended to be the teachers of the people, had been widely dispersed among the different tribes, and dwelt chiefly in the smaller towns. As they owned no lands, and were generally destitute, they exerted no great influence upon the people.

One poor Levite, a grandson of the great Lawgiver, took priestly service at the shrine of a newly manufactured idol, in order to obtain food and raiment. The further spread of such worship was favoured among the Israelites by the force of sensuality, by habit, and by the love of imitation.

At this time the marvellous occurrences in Egypt and in the desert were still vividly remembered by the several tribes, and formed a link of fellowship among them, notwithstanding the disintegrating effect of idolatry. The ancestral history continued to be handed down from father to son, and nursed the sentiment of a common nationality. An individual or an entire family immersed in affliction would then ask, "Where are all his miracles of which our fathers told us, saying, Did not the Lord bring us up from Egypt?"[1]

The events witnessed on Mount Sinai remained engraven upon the hearts of thoughtful men; nor were warning voices wanting to recall the olden days of divine mercy, and to rebuke the people on account of their idolatry. It appears that the utterances of reproof came from the Levites. They, as custodians of the tables of the covenant, and as servants in the Sanctuary of Shiloh, stood up in days of national misfortune, and on other occasions, to expose the corruption of their people. Sometimes they may have succeeded in making a deep impression, when they described past glories or present sorrows; but the effect of such addresses was only evanescent. The people were always predisposed to fraternise with strangers and to imitate their practices. One adverse condition produced another. The selfishness of the men of Ephraim induced their brother tribes to care only for self-preservation. The chances of uniting the Israelites under one commander were neglected. This again drove the divided tribes to confederacies with the pagans, and they became more closely united with them through the ties of family and of superstitious worship; hence came internal disunion and national degeneracy. The indigenous population of Palestine no sooner discovered the influence they were able to exercise, than they began to treat the Israelites as intruders, who should be humbled, if not crushed altogether.

[1] Judges vi. 13.

Sorrowful days befell the Israelites after Joshua had closed his eyes. One tribe after another was reduced to servitude. At length, when the sufferings of the people became unendurable, public-spirited men came to the rescue, and performed deeds of remarkable valour. These heroic deliverers were commonly known as "judges" (*Shofetim*). In an emergency they would lead one tribe, or several tribes to battle; but they were incapable of uniting the entire people of Israel, or of keeping the collected tribes under permanent control. It was altogether beyond the ability of these deliverers to bring order into this national disorganisation, or to abolish the abuse of idolatry, and enforce a strict observance of religion. They, in fact, shared the failings of their age, and had only a faint comprehension of the Sinaitic doctrines.

CHAPTER IV.

THE JUDGES.

Animosity of the Idumæans—Othniel, a Deliverer—Eglon, King of Moab—The Canaanite King, Jabin—Sisera, his General—The Prophetess and Poetess Deborah—Barak—Victory near Tabor—Early Hebrew Poetry—Sufferings through Nomads—The Hero Gideon (Jerubbaal)—Victory in the Plain of Jezreel—Commencement of Prosperity—Abimelech—Feud with the Shechemites—Jair the Gileadite—Hostilities of the Amalekites and the Philistines—Jephthah—Samson—Zebulunite Judges.

OTHNIEL, the son of Kenaz, a brother, and at the same time the son-in-law of Caleb, was the first warrior-judge. Having collected a brave band of combatants, he advanced against an Idumæan[1] king, and delivered the southern tribes of Judah and Simeon. But his enterprise did not bring the least advantage to the rest of the tribes, and remained almost unknown on the other side of Mount Ephraim. The daring act of the Benjamite, Ehud, the son of Gera, was of greater significance. The Israelites being oppressed by the Moabites, Ehud did not immediately invite his injured companions to make an open attack upon the foe. He first sought to put the hostile king, Eglon, out of the way. One day he presented himself before the king under the pretext that he was the bearer of a gift from his people in token of their submission. Being alone with Eglon, he thrust a double-edged sword into the body of his victim, and fled after having locked the door of the audience chamber. He then summoned the men of Ephraim and Benjamin, and occupied the fords of the Jordan so as to cut off the retreat of the Moabites, who had established themselves on the west side of that river.

[1] Judges iii. 8 and 10 must be read "king of *Edom*" (אֱדוֹם) instead of *Aram* (אֲרָם).

The Moabites were then totally routed. After this victory, the western tribes of Israel remained for a long time unmolested by the people of Moab.

From another quarter, the Israelites were harassed by the Philistines. Shamgar, the son of Anath, probably of the tribe of Benjamin, chastised the assailants with a weapon extemporised out of an ox-goad. Such sporadic acts of bravery, inadequate to improve the situation of the Israelites, tended only to aggravate their troubles. Jabin, a Canaanite king, joined by some of the neighbouring rulers, seemed bent upon exterminating the Israelites. The high-roads became insecure, and wayfarers had to seek devious by-ways. At that juncture, Israel was without a leader, or a man of tried courage. A woman, a poetess and prophetess, Deborah, the wife of Lapidoth, then came forward as "a mother in Israel." With her inspiriting speech she animated the timorous people, and changed them from cowards into heroes. Urged by Deborah, Barak, the son of Abinoam, reluctantly undertook to lead the Israelites against the enemy; and, at her bidding, the most valiant men in Israel joined the national army. Meeting near Mount Tabor, they discomfited the Canaanites, who were commanded by Jabin's general, the hitherto unvanquished Sisera. The power of Jabin was henceforth broken. The commander himself now had to flee for his life, and was slain by Jael, the wife of Heber, a member of the Kenite tribe, which maintained an amicable alliance with the Israelites. In a hymn known as " The Song of Deborah," the praises were sung of this unexpected victory, and of the mercy which God had bestowed upon His people. But these hostilities had not yet reached their end. The restless nations of the neighbourhood continued to inflict heavy blows upon the Israelites, who either were too weak or too disunited to resist such attacks. The roving Midianites periodically ravaged Palestine. At harvest time, they would cross the Jordan with their irresistible hordes, bringing with them their tents, their camels, and their herds. They came "like a flight of locusts," emptied the barns, led off the flocks, the herds and the asses, and then quitted the impoverished and despoiled land. The rich and fertile plain of Jezreel, with the adjacent northern and southern territory, was especially exposed to these incursions. To save their scanty means of subsistence, the owners of the land concealed their provisions in caverns and other hiding places. The insignificant gleanings of wheat had to be threshed in caves intended for wine-presses. In their severe trials the tribes prayed unto the God of their fathers, and assembled at Shiloh, where they were reproved for their sinfulness by "a man of God"—probably a Levite—who reminded them that their misfortunes were the consequence of their iniquities. Exhortations of this kind seem to have made a deep impression upon at least one man of note. This man was Jerubbaal, also named Gideon, of the tribe of Manasseh. In Ophrah, his native place, in a grove consecrated to Baal or to Astarte, there was an altar, which Jerubbaal destroyed, and he then raised another in honour of the God of Israel. The men of Ophrah, enraged at this sacrilege, were about to stone Jerubbaal, but he gathered round him tribesmen of Manasseh, Asher, Zebulun and Naphtali, and encamped at Endor to the north of Mount Moreh; there he dismissed the timid and faint-hearted, retaining only a picked force of 300 warriors. In the dead of night he fell upon the sleeping enemy, whom he terrified with the shrill blast of horns, the brandishing of burning torches, and the war-cry, "For God and for Gideon." The unprepared Midianites were utterly routed, and were forced to retreat across the Jordan. During many ages "the day of Midian" was remembered as a triumph which a handful of brave Israelites had accomplished.

Gideon then pursued the two fugitive Midianite kings, Zebah and Zalmunna, on the other side of the Jordan, chastised those Israelites who refused him and his famishing warriors the needful provisions, and inflicted a crushing defeat upon the Midianites, from which they never recovered. The people thus delivered offered to make him their king, an honour which he declined, both for himself and his descendants. It appears that he made Ophrah a centre for pilgrims, to the detriment of the less conveniently situated sanctuary of Shiloh. This aroused the jealousy of the men of Ephraim, who, after the death of the hero, were involved in violent conflicts with the men of the tribe of Manasseh. Gideon had, after his great victories, carried the rich treasures of the vanquished enemies into the land. The towns of Israel became seats of wealth and luxury. Phœnician caravans could henceforth safely journey through the land. Covenants were concluded with the trafficking strangers, who were placed under the protection of the tutelar Baal-Berith (Baal of the Covenant). The jealous men of Ephraim, who sought to foment dissension among the seventy sons and grandsons of Gideon, found in Abimelech, one of his sons, an unscrupulous ally. This Abimelech, being the son of a woman of Shechem, was elected by the Shechemites to be their leader. His first act was to put his brothers to death. Only Jotham, the youngest of them, escaped. On Mount Gerizim, Jotham pronounced his trenchant parable of the trees, who, in their search of a ruler, met with refusals from the fruitful olive, fig, and vine trees. The prickly bramble (Atad) was the only one who would accept the government; but he warned the trees that if they refused to acknowledge him as ruler, he would send forth a fire to consume all the trees of the Lebanon. The parable found its application in the subsequent hostilities between the men of Shechem and Abimelech, whose cruelty ended in his death at the hand of his own armour-bearer

After the fall of Abimelech the cis-Jordanic tribes seem to have retrograded, while the men of Manasseh or Gilead, on the other side of the Jordan, invaded the high land of the Hauran, and took possession of sixty rock-built cities. This district then received the name Havvoth Jair. At that time the Israelites suffered a shock from two sides, which caused further disintegration among them. On the one hand they were attacked by the Ammonites, and on the other, by the Philistines. These attacks distracted them, and rendered them incapable of resistance. The Ammonites appear to have driven the Israelites from their open places, after which they attacked the strongholds. These incursions were successful against the tribes of Ephraim and Judah.

On the opposite side, the Philistines assailed the neighbouring tribes of Israel, and sought to subdue them. They first attacked the tribe of Dan ; nor did they spare the tribes of Benjamin and Judah. Even these disasters did not arouse the tribes to make a combined resistance. The trans-Jordanic tribes had turned to the Ephraimites for help; but the latter took no part in the contest, either from selfishness or because the inhabitants of Shechem and other Ephraimite towns had been enfeebled by Abimelech.

In those troubled times there arose two deliverers, who drove off the enemy, and procured temporary relief. Jephthah and Samson, two adventurers, disregarding order and discipline, brought their powers to bear, as much for evil as for good. They both displayed extraordinary activity; but while Jephthah was a warrior who conquered his enemies by warlike measures, Samson, though endowed with great strength and daring, appears to have overcome his enemies by stratagems and unexpected attacks.

Jephthah, the Gileadite, of the tribe of Manasseh, having been banished by his tribesmen, began to lead the life of a highwayman. Daring associates.

who thought little of law and order, joined him and appointed him their leader. When attacked by the Ammonites, the men of Gilead remembered their outlawed kinsman, whose bold deeds had come to their knowledge. Some of the elders of his tribe went to him, and urged him to aid them with his troops, and help them to expel the enemy from their territories. Full of proud indignation, Jephthah rebuked them with the words, " You hated me, and drove me from my father's house; wherefore do you come to me now when it goes ill with you ? "[1] The Gileadite elders, however, entreated him more urgently, and promised, if he should vanquish the enemy, that they would recognise him as chief in Gilead. Upon this Jephthah determined to return with them. He then sent a formal message to the Ammonites, demanding that they should desist from their incursions into the territory of the Israelites; and when they refused on the pretext of ancient rights, he traversed the districts of Gilead and Manasseh in order to enlist warriors. Jephthah knew well how to gather many brave youths round him, and with these he proceeded against the Ammonites, defeated them, and wrested twenty cities out of their hands. After Jephthah had gained these decisive victories, the Ephraimites began a quarrel with him; and as previously, in the case of the heroic Gideon, they were displeased that he had obtained victories without their aid.

This led to a civil war, for Jephthah was not so submissive to the proud Ephraimites as the judge of Ophrah had been. The men of Ephraim crossed the Jordan, near the town of Zaphon, and assumed a warlike attitude; but Jephthah punished them for their presumption, defeated them, and blocked their road of retreat on the banks of the Jordan. Jephthah might have strengthened the tribes beyond the

[1] Judges xi. 7.

Jordan, but his rule lasted only six years, and he left no son to succeed him. He had only one daughter, and about her a deeply touching story has been preserved, which describes how she became the victim of her father's rash vow.

Whilst the hero of Gilead was subduing the Ammonites by force of arms, Samson was fighting the Philistines, who claimed from the tribe to which Samson belonged the coast-line of Joppa, formerly a part of their possessions. The tribe of Dan smarted under their yoke, but had not the power to effect a change. Samson was not supported in his enterprises by the various tribes, as Jephthah had been. They greatly feared the Philistines; thus Samson was compelled to have recourse to stratagems, and could harm the enemy only by unexpected onslaughts. This mode of warfare was censured in the words, " Dan shall judge his people like one of the tribes of Israel. Dan shall be as a serpent by the way, and as an adder in the path, that biteth the horse's heels, so that his rider shall fall backwards." [1]

Samson is supposed to have fought during twenty years for Israel, without, however, improving the state of affairs. Long after his death, the Philistines kept the upper hand over the tribes of Dan and Benjamin, and also over Judah and Ephraim. The rule of the Philistines pressed with increasing weight upon Israel. After Samson there arose successively three other deliverers, two in the tribe of Zebulun, and one in the tribe of Ephraim; but their deeds were of so insignificant a character that they have not been deemed worthy of mention. Of the two hero-judges in Zebulun, only the names and the territory or town in which they were buried have been preserved: Ibzan, of Bethlehem in Zebulun, and Elon, of the town of Ajalon. Also of the Ephraimite judge, Abdon, son of Hillel, the Pirathonite, little is

[1] Genesis xlix. 16, 17.

known. It is not even stated against what enemies they waged war; but the fact that the men of Zebulun, who at first lived far away from the sea, afterwards extended their dwelling-places to the shore, leads us to suppose that they supplanted the Canaanite inhabitants.

CHAPTER V.

ELI AND SAMUEL.

Importance of the Judges—Public Feeling—Sanctuary in Shiloh—
Eli and his Sons—Defeat by the Philistines—Capture of the
Ark—Destruction of Shiloh and the Sanctuary—Flight of
the Aaronites and Levites—Death of Eli—The Ark in Philistia
and in Kirjath Jearim—Prophecy re-awakened—Samuel in
Ramah—The Order of Prophets or Singers—Popular revulsion—
The tribe of Judah—Repeated attacks of the Philistines—Meet-
ing at Mizpah—Samuel's activity—Nob as a place of worship—
Increase in the power of the Philistines and Ammonites—The
tribes desire to have a King—Samuel's course of action.

1100 ?—1067 B. C. E.

THE twelve or thirteen warrior-judges had been
incapable of keeping off the hostile neighbours of
Israel for any length of time, much less had they
ensured the permanent safety of the country. Even
the celebrated Barak, with all his enthusiasm, and
Gideon and Jephthah with their warlike courage
could succeed only in uniting a few of the tribes, but
were unable to secure or restore the union of the
entire people. The warrior-judges were, in fact,
of importance only so long as they repulsed the
enemy, averted danger, and ensured safety in daily
life. They wielded no real power, not even over
the tribes to which their prowess brought help and
freedom; nor did they possess any rights by which
they could enforce obedience. The isolation of each
tribe, and the division amongst the several tribes continued, in spite of temporary victories; the actual weakness of the country increased rather than diminished.
Samson's "serpent-like attacks and adder's bites" did
not deter the Philistines from considering the tribes
within reach as their subjects, or more correctly
speaking as their slaves, nor did it prevent them from

ill-treating the Israelites. Jephthah's victories over
the Ammonites did not cause the enemy to relinquish
his claims over the eastern tribes of Reuben, Gad,
and the half of Manasseh.

After the deaths of Jephthah and Samson, the
state of affairs became still more dismal. It was,
however, precisely this sense of extreme weakness
which led to a gradual recovery of strength. Several
tribal leaders must have come to the conclusion that
this connection with neighbouring populations, and
the adoption of idolatrous customs had brought
the people to the verge of ruin. The remembrance
of the God of their fathers no doubt once more
revived in their hearts, and awakened their sleeping
consciences to a sense of duty. The men who had
been thus aroused called to mind the Sanctuary
dedicated to their God at Shiloh, and they repaired
thither.

Towards the close of the judges' period, Shiloh
once more became a general rallying point. Here
the Levites, the guardians of the Law, still resided,
and they used their opportunities to urge, at the
meetings held in times of distress, that a denial of
Israel's God and the worship of Baal had brought
all this misery upon the people. There also lived
in Shiloh a priest who was worthy of his ancestors
Aaron and Phineas. He was the first Aaronite,
after a considerable time, whose name has been
recorded for posterity. He was simply called Eli,
without the addition of his father's name, and the
only title of honour he bore was that of the priest
at Shiloh. Eli is described as a venerable old man,
on whose lips were words of gentleness, and who
was incapable of giving utterance to severe censure,
even of his unworthy sons.

This aged man could not fail to exercise a beneficial influence, and win warm adherents to the Law
which he represented, if only by the example of his
moral worth, and by the holy life he led. When

Shiloh was visited, in ever-increasing numbers, by desponding worshippers from the tribes of Ephraim and Benjamin, as also from the tribes on the trans-Jordanic side, some were murmuring at the sufferings imposed upon them, and others complaining of the hard treatment they endured at the hands of the Ammonites; but Eli would exhort them to rely on the ever ready help of the God of Israel, and to give up the worship of strange gods.

By such exhortations he might have brought about a better state of mind among his hearers, if the respect felt for him had been likewise enjoyed by his two sons, Hophni and Phineas. They, however, did not walk in the ways of their father; and when the people and Eli were overtaken by severe misfortunes, these were supposed to be a punishment of heaven for the sins of Eli's sons, and for the weak indulgence displayed by the High Priest.

The Philistines still held sway over the tribes in their vicinity, and made repeated attacks and raids on Israel's lands. The tribes attacked became so far skilled in warfare that they no longer sought to oppose the enemy in irregular skirmishes, but met them in open battle. The Israelites encamped on the hill Eben-ha-Ezer, and the Philistines in the plain near Aphek. As the latter possessed iron warchariots they proved superior to the Israelites, of whom four thousand are supposed to have fallen in battle. The Israelite warriors, however, did not take to flight, but kept to their posts.

In accordance with the counsel of the elders, the Ark of the Covenant was brought from Shiloh; it being believed that its presence would ensure victory. Eli's sons were appointed to escort it. Nevertheless, the second battle was even more disastrous than the first. The Israelite troops fled in utter confusion; the Ark of the Covenant was captured by the Philistines, and Hophni and Phineas, who attended it, were killed. The Philistines pursued the fleeing troops, and spread terror in every direction. Breathless with fear, a messenger of evil tidings arrived in Shiloh, and brought the sad news to the anxious people, and to the high priest Eli, who was sitting at the gate.

The news that the Ark of the Covenant had been captured affected the aged priest even more than that of the death of his sons; he dropped down dead from his seat. It now seemed that all glory had departed from the house of Israel. The victorious Philistines, no longer content to make foraging expeditions through the country, forced their way from west to east until they reached the district of Shiloh. They destroyed that town, together with the Tabernacle, which had been a witness to the blissful days of Moses. A later poet describes this time of trial with a heavy heart.[1]

The strength and courage of the people were entirely overcome by this defeat. Those tribes which until now had been foremost in every encounter were crushed. The tribe of Ephraim suffered— though not undeservedly—most severely by the overthrow of the Sanctuary, which, in Eli's time, had been recognised as a place for popular meetings. Every chance of union, especially amongst the northern tribes, who, however, had not been concerned in the disastrous strife, seemed to be cut off.

The Philistines were impressed with the idea that by capturing the Ark of the Covenant—which they supposed to be the safeguard of the Israelites—and by destroying the Sanctuary, they had vanquished the Israelite people. But they were painfully undeceived. As soon as they had carried off the Ark of the Covenant to the neighbouring town of Ashdod, the country was visited by various plagues. In their terror, the Philistine princes determined to follow the advice of their priests and magicians, and send back

---

[1] See Psalm lxxviii. 60–64; Jeremiah vii. 12.

the Ark, accompanied by expiatory offerings, after it had been in their possession for seven months. It was accordingly sent over the boundaries, and taken to the town of "Kirjath Jearim" (Forest Town), situated on a hill, where it was guarded by the Levites of the district; but it was so little missed by the people that decades passed before they even remembered their loss. In the eyes of the untutored Israelites, neither the contents nor the great age of the tablets of the Law preserved in the Ark were of great importance. Meanwhile these misfortunes—the destruction and loss of the Sanctuary at Shiloh—had aroused a desire for a better state of things. Those who were not utterly indifferent could perceive that the true cause of the evil lay in the religious and political dissensions. The Levites, who had escaped during the destruction of Shiloh, and had settled in other towns, probably prepared the public mind for a return to the belief in God. Perhaps also the return of the Ark of the Covenant from the land of the Philistines exercised an animating influence, and raised hopes of better days. The longing for the God of Israel became daily more widely diffused, and the want of a steadfast and energetic leader was keenly felt—a leader who would bring the misguided people into the right path, and raise up those who were bowed down with sorrow. And just at the right moment a man appeared who brought about a crisis in Israel's history.

Samuel, the son of Elkanah, was the man who reunited the long-sundered bonds of communal life amongst the Israelites, and thereby averted the threatening decay and internal corruption. His greatness is illustrated by the circumstance that he is placed second to Moses not only in chronological sequence, but also in prophetic importance.[1]

Samuel was an elevated character. He displayed the same unbending conscientiousness towards him-

---

[1] Jeremiah xv. 1 ; Psalms xcix, 6.

self as towards others. Living amidst the people, coming into daily contact with them, he surpassed the men of his time in love of God, purity of heart, and unselfishness. In addition to these qualities he was distinguished by the gift of prophecy. His spiritual eye pierced the clouds which hid the future. He proclaimed his prophetic visions, and they came to pass. Samuel was descended from one of the most distinguished Levitical families, from the same Korah who had incited the rebellion against Moses in days of old. Samuel inherited intensity of feeling from his mother Hannah, whose fervent though inaudible prayer has formed a model for all ages. At a tender age his mother secured a place for him as one of the attendant Levites in the Sanctuary at Shiloh. He had daily to open its gates; he took part in the sacrificial service, and he passed his nights within the precincts of the tabernacle.

At an early age the gift of prophecy, unknown to himself, was awakened within him. Whilst wrapped in deep sleep he heard himself called from the inner recess of the Sanctuary where the Ark of the Covenant reposed. This was Samuel's first vision, and happened previous to the defeat of the Israelites by the Philistines, the capture of the Ark of the Covenant, the death of Eli and his two sons, and the destruction of the Sanctuary. Samuel's services ceased with the last-named event, and he returned to his father's house at Ramah in deep affliction.

The misfortunes which had befallen his people, and especially the ruin of Shiloh made an over-powering impression on Samuel, whose youthful mind was filled with the highest aspirations. In the Levitical circle, in which he had grown up, it was a fixed belief that the trials undergone by the people resulted from their denial of the God of Israel. To have no Sanctuary was considered equivalent to being without God.

The sacred writings enshrined in the Ark enjoined righteousness, justice, mercy, and the equality of all Israelites without distinction of class, as commanded by God; but little or nothing was said of sacrifices. Samuel, who was nearer by many centuries to the origin of the Israelitish nation than were the later prophets, was, like them, convinced of the fact that God had not ordained the deliverance of His people solely in order that they might sacrifice to Him only, but that they might carry His laws into effect. The contents of these records of the Law represented the will of God which the Israelites were to follow with implicit obedience. This Law was a living force in Samuel's heart, and he grew to be the medium by which it became indelibly impressed on the people; to give effect to its teaching was the task of his life.

The fact of having no Sanctuary was, as has been shown, deemed equivalent to being abandoned by God. Gradually, however, Samuel seems to have taken up a different train of thought—*No Sanctuary, no burnt-offerings*. "Is sacrifice absolutely necessary for a pure worship of God, and for a holy life in His ways?" This thought became matured within him; and later, on a fitting occasion, he preached on this theme thus: The sacrifices are of little importance; the fat of rams cannot win God's approbation; in what, then, should the service of God consist? "In strict obedience to all that He has commanded." During his sojourn in Shiloh, Samuel had not only made himself acquainted with the contents of the stone tablets which were kept in the Ark of the Sanctuary, but he became versed also in the book of the Law emanating from Moses, and he was entirely filled with their spirit. The living word was the means which he employed to attain his end, for he was endowed with impressive eloquence. From time to time he had prophetic dreams and visions. These revealed to him that his convictions were not the mere suggestions of his own mind or heart, but were sanctioned or inspired by a higher Being. The prophetic inspirations consisted of teachings or commands; they were combined with an unveiling of the near future, and bore the character of revelations. Animated by his prophetic visions, Samuel communicated them to his hearers, probably at his native place, Ramah, where his reputation had preceded him. These communications, which foreshadowed extraordinary events beyond the limits of common foresight, he seems to have expressed in orations and in rhythmic utterances, abounding in poetic metaphors and similes.

Whilst in Shiloh, he had been repeatedly vouchsafed prophetic visions, and these had been confirmed. It soon went forth in the environs of Ramah, and in ever-widening circles that a prophet had arisen in Israel, and that the spirit of God, which had rested on Moses and had led him to deliver the children of Israel from Egypt, had now descended on the son of Elkanah. In the interval, during a long succession of centuries, no prophet, in the full sense of the word, had arisen. The fact that God had raised up a second Moses encouraged the hope that better times were at hand. Samuel's first endeavour was to reclaim the nation from the idolatrous worship of Baal and Astarte, and from a superstitious belief in the oracular powers of the Teraphim.

The desire of a portion of the people to abandon their evil ways materially assisted Samuel in his efforts. His irresistible eloquence was concentrated in the one theme that the gods of the heathen were nonentities who could neither help nor save. He declared that it was folly and sinful to consult the lying oracles and the jugglery of the soothsayers, and that God would never desert the nation whom He had chosen. These words found a powerful response in the hearts of those who heard them. Samuel did not wait for the people to come to him in order that he might address them, but he went forth to them. He travelled through the whole land, appointed public meetings, and announced to the multitudes the lessons revealed to him by the spirit of God; and the people, stirred by his prophetic utterances, and roused from the lethargy into which they had been plunged ever since their misfortunes had commenced, now began to revive. The right man had come, whose words could be followed in days of care and trouble. The eyes of the nation naturally turned towards him.

Had Samuel stood alone, he would scarcely have been enabled to effect so desirable a transformation. But he had a number of assistants on whom he could rely. The Levites, whose home was in Shiloh, had fled when the town and the Sanctuary were destroyed. They had been accustomed to surround the altar and to serve in the Sanctuary. They knew no other occupation. What were they to do now in their dispersion? Another place of worship had not yet been founded to which they might have turned. Several Levites therefore joined Samuel. His greatness had impressed them when he lived in Shiloh, and he now employed them to execute his plans. Gradually their numbers increased until they formed a band of associates (*Chebel*), or Levitical guild (*Kehillah*). These disciples of prophecy, headed by Samuel, contributed materially to the change of views and manners among the people.

Another circumstance served at that time to rouse the nation from its apathy. During the entire period of the Judges' rule, the men of Judah had not taken the slightest share in public events. Dwelling far away in their pasture-fields and deserts, they seemed to have no part in the life of the other tribes. They called themselves by the name of Jacob. Utterly secluded, they led a separate existence, untouched by the sorrows and joys, the battles and conquests, of the tribes living on both sides of the Jordan. The

Jebusites, who possessed the district between the mountains of Ephraim and Judah, formed a barrier between these tribes and the Israelites dwelling in the north.

It was only the repeated incursions of the Philistines on Israel's territory which seem to have aroused the tribe of Judah, and forced it out of its retirement. It was probably to strengthen themselves against the attacks of their enemy, who sought to lay the yoke of serfdom on their necks, that the men of Judah stretched out a helping hand to the neighbouring tribes. Whatever circumstance may have influenced them, it is certain that in Samuel's days, the tribe of Judah with its dependency, the tribe of Simeon, took part in the common cause. Jacob and Israel, divided during all the centuries since they first entered Canaan, were now at length united. It was, without doubt, Samuel who brought about this union.

Judah's or Jacob's entry into history marks the accession of a new, vigorous and rejuvenating element. The tribe of Judah had found but few towns, and by no means a developed town life in the territories it had acquired. The only city worthy of note was Hebron; the other places were villages for cattle-breeders. Both the refinement and the depravity resulting from the influence of the Philistines had remained unknown to the tribes of Judah and Simeon. The worship of Baal and Astarte, with its coarse and sensual rites, had not established itself among them. They remained, for the most part, what they had been on their entry into the land— simple shepherds, loving peace and upholding their liberty, without any desire for warlike fame or for making new conquests. The simple customs of patriarchal life seem to have endured longer in Judah than elsewhere. This accession of strength and religious activity could certainly not have been rendered possible without Samuel's commanding and energetic intervention. The son of Elkanah, though no warrior, was looked upon as a firm supporter on whom both houses could lean. For many years Samuel, assisted by the prophetic order of Levites, pursued his active course with zeal and energy; the people regarded him as a leader, and he, in fact, by his inspired zeal, led them on to conquest. A victory gained near Eben-ha-Ezer, where, many years before, the Philistines had overcome the Israelite troops and had carried off much booty, now produced a mighty effect: it revived the courage of the Israelites and humbled the Philistines.

During the next decade the people once more enjoyed the comforts of peace, and Samuel took measures that prosperity should not efface the good results of previous misfortunes. It was his earnest endeavour to consolidate the union between the tribes, which was the true foundation of their strength. Year after year he called together the elders of the people, explained to them their duties, and reminded them of the evil days which had befallen the Israelites through their godlessness, their intermarriage with strange nations, and their idolatrous excesses; he also warned them against a return to these errors. Such assemblies Samuel held by turns in the three towns which came into notice after the destruction of Shiloh—namely, in Bethel, in Gilgal, and in Mizpah where prayers for victory over the Philistines had been offered up in the former campaign. At Ramah, the place of his residence, frequent meetings of the various tribes took place; and here the elders sought his advice in all important matters. At divine services Samuel not only caused sacrifices to be offered up, but with the aid of the Levites he introduced the use of stringed instruments in order to arouse the devout feelings of the people.

Through him a new element was introduced into the divine service of the Israelites—viz., songs of

praise.   Samuel, the ancestor of the celebrated
psalmists, the sons of Korah, was the first who composed songs of praise for divine service.   His grandson, Heman, was considered the chief psalmist and
musician, and he ranked in fame with Asaph and
Jeduthun, who flourished in the subsequent generation.   The charms of poetry and music were by
Samuel brought to bear upon the religious service,
and they left a lasting and ennobling impression on
the minds of the people.   The employment of choirs
of Levites and singers rendered the sacrificial rite of
minor importance.

The priests, the sons of Aaron, took up a less
respected position, and were, to a certain extent,
neglected by Samuel.   Achitub, a grandson of Eli,
had saved himself after the destruction of Shiloh by
taking refuge in the small town of Nob, near Jerusalem.   He had carried away with him the high
priest's garments; and various members of the
house of Aaron having assembled there, Nob became a sacerdotal town.   Here, it seems, Achitub
had erected an altar, and also a tabernacle on the
model of the one which had been destroyed in
Shiloh.   He even appears to have made an Ark
of the Covenant in Nob, instead of the one carried
off by the Philistines.   The Israelites apparently
disregarded the fact that the new ark was wanting
in the essential contents,—the stone tablets of the
Covenant.

Notwithstanding the eventful changes effected by
Samuel through his great gifts and untiring energy,
the condition of the people was anything but satisfactory.   He had given special attention to the central and southern districts, and had appointed his two
sons, Joel and Abijah, to act as judges—the one in
Beer-sheba, the other in Bethel—but the north was
left unrepresented.

With increasing years Samuel could not display
the same activity as in his youth and riper man-

hood. His sons were disliked, being accused of misusing their power and of accepting bribes. There were no men of energy amongst Samuel's followers, and thus the ties which held the people together gradually slackened. In addition it must be noted that just at this period the country of Israel's greatest enemies was transformed into a kingdom. The Philistines had either of their own free will chosen a king, or had been forced to do so by one of the rulers of their five cities. The town of Gath became the capital. The ambition of the Philistine king now turned in the direction of fresh conquests; he seems to have made successful attacks on the Phœnicians, and to have laid waste the town of Sidon. In consequence of their defeat the Sidonians took refuge in their ships, and on a rock which projected far out into the sea they built a town which they called Zor (Tyre), the city of the rock. Meanwhile the Philistines became possessors of the entire territory between Gaza and Sidon, and it seemed easy to them, with their increased power, to subjugate Israel; hence a fierce warfare ensued between them and the Israelites. The Ammonites also, who had been humiliated by Jephthah, now rose again under their warlike king Nahash, and began to invade the possessions of the tribe of Gad and the half of Manasseh. Powerless to defend themselves, these tribes sent messengers to Samuel, entreating him to supply efficient aid. They at the same time expressed a wish which, though entertained by the entire people, was deeply painful to the prophet. They demanded that a king should be placed at the head of the Israelite community, who could compel the various tribes to unite in joint action, and might lead them to battle and to victory. There was now to be a king in Israel. Samuel was amazed when he heard these demands. A whole people was to be dependent on the whims or the will of a single individual! Equality of all members of the nation before

God and the law, the entire independence of each family group under its patriarchal head, had become so identified with their mode of life, that any change in their condition seemed incomprehensible and fraught with the heaviest misfortunes.

It was now necessary to give a new direction to the destinies of the people. Samuel's clear intellect disapproved of the radical change; yet his inherent prophetic gift compelled him to accede. The kingdom of Israel was brought forth in pain: it was not the offspring of affection. Therefore it never could find a natural place in the system of Israel's organisation, but was at all times considered by more discerning minds as a foreign element.

CHAPTER VI.

THE APOGEE.

Establishment of a Kingdom—Saul—His Position and Character—
His secret Election at Mizpah—Humiliating Condition of the
Nation under the Philistines—Declaration of War—Assemblage
in Gilgal—Battle of Michmash—Defeat of the Philistines—
Severity of Saul—Victory over the Ammonites—Saul's Election
as King confirmed—His Court and Attendants—His Officers
and Standing Army—Victory over the Amalekites—Disputes
between Saul and Samuel—Saul's Attacks on the neighbouring
People—War with the Gibeonites—Place of Worship in Gibeon—
War against the Philistines in the Valley of Tamarinths—Goliath
and David—Meeting of Saul and David—Saul's Jealousy turns
into Madness—The Persecution of David—Saul's last Battle
against the Philistines—Defeat and Death.

1067—1055 B. C. E.

THE king who was placed at the head of the people
through their own eager insistence, and with the
unwilling consent of the prophet proved, more
effectually than any objections could do, how little a
monarchical constitution was fitted to realise the
expectations founded on it; for the king, until his
accession a simple and excellent man, with no
thoughts of ambition or arbitrary power, did not
shrink from cruelty and inhumanity in order to
assert his dignity.

By the aid of prophetic guidance, care was taken
that he should not resemble the repulsive prototype
drawn by Samuel, or become so independent as to
place himself above all laws and rules, but that he
should ever remain mindful of his lowly origin.
Samuel did not select a king from the haughty tribe
of Ephraim, lest he should act like Abimelech, who,
in his presumption and ambition, had killed his own
brothers, and laid waste whole districts; but the king
was chosen from the smallest of the tribes, the tribe

of Benjamin. His family, that of Matri, was one of the lowliest in Benjamin. His father, Kish, was not in any way distinguished ; he was a simple country-man ; and nothing could be said in his praise, except that he was an upright man. Saul was chosen because he was content to work at his plough, and watch the increase of his father's flocks. He had no thought beyond the village in which he was born, and barely an idea that there were human beings to whom the possession of power was an attraction. In his shyness he displayed the ways of a true peasant; these circumstances, and the personal qualities of Saul seemed to be a security against any presumption or pride on the part of the first king of Israel.

The circumstances attending the choice of a king left a deep and pleasing impression. " See," said Samuel, " this is the man whom God has chosen as king; his like is not to be found in all Israel." Most of the bystanders, carried away by the solemn proceeding and by Saul's appearance, shouted, " Long live the king!" Samuel then anointed the newly elected king with holy oil, by which he was believed to be rendered inviolable. The elders rejoiced that their heartfelt wish of having a king to rule over them was at length realised. They looked forward to happy days. This choice of a king was an important epoch in the history of the Jewish people; it determined their entire future. Yet during the joyful and solemn proceedings, discord had already arisen. Some discontented people, probably Ephraimites, who had hoped to have a king chosen from their own ranks, loudly expressed their disappointment. " How can this man help us!" Whilst all the other elders, according to universal custom, brought the king gifts of homage, and a few of the most courageous followed him to Gibeah to assist him against the enemies of Israel, the malcontents kept apart and refused their allegiance.

Saul's courage, after his elevation to the throne, must have increased greatly, or he must have felt himself guided by God after his unexpected elevation. He now boldly confronted the task of opposing his mighty enemies, and of settling the disorganised affairs of the commonwealth. The position of the people at his accession was very sad and humiliating, almost worse than in the days of the Judges. Their arms, such as bows and arrows, swords, etc., had been carried off by the victorious Philistines, who left no smith in the land to make new weapons. The newly elected king lacked a sword,—that symbol of royalty among all nations and at all times. His election was probably conducted so secretly that the Philistines knew nothing of it. The Philistine tax-gatherers exhausted the strength of the country, and at the same time repressed every attempt at revolt. So greatly were the Israelites humbled that some of them had to accompany the Philistines on expeditions against their own brethren. Nought but a miraculous event could have saved them, and such an event was brought about by Saul with his son and kinsmen.

Saul's eldest son, Jonathan, was perhaps worthier of the kingly dignity than his father. Modest and unselfish perhaps to a greater extent even than his father, courageous in the very face of death, he combined with these qualities an almost excessive kindliness and gentleness,—a feature which endeared him to all, but which would have been a serious failing in a ruler who had to display a certain amount of firmness and severity. Jonathan was, besides, endowed with an enthusiastic nature which appealed to every heart. He was truthful, and an enemy to all deceit; he uttered his opinions freely, at the risk of displeasing, or of losing his position and even his life, all of which qualities made him a favourite with the people. Abner, the cousin of Saul, was of an entirely different disposition; he was a warrior of unbending firmness, and possessed a considerable degree of artfulness. To the inexperienced king and the people he, too, rendered important service in their distress. Surrounded by these and other faithful adherents of his family, and by the tribe of Benjamin in general, who were proud to gain importance through him, Saul set forth on the unequal contest with the Philistines. Jonathan commenced hostilities. In the town of Geba, or Gibeah of Benjamin, lived the Philistine tax-gatherers, surrounded by a host of warriors. Jonathan attacked this post and killed the garrison. This was the first declaration of war; it was made at Saul's command and with his full approval. The king now ordered that the trumpet-blast, announcing that the war with the Philistines had commenced, should sound throughout the land of Benjamin. Many heard the news with joy, others with sadness and dismay.

All who had courage assembled in order to stand by their king, determined to aid him in casting off the disgrace of Israel, or to perish in the attempt. Those who were cowards escaped to the opposite side of the Jordan, or hid in caverns, in clefts of the rocks, or in subterranean passages. A feeling of intense anxiety filled all minds as to the result of the contest. The meeting-place of the Israelites was then in Gilgal, the town most remote from the land of the Philistines. This place of meeting had been appointed by the prophet Samuel. He had directed Saul to repair thither, and tay there seven days to await his arrival and further instructions. Gilgal probably contained the choir of musicians and prophets, whose psalms and songs were to inspire the Israelite warriors with martial courage and with trust in the deliverance of their fatherland. Meanwhile the Philistines prepared themselves for a war of extermination against the Israelites. The news of Jonathan's attack on their outposts had exasperated them; they were, however, more surprised than terrified. How could the cowardly, weaponless, unarmed Israelites dare to attack the Philistines, their masters? A numerous band of warriors, supported by cavalry, passed through the valleys of the southern mountain-range of Ephraim, and through the entire breadth of the land as far as Michmash; from this camping-place they spread their marauding bands in three directions, the most humiliating circumstance being that many Israelites were compelled to assist the Philistines in subduing their own tribesmen.

This was a critical time for the people of Israel. Whilst the Philistines were gradually pushing forward to Michmash, Saul, surrounded by the brave men of his tribe, awaited in Gilgal the prophet who was to give the warriors his inspired directions, and thus endow them with courage. But day after day passed and Samuel did not appear. Every hour spent in idleness seemed to destroy the chance of a successful issue. Saul feared that the enemy would descend from the mountains into the valley, attack Gilgal, and destroy or put to flight the small body of Israelites. Not a few of his soldiers had already deserted, looking on Samuel's absence as an inauspicious omen. Saul, becoming impatient, determined on the seventh day to attack the enemy on his own responsibility. According to ancient practice, he made a sacrifice in order to propitiate the Deity, and to ensure his success in the battle. Just as he was preparing the burnt-offering, Samuel suddenly appeared. and upbraided the king severely for being carried away by impatience. He resented this error with great austerity, departed from Gilgal, and left Saul to his own resources—a hard blow for him, as he had reckoned confidently on the prophet's assistance at this dangerous juncture. After Samuel had departed from Gilgal, Saul found it useless to remain there. He therefore repaired with the remnant of his troops to Gibeah. On reviewing his soldiers here, he found them to amount to not more than six hundred. It is not surprising that Saul and Jonathan became dispirited at the sight of this slight force, which was unarmed and had to fight the well-appointed armies of the enemy. Saul and Jonathan alone possessed swords. It was indeed a sad honey-moon for the young kingdom. The most painful blow for Saul was that, through Samuel's absence, he was deprived of the means by which the people might ascertain the will of God.

Jonathan, however, made a good beginning at Gibeah, where Saul and his troops lay encamped, at scarce an hour's distance from Michmash, the site of the Philistine camp. Between the two armies lay a valley, but the road which led from one place to the other was impracticable, the valley being bordered by steep, almost perpendicular walls of rocks and precipices, which closed it up on the east till it became a mere gorge of about ten feet in width. On the west side, where the valley formed a wide pass, the Philistines had stationed their outposts. Thus the Philistines and Israelites could only come to an encounter in the narrow path. At last Jonathan determined to ascend the steepest part of the pass, and, accompanied by his sword-bearer, he climbed, on hands and feet, up the steep sharp points of the rock on the side of Michmash. One false step would have precipitated him into the depth, but happily he and his man arrived safely at the highest point. When the Philistines beheld them, they were not a little surprised that, on this rocky road, a path had been found to their camp. Deceived by this ruse, and fearing that other Israelites would follow, they called out scornfully, "Look at the Hebrews, they are crawling out of their hiding-places; come higher up, we wish to become better acquainted with you."[1] It had been previously agreed between

---

[1] 1 Samuel xiv. 12.

Jonathan and his sword-bearer that, should they receive such a challenge, they would press on and bravely commence the attack. The Philistines who first beheld the daring climbers, soon left off scoffing, for twenty men were killed at the first attack with pieces of rock and sling-stones. The Benjamites were very skilful in the use of the sling, and Jonathan and his sword-bearer advanced further, and continued hurling masses of rock at the Philistines. Terror-stricken by this sudden attack from a side where approach had seemed impossible, they could only imagine themselves attacked by supernatural beings, and, seized with fear, they fought each other, or broke the ranks in the wildest confusion. Saul, who was watching from a high eminence, no sooner perceived the enemy beginning to flee than he hurried to the scene of action, followed by his six hundred warriors, and completed the defeat of the Philistines. Those Israelites who had until then been compelled by the Philistines to fight against their own brethren turned their arms against their oppressors. Others who had hidden themselves in the clefts and grottoes of the mountains of Ephraim took courage, when they witnessed the flight of the Philistines, and swelled the ranks of the aggressors. Saul's troops, thus increased, numbered ten thousand. In every town of Mount Ephraim through which the Philistines passed in their flight, they were attacked by the inhabitants, and cut down one by one. Though tired and exhausted, Saul's troops pursued the retreating foe for eight hours.

An occurrence of apparently slight consequence, but which proved to be of great importance, put a stop to further pursuit. Saul had impressed on his soldiers that the destruction of their enemy was not to be interrupted even for food or refreshment, and he pronounced a curse on him who should take the slightest nourishment. Jonathan, who was always foremost, had heard nothing of this curse. Exhausted by the long fight and pursuit he could not restrain himself, and tasted wild honey into which he had dipped his staff. When his attention was drawn to his father's peremptory command, he openly avowed his act. Saul, however, made a serious matter of it, and determined to condemn Jonathan to death. But the people protested vehemently. "What!" cried the warriors, "shall Jonathan, to whom the people owes its great victory, be killed? No, not a hair of his head shall be touched."[1] The people offered a sin-offering for Jonathan, and thus released him from death. Through this episode, the pursuit of the Philistines to the west of Ajalon was suspended. Great was the joy of the Israelites at the victory they had so unexpectedly obtained. The battle of Michmash fully restored their reputation. They also had regained their weapons, and felt strong enough to fight under a king whose firmness of resolve they had experienced. But Saul returned humbly and modestly to his dwelling place in Gibeah, and ploughed, as heretofore, his father's fields. He was not yet blinded by his new dignity. Meanwhile the hostilities of the Ammonites against the tribes on the other side of the Jordan had increased. Nahash, king of the Ammonites, besieged the fortress of Jabesh-Gilead. The inhabitants were unable to hold out for long, and negotiated with Nahash about a capitulation. He offered a hard, inhuman condition to the Gileadites of Jabesh. As a disgrace to Israel, all men should consent to lose their right eye. What were the Gileadites to do? They treated for a delay of seven days in order to send messages to their fellow-tribesmen. When Saul was one day returning home with his yoke of bullocks from the field, he met the inhabitants of Gibeah in great excitement and bathed in tears. Astonished at this, he asked the cause of their grief, and the messengers

[1] I Samuel xiv. 45.

from Jabesh-Gilead related what would befall their town if speedy assistance were not at hand. Incensed at the disgraceful condition imposed by the king of the Ammonites, Saul immediately determined to bring aid to the Gileadites of Jabesh. For the first time he exercised his royal prerogative by summoning all Israel to take part in the campaign against the Ammonites.

Samuel supported this summons by declaring that he too would join in the expedition. By Saul's command all the warriors assembled at the meeting-place. The anarchy of the era of the Judges was now at an end, and a stern will ruled. A large body of Israelites crossed the Jordan; the Ammonites, attacked on the south, north, and west, fled in all directions, and no two of them remained together. The people of Jabesh were saved, and ever after displayed the deepest gratitude to Saul and his house for the help so quickly and energetically rendered to them. On his recrossing the Jordan, after his second victory over the enemy, Saul was greeted with tumultuous joy. Samuel, who was a witness to these expressions of delight, thought it wise to remind the king and his people that their triumph should not turn into pride, and that they should not consider the kingly dignity as an end, but only as a means. He therefore summoned a large gathering of the Israelites, and determined to call the king's and the people's attention to their duties. Samuel again anointed Saul as king ; the people renewed their homage, and made joyful offerings.

In the midst of these rejoicings Samuel delivered an address, which bears testimony to the powers of his mind and to his greatness as a prophet.

Saul's two important victories, and the assemblage at Gilgal, where homage had been rendered to him by nearly all the tribes, confirmed his power, and the royal dominion was placed on a permanent basis. Although Samuel praised and extolled the days of the Judges, yet the people felt that it could better appreciate a king than a hero-judge. The nation willingly exchanged its republican liberty for the prize of unity and the power obtained thereby. The kingly estate led to various changes. Saul had to employ responsible men for the execution of his commands; he required a number of officers and servants. Officers of war were appointed to rule over hundreds and thousands respectively, and councillors, who were admitted to the king's table. A special band of men served as runners (*razim*), an armed force who became the obedient instruments of the king's will. These and their chief formed the king's court. Saul's leader of the guard was named Doag, an Idumæan by birth. Owing to the presence of the standing army and attendants, Gibeah, till then only a small town, now became the capital. Towards Samuel, Saul at first showed submission. When the prophet, in the name of God, commanded him to declare war to the death with the Amalekites, Saul immediately made preparations, and summoned his warriors. The Amalekites were the implacable and hereditary enemies of the Israelites, and had displayed the greatest cruelty towards them during their wanderings in the desert, and on their entry into the Holy Land. These enemies often joined other nations in order to crush the Israelites. The Amalekite king Agag appears to have caused great trouble to the tribe of Judah in the days of Saul.

It was, however, no light task to undertake hostilities against the Amalekites. Agag was considered a great hero, and inspired all around him with fear; but although the Amalekites were renowned for their courage and power, Saul did not hesitate to prepare for this hazardous campaign. He appears to have carried on the strife with skill and courage, and to have drawn the enemy into an ambush, by which he was enabled to obtain a complete victory. He took the capital (possibly Kadesh), killed the men, women and children, and captured the dreaded king Agag. Only a few of the people who escaped with their lives took refuge in the great neighbouring desert which leads to Egypt. The Israelite warriors carried off rich booty, including flocks of sheep, herds of cattle, and camels. According to Samuel's command, this spoil was to be destroyed, so that every trace of the memory of Amalek might be lost. The soldiers, however, did not wish this rich spoil to be given up to destruction. Saul, ordinarily so rigid in his discipline, permitted the preservation of the booty, and thus transgressed the prophet's directions. Saul was very proud of his victory over the dreaded Amalekites, and he caused the king Agag to be led in chains as a living sign of triumph. His success in battle intoxicated him, and caused him to forget his former humility. On his return he erected a monument of his victory in the oasis of Carmel. Meanwhile, Samuel, in a prophetic vision, had learned that the king had not fulfilled the instructions given him, and was therefore to be punished.

Samuel had to announce this to the victorious king; but the task was difficult, and he struggled and prayed a whole night. At last he determined to proceed to meet Saul. But hearing on the way that Saul was so dominated by pride as to cause a monument to be raised, he turned back and repaired to Gilgal. When Saul heard of this journey, he followed him thither. The elders of Benjamin and the neighbouring tribes also proceeded to Gilgal to salute the victorious king. Here they were witnesses to a strife which foreboded evil times.

As though nothing had occurred, the king met the prophet with these words, "I have fulfilled God's commands." On which Samuel sternly replied to him, " What is the meaning of the bleating of the sheep which I hear?" " It was the people," answered Saul, " who spared the best of the sheep and the

oxen, in order to sacrifice them on the altar at Gilgal."
At these words the prophet Samuel could no longer
repress his anger, and he replied in winged words:
" Hath the Lord as great delight in burnt-offerings
and sacrifices, as in obeying His voice?   Behold, to
obey is better than sacrifice, and to hearken, than the
fat of rams.   For the sin of witchcraft comes from
rebellion, and the iniquity of Teraphim from stubborn-
ness.   Because thou hast rejected the word of the
Lord, He hath also rejected thee from being king."

Saul was so deeply humiliated by these words and
by the stern and austere attitude which the prophet
adopted that he confessed his fault and, in the
effort to prevent him from going away, he seized
Samuel's robe so firmly that it was torn.   Samuel
then said, " This is a sign : God will tear thy kingly
dignity from thee and will give it to a better man,
even though Israel be torn asunder in the act."   Once
more Saul entreated the prophet.   "At least honour
me now before the elders of my tribe and of Israel,
and return with me."[1]

In consideration of this entreaty, Samuel accompanied him to the altar, where the king humbled
himself before God.   Samuel then ordered that the
fettered king Agag should be led forth.   The Amalekite king exclaimed in his fear, "Oh! how bitter,
how bitter is death!"[1]   To this exclamation Samuel
replied, "As thy sword hath made women childless,
so shall thy mother be childless among women," and
Samuel hewed Agag in pieces before the king in
Gilgal.[1]

After this scene in Gilgal, the king and the
prophet avoided each other.   The victory which
Saul obtained over Amalek was a defeat for him--
his pride was crushed.   The announcement that
God had abandoned him threw a dark shadow
over his soul.   His gloom, which later on developed

---

[1] I Samuel xv. 12 to 33   In the 32d verse read *mar mar hammavein.*

into madness, owed its rise to the threatening words of Samuel, "God will give the kingdom of Israel to a better man."[1] These terrible words were ever ringing in Saul's ears. Just as he had at first hesitated to accept the reins of government, so he was now unwilling to let them pass from his hands. At the same time he felt himself helpless. What could he do against the severity of the prophet? In order to divert himself, he plunged into warfare. There were many enemies on the borders of Israel whom he wished to subdue. He also pursued another course in order to impress the people with a sense of his importance.

There still lived amongst the Israelites a few Canaanite families and small clans who had not been expelled when the country was conquered, and could not be ejected now. These had led the Israelites to honour false gods, and to indulge in idolatrous errors. Saul therefore thought that he would greatly benefit the nation, and serve the law of Israel, if he removed these idolatrous neighbours, and everything that was foreign. Among the strangers who had been suffered to remain were the men of Gibeon, they having voluntarily submitted to the conquering Israelites. Saul did not respect the oath given to the Gibeonites, but ordered a wholesale massacre amongst them, from which but few escaped.

Together with the foreign Canaanite nations he also persecuted the sorcerers who took part in idolatrous practices. Whilst Saul, on the one hand, endeavoured to acquire the good will of his people, and showed himself the severe champion of the laws given by God, he tried, on the other hand, to impress the nation with submissive dread of the kingly power. He wore a golden crown on his head, as a sign of greatness and exaltation above the masses. His contemporaries, who had known him as a plough-

---

[1] I Samuel xv. 28.

man, and might have been inclined to treat him as their equal, were to forget his past and become accustomed to gaze at him with awe as the anointed wearer of the holy crown. Saul also indulged in the royal luxury of polygamy. He took wives in addition to his first wife Ahinoam, whom he had married when he was still a peasant. Among them was the beautiful and courageous Rizpah.

Saul showed much energy in his raids against the enemy and, no doubt in order to dissipate the fears aroused by the prophet's harsh words, displayed great pomp and ostentation, until then foreign to his nature. But sooner than he had anticipated, the evil spirit of his imagination took form in the shape of a youth that charmed him despite himself.

It happened during one of the frequent fights with the enemy that Saul's troops were drawn up in martial array against the Philistines, and the two armies stood face to face, separated from each other only by a deep ravine. Both were fearful of taking the first decisive step. At length the Philistines made the proposal that the battle should be settled by single combat, and they sent forth as their champion the gigantic warrior Goliath. King Saul would gladly have seen one of his army go forth to the duel, and he promised the victor rich presents, exemption from taxes, freedom from compulsory service, and the hand of one of his daughters. But not even at such a price did any one of the Israelite army dare to oppose himself to Goliath. Then, as if by chance, a shepherd boy of Bethlehem, a town near to the field of battle, presented himself, and brought about a decisive issue.

This shepherd of Bethlehem, directly or indirectly, was the cause of a revolution in the history of Israel, and in the history of the human race. David, then known only to the inhabitants of the village or town of Bethlehem, has since become a celebrated name throughout the world. After his disagreement with Saul, Samuel had received the prophetic mission to repair to Bethlehem in order to anoint the future king of Israel from amongst the eight sons of the aged Jesse as successor to Saul. Samuel set out in secret, lest he should be pursued by the king. The prophet selected David as the future king chosen by God, and anointed him as king of Israel in the presence of his brothers. This simple but important act was naturally performed in privacy, and was kept secret by David's father and brothers.

Jesse, the father of David, was not descended from a distinguished house of Judah, but, like all the inhabitants of Bethlehem, belonged to a very humble family. David was about eighteen years old when he was anointed, and was not distinguished either by his experience or by any deed. The beautiful pasture-land round about Bethlehem had till then composed his world. But faculties lay dormant in him which only needed to be aroused to make him excel his contemporaries intellectually as Saul surpassed them physically. David was pre-eminently gifted with poetic and musical talent, and whilst he yet tended his flock, his harp awakened the echoes of the mountains. A single circumstance, however, sufficed to change this youth into a man.

Samuel returned to Ramah as secretly as he had left; but he kept an eye on the youth whom he had anointed, and drew him into the circle of his disciples. Here David's poetic talents were developed. Here he was able to perfect himself in the use of musical instruments. But he learnt something more in Samuel's surroundings; he learnt "to know God." His spirit was pervaded with the Divine presence, and became instinct with that piety which refers all things to God, and submits in all things to Divine guidance. This reliance on God had been awakened and strengthened in him by the influence of Samuel. David frequently journeyed from Beth lehem to Ramah, and from Samuel's house to the flocks of his father. The noble courage, with which his anointment and the influence of Samuel inspired him, did not desert him when he tended his flocks in the meadows of Bethlehem. When war with the Philistines broke out, in the neighbourhood of Bethlehem, David could no longer remain a shepherd of his flocks, and he gladly undertook to deliver a message to his brothers who were serving in the army, so as to have an excuse for entering the camp. On his arrival there, he timidly told the bystanders that he was willing to risk an encounter with the blaspheming Philistine that reviled the army of the living God. The news soon reached the king's ears that a youth had offered himself for the combat. Half convinced, half in scorn, Saul gave him permission to engage in the duel, and offered him his own armour. The first stone, cast with his skilled hand from the sling, struck the heavily-armed giant from afar; he fell to the ground. David threw himself upon Goliath, drew the sword out of the scabbard, and cut off the giant's head. The Philistines, from the hilltops, had witnessed the fall of their champion, whom they had thought invincible; they declared themselves conquered, and no longer sought to prolong the war, but fled to their fastnesses. The troops of Israel, on the other hand, carried away by David's victory, followed their enemy in hot pursuit.

Holding the bleeding head in his hand, the youthful victor was led before Saul, to whom he had till then been unknown. He had not the remotest suspicion that this youth, from whom he could not withhold his admiration, might become a dreaded rival. He felt great joy at the signal victory. His son Jonathan, who had an open, tender and unselfish heart, was enchanted with the young victor. His love and attachment for David became stronger than man's love for woman. The fame of David's name and the victory he had obtained in Ephes-Damim

soon resounded throughout the valley of Terebinths,
and in the territories of all the tribes. David, however, returned to his father's house as though nothing
had happened, and merely took Goliath's shield and
armour with him as memorials. But he did not
long remain at home. The destiny of Saul had
begun to be fulfilled, and David was its chosen
instrument. The gloom of dejection, which had
obscured the soul of the king since his breach with
the prophet, became still darker. His ill-humour
deepened into sadness and melancholy, and sometimes paroxysms of wild madness took hold of
him. "An evil spirit hath entered the king," his servants whispered to each other. Instrumental music
alone was capable of rousing him; his faithful servants therefore proposed that a skilled musician and
poet should come to the court, and they advised him
to select the son of Jesse, who was handsome, brave,
eloquent, and a harpist. David came, and his musical talent, as well as his general bearing, delighted
the king. Whenever Saul fell into melancholy, David
touched the harp, and the king was relieved from his
depression. Saul felt himself enchained by David.
He began to consider him as a son, and at length
entreated David's father to leave him permanently at
court. Saul appointed him his armour-bearer, thus
securing to himself the cheering influence of his presence. This was the first step towards David's rise.
But not only was the king attracted by him, David
exercised an influence over the entire court, and all
hearts turned towards him. Jonathan, however, loved
him best of all. Saul's second daughter, Michal,
was also secretly devoted to him. At the court, David
learnt the use of weapons, and exchanged the harp
for the sword. As he was full of courage, he soon
distinguished himself in the small frays in which he
took part, and came off victorious and successful.
On one occasion, when David had inflicted a signal
defeat on the Philistines, and when there were great

rejoicings throughout the Israelite territory, the women and maidens of the various cities which he traversed on his return came forth to meet him with songs, timbrels and cymbals, dancing around him, and joyfully proclaiming him victor, saying: " Saul has killed his thousands, but David his tens of thousands." These honours, unanimously and enthusiastically offered to the youthful hero, at length opened Saul's eyes. This was "the better man," the one whom God had chosen as king over Israel; the rival with whom Samuel had threatened him, whom he dreaded so greatly, but who had hitherto only appeared to him as a visionary being, was now actually before him in the person of his own favourite and that of his people.

It was a terrible disillusion for Saul. "To me they give but thousands, and to him tens of thousands—they place him above me. What is yet wanting to make him king?" The joyous shouts of the singing and dancing choruses of women rang in his ears from that time and brought to mind the words of the prophet: " Thou art deserted of God." Saul's love for David now changed to bitter hate, which soon turned to madness.

On the very day succeeding David's return from his triumphal procession, Saul was seized with frenzy, and twice hurled a spear at David, who skilfully avoided the thrust. When the mad fit had left Saul, the failure of this attempt seemed to him a proof that God was protecting his enemy. From that time he sought to destroy his rival by stratagem. He pretended to honour David; made him the leader of the picked detachment of a thousand men, ordered him to direct attacks of great importance and danger, and offered him his eldest daughter, Merab, as a wife. Saul hoped to bring the man whom he hated to ruin by these apparent marks of favour. David, however, avoided the danger by refusing to marry Merab, and, on the other hand, he had the good fortune to defeat the Philistines. He was to have the king's second daughter in marriage, if he brought proofs of having killed one hundred Philistines. He brought evidence of having slain double the number, and Saul was obliged to keep his promise, and give him his daughter Michal. She and Jonathan sided with David against their father, thus incensing Saul still more. He sought to take David's life, at first secretly, and then openly by leading his forces against him. David was proclaimed an outlaw, and became utterly desperate. He was now joined by youths and men as forlorn as himself, and anxious for war. Chief amongst these was his kinsman, Joab, who, with his two brothers, formed the nucleus of the body of *heroic warriors* (*Gibborim*), by whose assistance David was to rise step by step to the throne. A prophet, named Gad, belonging to the school of Samuel, also joined him. The last representatives of the sacerdotal family of Eli, the high-priest, were driven by Saul into the arms of his supposed enemy. Saul, hearing that the priests of Nob, the relations and descendants of Eli, had been aiding David, caused them to be cruelly murdered, and the priestly city to be destroyed. One family alone, that of Abiathar, escaped death, and fled to David, who received the fugitives with open arms. Hatred of his rival made Saul cruel and bloodthirsty. All attempts on the part of Jonathan, who desired to mediate between his father and his friend, proved fruitless, and only served to widen the breach. Saul being clearly in the wrong, a part of the nation sided with David; but unable to assist him openly, they gave him secret help, by which he was enabled to escape from repeated persecutions. It is to be deplored that David, in his wanderings and privations, was obliged to form friendly relations with the enemies of his country—with the king of Moab, with the Ammonite king, Nahash, and with the king of the Philistines,

Achish. He thus incurred the suspicion of having become a traitor to his country, and apparently justified Saul's enmity towards him. The terms of David's alliance with Achish, by whom he had been at first refused protection, but with whom he had, on the second occasion, found refuge, seemed especially apt to implicate him. Achish granted him protection on the condition that he would break entirely with Saul and his country, so that, in case of war, he and his troops, amounting to six hundred men, might join the Philistines against his own tribe, and, in times of peace, make incursions on the remote portions of Judah, and deliver up a part of the booty to his liege lord. David, it is true, appears to have determined to evade these conditions, and eventually even to join his own people against his allies. But thus he was compelled to enter upon crooked ways, and to give up the honesty of purpose which had hitherto distinguished him. It is probable that the wild appearance of David's troops did not make a very pleasant impression on the inhabitants of Philistia. The Philistine chiefs were displeased that their sovereign should ally himself with a leader who owed his glory to victories over their own people. King Achish, however, expected so much from this alliance that he paid no heed to the warning of his counsellors. But David himself felt the discomfort of living amongst the Philistine population. He therefore begged Achish to assign to him and his followers a dwelling-place in one of his citadels. This proposition being agreeable to the Philistine king, he gave David the town of Ziklag. No sooner had the news spread that a special city had been appointed for David's occupation, than warlike men, both strangers and natives, joined him, many of whom distinguished themselves by their heroism later on. Achish believed that, in David, he had secured a faithful ally, who was employing his military knowledge and courage against members of his own tribe, and who, consequently, could never again make peace with his own people.

Thus adroitly deluded by David, Achish thought himself secure in undertaking a decisive war against the Israelites. Saul was sunk in melancholy, and since his quarrel with his son-in-law had lost his former energy in warfare. The strong arm which had fought for him, and the quick brain which had planned for him, were now turned against him. The bravest youths and men in Israel had placed themselves under David's command. Achish summoned all his troops, in order to inflict a decisive blow on Israel. Marching through the plain along the coast of the Mediterranean (which belonged to the Philistines since their victory over the Phœnicians), he led his army right into the valley of Jezreel. This territory, apart from political considerations, offered a better field than the mountain regions for employing the cavalry and chariots. In consequence of their treaty, Achish demanded that David should aid him in this great war against Saul, and unite his troops with the Philistine army. David's heart must indeed have been heavy when he joined the army, but he had no choice; he had sold himself to the enemies of his nation. The Philistine nobles, however, delivered him from his equivocal position. They loudly and vehemently demanded that the king should send away David and his soldiers, whose fidelity they mistrusted. The Philistine king was forced, by their almost rebellious demand, to dismiss David. After giving him the assurance of his unshaken confidence in his fidelity, he sent him back to Ziklag. This was fortunate for David, as he was thus saved from the dilemma of either becoming a traitor to his own people, or breaking faith with his ally Achish.

The Philistines meanwhile went forth to the number of thousands, and encamped near the town of Shunem. Saul, who had received news of the preparations of

the Philistines, and of their final expedition, called
together the Israelitish troops, advanced in forced
marches to meet the enemy, and encamped at first at
the foot of Mount Gilboa. He then marched around
the opposite heights, and, having proceeded north-
ward, encamped at the northwest base of the mountain range near Endor.

Saul lost heart at the sight of the great number
of Philistines, especially when he beheld their cavalry; the evil days which he had brought on himself had deprived him of his former courage. He
felt himself deserted by God, since neither priest
nor prophet gave an answer to his inquiry as to
the result of the war. Having waited in vain for an
inspiration to come to him in a dream, he finally, in
despair, went to a ventriloquist in Endor, who had
escaped persecution, and practised her witchcraft in
secret. It was peculiar that Saul had to have
recourse to the arts of jugglery, which formerly he
had desired to banish from his dominions. Discouraged by the ominous predictions of the witch, Saul
went into battle with a heavy heart, and as though
his fears had infected his troops, the result proved
disastrous. The Israelites, indeed, fought bravely,
and the battle lasted the whole day, but they could
not contend with the cavalry and war chariots on
the plain. They fled to the mountains of Gilboa,
but they were pursued, and routed by the Philistines. Saul's three sons, the amiable Jonathan, Abinadab and Malchishua, all fell, and the father found
himself suddenly alone, attended only by his armour-
bearer, whilst the Philistine bowmen pressed on him.
He did not wish to flee nor to be taken prisoner,
and exposed to the scorn of the Philistines. He,
therefore, entreated his servant to give him the
death-blow, and when the latter refused to lay hands
on the king, Saul had no alternative but to fall on
his own sword, and die a death worthy of a king.
The destruction was fearful. The flower of the

Israelite troops lay strewn on Mount Gilboa and the plain of Jezreel.

After resting during the night from their hard day's work, the Philistines revisited the battle-field, and stripped the slain of their clothing and ornaments. Here they found the corpses of Saul and his three sons. The king's head and his weapons they sent as trophies to Philistia; the skull they preserved in the temple of Dagon, and the weapons, in a temple of Astarte to commemorate the great victory over Israel. They then forced their way into the towns in the plain of Jezreel, and into those in the north-eastern territory near the Jordan and occupied them. The inhabitants, on hearing of the defeat at Gilboa, had fled to the opposite side of the Jordan. The Philistines, as an insult to the Israelites, hung the headless bodies of Saul and his son Jonathan on the walls of Bethshan. It appears that the Philistines, following up their victory, turned to the south of Mount Gilboa and Bethshan, and occupied every town of importance. Saul's capital, Gibeah-Saul, was filled with terror at the approach of the Philis-tines. The inhabitants fled to the mountains, and while attempting to save Jonathan's son, Mephi-bosheth, then five years old, his nurse dropped him, and he was lamed for life.

At his death, Saul left the country in a deplorable position, for things were even worse than they had been at his accession. The defeat was so thor-ough and unexpected that, at the moment, there was no thought of resistance, all courage having vanished. It was even considered an act of daring that some men of Jabesh-Gilead (from the opposite side of the Jordan), ventured, out of gratitude to Saul who had brought aid to their town, to rescue the king's body from its disgraceful exposure. They crossed the Jordan, at Bethshan, by night, took Saul's and Jonathan's bodies from the walls, buried them under a terebinth, and mourned for them during seven days. The tribes on this side of the Jordan were not equally courageous, or perhaps felt no gratitude to Saul, who had brought misery on the land by his persecution of David. Such was the end of a king whose election the nation had hailed with so much hope and joy.

CHAPTER VII

DAVID AND ISHBOSHETH.

Burning of Ziklag—Defeat of the Amalekites—Judah elects David as King—Abner and Ishbosheth—War between the houses of Saul and David—Murder of Abner—Death of Ishbosheth—David recognised as sole King—Capture of Zion—Fortification of Jerusalem—War with the Philistines—Victory of David—The Heroes —Alliance with Hiram—Removal of the Ark of the Sanctuary to Jerusalem—The High·Priest—Choral Services of the Temple— Internal Government of Israel—The Gibeonites and Rizpah— Mephibosheth.

1055—1035 B. C. E.

DAVID, too, in whom the people had once set high hopes, seemed to be forgotten by them. What had he done while his fatherland was bleeding? Whether or not his expedition with the Philistines was known, it must have appeared strange to all that, in this sad crisis, he was keeping himself aloof from every danger, only caring for his own safety, and that, instead of hastening to the aid of his oppressed people, he was holding to his treaty with the Philistines. It is true, he was himself at that time in distress, but the events which concerned him became known only later on. Meanwhile it must have been mortifying to those who cared for the weal of the kingdom that David was allied with the enemy, and that, during the absence of king Achish, in the war against Israel, David seemed in a measure to guard the enemy's frontiers. When David was sent back from his intended expedition with the Philistines on account of the suspicions of the nobles, he found that his town of Ziklag had been burnt down, and the women and children and all those who had joined him had disappeared. The Amalekites, who had suffered from David's incursions, had made use of his absence

to undertake a raid against him. The grief of the
troops was so great when they found that their
belongings had disappeared and their town had
been destroyed that they turned on David in their
anger, and threatened him with death. However,
they were encouraged by the oracular words of
Abiathar, the priest, and permitted themselves to be
appeased. Hurriedly David and his men then followed in pursuit. They discovered the camp of the
Amalekites by the aid of an Egyptian slave whom
they had found ill and deserted by the wayside. They
pursued the Amalekites, and David's angry soldiers
routed them so completely that most of them were
left dead on the field of battle, and only a few could
escape on camels. David and his troops returned to
Ziklag, buoyed up by victory. They commenced to
rebuild their town, and to settle down. Parts of the
booty taken from the Amalekites David sent as gifts
to the elders of the people and to his friends in
many towns from Beersheba to Hebron, so as to
spread the news of his victory, and, at the same time,
gain partisans for himself. Hardly had he regained
a firm footing in Ziklag, when he heard the evil
tidings of the defeat and death of Saul.

The chief men of the tribe of Judah, at the instiga-
tion of those friends whose interest he had won by his
attention, chose David as king. He then entered into
communication with the tribes on the other side of the
Jordan, in order to win also their affection. To the tribes
on this side of the river he could not appeal, as they
were still under the yoke of the Philistines. To the
inhabitants of Jabesh-Gilead, he expressed his contentment and his thanks for having shown their fidelity
towards Saul even after his death, and for having rescued the corpse of the king from ill usage. He also
informed them of the fact that the tribe of Judah had
elected him as Saul's successor.

His unhappy fate, however, still kept him in alliance with the Philistines, and his prudence was strug-

gling with his patriotism. The latter incited him to
risk everything, in order to release himself from the
fetters which bound him, whilst the former, on the
other hand, warned him not to arouse the anger of his
powerful neighbour. Achish gave David full permission to consider himself king of Judah, and to
make incursions on the border lands of the desert, on
condition that he received his share of the booty. But
beyond this David was not permitted to advance a
step. The deliverance of the land from the Philistines, which David, whose hands were bound, was
unable to carry out, was effected by Abner, Saul's
general. He had succeeded in escaping in the great
defeat at Gilboa, and he did not lose courage, but
saved what he could from the ruin which befell the
house of Saul. Attended by some fugitives, he took
refuge on the other side of the Jordan (beyond the
reach of the Philistines), where many hearts were
still faithful to Saul and his house. Abner conducted the surviving son of Saul, Ishbosheth, and
the remaining members of the helpless royal family
to Mahanaim, and induced the tribes residing on
that side of the river to acknowledge Ishbosheth as
Saul's successor. Having collected a powerful force
from among the tribes and the Benjamites who
joined him, he commenced his contest with the
Philistines. Abner was successful in ousting the
Philistines from the neighbouring border towns, but
it was only after a struggle of four or five years that
he was enabled to free the whole country (1055–1051),
so arduous was the contest. The tribe of Benjamin
was the most difficult to reconquer, as the Philistines
could most easily march their troops into its territory.
Every tribe which Abner delivered was eager to pay
homage to the son of Saul. Abner achieved great results: he not only regained independence, but even
induced tribes, which had shown themselves unruly
under Saul's government, to join the commonwealth.
He was the actual founder of the kingdom of the Ten

Tribes of Israel, and he firmly welded the links which bound them to one another. But, notwithstanding his victory and his exertions, the nation was suddenly divided into two kingdoms—that of Israel and that of Judah—and two kings ruled them. The tribe of Judah, which the energy of Samuel and of Saul had drawn from its seclusion, and reunited with the other tribes, was thus again separated from the whole.

Abner's victories aroused no feelings of joy because they led to disunion. The historian's pen hurries over his deeds, and touches but lightly on the hero's achievements. The state of affairs made an amalgamation of the houses of Judah and Israel impossible. Not only were the two kings, David and Ishbosheth, averse to the reunion of the several tribes (as in this case one of the two would have to resign his kingly dignity), but their adherents, and especially their respective generals, Joab and Abner, displayed a great degree of mutual jealousy. The scales were turned by the fact that the house of Judah was led by a brave and martial king, who had been consecrated by Samuel, and whose person was therefore considered holy, whilst Ishbosheth, a king only in name, had not been confirmed in his dignity by the voice of God, and besides, it seems, was by no means of a warlike disposition. The whole power rested in the hands of his general Abner, while Ishbosheth remained in some remote corner of his possessions, whereas David had his dwelling-place in the midst of his tribe, and thus could direct everything from his residence in Hebron.

After Abner had won or reconquered all the tribes, with the exception of Judah, a civil war broke out between the houses of Israel and Judah, or, more correctly speaking, between the houses of Saul and David. This war lasted two years (1051–1049), and raged very fiercely. At length Abner called upon Joab to put an end to the slaughter of the masses. He cried, " Must the sword slay for ever; dost thou

not know that only misfortune can arise from this
warfare? Why dost thou not command thy people
to hold off from their brethren?" At length Joab
also found it advisable to put aside his weapons, and
to proclaim an armistice. He and his people bore
the corpse of his brother Asahel, whom Abner had
slain against his will, to Bethlehem, in order that it
might be interred in the ancestral tomb, and thence
they repaired to Hebron. Abner and his followers
crossed the Jordan, and went to Mahanaim. But a
tragical destiny threatened the house of Saul. Abner
had cast covetous glances at Rizpah, the beautiful
slave of Saul, who dwelt in Mahanaim with her
two sons. Although Ishbosheth allowed his general
many liberties, he could not permit him to maintain
intimate relations with his father's widow, which im-
plied the intention of laying claim to the throne.
Abner, feeling himself slighted by the rebuke he
received, reproached this mock-king with ingratitude, and turning away from him, entered into
secret negotiations with David, offering to secure
to him the homage of all the tribes. In return for
this service, he probably stipulated that he should
retain his office of commander-in-chief of the Israelitish
tribes. David gladly entertained his proposition,
but demanded, as a preliminary concession, that his
favourite wife Michal, who had been torn from him by
Saul, and married to a Benjamite, should be restored
to him. Ishbosheth himself no doubt saw the justice
of this demand, and did not perceive in it any evil
intention towards himself. Thereupon Abner, leaving
the king under the pretext of bringing about Michal's
separation from her husband, entered the Benjamite
territory, compelled Phaltiel, Michal's husband, to
give up his wife, whom he followed, with many tears,
till Abner's angry threats compelled him to turn back
in sorrow, and David recovered the beloved wife of
his youth. Abner then wandered about amongst
the tribes trying to obtain secret adherents for David.

Many Israelites no doubt privately wished that the luckless civil war would end with submission to the king of Judah; even some of the Benjamites were not averse to a union. Attended by twenty trusty followers whom he had secured for David, Abner secretly entered Hebron; David had succeeded in sending away Joab and his brothers (the distrustful and jealous sons of Zeruiah) on a predatory expedition. During their absence, David personally arranged with Abner and his twenty followers the manner in which the elders of the tribes should be won over to his side, and how the dethronement of Ishbosheth should then be effected. Abner had already left Hebron in order to call upon the elders of the tribes to follow his example, and do homage to the king of Judah. When Joab returned from his expedition, he heard the astonishing intelligence that Abner, the enemy of David's house, had been received, and permitted to depart in full favour, and that the king had made a secret treaty behind his back. As it seemed to him inevitable that he must be the victim of such a compact, he quickly decided on his course, and sent messengers after Abner, who induced him to return. Joab and Abishai lay in wait for him at the gates of Hebron, and Abner, unaware and unwarned, was felled to the earth by their swords. David felt the death of Abner acutely. The man who alone was able and willing to obtain for him the adherence of all the tribes by peaceful measures was thus foully murdered, on the very eve of the realisation of his plan. David was placed in an awkward position. In order to destroy any suspicion which might arise against him, David gave solemn expression to his sincere grief at Abner's loss. He commanded a grand, imposing funeral in Hebron for Israel's fallen hero, ordered all his followers to attend the funeral procession, and accompanied it himself. He breathed forth his tearful grief in an elegiac poem, the beginning of which has been preserved, and which made a powerful impression on all hearers. All burst into tears, and were convinced of the sincerity of his sorrow by the manner in which he recited his threnode. On the other hand, David feared to take the sons of Zeruiah to account, or even to reproach them for their conduct; he could not spare their assistance. In the circle of his intimates only, uttering bitter complaints of them, he said, " Know that a great prince in Israel has fallen to-day."

The news of Abner's murder made a deep impression on Ishbosheth. He had no knowledge of his fallen general's treacherous league with David, and he therefore deeply mourned the death of a hero whom he supposed to be faithful, and whose loss seemed to be irreparable, for he considered Abner as the chief support of his throne.

After Ishbosheth's death the kingdom of the ten tribes naturally fell to David. Among them, too, he had adherents of long standing, who remembered his warlike deeds against the Philistines in Saul's time, and who honoured him as the chosen one of God through his prophet Samuel. Others had been won over to his side by Abner. Even those who took offence at David's league with the enemies of Israel, could not hide from themselves the consideration that no choice was left them but to do him homage. The Benjamites also acknowledged him, but with a secret grudge, which they could hardly conceal. David's dearest wish was now realised; from having been the ruler of a little, insignificant tribe he had become, after many obstacles and troubles, the king of all Israel. The breach between the houses of Judah and Israel was healed apparently, and everything seemed favourable to him. The priesthood and the prophets did not take a hostile attitude towards him, as they had done towards Saul, but joined with heart and soul in his cause. A descendant of the house of Eli, named Abiathar, who had shared David's troubles, belonged to his court; and the prophets welcomed in him the man who had been anointed by Samuel, and had belonged to that great man's circle of disciples. The prophet Gad was also a member of the court; and another prophet of the time, named Nathan, was to a certain extent the keeper of David's conscience. Thus encouraged in all his undertakings by his spiritual advisers, everything tended to level the way for him, as far as the internal government was concerned. But his foreign relations occasioned him great difficulties, which had to be overcome before he could rule as an independent king.

In the first place, David was forced to break with the Philistines, if he wished to be independent, and to win back the love of his people. He had to prepare himself for fierce warfare with his former auxiliaries. But he did not immediately commence hostilities with them; they were too powerful for him. He wished first to free himself from other bonds. In the midst of the Benjamite territory was an enclosure, which had remained in the possession of the Jebusites, because the Israelites, on their entry into the land, had not conquered it. The high hill of ZION was rendered inaccessible on three sides by narrow valleys and artificial fortifications. The most impregnable point was the south side, where the rocky wall of the hill rose almost in a vertical line from an abyss below. From this mountain fortress, the Jebusites ruled the entire surrounding territory, and felt themselves secure from all intruders. They appear to have lived in a state of peace with the surrounding Benjamites and Judæans, as even Saul did not disturb them in the possession of their territory. David, however, considered it conducive to his interest to obtain possession of this citadel of Zion before commencing hostilities with the Philistines. He therefore resolved to storm the citadel, and subdue its defenders. As soon as the Jebusites found all opposition useless they sued for peace, which was granted them by David. They were allowed to remain in their city, but not in the fortress; he permitted them to settle in the east of the town, on Mount Moriah. This victory, which had appeared so difficult, and had, in fact, been easily obtained, had been preceded by the boast of the Jebusites about the blind and the lame, which gave rise to a proverb.

After its conquest, David removed his capital from Hebron to Mount Zion, and it was henceforth known as the town of David. The city itself lost its old name of Jebus, and received the new name Jerusalem (*Jerushalayim*), the meaning of which is not known. Hither David removed with his warriors and their families, and his courtiers. The spot where the bravest soldiers had their dwellings was called after them the house of the brave (*Beth-ha-Gibborim*). Such was the beginning of the place which since then, and for centuries, was to be known as the " Holy City." The choice of this spot as a capital was a happy stroke, as circumstances soon proved. It is true, Shechem would have made a better metropolis, on account of its position in the midst of the tribes, and the fruitful territory around it. But David found it impossible to move his dwelling to the town of the Ephraimites. The inhabitants were not especially well disposed towards him, and rather unwilling that the half-savage king, who sprang from Judah, should prescribe laws to them. Besides, he needed the support of his own tribe, and this he could have in Jerusalem, which was situated on the boundaries of Benjamin and Judah, and which would serve as a protection in the event of unruliness on the part of the other tribes. The territory on which the new capital was erected was not sterile, though it could bear no comparison with the part of the country in which Shechem lay. In the valleys flow everlasting springs, the springs of Siloah and En-Rogel in the south, the Gihon in the west; so that in the dry season the town and fields can always be supplied with water. On three sides Jerusalem is surrounded by a range of hills which protect and embellish it.   On the east is a high watershed (2724 feet), Mount Olivet, so named from the olive trees which cover it.   In the south the hills are not so lofty, and the valley dividing them from the city is narrower.   The valley is that of Henna (Ge-henna), which was thus named after an individual or a family, and which was destined to acquire a sad renown, and to supply another appellation for hell (*Gehenna*).   On the west the summits are also low, and can hardly be called hills.   On the north, the hills gently slope down to the plain.   By these hills and valleys, which form natural walls and ditches, Jerusalem is sheltered on three sides.   Within Jerusalem, on the high plateau and between the three valleys on the east, south, and west, there are three ranges of hills rising above the plain.   On the west is Zion, the loftiest summit.   On the north is a hill of no great height; and opposite the third is Mount Moriah, which has an offshoot towards the south, called "Ophel."   Moriah, though much less lofty than Zion, was destined to eclipse it and the greatest heights on earth in importance.

The Philistines could not ignore the fact that the choice of David as king of the entire Israelite nation had not only greatly loosened the bond which united him to them, but that it must in the future force him to take up a hostile attitude towards themselves. They did not, however, wish to break with him.   But when the conquest of Jebus (Jerusalem) took place, they considered the fact of his removing his dwelling thither as a premonitory sign.   They hastened to join with him in battle, before he had time to arm the available troops of the various tribes.   A Philistine band pressed forward across the plain into the mountains, and approached Jerusalem.   Whether David was surprised by their attack, or whether he wished to avoid an action near his capital, is

unknown, but he left it with his troops, and moved
southwards to Adullam. Encouraged by this retreat,
the Philistines pressed on to Bethlehem, David's birth-
place, where they encamped, and whence they sent
out predatory expeditions to ravage the land of
Judah. David delayed attacking the Philistines; his
army was probably too weak, and he expected reinforcements from the tribes. In order to stimulate
his warriors to trials of strength during the pause
before the decisive contest, David expressed a wish
to drink water from a well in Bethlehem, which was
in the possession of the Philistines. Three of the
chief warriors, Jesheboam, Eleazar, and Shammah,
immediately set out against the Philistines, daringly
drew water from the well, and brought it to David
at Adullam. David, however, would not drink the
water for which his warriors had risked their
lives. He had only put them to the test. At
length the Israelite troops went forth to meet the
Philistines, and utterly routed them at Mount Baal-
Perazim. This victory was so decisive that it was
compared with Joshua's at Gibeon. In their hurried
flight, the Philistines left behind them their idols,
which were burnt by the Israelites. The enemy did
not, however, relinquish their intention of subduing
David and his people. They made repeated attacks,
once in the valley of Rephaim, another time near
Ephes-dammim in Terebinthea; David's troops
and warriors performed miracles of bravery, they
defeated their enemies, and pursued them as far as
Gaza. David did not content himself with mere
defence, but he determined on attacking the Philistines. If he wished to protect his people, it was
necessary either constantly to harass, or to subdue
the small but powerful nation which depended on
incursions and warfare for its maintenance. He
therefore proceeded with his soldiers as far as Gath,
the former capital of the Philistines, which was
situated nearest to the land of Judæa. The Phil-

istines made a very obstinate resistance, and violent conflicts arose, in which David's heroes had ample opportunity for distinguishing themselves. It appears that the Philistines suggested, according to their custom, that there should be combats with the remnant of their Rephaitic giants. Times had changed, however, and whilst in David's youth the Israelitish troops had not had among them a single soldier who would accept Goliath's challenge, there were now more than thirty who burned with eagerness to take part in the duels. On this occasion the warriors entreated the king not to expose himself in battle, and, in fact, not to go to war himself, in order that " the light of Israel " might not be extinguished.

At length the Israelites succeeded in utterly routing the Philistines, so that they were obliged to surrender their capital Gath, and its villages and the surrounding territory. The town in which the son of Jesse had first appeared, entreating help in the guise of an imbecile, thus fell before him. One of the thirty warriors, Sibbechai of Hushah, killed the giant Sippai of Gath; another man from Bethlehem named Elhanan, killed the brother of Goliath, named Lahmi, who had sallied forth to the contest like Goliath, laden with armour. David's nephew Jonathan killed a giant who had an additional finger on each hand, and an additional toe on each foot. David himself was once, when exhausted from the long struggle, in imminent danger of being overcome by the giant Ishbi of Gath; Abishai, however, Joab's brother, hurried to his aid, defeated the giant, and killed three hundred Philistines with his spear. The overthrow of the Philistines was an event of the greatest importance; it ensured lasting peace and freedom of action to the people, for none of the other enemies of Israel harassed it so persistently. David did not push his victory further; he left the important cities of Gaza, Askelon, Ashdod and Ekron undisturbed, and even the town of Gath he appears later on to have restored to its king. No doubt he had reasons for not using extreme measures with the Philistines. It appeared to him better to rule them as a tributary power than to drive them to a war of desperation.

By his victory over the Philistines, David attained great importance and respect in the eyes of the neighbouring peoples. Hiram, the king who had transferred the Phœnician power from Zidon to Tyre, despatched ambassadors to David, offering to make an alliance with him. He also offered to send supplies of cedar wood and building materials for adorning the new capital of Jerusalem in a fitting manner. He rejoiced at the subjection of the Philistines, probably because they would no longer be able to cast covetous glances at the Phœnician coast-lands. It was a matter of great interest to the king of Tyre to secure an alliance with David, in order that the Phœnician caravans might have free passage, and find protection for their goods when they passed backwards and forwards between Phœnicia and Egypt. David willingly accepted his advances, and thus a sort of friendship arose between him and Hiram. He accepted Hiram's offer in order to fortify the capital which had been founded by him, and to obtain materials for adorning it with architectural works, so that Jerusalem might vie in outward appearance with the other capitals of those times. In the first place Jerusalem was fortified, especially on the north, where it was most liable to be attacked. The hill of Zion, or City of David, was, in fact, not sufficiently extensive to contain all the inhabitants who had already settled there, and it had become necessary to take measures to provide for the increasing population. For this reason, the hill which lay to the north of the town was included in its boundaries. Between Zion and this hillock lay a narrow valley. The northern elevation of the town was called *Millô* (border); it was considered the newer quarter of the town, in comparison with the more ancient city of David.   Mount Moriah and its offshoot Ophel remained outside the circuit of the city, and in those days was not considered as belonging to Jerusalem, but was inhabited by the surviving remnant of the Jebusites.   David also built a palace of cedar, the wood for which was procured from Lebanon.   To Joab and the other important personages of David's court were assigned roomy and well-built houses, which were not constructed of cedar wood, but of cypress.

David further sought to make Jerusalem the centre of religious life, in order that the eyes of the whole nation might be turned towards it.   He therefore took measures to remove the ark of the sanctuary from the house of Abinadab at Kirjath-Jearim, where it had remained since its recovery from the hands of the Philistines.   A splendid tent was built for its reception in the city of David. David had vowed not to remain in his house, nor to rest on his bed, nor to close his eyes in sleep until he had found a resting-place for the ark of the covenant.   Accompanied by a great concourse, the king repaired to Kirjath-Jearim (which lay at about an hour's journey to the north-west of Jerusalem), and many Levites followed in the king's train.   The ark of the sanctuary was placed on a new carriage drawn by bullocks, which were led by two sons of Abinadab. Choirs of Levites sang hymns, and accompanied themselves on stringed instruments, and David also assisted them with all his might.   An accident, how-ever, occurred on the road.   Uzzah, who walked next to the chariot, suddenly fell down dead.   David was so shocked at this catastrophe that he hesitated to carry the ark of the covenant into Jerusalem.   He feared that it might bring down misfortune on the people, as it had done in the case of the Philistines.   It was therefore placed in a house for three months, and, seeing that no evil came of it, David determined on

making a second attempt at bringing it to Mount
Zion.   On this occasion, however, it was not placed
on a chariot, but was carried by Levites.   Followed
by a mass of people, and amidst shouts of joy, blasts
of trumpets, and dancing, the ark was conveyed to
the tent appointed for it.   The king himself, oblivious
of his dignity, sang and danced in exultation before
the ark.   His conduct called forth a rebuke from his
wife Michal, who scoffingly charged him with be-
having like a public clown.

As it had done in the case of Shiloh, the arrival of
the Ark raised Jerusalem to the dignity of a holy
city.   In such a place of public worship, it was neces
sary to maintain a priest, or rather a priesthood.
Abiathar, David's faithful follower in all his wanderings,
was, as a matter of course, raised to the office of High
Priest to the sanctuary in Zion.   There was, however,
another high priest in Gibeon, whom Saul had placed
there after the destruction of Eli's family in Nob.
David could not entirely displace him, for such a
course would have led to dissensions.   He therefore
confirmed his predecessor's appointment, and thus
retained two high priests in office at the same time—
Abiathar in Jerusalem, and Zadok in Gibeon.   A
former pupil of the Levitical choirs, himself a poet
and a musician, David naturally followed Samuel's
example and introduced choral singing into the
solemn religious services.   He also composed hymns
of praise at times, when a victory over the enemy, or
some other success filled his heart with thankfulness,
and animated him with poetical fervour.   It may be
said that his songs have become the prototypes of this
lofty and inspiring style of verse.   Besides the royal
psalmist there were other poets and musicians, such
as Asaph, Heman, a grandson of Samuel, and Jeduthun.   Their descendants were the Asaphites and
Korachites (Bene Korach), who are named with
David as the most famous composers of psalms.
David arranged that Asaph and his choir should lead

the choral service in the sanctuary at Jerusalem, whilst his fellow-musicians, Heman and Jeduthun, performed the same functions at the altar in Gibeon. Samuel's creation of a spiritual divine service was thus firmly established by David; and though he was an upholder of sacrificial rites, he valued the elevating and refining influence of psalmody too highly not to make it an integral element of the public cult. At a time when poetry as an art had hardly awakened amongst the other nations, it already occupied a prominent place in the divine service of Israel.

As David was the actual founder of a sanctifying divine worship, he was also the creator of a system of government which was based on justice. He presided at the tribunal, listened untiringly to the disputes of individuals or of tribes, and administered justice with strict impartiality. His throne was not only the high seat of government and power, it was also that of order and justice. Succeeding generations pronounced David the ideal king. His throne was looked upon as the prop of justice, and his sceptre as the standard of civic peace. Jerusalem was by him made an ideal city, where a pure worship of God had been established, and justice, in its most exalted form, had found its earthly resting-place. A later psalmist says—

> "Jerusalem, that art builded as a city that is compact together,
> Whither the tribes go up, even the tribes of the Lord;
> For a testimony unto Israel,
> To give thanks unto the name of the Lord.
> For there are set thrones for judgment,
> The thrones of the house of David." PSALM cxxii. 3-5.

Jerusalem was considered "a faithful citadel—full of righteousness—where justice had its dwelling-place." These circumstances, the deliverance from the yoke of the Philistines, the universal safety, and the establishment of justice under David's rule, rendered him again the favourite of the people, as he had been in his youth. A feeling of loyalty to him prevailed, which was of spontaneous growth, and in which force had no share.

David partly altered the internal arrangements of the country. The constitution of the tribes remained intact. The elders represented the families, and the head of the oldest family was also the prince of his tribe (Naszi-Beth-Ab). The princes were the representatives of the tribes with the king. But it was necessary to limit the freedom, or rather the arbitrariness of the tribes, in regard to military arrangements. Each tribe, in case of war, was bound to contribute a number of capable soldiers (over twenty years of age) as its contingent to the national army (*Zaba*). A special officer was appointed over this contingent, who was called the enumerator (*Sopher*), or the keeper of the rolls. He wrote down on a list the names of the men fit for active service, looked to their enrolment, and compelled the attendance of all defaulters. This duty David delegated to a man named Shavsha, from whom it passed on to his heirs. As soon as the army was assembled, it was commanded by the field officer (*Sar-ha-Zaba*), who at this conjuncture was Joab. David also supported a troop of mercenaries whom he recruited from the heathen soldiery, the Cherethites, who came from a territory belonging to the Philistine dominions, and the Pelethites, whose origin is unknown. Benaiah, son of Jehoiada, one of the bravest of David's soldiers, was their commander. David also appointed a special officer on whom devolved the duty of reporting to the king all important, or apparently important events. He was called the recorder (*Maskhir*). As favouritism is inseparable from kingly will, David also had a favourite (named Hushai the Arkhi) on whom he could rely under all circumstances, especially in cases requiring discretion. He was also fortunate in having an adviser at hand, who could give suitable counsel in various emergencies; his name was Ahithophel, and his birthplace

was the Judæan town of Gilo. At that time his
advice was currently said to be as infallible as the
oracles uttered by the lips of the high priest. This
wise and over-wise councillor of David was destined
to exercise a great influence over his royal master.
At one time David's judicial conscience was put to
a severe test. A famine of long duration overspread
the land on account of a two years' drought. The
distress continued to grow when, at the commencement of the third year, no rain had fallen, and the
people turned to the king for help. This misfortune,
in which the entire country shared, was interpreted
as being God-sent retribution for some secret and
unavenged sin. David therefore inquired of the
priest Abiathar what sin required expiation, and the
answer came, "on account of Saul and his ruthless
persecution of the Gibeonites." David then sent to
the remnant of the Gibeonites, and inquired of them
what atonement they desired. Not satisfied with an
expiatory sum of money, they demanded that seven
descendants of Saul should be hanged in Gibeah-Saul.
The demand of the Gibeonites seemed just, for
according to the views of the time, only blood could
atone for the shedding of blood and a breach of faith.
With a heavy heart David had to comply with the
demand of the Gibeonites, and satisfy the desire of
the nation. The two sons of Saul's concubine
Rizpah, and his grandson, the son of his daughter
Merab, were sought out, handed over to the
Gibeonites, and killed by them in cold blood, in
Gibeah-Saul, the town in which their father had won
a crown.

David spared only Mephibosheth, the son of
Jonathan, for he remembered the oath made to his
friend, that he would always protect his descendants.
The corpses of the seven victims were to remain on
the gallows until rain should fall from the heavens,
but it was long ere the rainfall came. It was in those
dire days that the beautiful Rizpah, for whose sake

Abner had quarrelled with Ishbosheth, showed of
what a mother's love is capable.   In order to prevent
her sons' corpses from being devoured by eagles and
jackals, she made her couch on the rocks on which
the bodies were exposed, and guarded them with a
watchful eye through the heat of day.   Nor did she
relax her vigilance in the night, but continued her
work of scaring away the beasts of prey from the
dead.   When at length in the autumn the rain fell,
the seven bodies were taken down, and at David's
command the last honours were bestowed on them.
He also seized this opportunity to remove the
remains of Saul and Jonathan from Jabesh-Gilead,
and to bury them, together with the remains of
their kindred, in the family tomb of the house of
Kish at Zelah.   It appears that, on this occasion,
David caused his deeply touching lament for the
death of Saul and of Jonathan to be reproduced, in
order to express publicly how deeply the destruction
of the royal house of Benjamin had affected him.
He directed that the elegy should be committed to
memory by the youths of the country.   Jonathan's
surviving son, Mephibosheth (who had been living in
the house of a much-respected man on the other side
of the Jordan) was brought to Jerusalem, and David
received him in his own house, placed him at his own
table, and treated him as one of his own sons.   David
also restored to him Saul's lands in the tribe of
Benjamin, and entrusted the management of them
to one of Saul's slaves, named Ziba.   Notwithstanding this, the Benjamites accused David of
destroying the house of Saul, and of having preserved Mephibosheth, because he was lame and unfit
o rule.   When David's fortune was on the wane,
the embittered Benjamites cast stones at him.

CHAPTER VIII.

DAVID.

War with the Moabites—Insult offered by the king of the Ammonites—War with the Ammonites—Their Defeat—Battle of Helam—Attack of Hadadezer—Defeat of the Aramæans—Acquisition of Damascus—War with the Idumæans—Conquest of the town of Rabbah—Defeat of the Idumæans—Conquered races obliged to pay tribute—Bathsheba—Death of Uriah the Hittite—Parable of Nathan—Birth of Solomon (1033)—Misfortunes of David—Absalom—Wise Woman of Tekoah—Reconciliation of David and Absalom—Numbering of the Troops—Pestilence breaks out in Israel—Absalom's Rebellion—Murder of Amasa—Sheba's Insurrection—David and Nathan—Adonijah.

1035—1015 B. C. E.

WHEN David had completed two decades of his reign, he became involved in several wars, which withdrew him from the peaceful pursuits of regulating the internal affairs of the country, and of attending to the administration of justice. These wars with distant nations, forced on him against his will, gave him an immense accession of power, and raised the prestige of the people in a surprising degree. David first began a fierce warfare with the Moabites, who dwelt on the opposite side of the Dead Sea. With them he had been on friendly terms during his wanderings, and amongst them he had met with a hospitable reception. It is probable that the Moabites had ousted from their possession the neighbouring Reubenites, and that David hurried to their rescue. It must in any case have been a war of retribution, for, after his victory, David treated the prisoners with a severity which he did not display towards any of the other nations whom he conquered. The Moabite captives were fettered, and cast side by side on the ground, then measured with a rope, and two divisions were killed, whilst one division was spared. The whole land of Moab was subdued, and a yearly tribute was to be sent to Jerusalem.

Some time afterwards, when Nahash, king of the Ammonites, died, David, who had been on friendly terms with him, sent an embassy to his son Hanun, with messages of condolence. This courtesy only roused suspicion in Rabbath-Ammon, the capital of the Ammonites. The new king's counsellors impressed him with the idea that David had sent his ambassadors as spies to Rabbah, in order to discover their weakness, to conquer them, and to deliver them over to the same fate that had befallen the Moabites. Hanun was so carried away by his suspicions that he offered an insult to the king of Israel which could not be passed over unnoticed. He obliged the ambassadors, whose persons, according to the laws of nations, were inviolable, to have their beards shaved off on one side, and their garments cut short, and thus disgraced he drove them out of the country. The ambassadors were ashamed to appear at Jerusalem in this guise, but they informed David of the occurrence. He immediately prepared himself for battle, and the militia was called out; the old warriors girded their loins, and the Cherethite and Pelethite mercenaries sallied forth with their heroic leader Benaiah at their head. Hanun, who feared the valor of the Israelites, looked around for help, and engaged mercenary troops from among the Aramæans, who lived in the regions between the mountains of Hermon and the banks of the Euphrates. Hadadezer, king of Zobah on the Euphrates, contributed the greatest number—20,000 men. David did not personally conduct this war, but left the supreme command with the careful and reliable Joab. Having led the Israelite army across the Jordan, Joab divided it into two bodies. With the one he attacked the Aramæans, the other he left under the command of

his brother Abishai.   He aroused the enthusiasm of
his army by inspiring words : " Let us fight bravely
for our people and the city of our God, and may the
Lord God do what seemeth good unto Him."   Joab
then dashed at the Aramæans, and put them to flight.
On this, the Ammonites were seized with such fear
that they withdrew from the field, and took shelter
behind the walls of their capital.   It was a most successful achievement.   Joab hurried to Jerusalem to
report to the king, and to lay before him a plan by
which the Aramæans might be totally annihilated,
and any future interference on their part prevented.
The victorious army, having been recalled from the
Ammonitish territories, was reinforced, and with the
king himself at its head pursued the Aramæan enemy
on the other side of the Jordan.   King Hadadezer, on
his part, also sent fresh troops to the aid of his defeated forces, but in a battle at Helam, the Aramæan
army was again defeated, and its general, Shobach,
fell in the encounter.   The vassals of the mighty
Hadadezer then hastened to make peace with David.

Tôi (or Tou), the king of Hamath, who had been at
war with Hadadezer, now sent his son Joram to
David with presents, congratulating him on the victory over their common foe.   David followed up
his successes until he reached the capital of king
Hadadezer, situated on the banks of the Euphrates.
The Aramæans were then defeated a third time ;
their chariots and soldiers could not withstand the
attack of the Israelite army.   The extensive district
of Zobah, to which various princes had been tributary, was divided into several parts.

The king of Damascus, an ally of the king of
Zobah, was also defeated by David, and the ancient
town of Damascus henceforth belonged to the king
of Israel.   David placed land-overseers in all the
Aramæan territories from Hermon to the Euphrates,
in order to enforce the payment of tribute.   David
and his army themselves must have been astonished

at the wonderful result which they had achieved. It rendered the king and his army objects of fear far and wide. Meanwhile the king of the Ammonites had escaped punishment for his insults to the ambassadors of Israel. In consequence of the campaign against the Aramæans, which lasted nearly a year, the Israelitish army had been unable to resume the war against Hanun. It was only after the great events narrated above that David was again enabled to send his forces, under Joab, against Ammon. Yet another war arose out of the hostilities against this nation. The Idumæans, on the south of the Dead Sea, had also assisted the Ammonites by sending troops to their aid, and these had to be humiliated now. David deputed his second general, Abishai, Joab's brother, to direct the campaign against the Idumæans. Joab was in the meantime engaged in a long contest with the Ammonites, who had secured themselves behind the strong walls of their fortified capital, and were continually making raids on their foes. The Israelitish army had neither battering rams nor other instruments of siege. Their only alternative was to storm the heights of the city, and in their attempts to carry out this plan they were often repelled by the bowmen on the walls. At length Joab succeeded, after repeated attacks, in gaining possession of one part of the city—the Water-Town; he reported this victory to David at once, and urged him to repair to the camp in order to lead in person the attack on the other quarters, so that the honour of the conquest might be entirely his own. When David arrived at Rabbah with fresh troops, he succeeded in subduing the whole town, and in obtaining rich booty. David himself put on his head the golden diadem, richly adorned with precious stones, which had heretofore crowned the Ammonitish idol Malchom (Milchom). It appears that David did not destroy the city of Rabbah, as he had intended. He merely condemned the male inhabitants, or perhaps only the prisoners, to do hard work, such as polishing stones, threshing with iron rollers, hewing wood with axes, and making bricks. He treated the other prisoners from the various towns in a similar manner. Hanun, the original cause of the war, who had so deeply insulted David, was either killed or driven out of the kingdom. In his stead David appointed his brother Shobi as king. Meanwhile Abishai had been engaged in a war against the Idumæan king, and had utterly routed him in the Valley of Salt—probably in the neighbourhood of the rock-salt mountain, near the Dead Sea. Eighteen thousand Idumæans are said to have fallen there. The rest probably submitted; and for this reason David contented himself with placing excise officers and a garrison over them, as he had done in Damascus and the other Aramæan provinces. The Idumæans, however, seem later on to have revolted against the Israelitish garrison and the tax collectors, and to have massacred them. Joab therefore repaired to Idumæa, caused the murdered Israelites to be buried, and all Idumæan males to be put to death. He was occupied with this war of destruction during half a year, and so thoroughly was the task executed that only a few of the male sex could save themselves by flight. Amongst them was a son or a grandson of the Idumæan king.

By these decisive victories, in the west over the Philistines, in the south over the Idumæans, in the east (on the opposite side of the Jordan) over the Moabites and Ammonites, and in the north over the Aramæans, David had raised the power of Israel to an unexpected degree. While, at the commencement of his reign, when he was first acknowledged king of all Israel, the boundaries of the country had been comprised between Dan and Beersheba, he now ruled over the wide-spread territory from the river of Egypt (Rhinokolura, El-Arish) to the Euphrates, or from Gaza to Thapsacus (on the

Euphrates). The nations thus subdued were obliged annually to do homage by means of gifts, to pay tribute, and perhaps also to send serfs to assist in building and other severe labour.

These wars and victories were better calculated than his early hardships to bring to light the great qualities of David's mind. Strong and determined as he was in every undertaking in which the honour and safety of his people were involved, he remained modest and humble, without a spark of presumption, after success had been attained. He erected no monument to commemorate his victories as had been done by Saul; like his general, Joab, he was imbued with the thought that to God alone was to be attributed the victory. The faith in God, to which David had given utterance when he prepared himself for the duel with the Rephaite Goliath (1 Samuel xvii. 47), he preserved in all great contests. David elaborated this guiding thought in a psalm, which he probably chanted before the ark at the close of the war, and in which he gives a retrospect of his entire past life.

In consequence of their great victories, two firm convictions were impressed on the minds of the people, and these actuated and possessed them in all times to come. The one idea occurs in various forms: "A king cannot escape by the multitude of his army, nor a warrior by his power; vain is the horse for safety." God alone decides the fate of war, brings it to a close, gives victory or defeat, and "to Him it is equally easy to conquer with few or with many." The other idea, in closest connection with it, is that God leads the armies of Israel to victory, if they go forth to glorify His name or to save His people. The God of Israel was, in accordance with this idea, designated by a special name which fully expresses this thought; He was named the *God of hosts* (Adonai Zebaoth), the God who gives victory unto Israel in its conflicts. The King

Zebaoth was invoked before every battle, and the Israelitish troops went forth with the firm conviction that they could never be defeated. This confidence, certainly, worked wonders in the course of time.

Severely as David treated the idols of the nations whom he had conquered, he behaved with comparative leniency to the conquered idolaters. The Moabites alone were cruelly punished, and the Ammonites were enslaved, but the other conquered races were merely obliged to pay tribute. The offences of the former must have been very great to have deserved so heavy a punishment. The foreign races residing in the country were not molested; thus we find Jebusites in Jerusalem, and Canaanites and Hittites in other parts of the country. Hence we find many strangers and natives not of Israelitish descent enrolled in his corps of warriors, or leading their own troops in his service. The Hittite Uriah, one of David's thirty heroes, who was destined to play a melancholy part in David's career, was deeply attached to the Israelitish nation.

The joy over these great achievements remained, however, but for a short time unmarred. The happiness of a state, like that of individuals, is but seldom of long duration, and days of sunshine must be followed by periods of darkness, to prevent the enervation of the national vigour. By one false step David lost not only his own inward contentment and peace, but shook the very foundations of that state which it had cost him such exertions to establish. When David returned home from the Aramæan war, and was resting from the fatigues of battle, which Joab and his army were still undergoing in the land of Ammon, he beheld from the roof of his palace a beautiful woman, who was bathing. She was the wife of one of his most faithful warriors (the Hittite, Uriah), and her name was Bathsheba. The houses of the warriors were built on Zion in the vicinity of the king's palace, and thus he happened to

see Bathsheba. Carried away by his passion, he sent
messengers to command her to repair to the palace,
and Bathsheba obeyed. When David, some time
after, found that this violation of the marriage tie
had not been without consequences, his only thought
was to save his honour, and thus he involved himself
in deeper sin. He commanded Uriah to return to
Jerusalem from the camp at Rabbah. He received
him in a friendly manner, and gave him permission
to rest, and enjoy the company of his wife. Uriah,
however, made no use of this permission, but remained with the guard, who slept at the entrance of
the king's palace, and protected his person. David
was disappointed. He sought an escape from the
dilemma, and this led him into a heinous crime.
As he could not save his honour, he determined that
Uriah should lose his life. David therefore sent him
to the camp with a letter to Joab, saying that the
bearer should be placed in a post of extreme danger
—nay, of certain death—during one of the sorties of
the Ammonites. This command was fulfilled, and
Uriah fell, struck dead by an Ammonite arrow.
Bathsheba fulfilled the customary time of mourning
for her husband, and was then received into the
palace by David as his wife.

In every other State the court circle would have
discussed a king's fancy with bated breath; it would
hardly have been blamed, and certainly it would soon
have been forgotten. But in Israel there was an eye
which could pierce this factitious darkness, and a conscience which declaimed in a loud voice against the
crimes of even a royal wrong-doer. Prophetism possessed this clear sight which never failed, and this conscience which never slept. It was its foremost duty not
to allow sin to grow into a habit by hushing it up and
screening it, but to expose it in glaring colors, and
brand it with the stamp of public condemnation.

David no doubt believed that Bathsheba alone was
cognisant of his sin, and Joab the only accessory to

the plot against Uriah's life. But this error was suddenly and rudely dispelled. The prophet Nathan one day came to David, and requested permission to bring a certain case to his notice. He then related the following parable:—In a great city there lived a rich man, who possessed great flocks and herds; and near him lived a poor man who possessed but one little lamb, which he had reared for himself. One day, when a guest came to the rich man, he was too stingy to kill one of his flock for the meal, but he took the lamb of the poor man to feast his friend. On hearing this complaint, David's sense of justice was aroused, and he said indignantly that the heartless rich man deserved to die, and should pay the poor man four times the value of the lamb. Then the prophet replied, "Thou art the man!"

Any other king would have punished the moralist who had dared speak the truth to a crowned head, to the representative of God on earth. David, however, the pupil of the prophet Samuel, when the picture of his misdeeds was thus placed before him, penitently answered, "Yes, I have sinned." He certainly did not fail to offer up heartfelt prayers, and to make atonement in order to obtain God's forgiveness. The child which was born died in early infancy, although David had worn himself away in fasting and prayers for its life. Bathsheba afterwards had a second son named Jedidiah, or Solomon (1033), who became the favourite of his father.

But though God pardoned the king for his heinous sins, humanity did not forgive them, and they proved fatal to domestic peace. Bathsheba, the wife of Uriah, was the daughter of Eliam (one of David's warriors), and the granddaughter of his counsellor Ahithophel. The father and grandfather felt their honour disgraced through their daughter's seduction, which they could never forgive, although they kept silence, and did not betray their hatred. Ahithophel especially nursed his vengeance in secret, and only awaited an opportunity to wreak it on the king. David did all in his power to appease them. He elevated Bathsheba to the rank of first queen, promised her secretly that her son should be his successor, and solemnly swore to fulfil this promise. He wished at any cost to make peace with Ahithophel, whose counsel was precious to him. Ahithophel, however, remained immovable. A scandalous event in the house of David involved matters to a still greater extent, and robbed his remaining years of all tranquillity. His eldest son Amnon seduced his half-sister Tamar, and thereby aroused the fierce anger of her brother Absalom, who determined to avenge her. Each of the king's sons, six of whom had been born in Hebron, and eleven, in Jerusalem, had, when he attained manhood, his own house, household and lands. Absalom's lands and herds were situated at Baal-Hazor, not far from the capital. Thither he invited all the king's sons to the feast of sheep-shearing. Whilst they and their guests were enjoying the feast, and drinking freely, Absalom's servants, at their master's command, attacked Amnon, and dealt him his death-blow. Absalom served a double purpose by this murder. He avenged the insult offered to his sister, and hoped to secure his own succession to the throne by ridding himself of his elder brother. The son of Abigail, the second in succession, was already dead, and so it seemed inevitable that he, as the third son, must be the successor. David's son a fratricide!—What will be the consequences of this bloody deed? Only his faith in God saved him from becoming, like his predecessor, a victim to insanity, although the dire fate which had befallen him was but too real, and not merely the effect of a distrustful imagination.

David's first impulse was to seek out the murderer, who had taken refuge with his grandfather, King Talmai, of Geshur, on the south-west boundary of Judæa,

in order to deal with him as he deserved, even at the
risk of going to war on his account. But there were
various influences at work against such a policy. In
fact, since the affair with Bathsheba, intrigues had
been rife at David's court. Joab was opposed to the
succession of the last-born, Solomon, and was naturally on the side of Absalom, the eldest surviving
son. Ahithophel, David's infallible counsellor, also
favoured Absalom's claim to the throne, because he
could use him as a tool against his father. On the
other hand, Adonijah, David's fourth son, advocated
the infliction of condign punishment on Absalom.
Adonijah thought his prospects of displacing the infant
Solomon fairer than his chance with the remorseless
Absalom. If the latter were punished for fratricide,
Adonijah would be the next in succession. He and
his mother Haggith may perhaps, therefore, have
incensed David against Absalom, but Joab and
Ahithophel were wiser, and knew how to exert their
influence in favour of abandoning all warlike attempts
upon him or his grandfather, whose protection he
was enjoying.

When David had at length decided on seizing or
demanding the surrender of his guilty son (though
he had been absent for three years), Joab employed a
ruse to turn the king from his resolve. He sent for
a woman living in the adjacent town of Tekoah,
who had a reputation for adroit and clever speech.
With her he devised a plan to make the king
realise how horrible it was for a father to be willing
to put to death a son for the not altogether
unjustifiable murder of his brother. The wise
woman of Tekoah consequently appeared before
the king in mourning garments, and as though
invoking his mercy she called out in an entreating
voice and with deep prostrations, Help! O king,
help! When she stated her fictitious case, the
king readily recognised the hidden point of her
story, and the allusion to his own case, and he

demanded an open answer from her as to whether Joab had assisted her in her disguise and invention. When the woman of Tekoah had confessed the truth, the king sent for Joab, and assured him that he no longer entertained evil intentions against Absalom, and assigned to him the task of conducting his son to Jerusalem. The woman of Tekoah had, in her ingenious manner, made it clear to him that blood-revenge against his own son would be a contradiction in itself.

Joab himself brought Absalom from Geshur to Jerusalem. The son, however, was not permitted to appear before his father, but was obliged to remain in his own house. By this means Joab unconsciously sowed the seeds of dissension in the house of David. Night and day, Absalom, in his isolation and disgrace, brooded over the vile plan of deposing his father. But he dissembled in order to lull the latter's suspicion. To this end it was absolutely necessary that a reconciliation should be effected. Joab, who earnestly desired peace between father and son, became the mediator, and David decided that, after a two years' exile from his presence, his son might now be allowed to return. At this meeting, Absalom played to perfection the part of the penitent, obedient son; David then gave him a fatherly embrace, and the reconciliation was complete. Seven years had passed since the death of Amnon. But now Absalom's intrigues commenced. No doubt he had frequent meetings with Ahithophel, and was following his advice. He obtained chariots and horses from Egypt, procured a guard of fifty men, and displayed regal grandeur. He arose betimes in the morning, listened to disputes, and found every one's case just, but regretted that the king would not listen to all, and would not give justice to all. He hinted that were he the judge, no one would have to complain of difficulty in obtaining his dues. Absalom pursued this course for four years after the reconciliation with his father. He was the handsomest man of his times. He was then about thirty, and in the full pride of his strength. His beautiful thick hair fell in waves over his neck and shoulders, like the mane of a lion. His affability won him the hearts of all who approached him. David was so blinded that he did not see how his crafty son was alienating the affections of the people from their sovereign, whilst Absalom merely awaited a favourable opportunity to proceed against his father, to dethrone him, and perhaps to attempt his life. This opportunity soon offered itself.

It appears that David was occupied, in the last decade of his reign, with a comprehensive plan, apparently that of a great war which would require a numerous body of soldiers. He had already enlisted bands of mercenaries, six hundred Hittites, who, with their general Ittai, (whose admiration for David secured his unswerving attachment), had arrived from Gath. The king also wished to ascertain the number of able-bodied men over twenty years of age in all the Israelitish tribes, in order to determine whether he could undertake with their aid a campaign which would probably prove severe and tedious. The king delegated the office of numbering the men who could bear arms to his commander-in-chief, Joab, and the other generals. The work of enumeration lasted nine months and twenty days. From the numbers which were handed in, supposing them to be correct, it appears that, out of an entire population of 4,000,000, there were 1,300,000 men and youths capable of bearing arms.

This counting of the nation, however, proved to be a mistake for which David had to pay heavily. The people were highly incensed against him. In itself the act was displeasing to them, as they saw in it the preliminaries to enlistments for a war of long duration; added to this was the fear that the counting itself must be attended by evil results, for such was the view held in those days. A fearful pestilence broke out, which carried off great numbers, and confirmed all minds in the belief that it had arisen in consequence of the numbering of the people. The capital, being densely populated, naturally suffered the greatest loss from the pestilence. On seeing the heaps of corpses, or, to speak in the metaphorical language of those days, at sight of " the angel of Destruction " that had snatched away so many, David exclaimed:—" I have sinned and done wrong, but what has my poor flock done ? Let thy hand strike me and the house of my fathers." The plague having spared Mount Moriah, where the Jebusites had settled, the prophet Gad bade the king erect an altar, and offer up sacrifices on that mountain, and he announced that the pestilence would then be averted from Jerusalem. Without hesitation, David and his entire court repaired thither. When the chief of the Jebusites, Ornah (Araunah), saw David approaching, he hurried to meet him, saluted him humbly, and asked what was his desire. David then informed him that he wished to buy the mountain in order to build an altar on it. Ornah graciously offered him the spot and all appertaining to it as a gift, but David refused to accept it. No sooner was an altar hastily erected there and a sacrifice offered, than the pestilence ceased in Jerusalem. From that time Mount Moriah was considered a sacred spot, which destruction could not approach; it was also the mountain on which Abraham was supposed to have offered his son Isaac as a sacrifice.

In consequence of this plague the nation conceived a dislike to David; it condemned him for the loss of the thousands of human beings whom the Angel of Destruction had snatched away. Ahithophel made use of this dislike in order to avenge himself on David, and he employed Absalom as his tool, and, with him, contrived a conspiracy which could not fail to succeed

Absalom secretly despatched messengers in every direction, in order to give those adherents who were already attached to him the necessary signal. The insurrection was to be set on foot in Hebron, an out-post of the tribe of Judah, whose elders had already been won for Absalom. The latter invented subter-fuges by which to deceive David as to the true purpose of his visit to Hebron, and the king per-mitted him to depart without suspicion.

Absalom arrived at Hebron, attended by his friends and guards, and by two hundred prominent men of Jerusalem, whom he had invited under some pretext, and who did not suspect his real aims. These two hundred men, through their very ignorance of mat-ters, contributed to the success of the project. The people of Hebron, seeing that even prominent men had joined Absalom's party, gave up David's cause as lost. Ahithophel, who had likewise invented a pretext to absent himself from court, openly declared for Absalom, thus giving his cause an immense ac-cession of power, as he was known to be David's right hand.

The traitorous plan succeeded but too well. The Hebronites and others present saluted Absalom as king, forswore their allegiance to David, and sacri-ficed burnt-offerings. Ambition prompted various members of David's family also to join Absalom. This was more especially the case with Amasa, his cousin, who considered himself a great commander, and thought that Joab had unjustly been preferred to him. The messengers then gave the signal previously agreed upon, and the conspirators who sided with Absalom gathered together, and shouted "Long live King Absalom!" They carried with them all who had been incensed against David for taking a census of the people, and in fact all who hoped to gain some advantage from changes and dissension. The Benjamites, whom the accession of David had deprived of supremacy, and the ever-dissatisfied Ephraimites, were more particularly delighted at David's downfall, and willingly did homage to the usurper; they hoped to regain their former freedom through David's misfortunes. They had greater chances of obtaining power under Absalom, who was very vain, and not likely to retain the favour of the nation for a long time, than under the rule of David. The chief towns of all the tribes sent ambassadors to Hebron to salute the new king, and his adherents daily increased in number. At first the conspiracy was kept secret from those in authority; no one was permitted to journey to Jerusalem, lest the news spread. David received the information of his own dethronement and the accession of his son simultaneously with the news that the houses of Judah and Israel had renounced their allegiance to him.

It was a terrible blow for the king. But his resolve was soon taken; he would not resort to a civil war, as the sons of Zeruiah and many other faithful followers probably urged him to do. Deserted by all the tribes, he would be obliged to shut himself up in his capital. The city would not be able to resist the attack of so large an army; and he saw, now that he was undeceived, that Absalom would not scruple to turn Jerusalem into a sea of blood. David felt deeply wounded by the alliance of Ahithophel with his usurping son, and he was greatly discouraged by it. He saw, too late, that the conspiracy was of long standing, that the plan had been maturely considered, and that resistance on his part would only lead to his own destruction. He therefore announced to his people that he would depart from Jerusalem in all haste, before Absalom could leave Hebron with his numerous followers.

This step was instrumental in proving to David that he still had faithful friends, who would be true to him till death. When, on leaving his palace, he passed the Place of the Sellers of Ointment, he ob-

served to his great joy that a great concourse followed him.   Not only his general, Joab, with his
brother, Abishai, and their followers ; not only a great
number of the warrior-corps (Gibborim), the hired
troops, Cherethites and Pelethites, with Benaiah their
leader, but also Ittai the Hittite, with six hundred men,
whom David had only a short time before enlisted
The entire population wept aloud, whilst David withdrew to the Vale of Kedron, where he mustered his
followers before taking the road over the Mount
of Olives to the desert near the Jordan.   He did
not venture to take refuge in a city from fear of
treachery.

Later on the two high priests Zadok and Abiathar
with all the Levites hurried after him, bearing the
ark of the covenant with them.   David, however,
urged the priests to return to Zion with the ark, saying,
" If by God's mercy I shall be permitted to return
to Jerusalem, then I shall again behold the ark of the
covenant and the sanctuary; if not, if God rejects
me, I am ready to endure what seemeth good unto
Him."   It also appeared to him that the priests could
be of more service to him if they remained in Jerusalem than if they joined him in exile.   Whilst, then,
the priests hastily took the ark back to Jerusalem,
David ascended the Mount of Olives barefoot, his
head covered, and his face bathed in tears.   All his attendants wept bitterly.   But when his grief and despair
had reached their climax, a friend, who was to give him
help, came from the other side of the Mount of Olives,
and met him at its highest point.   Hushai from the city
of Erech was a confidant of David, and a counsellor
of no less wisdom than Ahithophel.   He advanced
in mourning array, his garments torn, and earth
upon his head, prepared to share the king's flight.
David, however, refused to permit this, because, being
an aged man, he would only be a burden.   In
Absalom's vicinity he might do valiant service by
counteracting Ahithophel's counsels, and by keeping

David informed of all that occurred. Hushai therefore repaired to Jerusalem.

The first town through which David passed in his
flight was the Benjamite city of Bahurim. Far from
meeting with a friendly reception there, he was received
with insult and neglect. A Benjamite named Shimei,
of the house of Gera, reviled and cursed him, saying,
" Thou outcast and man of blood, God will repay thee
for thy treatment of the house of Saul, whose crown
thou hast stolen." He followed David's march for
a long distance, throwing stones and earth at him, so
that the soldiers had to shield the king. David, however, had some friends in Bahurim also. Humbled
and exhausted, the king at length accomplished the
journey through the desert, and reached the neighbourhood of Jericho with his forces.

Here he could recruit his energies after his recent
bodily and mental exertions, while awaiting the news
which his faithful adherents would transmit to him
from Jerusalem.

When David was approaching the banks of the Jordan, Absalom arrived in Jerusalem with his traitorous
adherents, among them Ahithophel, the faithless counsellor. Ahithophel urged the usurper to commit ever
greater crimes in order to widen the breach between
him and his father, and render a reconciliation impossible; he advised him to take possession of his
father's harem. It mattered little to Ahithophel
that Absalom would incur the hatred of the people
through this fresh misdeed. His sole object was to
revenge himself on David, and to ruin him. The
weak-minded sinner who called himself king, and
who was incapable of undertaking anything, unless
incited thereto by others, allowed himself to be
induced to commit this crime. But, whilst Absalom
was revelling in sin, the man who was destined to
frustrate all his ruthless plans was near at hand.
Hushai had apparently submitted to the new king,
and had assured him that he would serve him as

faithfully as he had served his father, and Absalom relied on this promise. He called a council to consider the most expedient plan for defeating and ruining his father. The elders of the tribes, who were in the city, were invited to attend. Ahithophel gave the diabolical advice to attack David that very night with a strong army, to disperse his following in a sudden onslaught made by a force its superior in point of numbers, and to capture and slay the king, whom he imagined to be utterly worn out and dispirited. But Absalom also consulted Hushai with regard to the campaign against his father, and Ahithophel's advice was rejected by him as impracticable. Hushai urged such plausible objections that Absalom was duped by them; he advised that David should not be attacked with a small force, but that Absalom should raise from the entire nation —from Dan to Beersheba—an army whose numbers would render it irresistible. Hushai's advice was more favourably received than Ahithophel's, and steps were forthwith taken to act upon it. The attack was postponed, and the campaign was deferred till the numerous forces could be assembled. Hushai immediately conveyed the results of the meeting to David by means of Jonathan and Ahimaaz, the sons of the High Priest.

The first result of these events was favourable to the cause of David, for Ahithophel departed from Jerusalem, and hanged himself in his native town of Gilo. He was led to this course either by disgust at Absalom's conduct in setting aside his counsel, or by the conviction that Absalom's cause would be lost through delay, and that he himself would reap well-deserved punishment. This suicide was a severe blow to the usurper, for he had no capable man amongst his followers, and he himself was neither warlike nor prudent. His general Amasa had but little military genius. The enrolment of soldiers was actually begun, but before it could be completed David had obtained an important advantage. He went to Mahanaim, the inhabitants of which town received him with a welcome as cordial as that which in former times they had extended to the fugitive son of Saul. All the Israelites on the opposite side of the Jordan offered their assistance, and placed themselves under his command. Two men of Gilead outvied each other in attentions to the unhappy king and father, and provided him and his followers with all necessaries. They were old men—Barzillai from Rogelim, and Machir from Lo-debar—and help came also from Shobi, king of Ammon, the son of Nahash. When at length Absalom or Amasa had succeeded in collecting a large force, they crossed the Jordan by means of rafts, and approached Mahanaim. The Absalomites encamped opposite the wood without any particular plan or order. David, on the other hand, divided his army into three divisions, commanded respectively by Joab, Abishai and Ittai, who were all proved and competent soldiers. David himself was not permitted to accompany them, as his generals knew too well his love for his wicked son. The contest cost many human lives. Although Absalom's forces exceeded those of David in point of numbers, yet they were defeated, for they were not well disciplined, and were not able to find their way in the forest. David's troops, on the other hand, fought valiantly. The forest was more destructive than the sword. Twenty thousand warriors are said to have fallen there. The forest of Rephaim was also the cause of Absalom's personal destruction. His long hair, of which he was very vain, caught in the branches of an oak, and the mule he had been riding galloped away. It seems providential that the death-blow was dealt by Joab, who had formerly favoured him, and who had thus unwittingly assisted him in his conspiracy. Joab then sounded the horn as a signal for David's army to cease from the contest, and the adherents of Absalom took to flight, and crossed the Jordan.

Thus ended the second civil war of David's reign, a war which was the more unnatural because of the close relationship between the rival combatants, and the sad causes which led to the contest. The first duty of the victors was to transmit the news of their triumph to David. This was in itself a painful office, for all knew how deeply David would feel the death of his wicked son. David was terrified at the news, wept and sobbed, and cried repeatedly, "My son, my son, Absalom; would, I had fallen instead of thee!" The depths of a father's heart are unsearchable. Perhaps, he considered Absalom in the light of a victim whom Ahithophel had inveigled and urged on to rebellion. The warriors dared not enter Mahanaim as victors, but repaired homewards stealthily, as though humiliated after a defeat. David would see and speak to no one, but mourned continually for his son's loss. At length Joab took heart, and reproached him in harsh terms for indulging in continued mourning, and thereby manifesting ingratitude towards his soldiers. In order to rouse the king, Joab further threatened that if he did not immediately show himself to his soldiers, and address them kindly, his faithful followers would leave the same night, and he would remain alone and helpless. These sharp words of the rough but faithful Joab induced David to rouse himself, and appear before the people. The corpse of Absalom was thrown into a cave, and covered with a heap of stones. He left a beautiful daughter, but his three sons had been snatched away by death before his revolt, as though it were destined that no son of his should witness the attempt against his father's life. During his short reign at Jerusalem, he had erected a splendid monument in the "King's Valley," to perpetuate his own name. Intended for his glorification, it became the commemoration of his disgrace. After the close of the war, David contemplated returning to Jerusalem. He did not wish, however, to force the tribes into submission, he preferred to await their repentant return to him, and the renewal of their oaths of allegiance. It was a curious fact that the tribes of the north were the first to take this course. The voice of the people appealed to the elders to lead them back to their king. They cried, "The king who delivered us from our enemies, and freed us from the yoke of the Philistines, was forced by Absalom to flee from his own country. Absalom is now dead. Why do you not hasten to bring back our king? Come, let us lead him home." Thereupon the elders of the tribes invited David to return to his capital; and thus, a second time, they acknowledged him as king. Contrary to all expectation, the tribe of Judah, and naturally the tribe of Benjamin were still holding back. They did not move one step to welcome their king. Probably the men of Judah felt bitterly ashamed of the revolt they had started in Hebron, and did not venture to entreat David's pardon. Perhaps, too, the discontent which had incited them to forswear their allegiance was still at work amongst them. It seems that Amasa, who had fled to Jerusalem after the defeat in the forest of Gilead, still exercised great influence over the men of Judah.

When David saw that the tribe of Judah was still holding aloof from him, he commanded the two priests, Zadok and Abiathar, who had remained in Jerusalem, to admonish the elders of Judah to invite their king to return. He told the priests to assure Amasa that he would not only receive a free pardon, but even retain his rank as general. With this prospect before him, Amasa determined to accept David's offers, and he persuaded the elders to accede to the king's proposal. The men of Judah thereupon sent an invitation to David, and an embassy went forth to meet the king, and receive him at Gilgal. The men of Benjamin were sorely puzzled by this conduct. What were they to do? The Benjamites had publicly shown themselves inimical to David when he had fled from Jerusalem through their territory; they had not thought it possible that he would ever return, and reclaim his throne. Now affairs had changed, and not only the northern tribes, but even Judah was preparing to do him homage. The Benjamites felt no attachment to David, but they could not isolate themselves, for then the king's wrath would fall heavily on them. Shimei, whose insults had caused David such bitter pain during his flight, and who, in consequence, had most cause to fear the king's anger, advised that they should display intense enthusiasm for David's cause, exceeding that of the other tribes, since, by appealing to his generosity, they might incline him favourably towards them. In obedience to this advice, one thousand Benjamites went forward to meet David, joined the Judæan embassy, and, on arriving at the bank of the Jordan, threw a bridge across the river in order to facilitate the king's transit. Meanwhile the king had left Mahanaim, and was approaching the Jordan, attended by his court, his servants, and the faithful followers who had joined him on the opposite shore. Shimei advanced before all the others, threw himself at the king's feet as he was about to cross the river, acknowledged his fault, and entreated David's forgiveness. David now returned with a larger concourse of followers than had accompanied him on his flight across the Jordan: he was attended by the Judæan embassy, by a thousand Benjamites, and by the faithful friends who formed his guard of honour. The first town reached after crossing the Jordan was Gilgal. Here the ambassadors of the different tribes on this side of the river were assembled to renew their homage; they felt surprised and annoyed that the Judæans had stolen a march on them by meeting the king at the very shore of the Jordan.

They saw in this eager display of loyalty, which they could not consider sincere, an effort on the part of the house of Judah to regain the king's favour, to the detriment of the house of Israel.

The elders of Israel made no secret of their displeasure, and gave vent to it in David's presence; the Judæans, however, retaliated on them. The question of precedency degenerated into a violent quarrel, the Judæans making angry retorts, thus offending the northern tribes still more. Bitter animosity arose between the contending parties; David appears to have inclined to the side of the Judæans. Sheba, a Benjamite of the family of Bichri, taking advantage of the general confusion, sounded the trumpet and cried, "We have no portion in David, and no share in the son of Jesse; let every Israelite return to his tent." Heeding this cry, the elders of the northern tribes withdrew, and followed Sheba the Bichrite. The men of Judah alone remained faithful to David, and accompanied him to Jerusalem. The joy of their return was mingled with annoyance: a fresh breach had arisen, a civil war was imminent. At this sad juncture David had recourse to a step which may be considered either very wise or very foolish. Joab had become obnoxious to him since the king had learned that he had killed Absalom, and David did not wish him to fill the office of general any longer. Besides this, he desired to keep his word with Amasa, and to appoint him to the office of commander-in-chief. David, being now dependent on the tribe of Judah, felt the necessity of retaining Amasa's good-will, as the latter's influence had immense weight with the Judæans. Without consulting Joab, he commanded Amasa to summon the forces of the tribe of Judah within three days, in order to proceed against the rebels. The time expired, and Amasa did not return. David became uneasy; he thought Amasa might have deceived him, and made common cause with the insurgents. It was necessary to be expeditious, lest Sheba's followers increase in numbers, and also gain time to occupy fortified cities. David had no choice but to turn to the sons of Zeruiah, who, in their unswerving fidelity, had remained true to him in spite of frequent slights, and whose skill in matters of war he had amply tested. David would not, however, give the supreme command to Joab, but entrusted it to his brother Abishai. He set out with the Cherethites and Pelethites, who were to form the nucleus of the army which he hoped to collect on the way. Joab overlooked the insult which had been offered him, and joined the troops, or rather became their leader. He appears to have issued an appeal to the people to gather around him. When Amasa joined them in Gibeon, Joab killed him with one stroke of his sword, and the Judæans, whom Amasa had collected, followed the sons of Zeruiah. In all the towns, fresh partisans and followers attached themselves to David's cause. Sheba found but few adherents, the northern tribes being unwilling to begin a civil war for the sake of a man who was but little known, and who was followed only by a small band of soldiers. He had thrown himself into the fortified town of Abel, and a part of his followers occupied the town of Dan, which lay at an hour's distance from the base of Mount Hermon, not far from the source of the Jordan. Joab quickly ordered a trench to be dug round the town of Abel, and without calling on the inhabitants to surrender, he began to undermine the walls. The inhabitants became greatly alarmed. Then a wise woman called from the wall to the sappers below to summon Joab. When he approached, she addressed him reproachfully, " Thou shouldst have asked first in Abel and Dan that thou mightest have heard, whether all those who are faithful and peace-loving have departed from Israel. Why wilt thou slaughter the mothers and the children of Israel? Why wilt thou destroy the inherit-

ance of Jacob?" Joab replied that he did not wish
to do this, that he merely desired to capture the man
who had lifted his hand against the king. On this
the woman promised that the head of the rebel should
soon be thrown over the wall. She kept her word,
for she secretly persuaded her fellow-citizens to separate Sheba from his few followers, and to kill him.
His gory head was cast over the wall, and Joab
raised the siege, dismissed his soldiers, and returned
to Jerusalem with the news of his victory. The king
was obliged, against his will, to leave him in command
of the army.

David returned to his capital with a purged soul.
He had suffered and atoned heavily for his sins.
He had taken away the wife of his faithful servant,
and his son had taken away *his* wives. He had spilt
Uriah's blood, and the streams of blood shed in his
own house had almost overwhelmed him. He had
found by bitter experience that even the best king
cannot build on his people's love. His plan of
undertaking a great war against his heathen foes
was shattered. He, therefore, in his old age, during
the last years of his reign, confined his attention to the
internal affairs of his kingdom. He wished to carry
out, before death overtook him, an idea he had long
cherished. He wished to build a magnificent temple
to the God of Israel, who had rescued him in his many
troubles. Before commencing, David consulted
Nathan, the prophet; for in those days the prophet
ranked higher than the priest. He said, "I live in a
palace of cedar wood, whilst the Ark of God is
only in a temporary tent. I will build a temple of
cedar for it!" Nathan approved the plan and said,
" Carry out all that is in thy heart, for God is with
thee!" The next day, however, the prophet came
to him, and revealed to David that he was not destined to build a temple, because he had shed blood,
but that this task would be reserved for his son. At
the same time David was informed that his throne

was established for many years to come,—that a long succession of kings would descend from him, and occupy his throne, provided that they walked in the ways of God.   Much as David had wished to build a stately temple in Jerusalem, he bowed humbly to the divine decree revealed to him by Nathan, and gave up his project.   Before the ark of the covenant, he thanked God in a heartfelt prayer for the mercies bestowed on him, who had been raised up from the dust.   His heart was filled with gratitude that his royal house and his throne were to be established for many years to come.   David gave expression to this feeling in a psalm, which, however, has not the same *verve* as his former songs; it was, perhaps, his last poetic prayer.

Although David did not commence the erection of the temple himself, he began to make the necessary preparations.   He devoted to the sanctuary a part of the booty which he had acquired from the conquered nations.   He also regulated the order in which divine services were to be conducted, by having, according to Samuel's method, choirs of Levites to play on the harp and sing psalms, in addition to the ordinary sacrificial rites.   He is also considered the inventor of the various musical instruments which were later on introduced into the service.

David's vital energy began to decrease before he had attained his seventy-first year.   The anxieties of his youth, the constant warfare, the exciting events in his own family, Amnon's sinfulness and Absalom's revolt caused him to grow old at a comparatively early age.   He felt no warmth in his body; he felt cold despite the torrid heat of Jerusalem, and all the clothes which he could procure did not seem to supply him with the necessary vital heat.

Adonijah, the king's fourth son, endeavoured, by taking advantage of David's failing powers, to secure the succession.   He was the next heir after Amnon and Absalom, but he feared that he might be passed over if he awaited the death of his father, and he had probably heard of the secret understanding, according to which the son of Bathsheba, his youngest brother, was to succeed to the throne. Adonijah had no desire to rebel against his father as Absalom had done, he merely wished to have his right to the succession recognised by the chief dignitaries of the kingdom. He therefore took counsel with those of David's court who were opposed to Solomon's succession. Foremost amongst these was Joab, who supported him as he had formerly supported Absalom. Adonijah's other confidant was Abiathar, the second of the high priests, who seems to have been placed in an inferior position by David. Zadok, whose family had been appointed hereditary high priests by Saul at Gibeon, had been retained in that position by David, who wished to secure his support, and therefore bestowed upon him the highest rank in the sanctuary. Abiathar may have felt hurt by this neglect, and perhaps took the part of Adonijah in order to secure the position he could not hope to obtain under Solomon. The other sons of the king also wished to see the throne assured to Adonijah, and thus intrigues at the court commenced afresh. Adonijah was as handsome and as popular as Absalom had been, and also, it appears, as thoughtless and as unfit for governing. Like Absalom, he began to draw the eyes of the people upon himself by a truly royal display; he procured chariots and attendants on horseback, and kept a guard of fifty runners, who preceded him wherever he went. David was weak in his behaviour to him, as he had been to Absalom—permitted him to have his own way, and thus tacitly acknowledged him as his successor. One day Adonijah invited his confidants, Joab, Abiathar, and all the king's sons excepting Solomon, to a meeting. They offered up sacrifices near a well, and during the feast his followers cried, "Long live King Adonijah!"

The first to take exception to Adonijah's proceedings was Nathan the prophet. He knew of the secret promise, given by David to his wife Bathsheba, that Solomon should inherit the crown. He had also revealed to David that Solomon was appointed by God to be his successor. He seems to have had confidence in Solomon's character, and to have expected better things from him than from Adonijah. Nathan, therefore, went to Bathsheba, and they devised a plan by which Adonijah's scheme might be overthrown. Bathsheba then repaired to the king, reminded him of his oath, and directed his attention to the fact that, in the event of Adonijah's succession, she and her son both would be lost, and her marriage would be branded with ignominy.

Hardly had she ended the description of the sad fate which awaited her if Solomon's claims were set aside, when the prophet Nathan was announced, and confirmed her assertions. David's resolve was quickly taken, and carried into effect on the same day, for he was most anxious to keep his oath to leave the sceptre to Solomon. He called upon the dignitaries who had not conspired with Adonijah, on Zadok, Benaiah and the warriors, and announced to them his resolve that Solomon should be anointed king during his own lifetime, and they all solemnly promised to acknowledge Solomon. Thereupon, David summoned the Cherethites and Pelethites to attend his son. Solomon then mounted one of the royal mules, and proceeded to the valley of Gihon, to the west of the town. A crowd of people joined the procession, and when the high-priest Zadok and the prophet Nathan had anointed him with oil from the tent of the sanctuary, the soldiers blew their trumpets, and all the people cried, " Long live King Solomon ! "

Great excitement now prevailed in Jerusalem. While the eastern mountains echoed with the cry of " Long live King Adonijah ! " the western chain was resounding with shouts of "Long live King Solomon!" Had both the king's sons and their adherents remained obstinate, a civil war must have ensued. But Adonijah was not like Absalom—he did not wish to excite a rebellion. Nor would his chief supporters, Joab and Abiathar, have assisted him in such an attempt. No sooner did Adonijah hear that Solomon had been anointed king by his father's command than his courage failed him. He hastened to the sanctuary at Zion in order to seek refuge in the holy of holies. Solomon, however, who had immediately taken the reins of government, sent to inform him that he might leave the sanctuary, that not a hair of his head should be touched so long as he did not attempt any fresh revolt. Adonijah then repaired to the young king, paid him due homage, and was dismissed with presents. Thus the contest for the succession ended.

David's weakness gradually increased, until after a stormy reign of forty years and six months (1015), he expired peacefully. He was the first to occupy a place in the royal mausoleum which he had built in a rocky cave on the southern slope of Mount Zion.

David's death was deeply mourned. He had made the nation great, independent and happy, and death transfigured him. When he had passed away, the nation began to realise the true value of his work, and what he had been to them. He had reunited the various tribes, each of which had before followed its own special interests, and he formed them into one nation. The revolts of Absalom and Sheba proved sufficiently how strong the feeling had become which bound the tribes together. The house of Israel did not seize the opportunity offered by his death of severing itself from the house of Judah, and great as was their jealousy of each other, they held together. David had removed every inducement for party divisions, and had knit them together with a kind but firm hand. During his reign the priesthood and the prophets worked amicably together. Thus Solomon was anointed by the high priest Zadok in conjunction with the prophet Nathan. David maintained friendly relations between the priestly houses of Eleazar and Ithamar, represented by Zadok and Abiathar respectively. The nation had no reason to complain of oppression, for he dealt justly to the extent of his ability. By destroying the power of the Philistines, who had so long held the neighbouring tribes in subjection, and by conquering the nations inhabiting the banks of the Euphrates, he had not only established internal prosperity, but had also founded a great empire which could vie in power with Egypt, and had cast into the shade the Chaldæan and Assyrian kingdoms on the Euphrates and the Tigris. By this means he had roused the people to the proud consciousness that it constituted a mighty nation of the Lord, the possessor of the law of God, the superior of the neighbouring nations. David's sins were gradually forgotten, for his atonement had been both grievous and manifold. Posterity pronounced a milder judgment on him than did his contemporaries. The remembrance of his great deeds, his kindness, his obedience to God, caused him to appear invested with the traits of an ideal king, who served as a pattern to all later rulers,—one who had always walked in the ways of God, and never departed therefrom. The kings of his house who succeeded him were measured by his standard, and were judged by the extent of their resemblance to him.

David's reign shone through the ages as perfect, —as one in which power and humility, fear of God and peace were united. Every succeeding century added its tribute to David's character, until he became the ideal of a virtuous king and sacred poet.

CHAPTER IX.

SOLOMON.

1015—977 B. C. E.

DAVID had left affairs in Israel in such perfect order that his successor, unless he were a fool or a knave, or the victim of evil advice, would have but little trouble in governing. Solomon, however, carried David's work still further. He shed such lustre upon Israel that even the most distant generations basked in the light that emanated from his wise rule. Indeed, a king who solidifies and increases, if he does not actually found, the greatness of the State; who permits his people the enjoyment of peace; who sheds the bounties of plenty over his land, driving poverty away from the meanest hovel; who opens up new channels for the development of his people's powers, and who thus increases and strengthens them; a king who has the intelligence to arouse his subjects to exercise their mental gifts, and cultivate their love of the beautiful; who, by his material and spiritual creations, elevates his country to the dignity of a model State, such as had never been before him and scarcely ever after him;—such a monarch assuredly deserves the high praise which posterity has accorded to him.

Carried away by the greatness of his deeds—for all these grand characteristics were strikingly prominent in Solomon—men shut their eyes to his weaknesses, and considered them the inevitable result of human imperfection.　In the first place he strove to preserve peace for his country, though his father had left him ample means for making fresh conquests.　He was called the king of peace—" Shelomo."　By giving to his people the comforts of prosperity, he widened its horizon, and raised its self-respect.　He ruled it with wisdom and justice, and decided with strict impartiality all contests between individuals as well as tribes. He increased the number of towns, and secured the safety of the roads and of the caravans.　He filled the city of Jerusalem with splendour, and built therein a magnificent temple in honour of God.　He himself cultivated the fine arts and poetry, and thereby endowed them with fresh attractions in the eyes of the people.　Lastly, he set great aims before the nation, and was rightly called the wise king.

History, the impartial arbitress, cannot, however, be blinded by his dazzling virtues to the blemishes which attach to his government, and which must be accounted the cause of the unfortunate breach which commenced when his grave was scarcely closed. The beginning of Solomon's rule was not free from stains of blood, and its end was clouded with mists, which dimmed its brightness; his love of splendour became injurious to morality; it made him despotic, and imposed a burden on the people, which it bore for a considerable time, but shook off at the first favourable opportunity.　Solomon converted the kingly power into an autocracy, under which every will had to be subservient to his.　But these blemishes were entirely hidden by the greatness of the achievements under his rule.　It is impossible now to decide how far the responsibility of Solomon for these evils goes, how much of the blame rests with his too officious servants, and to what extent their existence must be attributed to the irresistible force of circumstances, to which the exalted and the lowly alike must submit. It is the curse of crowned heads that the worthiest wearer of a crown, in order to consolidate his power, is induced to take steps which his conscience would under other circumstances condemn, and the misdeeds of his servants are also added to his account.

Solomon was young—scarcely twenty—when he ascended the throne. After his accession, whilst visiting the altar at Gibeon, we are told, he had a vision in which God asked him to express the innermost wish of his heart, with the promise that it should be fulfilled. He did not choose long life, nor riches, nor honour, nor the death of his enemies; but he chose wisdom, in order that he might rule his people with justice. In fact, this wisdom, this power of entering into the feelings and minds of the dissenting parties who appeared before him, of seizing on the true state of the case in spite of exaggeration and subtle arguments, Solomon possessed to an extraordinary degree. The Solomonic judgment is well known. By giving a verdict which was well adapted to reveal the real feeling of a mother, he recognised, in a dispute between two women for the possession of a child, on which side was truth, on which side falsehood. "Cut the child in half," he said. But its real mother could not accept this decision, and offered rather to give up her child. He was determined that no one in his kingdom should suffer from injustice. Though he may not have been the first that uttered the saying, "through justice a throne is established," yet it was a maxim after his own heart.

The wisdom of Solomon is also displayed to great advantage in another direction, namely, in his poetic productions. These were chiefly allegorical poems (Mashal); in them he caused the lofty cedars of Lebanon, and the lowly creeping wall plants, to appear as the emblems of what is highest and humblest, quadrupeds, birds of the air, reptiles, and even dumb fish are given voice and speech. Each of these fables probably ended with an appropriate moral lesson. It has been related that Solomon composed three thousand of such fables and five thousand songs or proverbs.

But Solomon was by no means the originator of this style of fiction. Long before him such compositions had been common among the Israelites. Standing on Mount Gerizim, Jotham, the son of the Judge Gideon, addressed the misguided people of Shechem in an ingenious parable. The prophet Nathan had disguised his exhortation to David respecting his sin with Bathsheba in the form of a parable. But though not the inventor of this branch of poetry, Solomon is still deserving of praise for devoting the time left unoccupied by the cares of government to its further development. His rare qualities of mind were displayed in yet another direction. In some of his compositions he delineates types of persons and things by means of allusions, the hidden meaning of which is left to guessing. Such enigmas, presented in a poetic form, were in those days the favourite diversions of social gatherings and feasts, and Solomon possessed remarkable ingenuity in devising these recreations of the human mind.

He was, however, guilty of errors, the greater part of which arose from an exaggerated idea of his royal dignity, and from imitating the kings of the neighbouring states of Tyre and Egypt, with whom he was in constant intercourse. He claimed for himself a prerogative almost impious in a mortal, namely, that of being considered identical with the State,—all interests were to centre in him, and all else was to be of comparatively little importance. Solomon's wisdom ran aground on this rock. The truth of Samuel's prediction, at the time of the election of a ruler, was better proven by the wise king than by his predecessors.

Unfortunately Solomon was a younger son, to whom the throne had been allotted contrary to the ordinary laws of succession, whilst Adonijah, whom a portion of the people had recognised as king, was considered the rightful heir. So long as the latter lived, Solomon's government could not be on a firm basis, and he could never feel himself secure. Adonijah, therefore, had to be removed; the leader of the body guard, Benaiah, forcibly entered his house, and killed him. As an excuse for this act of violence, it was asserted that Adonijah had attempted to win the hand of Abishag, the young widow of David, and thus had revealed his traitorous intention of contesting his brother's right to the throne. No sooner had he fallen than Joab, the former adherent of Adonijah, feared that a similar fate would overtake him. This exemplary general, who had contributed so considerably to the aggrandisement of the people of Israel and the power of the house of David, fled to the altar on Mount Zion, and clung to it, hoping to escape death. Benaiah, however, refused to respect his place of refuge, and shed his blood at the altar. In order to excuse this crime, it was given out that David himself, on his deathbed, had impressed on his successor the duty of revenging the death of Abner and Amasa. Joab, who had killed them in times of peace, was not to be allowed, in spite of his venerable age, to die in peace.

It is uncertain whether Benaiah was Solomon's evil adviser, or merely his instrument. Joab's death was the cause of great joy amongst the enemies of Israel, and aroused in them the courage to plan a rebellion. Adonijah's priestly partisan, Abiathar, whom Solomon did not dare touch, was deprived of his office as high priest, and Zadok was made the sole head of the priesthood, and his descendants, invested with that dignity, maintained it for over a thousand years, whilst the offspring of Abiathar were neglected.—The Benjamite Shimei, who had pursued

David with execrations on his flight from Jerusalem, was also executed, and it was only through this three-fold deed of blood that Solomon's throne appears to have gained stability.

Solomon then directed his attention to the formation of a court of the greatest magnificence, such as was befitting the powerful king whose commands were obeyed from the boundaries of Egypt to the banks of the Euphrates. In those days many wives were considered a necessary adjunct to the king's dignity; David had about sixteen wives, but this was an insignificant number as compared with that of the kings of Egypt and Phœnicia, whom Solomon had taken for his pattern. It was only in compliance with this common but corrupt practice that Solomon formed an immense harem. His first wife was Naamah (the beautiful), an Ammonite princess; he also had other wives from the Moabite and Aramæan courts, and even from those of the Hittite and Caananite kings; but what most gratified his pride was that the Egyptian king Psusennes gave him his daughter in marriage. Solomon thought that in acting thus he had taken a wise step, and that his country and his dynasty would be benefited by the alliance. But the result proved the contrary. The daughter of Psusennes was naturally received with every mark of attention in the Israelitish capital; she became the first queen in Solomon's harem, but it seemed to him a disgrace that he could not place a magnificent palace at the disposal of this queen. What was the cedar palace built by David on Mount Zion, when compared with the gigantic edifices and labyrinthine palaces of the kings of Egypt? Solomon, therefore, determined to build a palace worthy of her.

Through the alliance with Egypt, innovations of great consequence were made in Israel, among them the introduction of horses and chariots.

Solomon also entered into close and friendly connection with Hiram, king of Tyre, with whom David had already established a neighbourly intimacy. He appears to have married a daughter of Hiram, too, and this close bond between Solomon and Hiram seems to have led to important and extensive undertakings.

The establishment of a large harem demanded an immense body of servants. Solomon maintained a most brilliant court. The ambassadors of tributary and friendly powers had to be received with great pomp, for Solomon laid great stress on the display of splendour, and the maintenance of his court demanded the expenditure of large sums of money. As he could not otherwise obtain means, the royal house not having extensive estates in its own right, the people had to defray his enormous expenses. The whole land was divided into twelve parts, and a Governor was placed over each division to see that the inhabitants contributed one month's provisions every year; the purpose of this division seems to have been that the old system of tribal organisation might cease. A superior, or Vizier, whose duty it was to see that the tribute of natural products was sent in regularly, was appointed over these twelve officials.

Solomon displayed heightened grandeur in his buildings. He was anxious in the first instance to raise a splendid temple to the God of Israel in the capital of his country. It could not be a matter of indifference to him that in the neighbouring lands of Egypt and Phœnicia, with the rulers of which he was intimately acquainted, gigantic temples were raised for the various gods, whilst in his country the sanctuary was merely placed in a tent. Solomon, therefore, immediately after his accession to the throne, made preparations for commencing the erection of a sacred edifice; the site was already chosen. It was to be on Mount Moriah, to the north-east of the city, where David had raised an altar after the pestilence had ceased. Silver and gold had been collected for the purpose, but building materials, stones and cedar wood still had to be procured. Freestones and blocks had to be hewn from the rocks in the quarries north of Jerusalem, where they were so dovetailed as to be easily joined after reaching the spot. But whence procure workmen for this troublesome business of hewing, preparing and conveying the stones? Solomon had learnt from Pharaoh Psusennes, his father-in-law, the means of obtaining workmen without incurring heavy expense. He employed the remnant of the Canaanite population still living in the country. Although Saul had begun to decrease their numbers, he could not proceed against them with his full strength, on account of his continual strife with David. David had left them undisturbed, so that they lived quietly, mixed peaceably with the Israelites, and served the king faithfully in his wars against the Philistines and other nations. Solomon, on the contrary, declared the remnant of the Ammonites, Hittites, Perizzites and Hivites, as well as the Jebusites (whom David had permitted to live in the outskirts of Jerusalem), to be bondmen, and compelled them to perform the hardest labour. They numbered 150,000 youths and able-bodied men, and comprised the working class. More than 3,000 Israelitish superintendents kept the enslaved natives to their work. A superior officer, Adoniram, watched over the superintendents and the workmen. Eighty thousand of these unhappy beings worked in the stone quarries day and night by the light of lamps. They were under the direction of a man from Biblos (Giblim), who understood the art of hewing heavy blocks from the rocks, and of giving the edges the necessary shape for dovetailing. Twenty thousand slaves removed the heavy blocks from the mouth of the quarry, and carried them to the building site.

Hiram, the King of Tyre, Solomon's friend, supplied cedar and cypress wood. The trees were felled on Lebanon, for which purpose Hiram placed skilled workmen at Solomon's disposal. The trunks were forwarded from Lebanon to Tyre or to the other harbours, whence they were conveyed in rafts to the port of Jaffa, and from there with much toil over hills and dales to Jerusalem, a distance of at least a ten hours' journey. As the Canaanite slaves were not sufficiently numerous to remove the cedar and cypress trees, and to convey them to their destination, Solomon employed Israelites to assist in the work, thirty thousand being impressed for the duty. Each ten thousand were sent for a month to work in the forests, to fell the trees, and convey them to their destination. After a month had passed, the workmen were relieved by another body of ten thousand. These thirty thousand Israelites were not enslaved—they remained free, and even received wages—but they were not allowed to withdraw voluntarily from the work.

It was not to be expected that Hiram would cut down his cedar and cypress forests, or that he would place carpenters and builders at Solomon's disposal without receiving some return. So long as the buildings were in course of erection, Solomon sent him annually a certain amount of corn, wine and oil, with the raising of which tribute the people were probably taxed. But Hiram was also obliged to advance gold for the adornment of the interior of the temple. Solomon's fleet had not yet imported the precious metal. In return for the supply of gold, Solomon yielded up to Hiram twenty towns of the borderland, in the tribe of Asher, between Phœnicia and the territory of Israel. Though these were not important, and did not please Hiram, still it was a transference of Israelitish territory to the Phœnicians Hiram permitted various races to colonise the towns, from whom the territory received the name " Gelil Haggoyim" (the district of nations), later Galilee.

As soon as the stones and blocks of wood had been removed to the building site of the temple, the erection of which was to occupy three years, the work was commenced.

The temple was built of freestone, and the walls were covered with cedar planks on the inside. On these were traced designs of palms, open flower cups, and cherubim (winged heads with human faces), and these designs were inlaid with gold. The temple was sixty cubits long, twenty cubits wide, and thirty cubits high. It was divided into the Holy of Holies (Debir, the inner chamber, a square of twenty cubits), and the Holy Place (Hechal, which was forty cubits long). The Holy of Holies seems to have been situated on higher ground than the sanctuary. At the sides were two cherubim of gilded olive wood, each ten cubits high, the wings of which were five cubits wide. At the entrance of the sanctuary was an open vestibule (Ulam), which was of the same width as the sanctuary, and ten cubits in length, and in front of this hall there were artistically wrought columns of bronze. The artist, Hiram, was a half-Jew, his father being a Syrian and his mother a Naphtalite. The Holy of Holies was to face the west, contrary to the custom of the Gentiles, whose temples faced the rising sun; the gates were of olive wood, adorned with gilded cherubim as well as with palms and flower-cups. The folding doors of the sanctuary, made of cypress wood, were ornamented in a like manner, and the floor was of cypress wood inlaid with gold. In the Holy of Holies nothing was visible but the cherubim, intended to enshrine the ark of the covenant, in which the tablets of the law were kept. In the sanctuary there was an altar of cedar wood gilded on all sides, with five gilded candlesticks at each side, and a large gilded table for twelve loaves. The temple was surrounded by an extensive courtyard. Inside the vestibule stood a large iron altar, and a spacious water reservoir, called the "iron sea," adorned with a border of open flower-cups and lily-buds, and on the lower part with colocynths. This reservoir was supported by twelve iron bulls, each three of which turned in a different direction. The water was intended for washing the hands and feet of the officiating priests whenever they entered the sanctuary, the flow of water probably being regulated by a faucet. Ten small basins on wheels, artistically engraved, could be pushed to any spot where they might be wanted. Vessels for the sacrificial rites were cast in large quantities by the order of the king. The whole building inside and outside was stamped with the impress of wealth and grandeur. At the completion of the building, it was consecrated (1007) with solemn rites. The erection of the temple had occupied seven years, and the month selected for the consecration was that in which the harvest and the vintage were completed. The chiefs of all the tribes and the elders of families were invited, and people streamed from every quarter to gaze in astonishment at the splendours of the temple, and to look upon the unaccustomed spectacle.

The solemnities commenced with the transfer of the ark from Mount Zion, the town of David, to Mount Moriah. The bars attached to the ark were those which had been used during the wanderings in the desert. They were so placed that all present could see that holy relic of past ages, the two stone tables inscribed with the ten commandments. During the transfer of the ark of the covenant, and during the consecration, many thousands of sacrifices were offered, and also psalms were sung. No sooner had the ark of the covenant been brought into the Holy of Holies than a thick cloud filled the body of the temple, so that the Aaronites were interrupted in their service. This was considered a token of God's mercy, and a sign that the consecration had been performed in accordance with His will. The vast assembly was thus swayed by the feelings of joy, piety and devotion. The king gave expression to the general sentiments in a few grave words: "God has promised to dwell in a cloud. I have built a dwelling for thee, O God—an abode for thee to dwell in for ever." Mount Moriah thus appeared like Mount Sinai, where the voice of God had spoken from out of a dense cloud. The temple became an object of veneration to the people, who believed that from between the two cherubim, God would make known to them the ways in which they were to walk. A prophet who was present (perhaps Ahijah of Shiloh) announced to King Solomon in the name of God, "If thou wilt walk in my law, and obey my commands, and fulfil my behests, then I will fulfil unto thee the promise I made unto David, thy father—' I shall dwell in the midst of the sons of Israel, and I will not desert my people.'"

The nation celebrated the autumn festivals, which occurred simultaneously with the consecration, most joyfully. Deep and lasting was the impression made by this temple, gleaming with gold and bronze, sumptuous and imposing in its structure, containing no visible image of the Deity, yet filled with His invisible presence. The house of God offered something tangible to those whose imaginations could not conceive of the spiritual, divested of material form. The temple was the pride and strength of Israel, and the delight of its eyes. At the time of the consecration there was inaugurated a religious service, such as had been impossible within the narrow limits of the sanctuary in Shiloh or, during the transition period, in the tent at Zion. A priesthood had certainly existed even in former times, and belonged exclusively to the descendants of Aaron. It was, however, only under Solomon that a high priest was put at the head of the others, and that gradations in rank were introduced. Azariah, the son of Zadok, was advanced to the office of high priest after the death of his father, and was assisted by the inferior priests. A new order of service was arranged for the Levites,

who were subordinate to the priests. A part of them
assisted at the sacrificial services. Another part
kept guard at four sides of the temple, and were
charged with the care of the sacred vessels, and with
all preparations for the temple service. Lastly, certain families took part in the singing and the instrumental music that accompanied the services. It was
the temple and the new order of worship introduced
there that actually raised Jerusalem to the position of
the capital of the country. Pilgrims from all the
tribes attended the autumnal festivals there, in order
to witness the solemn divine services, such as could
be held at no tribal altar. Jerusalem gradually becoming an important commercial town, in which foreign goods and curiosities were displayed, attracted
ever greater numbers of visitors from all the tribes.
Thus the youngest of the cities in the land of Israel
surpassed and outshone all the older towns. Solomon gave orders that the capital be fortified on all
sides, and that the temple also be included within
the line of fortifications.

The erection of the royal palace occupied a period
of more than thirteen years. It consisted of a series
of buildings which extended over a great area on the
northern hill, in the quarter called Millo. Next to
the entrance was the House of the Forest of Lebanon,
which took its name from the numerous pillars of
cedar, which were ranged in rows of fifteen each.
This house served as the Armoury for the king's
protection. Here thirteen hundred guards kept
watch; they were provided with spears and shields
of gold, and acted as the king's attendants when
he proceeded to the temple. Great attention was
given by Solomon to the fitting up of the Judgment or Throne Chamber. The walls from the
floor to the ceiling were covered with cedar wood,
and adorned with gold fretwork. In this hall
Solomon's throne was placed. It was considered
a marvel of workmanship. It was ornamented with

ivory, and inlaid with gold. Six steps led up to it, and on each step were two artistically wrought lions, the symbols of power and of royal dignity. The seat was supported on each side by arms, and on it also were two lions. In the hall of public justice Solomon heard contesting parties, and pronounced judgment: he considered his office of judge one of the holiest and most important connected with his kingly dignity. Here he also received the ambassadors of the various countries, who attended his court to offer their homage, or to negotiate new treaties. A special palace was built for the king, his servants and his wives, a separate house being reserved for the Egyptian princess. It appears that her removal from David's house to her own residence was effected with great pomp. Probably Solomon had also an aqueduct built so as to supply the town of Jerusalem and the temple with water from the rich spring of Etam, which was at a two hours' journey from Jerusalem.

The practice of building splendid edifices of cedar was not confined to Solomon ; the great nobles and princes who lived in Jerusalem, the high officers, and his favourites, all followed his example. With the wealth that streamed into the land through the opening of three important channels, the love of show, which spread from the king to the higher classes, could be freely gratified. Phœnician merchants of high standing, who carried on a large wholesale trade, money-changers, men of wealth who lent money on interest, now settled in Jerusalem. They composed a special corporation or guild, and were under the protection of the treaty between Solomon and Hiram. They were permitted to live according to their own laws, and were even allowed to practise their religious or, rather, idolatrous rites. The three great sources of wealth were the *Powerful Position of the State*, the *Alliance with Egypt*, and the *Indian Trade*. Those princes who had entered into treaties with David confirmed them with his successor, and other potentates sought his friendship. On swearing allegiance, all these princes and nations sent the customary tribute and rich gifts, such as gold and silver vessels, valuable garments, spices, horses and mules. The alliance with Egypt was also the source of considerable additions to the national wealth, as that kingdom furnished horses to the mountainous districts, and war chariots, which were in great demand in foreign parts. The princes of Aram and of the territories on the Euphrates who had formerly procured their horses and chariots from Egypt, were to buy these war materials from Solomon's merchant guild. The latter established a station for his own riders and horses on the plain not far from the sea. He kept twelve thousand horses and fourteen hundred war chariots (each drawn by two horses), and for these he erected spacious buildings, containing four thousand stalls. Solomon's greatest gains, however, were acquired in trade with India. To the Phœnicians the journey to this distant country was attended with insuperable difficulties, so long as the country near the Red Sea was rendered unsafe by the uncivilised and predatory bands that dwelt there. By his alliance with Hiram, Solomon had opened up a safer and nearer route to India. The strip of land extending from the southern border of Judah to the eastern coast of the Red Sea, the Points Elath and Eziongeber, had been rendered accessible. The caravans with their loaded camels could proceed in safety from Jerusalem and from the coast to the northern point of the Red Sea. At Hiram's suggestion, Solomon had a fleet of strong and large ships (ships of Tarshish) built, and equipped on the coast at Eziongeber. Hiram sent his most skilful sailors, who knew the route thoroughly, to man the vessels. Israelites of the tribes of Asher and Zebulun, who lived on the coast and were acquainted with the sea, were also employed.

When the Israelitish fleet was complete, it sailed out of the harbour of Eziongeber to the Red Sea, which separates Palestine from Egypt, Nubia, and Abyssinia, and proceeded along the coast to the Gulf which washes the shores of Southern Arabia, as far as the mouth of the Indus, in the land of Ophir (now called Scinde). After a period of two years, Solomon's fleet returned richly laden with the proceeds of this first expedition. Vast droves of camels carried the treasures to Jerusalem, to the great astonishment of the whole population. More than four hundred talents (kikhar) of gold, silver in great quantities, ivory, ebony, apes, and exquisitely coloured peacocks, sandal-wood, and sweet-smelling plants were thus transported. Solomon caused a throne to be made of the ivory, and the sandal-wood was used for ornamenting the harps and lutes of the musicians who played in the temple. The palings of the bridge which led from the palace to the temple were also made of this rare and costly wood. Solomon sent his fleet several times to Ophir or India, and each time new riches and curiosities were brought into the country. The port Elath became a place of great importance. Judæans settled there, and the land of Israel thus extended from the extreme end of the Red Sea to the Euphrates. In order to convey horses and chariots from Aramæa to the Euphrates, as also the various importations from Phœnicia, roads had to be made, and measures taken to ensure the safety of the caravans. In a mountainous country, it is not easy for beasts of burden, and certainly not for horses and chariots, to traverse great distances, obstructed as the way is by steep cliffs, abrupt precipices, and masses of rolling stones. Solomon, however, had roads made which led from Jerusalem to the north; these were the *king's high-roads*.

He probably employed the services of the Canaanite natives, who were obliged as bondmen to take part in this work. Heights were levelled, depths filled up, and stones removed. The roads were passable by carriages, which could proceed without hindrance from the south to the north, and the caravans passing from the Jordan to the sea could travel without difficulty. A chain of fortresses protected the roadways, and served as resting places. Besides these stations for riders and carriages, Solomon also founded towns for storing goods; these were also used to house grain for future years of scarcity.

Thus Solomon settled the affairs of Israel, and provided for its future security. He had no sharpsighted counsellor, such as David had had in Ahithophel, to assist him in establishing order; his own wisdom was his sole counsellor. But he had to choose responsible officers, who would give effect to his instructions, and carry out the plans which he devised. The great extent of his state and his court demanded the establishment of new offices. For the better reception of strangers he had placed over his vast household a major-domo (al-hab-Baith). Ahishar was the name of this officer. The twelve officials who provided for the wants of the household were supervised by a chief whose name was Azariah-ben-Nathan. A high official, Adoniram, the son of Abda, was also placed (al-ham-Mas) over the many thousand bondmen who worked on the roads and in the fortresses. Thus three high posts were newly created by Solomon.

Its great extent and the riches which Solomon had amassed enabled the kingdom of Israel to hold its place amongst the greatest nations in the ancient world. Princes and nations who lived in strife with each other sought the aid of the ruler of this mighty dominion, and called upon him to act as arbitrator, for his wisdom was famed far and wide. The greatest blessing in Solomon's reign was the peace and undisturbed quiet which obtained throughout the land. From Dan unto Beersheba the Israelites could peacefully enjoy their home, " every one under his own vine and under his own fig-tree."

The commercial treaties, the prosperity of the country, the security to life arising from the long peace maintained in Solomon's reign, all contributed to attract the surrounding tribes of Moabites, Ammonites, Idumæans, and even Egyptians to the country. It is probable, too, that the high religious culture of the Israelites, so superior to idolatry, and its splendid manifestation in the temple at Jerusalem influenced enlightened foreigners to seek shelter under the " wings of the God of Israel." The country, the people, and the God of Israel acquired widespread renown in Solomon's time. The Israelitish mariners, who visited so many harbours, coast-lands, and marts, and the Israelitish merchants who entered into connections with foreign parts carried reports of their fatherland to the remotest climes and nations. The praise of the wise, mighty, and brilliant king Solomon resounded far and wide in his times. In the eyes of the world he elevated the name of the God whom he honoured, and to whose glory he had erected a magnificent temple. The Israelitish sailors and merchants unconsciously became the first messengers and pioneers of the religion of Israel among the idolatrous nations.

One day Jerusalem was surprised by an extraordinary embassy. A wise queen, from the spice-bearing land of Sabia (Sheba), which is situated on the Arabian coast of the Red Sea, came to visit Jerusalem. As she had heard so much of the greatness of Solomon, and in praise of the God of Israel, she wished to see, with her own eyes, how much truth or falsehood lay in the reports which had come to her ears. She was received with marked attention by Solomon, and had many interviews with him. The queen (whom tradition calls Belkis) greatly admired his wisdom, and was much impressed by the temple which he had erected to God, and by the brilliancy of his court. It is said that she propounded enigmatic riddles to him in order to test his powers, and these he answered in a manner which excited her astonishment.

Solomon's brilliant rule, however, became the source of a serious division between the tribes, which he had unavailingly striven to consolidate into one indissoluble whole. Notwithstanding that the temple formed a bond of union for the whole people, and that Solomon tried to abolish the tribal isolation which prevailed, he succeeded only in the case of Benjamin, which became more closely united with Judah. This was owing to the fact that the temple was built on Benjamite territory, and consequently several Benjamite families settled in the capital. Probably Solomon also preferred the tribe of Benjamin and his own ancestral tribe to the other tribes. The mutual dislike of the houses of Israel and Judah, or the northern and southern tribes, had not ceased. Among the northern tribes a deep sense of discontent prevailed against Solomon, despite the prosperity to which he had raised them; they resented the pressure put upon them to forward regular supplies for the court, and to perform compulsory service in the erection of public buildings. Their discontent was not expressed aloud, but it needed only an occasion for it to vent itself. Wise as Solomon was, he had not sufficient foresight to perceive that his faults were sure to weaken the future security of the state. Amongst the officials whom Solomon employed to supervise the buildings was an Ephraimite, who was clever, courageous and ambitious. This was Jeroboam, the son of Nebat, from the town of Zereda or Zorathan, on the other side of the Jordan. He was the son of a widow; thus, free from paternal restraint, he could follow out his own impulses uncontrolled. Jeroboam had supervised the erection of the walls of Jerusalem, and had displayed great skill and firmness in managing the bondmen. Solomon was, in fact, so well pleased with him that he bestowed on him a high position in the territory of Ephraim and Manasseh. Here Jeroboam had the opportunity of becoming acquainted with the discontent of the people, which was probably strongest amongst the ever-discontented Ephraimites. The popular feeling accorded well with his ambitious plans, and he decided to utilise it when a favourable opportunity should occur.

Solomon was guilty of the folly of permitting sacrificial altars to be built for various idols. It may have been his foreign wives who induced him to make this concession, or perhaps it was due to the foreigners, the Phœnicians and other races, who had taken up their residence in Jerusalem, and had received permission to worship their gods in the land of Israel according to their custom. However this may have been, altars were raised on the high northern point of the Mount of Olives, in honour of Astarte of the Zidonians, Milcom of the Ammonites, Chemosh of the Moabites, and other idols. The religious convictions of the nation were not so deeply rooted that the people could witness all kinds of idolatrous practices without falling into the errors of idol-worship themselves. A prophet, Ahijah of Shiloh, had the courage to reprimand the king, and to warn him of the danger which his conduct rendered imminent. Solomon, however, seems to have given little heed to his representations, and the prophet, indignant at the king's obtuseness, determined to use Jeroboam (whose ambitious schemes he had probably divined) as the instrument of Solomon's destruction. When Jeroboam left Jerusalem, the prophet approached him, seized his garment, tore it into twelve pieces, and handing him ten of them, he said, "Take these ten pieces; they portray the ten tribes which will separate themselves from the house of David, and recognise thee as their king." Jeroboam wanted no further encouragement to mature his plans, since a prophet had commended them. He hurried to the territories of Ephraim, and called on the Ephraimites to separate themselves from the house of David. Meanwhile Solomon had received tidings of the event, and before the revolution could spread, he sent his guards to kill the rebel. Jeroboam then fled to Egypt, where a new dynasty now occupied the throne. Shishak (Sheshenk, Sesonchosis, 980–959) was the first king of the new line. Under his rule was severed the bond which had united Israel and Egypt since Solomon's marriage with the Egyptian princess. Shishak in fact was inimical to the Israelitish nation, which had become more powerful than was agreeable to him. He therefore received Jeroboam with kindness, intending to use him against Solomon. Shishak also gave a friendly reception and protection to an Idumæan prince, who had special reasons for avenging himself on the Israelitish nation. Hadad (or Adad) was a relation of the Idumæan king whom David had conquered. He had, when a boy, escaped the massacre ordered by Joab in consequence of a revolution in Idumæa. When Shishak ascended the throne, the Idumæan prince hurried to Egypt, and was graciously received. Shishak gave him the queen's sister in marriage, and his first-born son (Genubath) grew up among the Egyptian princes. Hadad also acquired possessions in Egypt, and was honoured in every way; notwithstanding this, he yearned to return to Edom, and to regain the territories which had been snatched away from him. He carried this desire into effect with the aid of Shishak, who was fully aware that the warlike spirit which had obtained under David and Joab, had diminished under Solomon's peaceful rule, and that petty warfare in the mountainous districts would be connected with little danger, while it might be productive of great benefit to himself. Hadad and the troops which he had mustered in Idumæa did great damage to Solomon's caravans, which carried goods between the bay of Elath and the Israelitish boundaries; and Solomon's warriors were powerless to prevent these attacks.

Unnoticed by Solomon, another cloud, which threatened Israel with destruction, was gathering in the north. Rezon (of Zobah), one of the servants of King Hadadezer, whom David had overthrown, had taken to flight after the defeat of his sovereign; he assembled a predatory troop, and made raids in the districts lying between the Euphrates and the northern ranges of the Lebanon. Rezon's troops gradually increased in numbers, and with their numbers grew his courage and power. At last he ventured to proceed against the ancient city of Damascus. He succeeded in capturing it and in having himself chosen king. Advancing from the north, Rezon also committed hostilities against the Israelites and their allies, without any opposition on the part of Solomon, who either had a dislike of war, or had no troops available to ward off the attacks from the north and the south. Thus arose, from small beginnings, powers inimical to Israel, which might easily have been nipped in the bud. Besides this, an internal breach was in store for Israel.

Solomon, however, did not live to see the development of the impending evils and the decay of his kingdom. He died in peace at the age of about sixty years (in 977). His body was buried, no doubt with great pomp, in the rocky mausoleum of the kings which David had built on the south of Mount Zion. It was said later on that Solomon, as well as his father, had heaped up untold treasures and wealth in these vaults and cells, which were discovered many centuries after by the later Jewish kings.

Although Solomon had numerous wives, it appears that he left but few children, a son named Rehoboam and two daughters, Taphath and Basmath, whom their father married to two of his officers. Posterity, which has greatly exaggerated Solomon's wisdom and ability, has also attributed to him power over mystic spirits and demons, who, obeying his will, could be invoked or dismissed as he chose.   Even a ring on which his name was engraven was supposed to exercise a mighty spell over the demons, and keep them in subjection.

The power to which Solomon had elevated Israel resembled that of a magic world built up by spirits. The spell was broken at his death.

CHAPTER X.

SECESSION OF THE TRIBES.

Accession of Rehoboam—Jeroboam's return—The King at Shechem —The Secession of the Ten Tribes—Election of Jeroboam—New Alliances—Rezon and Shishak—Fortification of Shechem— Jeroboam's idolatry—Ahijah's rebuke—Religion in Judah— Abijam—Asa—Nadab—Baasha—Wars between Asa and Baasha —Defeat of Zerah—Benhadad—Elah—Zimri—Omri—Civil war— Samaria built—Omri's policy—Alliances with Ethbaal and Tyre —Ahab: his character—Jezebel—The Priests of Baal—Elijah— Naboth's vineyard—Elijah at Carmel—War with Benhadad— Death of Ahab and Jehoshaphat—Ahaziah's Accession—Jehoram —Elijah and Elisha—Jehu—Death of Jezebel.

977—887 B. C. E.

FOR the first time since the monarchical government had been established in Israel, the next heir to the throne could succeed without disturbance or contest. Rehoboam, more fortunate than his father and grandfather, found himself, when he ascended the throne, ruler over a mighty and important country. Many nations bowed in allegiance to him, and he could indulge in golden dreams of power and happiness. His undisputed accession was perhaps owing to the fact that he had no brother, or that Solomon's strict laws regarding private property had also extended to the rights of succession. Whatever may have been the reason, Rehoboam ascended the throne of his father without opposition. In fact, disputes between brothers concerning the succession, such as had occurred at the death of David, did not occur again in Jerusalem. Nor would Rehoboam have been equal to such contests. He by no means resembled his father; indeed, his abilities were not even mediocre. Like all princes born in the purple, who are not gifted with striking personal qualities, he was thoughtless haughty, and at the same time so wanting in self-reliance that he could not decide for himself. He had neither martial abilities nor an appreciation of greatness of any kind. The throne was to secure for him power, peace, and the enjoyment of life's pleasures. If this was his dream, it was of but short duration. He was unexpectedly confronted with an enemy who robbed him of power and peace, and who caused a breach in the state of Israel which could never again be healed.

Jeroboam, the Ephraimite who had raised the flag of rebellion during the last years of Solomon's reign, and who, on the failure of his attempt, had fled to Egypt, returned to his native land immediately on receipt of the news of Solomon's death, with the intention of resuming his ambitious schemes, which had been approved by a prophet. Probably his protector, Shishak, the king of Egypt, assisted him, and permitted him to proceed by sea to the Israelitish port. No sooner had this bold Ephraimite arrived in Shechem, the second city of importance in the kingdom, than the Shechemites, ever ready for sedition, began a revolt. Jeroboam was invited to join the meeting of the people, or rather he instigated the holding of such an assembly in order to consider the steps necessary to attain the desired end without bloodshed.

The elders of other tribes were likewise invited to take part in the projects of the Shechemites, and thus their rebellious undertaking assumed the character of a national demonstration. It was first of all decided that the elders of the tribes were not, as heretofore, to repair to Jerusalem in order to pay homage to the new king, but that he was to be invited to receive their allegiance at Shechem. This was the first step in the rebellion. Rehoboam determined to accept their invitation, much against his will probably, in the expectation that his presence would put a stop to any intended insurrection. It was a disastrous hour, fraught with far-reaching results for the history of Israel.

Rehoboam was accompanied to Shechem by his council, consisting of the elder members who had served his father, and of younger members whom he himself had selected. In order to provide for all cases, he took with him Adoniram, the overseer of the slaves, whose angry glance and whose rod kept the unwilling labourers in submission. When Rehoboam arrived in Shechem, the representatives of the tribes came before him in order to explain their grievances. Jeroboam, who had been chosen as their mouthpiece, placed the troubles of the nation before the king in strong language: "Thy father put a heavy yoke on the people, and made them submit to heavy burdens. If thou wilt lighten this heavy yoke, we will serve thee." Struck by this bold language, Rehoboam concealed his anger as best he could, and told them to return for his reply in three days. He knew not what answer to give the representatives of the tribes. He therefore consulted his council. The older members were unanimously in favor of mild treatment, the younger men advocated severity, and the unwise king followed the advice of the latter. When, on the third day, Jeroboam and the elders came to him for his answer, he replied in words which he thought would annihilate them: "My little finger is stronger than my father's loins. If he scourged you with rods, I will scourge you with scorpions." Jeroboam had expected and reckoned on no other reply. Turning to the elders he said, "What share have we in David, and what inheritance in the son of Jesse? Return to your tents, O Israel, and thou, David, see to thine own house!" Jeroboam then unfurled the standard of rebellion, and assembled the Shechemites, who willingly mustered around him in order to display their enmity towards Rehoboam. All the jealousy and hatred that the Ephraimites had cherished during the reigns of David and Solomon, on

account of the oppression and supposed humiliation
to which they had been forced to submit, now burst
forth.   They seized the opportunity to free themselves from the yoke of David, and to place themselves, as they had done in the days of the Judges,
at the head of the tribes.   Sword in hand, the Shechemites, headed by Jeroboam, attacked the house in
which Rehoboam dwelt.   He sent Adoniram, the
overseer of the slaves, to chastise the ringleaders
like rebellious slaves.   A shower of stones over-
powered him, and he sank lifeless to the ground.
Rehoboam, whose life was in danger, fled from
Shechem in his chariot, and reached Jerusalem.   A
breach had been made which no one could heal.

Indignant and dispirited as Rehoboam was at the
turn affairs had taken in Shechem, he felt himself
obliged to ascertain, before taking any steps, how
far he could count on the fidelity of the nation.
What was he to do, if the tribes nearest to the capital,
induced by the example of the Shechemites, also
renounced their allegiance to him?   Where would the
secession end?   From this care, however, he was
soon freed.   The tribe of Judah, which was intimately
connected with the house of David, and considered
that house its most precious ornament, remained
faithful to Rehoboam.   The tribe of Simeon was
merely a subsidiary of that of Judah, and could not
be considered independent.   The tribe of Benjamin
also remained faithful to Rehoboam.   It was closely
connected with that of Judah, and their fortunes
could not again be parted.   There were more Benjamites than Judæans living in Jerusalem.   These
tribes, then, sided with Rehoboam.   No sooner was
he aware that two or three tribes would remain true
to him, than he naturally entertained the idea of
compelling the Shechemites and Ephraimites to return
to their allegiance by means of the sword, and he
would no doubt have succeeded, had not Jeroboam
taken measures to turn the secession to the greatest

advantage. He impressed on the Ephraimites that only a king could successfully resist Rehoboam's attacks, and that by no other means could they escape the severe punishment which awaited them as insurgents. They then determined to set up an opposition king. Who would be better suited for this post than Jeroboam? He alone possessed the needful courage and skill, and he was an Ephraimite. The elders of Ephraim therefore assembled, and with the co-operation of the remaining tribes, chose him as king. The latter paid homage to Jeroboam, possibly because they also had grievances against the house of David, and could expect no redress from Rehoboam. Thus the obscure man of Zereda became king over ten tribes (977–955), counting Manasseh of Machir as one, and Manasseh of Gilead as another tribe.

The tribes of Judah, Benjamin and Simeon alone remained attached to the house of David. The two last named, however, had no separate existence, they were merged into the tribe of Judah. The house of Israel, which had been joined with the house of Judah for barely a century, was thus again divided from it. To avoid continual warfare as well as the necessity of being constantly on the defensive, each of the two kings sought to strengthen himself by alliances, and thus frustrate all hostile plans. Rehoboam made a treaty with the newly elected king of Damascus, the state founded by Rezon, the bandit, in Solomon's time, having attained great power. Rezon, or his successor Tabrimon, had united various Aramæan districts to Damascus, and ruled over extensive territory. The treaty between Rehoboam and the king of Damascus prevented Jeroboam from attacking the kingdom of Judah, and visiting it with the horrors of a long war. Jeroboam, on the other hand, formed an alliance with another power, in order to exasperate and alarm the king of Judah.

A union of the two kingdoms was distasteful to

both.   The difference in their history prevented their coalescing.   The house of Israel, especially the tribe of Ephraim, willingly relinquished the advantages which might accrue from a union with the house of David, in order that it might not be forced to assume an inferior position.   The more worthy in both kingdoms were probably filled with grief at the breach which had occurred, but they were unable to avert it. The civil war which appeared imminent was prevented by the prophet Shemaiah, who, in the name of God, called on the Judæans and Benjamites to desist from fratricide.   Slight feuds, however, broke out between the contiguous kingdoms, as was unavoidable between such near neighbours, but they led to no serious result.

Jeroboam was effectually aided in his ambitious plans by Shishak (Sheshenk), who, it is said, married his wife's elder sister Ano to the fugitive Israelite, just as he had given another sister in marriage to the Idumæan prince who had taken refuge with him. Shishak probably had furnished Jeroboam with the supplies of money that enabled him to return to his fatherland, and now the new king seems to have formed an alliance with him against Judah.   Thus Rehoboam was prevented from undertaking any noteworthy steps against Israel.   In order to secure himself from Egyptian and Israelitish attacks, Rehoboam erected a chain of fortresses in a circuit of several miles round about the capital.   But they failed him in the hour of need.   Shishak, with an overwhelming force, undertook a war against Rehoboam in the fifth year of the Jewish king's reign (972).   Overcome by excess of numbers, the strongholds were taken one after another by the Egyptian armies, and Shishak pressed forward as far as Jerusalem.   It appears that the capital yielded without a struggle, and the Egyptian king contented himself with seizing the treasures which Solomon had deposited in the palace and the Temple.   He appropriated all the money then in Jerusalem, as well as the golden shields and spears which the king's guards used in royal processions to the Temple. He, however, left the kingdom of Judah intact, did not even touch the walls of Jerusalem, and left Rehoboam on his throne. On his return, Shishak commemorated his deeds of prowess and his victories over Judah and other districts by records and monuments. The alliance between Solomon and the king of Egypt was thus of but short duration. His son learned the futility of such a treaty, and experienced how little trust can be placed in plans and political measures, though apparently the outcome of the deepest calculation and forethought. Solomon, in spite of his wisdom, had acted thoughtlessly in regard to the union with the daughter of Pharaoh. He had built her a special palace, and within a few years after his decease, an Egyptian king ransacked this very palace and other monumental buildings of Solomon, and plundered them of all their treasures. The grandeur and power of Solomon's kingdom were at an end.

Jeroboam fortified Shechem and built himself a palace, which served also as a citadel (Armon) for purposes of defence. On the opposite side of the Jordan, he also fortified various towns, among them Penuel (or Peniel), to serve as a rampart against attacks from the south, where the Moabites and the Ammonites, in consequence of what had taken place, had separated themselves from the Israelites, in the same way as the Idumæans had shaken off the yoke of the Judæans. Internal embarrassments forced Jeroboam to introduce innovations. Guided either by habit or conviction, the families of the northern tribes continued to present themselves at Jerusalem in the autumn at harvest time, in order to take part in the service of the invisible God. This loyalty to the Jewish capital, even though manifested by only a part of his subjects, was a source of great anxiety to Jeroboam. How would it be if the people turned in ever increasing numbers to the temple in Jerusalem, and once more made peace with the house of David? Would he not be dethroned as quickly as he had attained to royalty? In order to avoid the possibility of such a reunion, Jeroboam matured a wicked plan, which caused Israel to fall back into the ways of idolatry and barbarity.

During his protracted stay in Egypt, Jeroboam had become acquainted with the system of worship established there, and he had observed that the worship of animals, particularly of the bull, tended to promote the aims of despotic government. He had observed that this animal worship served to stultify the nation, and Jeroboam thought he might turn to his own purposes a system so politic and advantageous. He therefore, in conjunction with his advisers, devised a plan by which these observances should be introduced in the Ten Tribes. He considered that this idol-worship might be of advantage to him in other ways, as it would keep him in favour with the court of Egypt. Israel would appear as a dependency of Egypt, and both countries, having common religious observances and customs, would also have common interests. The habits of Egypt were of special interest to him, as his wife was probably an Egyptian, and connected with the royal house of Egypt. Jeroboam also studied the convenience of the tribes. He wished to relieve those who lived far off from the necessity of making long journeys at the time of the harvest. At Bethel and at Dan, Jeroboam, therefore, put up golden calves, and issued a proclamation to the effect: "This is thy God, O Israel, who brought thee out of Egypt." In Bethel, where he himself intended to preside at the worship, he built a large temple, in which he also placed a sacrificial altar. To prevent the people from celebrating the Feast of Ingathering at Jerusalem, he fixed the festival a month later (in the eighth instead of the seventh month). Probably also a different time-reckoning was followed, according to the longer solar, instead of the shorter lunar year.

The nation, as a whole, appears to have taken no offence at this alteration, but to have actually regarded it as a revival of the ancient mode of worship. The fundamental principle, the *unity* of God, was in no way affected by it.   Jeroboam had not attempted to introduce polytheism, but had merely given them incarnations of the Deity, symbolising strength and fruitfulness.   The people, naturally sensual, were, indeed, well pleased to have a representation of the Godhead.   The *spirituality* of God, not admitting of ocular demonstration, was at that period more remote from their comprehension than the conception of His *unity*.   Sensual dissipation and depravity were not bound up with the worship of the bull as with the Canaanite service of Baal, and therefore it did not outrage the moral sense.

Thus the people gradually became accustomed to repair to Bethel or Dan for the high feasts; otherwise they made their offerings at home, or at the nearest place where sacrifices had been offered of old. Jeroboam fully attained his object; the nation became stultified, and bowed to him in servile obedience. The tribe of Levi, however, caused him anxiety. No Levite would consent to perform the office of priest at the worship of the bull; for Samuel's prophetic teachings had made a lasting impression on this tribe. That Jeroboam might not compel their services, the Levites, who had been living in the Israelitish towns, wandered forth, and settled in the kingdom of Judah. As he could not possibly manage without priests, he took any one who offered himself to serve in that capacity. At one festival he himself performed the priestly office, in order to elevate it in the eyes of the people, or, perhaps, in imitation of the Egyptian custom.   Jeroboam was thus led step by step to destroy the original principles of Judaism.

His conduct was not allowed to pass uncondemned. The old prophet, Ahijah, of Shiloh, who had incited Nebat's ambitious son to insurrection, now was too old and frail to lift his voice publicly against these proceedings. When, however, Jeroboam's wife visited him at Shiloh, to consult him about the dangerous illness of her eldest son, the prophet took the opportunity of announcing to her the approaching dissolution of the royal house. But a return was impossible, without paving the way to a reunion with the house of David. From motives of self-preservation, he was obliged to continue in the way he had chosen. The new worship was, therefore, retained during the existence of the kingdom of the Ten Tribes, and none of Jeroboam's successors attempted to make any alteration in its form.

In the kingdom of Judah (or House of Jacob), the conditions were quite different. Politically weakened by the severance of the tribes and the incursions of Egypt under Shishak, its wounds were too deep to heal before the lapse of a considerable time. But Judah had not sunk in religion or morals. Rehoboam appears to have troubled himself but little about religious or moral affairs; he was indifferent in every respect, and his pride having once received a blow, he seems to have passed his days in idleness. But the Temple, on the one hand, and the Levites, on the other, appear to have counteracted all deteriorating influences. In outward appearance all remained as it had been in the time of Solomon; the High Altars (Bamoth), on which families performed the sacrificial rites throughout the year, continued to be maintained, but at the autumn festivals the people repaired to the temple. Deviations from the established order of divine service were exceptional, and were accepted only by the circle of court ladies. As Solomon had permitted altars to be erected for his heathen wives, Rehoboam did not feel called upon to be more severe in his enactments. His mother Maachah, the daughter or granddaughter of Absalom, had a predilection for the immoral Canaanite worship; she erected a statue of Astarte in her palace, and maintained temple priestesses. Rehoboam permitted all this, but the unholy innovations did not spread very wide. Meanwhile, although idolatrous practices did not gain ground in the kingdom of Judah, there was no impulse towards a higher stage of moral culture under Rehoboam's government. A weakness seemed to have come over the people, as if they were in the last stage of senility. Nearly two centuries elapsed before traces of a higher spiritual force became evident. Rehoboam's reign of seventeen years was inglorious. The reign of his son Abijam (960–958) passed in a like manner. He also indulged in petty acts of hostility against Jeroboam, but without any important result. He, too, permitted the idolatrous practices of his mother Maachah. Abijam, it appears, died young, leaving no issue, and he was therefore succeeded by his brother Asa (957–918). He again was a minor, and the queen-mother Maachah held the reins of government. At first she seems to have desired to extend her idolatrous and immoral worship, but a revolution in the kingdom of the Ten Tribes put an end to her projects, and changed the course of events.

Nadab, who had succeeded to the throne on the death of Jeroboam (955–954), undertook a war against the Philistines, and besieged the Danite city of Gibbethon, which the Philistines had occupied. During this campaign a soldier by the name of Baesha (Baasha) conspired against the king in the camp, and killed him. From the camp Baasha proceeded to the capital, Tirzah, and destroyed the whole house of Jeroboam (954). The founder of this dynasty had not been anointed by the prophet; he was not considered inviolable, like Saul and David, and therefore the hand of the murderer was not restrained. Baasha was the first of the list of regicides in the Ten Tribes, and his act hastened the fate impending over the nation.

Having perpetrated the murder, he took possession of the throne and kingdom (954–933). He continued Tirzah as the capital, on account of its central position. It lay in the very heart of the kingdom, and possessed the additional advantage of being fortified. Had Baasha abolished the worship of the bull, he might have drawn to his side the worthier portion of the people of Judah. The latter were indignant at the idolatrous innovations of Maachah, which were more reprehensible than the bull-worship, as with them were connected the depraved habits of the temple priestesses. In Jerusalem the fear of eventual sympathy with Israel appears to have arisen; but Asa hastened to avert the calamity. Either on his own impulse, or urged thereto by one of the prophets, he snatched the reins of government from the hands of the queen-mother, forbade the worship of Astarte, removed the priestesses, and burnt the disgusting image which had been erected for worship in the valley of Kedron. Through these resolute acts Asa secured for himself the good-will of the well-disposed among his people.

The old inconclusive feuds between the two kingdoms were continued between Asa and Baasha. The former is said to have acquired several cities of Ephraim, and to have incorporated them in his own kingdom. In order to secure himself from the attacks of Judah, Baasha seems to have entered into a league with the king of Egypt, and to have urged him to carry war into the lands of his own foe. An Egyptian general named Zerah (Osorkon) sallied forth with a numerous body of Ethiopians, and pressed forwards as far as Mareshah, about ten leagues south-west of Jerusalem. Asa, however, marched against him with the combined forces of Judah and Benjamin, defeated the Ethiopian army north of Mareshah, pursued it as far as Gerar, and brought back enormous booty to Jerusalem.

Baasha was disconcerted by these proceedings,

and endeavoured to bring about an alliance with the
Aramæan king, Ben-hadad I., of Damascus, who,
hitherto friendly to the kingdom of Judah, had prevented all inimical attacks. Ben-hadad, the son of
Tabrimon, now cancelled his treaty with Asa, and
went over to Baasha's side. The latter conquered
Ramah, the birth-place and residence of the prophet
Samuel, which belonged to the Benjamites, and
fortified it so that it served as a base whence to
make raids on the neighbouring districts. Alarmed
at these doings, Asa endeavoured to revive the
treaty with the king of Damascus, and sent ambassadors to him, with quantities of treasure in silver
and gold, which he took both from the Temple and
from his palaces. Ben-hadad allowed himself to be
won over; it flattered him to be thus sought after
by both realms, to which his people had formerly
been obliged to pay tribute. He resolved to utilise
the weakness of both sides, and he commanded an
army to effect an entrance into the north of the
kingdom of Israel; he subjugated Ijon, Dan, and the
contiguous region of Abel-Bethmaachah; and also
reduced the district around the lake of Tiberias, and
the mountainous lands of the tribe of Naphtali. Asa
was thus saved at the expense of Judah's sister
nation; and Baasha was forced to abandon his desire
for conquest, and to relinquish Ramah.

Asa now summoned all the men capable of bearing
arms to assist in the destruction of the fortifications
of Ramah. The death of Baasha, which occurred soon
after this (in 933), and a revolution which ensued
in Tirzah, left Asa free from menace on that side.
Mizpah, a town having a very high and favourable
situation, was made an important citadel by Asa.
He also built a deep and roomy cistern in the rocks,
in order to have stores of water in case of a siege.

Meanwhile, in the kingdom of the Ten Tribes, terrible events were happening, which were productive
of changes in both kingdoms. Baasha was succeeded

by his son Elah (933–932), who was addicted to idleness and drunkenness. Whilst his warriors were engaged in battle with the Philistines, and were attacking Gibbethon, he passed his days in drinking-bouts. This circumstance was taken advantage of by his servant Simri (Zimri), the commander of one-half of the war-chariots, which had remained behind in Tirzah. Whilst Elah was dissipating in the house of the captain of his palace, Zimri killed him (in 932), at the same time destroying the entire house of Baasha, and not even sparing its friends. He then, as a matter of course, ascended the throne, but his reign was of short duration; it lasted only one week. No sooner had the news of the king's murder reached the army, then besieging Gibbethon, than they elected the Israelitish general Omri, as king. He repaired to the capital, but finding the gates closed against him, he laid siege to the city and effected a breach in the wall. When Zimri discovered that he was lost, he anticipated a disgraceful end by setting fire to the palace and perishing in the flames. He was the third of five kings of Israel who died an unnatural death, and only two of them were buried in the mausoleum for the kings, erected by Jeroboam. A fourth king was soon to be added to the list. Omri, a warrior, expected to obtain the vacant throne forthwith, but he met with opposition. One part of the population of the capital had chosen another king, Tibni, the son of Ginath; he was probably a native of the city. Thus two parties were formed in the capital, and the streets were no doubt deluged with blood. A civil war was the one thing wanting in the domains of Ephraim to make the measure of misery full to overflowing. For three years the partisan conflict raged (932–928); at length the party of Omri gained the upper hand. Tibni was killed, and Omri remained sole ruler (928). He, however, felt ill at ease in Tirzah; the palace was in ashes since the death of Zimri, and other depredations had no doubt taken place during the protracted civil war.

The conquered party was hostile to him, and Omri, therefore, determined to transfer the seat of the empire. He could not select Shechem, where the restless and rebellious spirit of the inhabitants would not permit him to live in safety, and there was no other important town situated in the heart of the country. Omri therefore conceived the idea of building a new capital. A high plateau, at a few hours' distance northwest of Shechem, seemed to him the fittest spot. He bought it of its owner, Shemer, erected buildings, a palace and other houses, fortified it, and called it *Shomron* (Samaria). Whence did he obtain inhabitants for the newly founded city? He probably adopted a course similar to David's in the case of Jerusalem, and caused the warriors attached to his cause to settle there. A year after his victory over the rival king, Omri left Tirzah, and removed to Samaria, which was destined to be the rival of Jerusalem for a period of two hundred years, and then, after two centuries of desertion, to revive, and once more wage war against Judah and Jerusalem. Samaria inherited the hatred of Shechem against Jerusalem, and increased it tenfold. The new city gave its name to the kingdom of the Ten Tribes, and the land was thence called the land of Samaria.

Omri, the first king of Samaria, was neither a strong nor a warlike leader, but he was a wise man. The crown which he had acquired, rather by the favour of circumstances than his own force of will, did not satisfy him. He wished to make his court and his people great, respected and wealthy, and he hoped that the prosperity of the days of Solomon might be restored to Israel. It is true that the nation was divided, and thereby weakened. But was it necessary for war always to be carried on between the two portions, and for the sword to destroy them? Connected as they were by reason of tribal relations and common interests, could they not henceforth pursue their course in friendly alliance?

Omri endeavoured, in the first place, to make peace with the representative of the royal house of David, and to impress upon him the advantages, to both of them, of pursuing an amicable policy. They might in that way obtain their former sway over the countries which had once been tributary to them. For a long time friendly relations were actually established between the two kingdoms; and they supported, instead of opposing, each other. Omri also cherished to a great, perhaps even to a too great degree, the hope of a friendly alliance with Phœnicia. He desired that a part of the riches which their extensive maritime expeditions and trade introduced into that country, might also flow into his own kingdom. At this time various kings had waded to the throne in Tyre through the blood of their predecessors, until at length Ethbaal (Ithobal), a priest of Astarte, ascended the throne, after the murder of his predecessor, Phalles. The disastrous occurrences in Phœnicia had greatly weakened the land. The great families had been compelled to emigrate, and had founded colonies on the north coast of Africa. The kingdom of Damascus, which had acquired great power, sought to obtain possession of the productive coast-line of Phœnicia; Ethbaal, therefore, had to strengthen himself by means of alliances. The kingdom of the Ten Tribes was nearest to him.

Omri and Ethbaal therefore had common interests, and formed an offensive and defensive treaty. The league, desired by both powers, was confirmed by an intermarriage. Omri's son Ahab married Ethbaal's daughter Jezebel (Jezabel or Izebel)—a marriage which was fraught with disastrous consequences.

Omri, fortified by this alliance, could now venture to think of undertaking warlike expeditions. He captured several towns of Moab, which had emancipated itself under Jeroboam's rule, and compelled it to become once more tributary. He forced the Moabites to send herds of oxen and rams every year

as tribute. As, however, a sort of alliance existed
between Moab and Aram, and an increase of Israel's
power was watched by Aram with a jealous eye, the
Aramæan king of Damascus, Ben-hadad I., declared
war against Omri, and recovered some of the cities
he had taken. Omri was forced to accept peace
with Ben-hadad on hard terms, and bound himself
to open the caravan-roads through the kingdom of
Israel, and to allow free passage through the land.

Omri thereupon entered into a closer alliance with
the kingdom of Tyre, and pursued the plan of as-
similating his people to their Canaanite neighbours.
Why should he endeavour to keep Israel separate
from the surrounding peoples? Would it not be
wiser and better to permit the kingdom of the Ten
Tribes to assume a Phœnician or Tyrian character?
United as they were in language and customs, might
not the two races become more closely welded together, if the Phœnician form of worship were introduced into the kingdom of Israel? Omri led the
way to this union. He introduced the service of
Baal and Astarte as the official mode of worship;
he built a temple for Baal in his capital of Samaria, ordained priests, and commanded that sacrifices should be universally made to the Phœnician
idols. He desired to see the worship of the bull,
as observed in Bethel and Dan, abolished. It
seemed to him too distinctly Israelitish in character, and to be likely to maintain the division between
the Israelites and Phœnicians. Jehovah, adored with
or without a visible image, was too striking a contrast to the Tyrian Baal or Adonis for Omri to permit His worship to remain. Omri's innovations
were of far greater import than those of Jeroboam;
or, to speak in the language of the Bible, he acted
yet more sinfully than his predecessors. He desired
to rob the nation of its God and of its origin; he desired it to forget that it had a special nationality in
contradistinction to that of the idolaters. History

has not recorded how these changes were received. His son Ahab (922–901) was destined to continue the work,—his father's bequest, as it were. In further-ance of the latter's projects he naturally kept up the close connection with Tyre and with the king of Judah.

But the execution of a charge involving the sever-est attacks on the inner convictions of man is, in spite of all one may do, dependent on circumstances or contingencies beyond the calculations of the wisest mind. Two kinds of obstacles intervened to prevent the Canaanisation of the Ten Tribes. The one was Ahab's disposition, and the other arose from an un-expected cause which weakened, if it did not entirely destroy, the effect of the terrible blow aimed at reli-gion. In order to accomplish this transformation of the nation into a mere appendage of Phœnicia, and the consequent loss of its own identity, the successor of Omri needed a powerful mind, an unbending will, and unyielding severity to crush all opposition with a strong hand. Ahab was, however, of an entirely different nature—weak, mild, loving peace and com-fort, rather disposed to avoid disturbances and obstacles than to seek or remove them. Had it rested with him alone, he would have abandoned his father's system and given himself up to such enjoy-ments as the royal power granted him, regardless of what the future might bring. Ahab was not even warlike; he permitted the neighbouring kings to treat him in a manner which would have excited the indignation and roused the most determined opposi-tion of any king not altogether destitute of the feel-ing of honour. But as he was forced against his de-sire and inclination to enter into a contest with an ambitious neighbour, so he was also compelled to enter upon a conflict with the Israelitish nation. His father had given him a wife in every way his oppo-site, with a strong manly will, who was determined to gain her ends by severity and cruelty, if necessary.

Jezebel, the Phœnician princess, whose father had filled the post of priest to Astarte before he obtained the throne, was filled with enthusiastic eagerness to carry out the plan of Canaanising the people of Israel. Either from a perverted idea or from political considerations, she desired to amalgamate the Israelitish people with her own, and make Tyrians and Israelites one nation. She continued the work commenced by Omri, with energy and mercilessness, and led her weak-minded husband into all kinds of oppressive and unrighteous actions. Jezebel's gloomy and obstinate character, with her uncontrollable energy, was the cause of a ferment and commotion in the kingdom of the Ten Tribes, which led to disastrous results, but which, like a destroying storm, performed the beneficent service of clearing the atmosphere. Jezebel's first step was to build a great temple to Baal in the capital of Samaria. In such a temple there were three altars, images and pillars, which were dedicated to a sort of holy trinity: Baal, his consort Astarte, and the god of fire or destruction (Moloch Chammon). For this worship, Jezebel introduced into the country a host of priests and prophets (450 for Baal and 400 for Astarte), who were supported at the expense of the royal house, and dined at the queen's table. Some of these priests attended to the sacrifices in Samaria, while others rushed madly through the country, celebrating their scandalous rites in the cities and villages. The Phœnician priests or prophets attired themselves in women's apparel, painted their faces and eyes, as women were in the habit of doing, their arms bared to the shoulders, and carried swords and axes, scourges, castanets, pipes, cymbals and drums. Dancing and wailing, they whirled round in a circle, by turns bowed their heads to the ground, and dragged their hair through the mud. They also bit their arms and cut their bodies with swords and knives till the blood ran, providing an offering for their bloodthirsty goddess. Doubtless they were accompanied by temple priestesses (Kedeshôth), who followed their shameful pursuit in honour of Astarte, and for the benefit of the priests. By means of this troop of priests of Baal and the ecstatic followers of Astarte, Jezebel hoped to wean the Israelitish people from the God of its fathers, and to carry into effect the plan of entirely transforming the national character. At the head of the Phœnician priesthood there was a high priest, who probably gave instructions and commands as to how they were to proceed. In the first place, the altars dedicated to God were destroyed, and others erected in the Canaanite fashion, with pointed pillars, the symbols of an obscene cult. The altars in Bethel and Dan were, no doubt, transformed in a similar manner. It was intended that the sacrifice-loving nation, for want of altars of its own, should bring its offerings to the temples of Baal and of Astarte, and thus become accustomed to this mode of worship. How easy it is to force a nation to give up its usages and peculiarities, and to accept those of strangers, if the rulers act with subtlety and force combined! The Israelites in the kingdom of the Ten Tribes had already been demoralised, owing to their half-century's separation from Jerusalem (the centre of intellectual activity), and to the bull-worship which they had long been practising. The cities had acquired a taste for luxury, and a love of dissipation, which the impure worship of Baal and Astarte only served to foster. The towns doubtless, for the most part, yielded to the new state of things, or, in any case, offered no opposition to it. Seven thousand individuals alone remained firm, and would not pay homage to Baal, nor adore him with their lips. A part of the nation, amongst them the villagers, meanwhile wavered in their ideas and actions, and not knowing whether God or Baal was the mightier divinity, they worshipped the one publicly and the other secretly. It was a period of uncertainty and confusion, such as usually precedes an historical crisis. It remained to be seen whether the ancient belief in the God of Israel, and the demands of holiness had taken sufficiently deep root, and had acquired enough vitality and power to conquer an opposing force and eradicate what was foreign. In such times a man of striking personality, in whom lives a pure faith, and who is entirely ruled by it, naturally assumes leadership, and by firmness, enthusiasm and heroic self-sacrifice convinces the waverers, strengthens the weak, incites the indifferent, and thus collects an army of defenders to rescue from imminent destruction their own national, peculiar endowments. When such an individual is roused by the very opposition of the enemy, and spurred on to action, he becomes a vivifying principle, and brings about a new state of things, a mingling of both old and new elements. Such an individual arose during this crisis in the person of the prophet Elijah (920–900).

Whence came this energetic, all-subduing prophet? In which tribe was his cradle? Who was his father? This is not known. He was simply known as Elijahu (shortened into Elijah). He was not a citizen of Transjordanic Gilead, but belonged to that class of tolerated half-citizens called Toshabim (dwellers). He was of a tempestuous nature, and was guided by no considerations of expediency; he would not have hesitated to offer his life for his creed. He was considered by his successors as the incarnation of moral and religious zeal (*kanna*). Like a tempest he made his entry, like a tempest he thundered forth his execrations against the weak, woman-led Ahab; like a tempest he rushed away, so that no one could seize him; and in a tempest he finally disappeared from his earthly scene of action. Elijah was imbued with the one thought, to save the belief in the God of Israel, which was passing away from the minds of the people. To this God he dedicated himself,

and to His service did his life belong solely and exclusively. Elijah was outwardly distinguishable by his
peculiar dress. In contradistinction to the effeminate,
luxurious dress of the worshippers of Baal and
Astarte, his undergarment was confined by a leather
belt, and over it he wore a black hairy cloak. He
wore his hair long, and touched no wine, and thus
gave rise to the institution of Nazarites, who were
not permitted to drink wine or to shave the hair of
the head. In this costume and with these habits he
appeared first in Gilead, and there announced the
all-embracing creed, "Jehovah alone is God." Here,
where the Jordan offered a barrier against the swarms
of the priests of Baal, and where the fear of Ahab and
Jezebel could not paralyze the conscience, there were
yet faithful adherents of the God of Israel. Amongst
these Elijah probably found his first auditors and
disciples, who were carried away by his enthusiastic
manner, and became his helpers.

In a short time a body of prophets or disciples
(Bene-Nebiim) had arisen, who were ready to give
up their lives for their ancestral tenets. They also
followed Elijah's way of living, and became Nazarites
The principles of this newly formed circle were to
lead a simple life, not to dwell in cities where luxury
and effeminacy ruled, but in village tents, not to drink
wine, not to till vineyards, to avoid agriculture generally, but, like the patriarchs and the tribes in earlier
times, to live by tending flocks. Jonadab, the son of
Rechab, who doubtless was one of the followers of
Elijah, was the first to establish these rules for himself and his household. He impressed on his
descendants the necessity of abstaining from wine,
from building fixed residences, from sowing seed,
and especially from planting vineyards. In this
way Elijah not only aroused and inspired a band
of defenders of the ancient law for his own time,
but opened the path to a new future. He set
simplicity and self-restraint against degeneracy and

love of pleasure. With his body of disciples he
eagerly commenced action against the priests and
prophets of Baal. He probably passed rapidly from
place to place, called the populace together, and
inspired them with his storm-like eloquence, the point
of which was " Jehovah alone is God, and Baal and
Astarte are dumb, lifeless idols." He may even have
incited attacks on those priests of Baal whom he
encountered. Jezebel could not long endure the
doings of the energetic Tishbite, which interfered
with her plans; she sent her soldiers against Elijah's
troop, and those who fell into their hands were
mercilessly slaughtered. They were the first martyrs
who died for Israel's ancient law. Jezebel, the
daughter of Ethbaal, the priest of Astarte, was the
first persecutor for religion's sake. Elijah himself,
however, on whom Jezebel was specially anxious to
wreak her vengeance, could never be reached, but
always eluded his pursuers. His zeal had already
produced an important effect. Obadiah, the superintendent of Ahab's palace, was secretly attached to
the ancient law. He who, perhaps, had the task of
persecuting the disciples of the prophet, hid one
hundred of them in two caves of Mount Carmel, fifty
in each cave, and supplied them with bread and water.
Obadiah was not alone—he had in his employ men
of his own faith, who executed his secret commissions.
How could Jezebel combat an invisible enemy that
found assistance in her own house?

One day, Elijah, though deprived of his followers,
ventured into the vicinity of King Ahab, whose
weak, pliable disposition he knew, in order to reproach
him for the misdeeds which he permitted. Ahab had
a passion for building and fortifying towns. It was
at his instance that Jericho, which had been deprived
of its walls since the entry of the Israelites, was fortified by Hiel of Bethel. Ahab also founded a new
capital in the beautiful table-land of Jezreel, where he
was desirous of passing the winter months. for

Samaria served only as a summer residence. This new town of Jezreel, which was destined to become the scene of tragic encounters, was built with great splendour. The royal couple had a palace of ivory erected there, which was to be surrounded by exten-sive gardens. For this purpose Ahab wished to have a beautiful vineyard which belonged to Naboth, one of the most respected citizens of Jezreel. Ahab offered him a compensation, either in money or land, but Naboth did not wish to part with the heritage of his fathers. Disappointed at his inability to surround his palace with park-like grounds, Ahab would not even take food. Finding him in this state, Jezebel contemptu-ously upbraided him for his childish vexation and his cowardly helplessness, but promised him that he should nevertheless possess the desired vineyard. She sent out letters in the king's name to those of the elders of Israel of whose slavish obedience she was cer-tain, and commanded them to produce two witnesses who would testify to having heard Naboth revile the gods and the king. When the council of judges had assembled at one of the gates of Jezreel, and Naboth, who was the eldest among them, had placed himself at their head, two degraded men appeared, and testi-fied against Naboth, under oath, as they had been instructed. Naboth was condemned to death by the elders, and the sentence was carried out not only on him, but also on his sons. The property of the executed fell by law to the king. Jezebel triumph-antly announced to her husband, " Now take Naboth's vineyard, for he is dead." When Eljah heard of this crime, he could no longer contain himself. He repaired to Jezreel and met the king just as he was inspecting Naboth's vineyard. Behind him rode two men, of whom one was fated to become the avenger of Naboth. The prophet thundered out to him, " Hast thou murdered, and dost now take posses-sion ?" " In the place where dogs licked the blood of Naboth, shall dogs lick thy blood, even thine."

(1 Kings xxi. 19; see 2 Kings ix. 25). This denunciation had an overwhelming effect on Ahab. He reflected
and meekly did penance, but ruthless Jezebel's power
over her weak-minded husband was too strong for
this change of mind to last.

Elijah, who had suddenly disappeared, now returned
a second time to Ahab, and announced that a famine
of several years' duration would befall the land. He
then departed and dwelt in the Phœnician town of
Zarephath (Sarepta), at the house of a widow, and
later in a cave of Mount Carmel. Meanwhile a famine devastated the land, and there was not fodder
even for the king's horses. One day, Elijah approached Obadiah, the superintendent of the palace,
and said to him, "Go, tell thy master, Elijah is here."
On his entrance, Ahab said to him, "Is it thou, disturber
of Israel?" Then the prophet replied, "Not I have
troubled Israel, but thou and thy father's house
have."

As though he had the right to give orders, he
bade the king command the priests of Baal to assemble on Mount Carmel, where it would be revealed
who was the true, and who the false prophet.

What occurred on Mount Carmel, where the contest took place, must have produced an extraordinary impression. Ahab, we are told, summoned all
the prophets of Baal to the mountain, whither many
of the people repaired, anxious to witness the result
of the contest between the prophet and the king,
and to see whether the prevailing drought would in
consequence come to an end. The hundred prophets who had hidden in the caves of Carmel, and
were maintained there by Obadiah, were probably also
present. Elijah presided at the assembly, which he
addressed, saying (1 Kings xviii. 21): "How long
halt ye between two opinions? If the Lord be God,
follow him; but if Baal, then follow him." He then
ordered the priests of Baal to erect an altar, offer
sacrifices, and call on their god for a miracle. The

priests did so, and according to their custom, they wounded themselves with knives and lances till the blood gushed forth over their bodies. They cried from morning till midday, " O Baal, hear us ! " When they at length ceased in confusion, Elijah erected an altar of twelve stones, performed his sacrifice, and prayed in a low voice. Then a miracle followed so suddenly that all present fell on their faces and cried, " Jehovah alone is God ! " A flash of lightning burnt the sacrifice and everything on the altar, even the water in the trench was dried up. Elijah determined to avenge himself on the priests of Baal, and commanded the multitude to kill them and throw their bodies into the river Kishon, which flowed hard by. Ahab, who was present, was so amazed and terror-stricken that he permitted this act of violence.

Jezebel, however, who was made of sterner stuff, did not look with equal unconcern on this scene. On receiving information of what had occurred, she threatened Elijah with a similar fate, if he should ever fall into her hands. He was, therefore, obliged to flee in order to save himself. In the desert near Mount Horeb he had a vision, in which it was revealed to him that the kingdom would pass away from the house of Ahab, whose descendants would be utterly destroyed, and that Jehu was to be anointed as king over Israel. Elijah himself was instructed to return on his way to the wilderness of Damascus, appoint a successor, and retire from the scene of action. The intemperate zeal which had led him to direct the slaughter of the priests of Baal was severely condemned on Horeb.

During Elijah's long absence there appears to have been a sort of truce between the royal house of Omri and the followers of the Tishbite. Ahab, who had been an eye-witness of the events at Carmel, had probably become more indifferent towards the worship of Baal, and as far as lay in his power had put a stop to the persecution of the prophets of the Lord.

The latter, on their part, also seem to have become less aggressive. Associations of prophets were formed in Jericho, Bethel and Gilgal, in which places they were permitted to dwell unmolested.

One prophet or disciple, however, remained inimical to Ahab—namely, Michaiah, son of Imlah. As often as the king sought out Michaiah to learn his prospects of success in some enterprise, the prophet foretold evil. Ahab, however, did not attempt his life, but merely imprisoned him. The ruler of the kingdom of the Ten Tribes had misfortunes enough to serve him as forewarnings. The king of Aram, Ben-hadad II., became daily more powerful, more presuming, and more eager for conquest. Besides his own horsemen and chariots, he had in his train thirty-two conquered vassal kings. With their assistance he attacked Ahab—doubtless in the hope of profiting by the famine and the discord which were weakening his kingdom. Ben-hadad subdued entire districts of the kingdom of the Ten Tribes, and besieged Samaria (904). In his distress, Ahab sued for peace, but Ben-hadad imposed such hard and disgraceful conditions that Ahab was forced to continue the contest. Finally, Ahab was victorious, and the Aramæan king, forced to surrender, was ready to promise anything in order to secure peace. The former enemies became friends, made a treaty and ratified it by many oaths, soon to be forgotten. This hastily-formed alliance was rightly condemned by one of the prophets, who predicted that Ahab had thereby created a fresh source of danger.

Ben-hadad, in fact, had no desire to fulfil the conditions and promises of the treaty. He restored, it is true, the captured town of Naphtali, but the Transjordanic cities, especially the important town of Ramoth-Gilead, he refused to cede, and Ahab was too indifferent to press the matter. The longer he delayed, the more difficult it became for him to insist on his claim, as Ben-hadad meanwhile was recovering his strength. Perhaps it would have been impossible for Ahab alone to regain possession of Ramoth-Gilead by force of arms. Just at this time he formed an alliance with King Jehoshaphat of Judah (918–905), and together with this king, he ventured to proceed against Ben-hadad. This alliance was a surprising one, seeing that Jehoshaphat detested the idolatrous perversions of Ahab and Jezebel, and could not approve of the forcible introduction of the Baal-worship into Samaria, nor of the cruel persecution of the prophets. Nevertheless, he formed an intimate connection with the house of Omri, and, guided by political reasons, even permitted his son Jehoram to marry Athaliah, the idolatrous daughter of Ahab.

When Jehoshaphat paid his visit to Samaria, in order to strengthen himself by an alliance with its king, Ahab probably solicited his royal guest to aid him in recovering Ramoth-Gilead; and the king of Judah promised the help of his nation and soldiery. Thus, after a long separation, the kings of Israel and Judah fought side by side. After crossing the Jordan with Jehoshaphat, Ahab was mortally wounded by an arrow as he stood in his war-chariot, but he possessed sufficient presence of mind to order his charioteer to drive him out of the turmoil of the battle. The soldiers were not informed of the king's condition, and fought until evening. Not until after the king had bled to death did the herald announce "Let each return to his own country and to his own town." The Israelitish and Judæan armies then recrossed the Jordan, and the Aramæans remained in possession of the mountain city of Ramoth-Gilead. Ahab's corpse was brought to Samaria and interred. But his blood, which had filled the chariot, was washed out at a pool and licked up by dogs.

Ahaziah, his son, succeeded Ahab, this being the first occasion on which the kingdom of the Ten Tribes descended in a direct line to a grandson. He reigned only a short time (901–900) and but little is

known of his character.   In spite of all warnings, he
followed in the evil ways of his parents.   Falling from
the window of his room, he took to bed, and sent to Ekron to consult the oracle of the reputed idol Baal-Zebub
(Bel-Zebul).   By this time Elijah had returned from his
sojourn on Mount Horeb, but in accordance with the
commands laid upon him, he had remained in seclusion, probably on Mount Carmel.   He no longer
interfered with the course of events, but had chosen
as his successor Elisha, son of Shaphat, who lived
near the Jordan.   The manner of choice was characteristic of Elijah.   While Elisha was ploughing a field
with a yoke of oxen, Elijah approached, threw over
him his dusky mantle (the distinctive garb of the
prophets), and went away.   If Elisha was indeed
worthy to succeed him, he would understand the
sign.   Elisha ran after him and begged him to wait
until he had taken leave of his parents.   " Go!
return!" said Elijah curtly.   Elisha understood that
a faithful prophet of God must leave father and
mother, and sacrifice the wishes of his heart and the
habits of his life.   Without returning to his father's
house, he followed Elijah at once, and became his
attendant, or, in the language of the time, " poured
water on his hands."   Only once again did Elijah
take part in public affairs.   He accosted the messenger whom Ahaziah had sent to Baal-Zebub, and said
to him, " Say to the king who sent thee, Is there no
God in Israel, that thou sendest to Ekron in order to
consult Baal-Zebub concerning thine illness?"   The
messenger returned to Samaria and related what he
had heard of the extraordinary man.   From the
description Ahaziah recognised Elijah, and dispatched
messengers for him.   After a long delay, Elijah went
fearlessly to Samaria, and announced to Ahaziah that
he would not again leave his sick bed.   As the king
died without leaving any children, he was succeeded
by his brother Jehoram (Joram, 899–887).   Elijah also
disappeared from the scene at about the same time.

His disciples and followers could not believe that the mortal frame of so fiery a soul could crumble into dust, and the belief arose that he had ascended to heaven in a storm-wind. His constant follower, Elisha, seeing that his master desired to avoid him, followed him the more closely. Elijah visited Gilgal, Bethel and Jericho, followed by Elisha, who did not venture to ask him whither he was going. At length they crossed the Jordan on dry ground, and then the teacher was withdrawn from his disciple's vision in a fiery chariot with fiery horses, which conveyed the prophet to heaven. The untiring activity of Elijah in preserving the ancient law under the most unfavorable circumstances, amidst ceaseless strife and persecution, surrounded by the idolatry and wickedness of the Baal and Astarte worship, could only be explained as the result of miracles. The greatest marvel, however, which Elijah accomplished, consisted in founding a circle of disciples who succeeded in keeping alive the teachings of the ancient law, and who raised their voices against the perversions of the mighty ones of the land. The members of the prophetic school founded by the prophet lived by the work of their own hands. After Elijah's disappearance, the disciples being without a leader, Elisha placed himself at their head. In the beginning of his career he followed closely in the footsteps of his master, keeping aloof from all men, and living chiefly on Mount Carmel. Gradually, however, he accustomed himself to mix with the people, especially after he had succeeded in rousing an energetic man to destroy the house of Omri, and put an end to the worship of Baal.

Jehoram, the third of the Omris, was not as fanatical in his desire to spread idolatry as his mother Jezebel, but nevertheless Elisha felt so profound an aversion for him that he could not bear to meet him face to face. After his brother's death, Jehoram undertook a war against King Mesa (Mesha) in order to punish him for his secession, and to reduce him to

subjection. Together with his brother-in-law, Jehoshaphat, he determined to proceed through Idumea,
whose king was also to supply auxiliary forces, and
south of the Dead Sea, towards Moab. By taking
this route Jehoram passed Jerusalem, where the heads
of the houses of Israel and Jacob met in a friendly
way. But it was merely an alliance of the chiefs.
By the advice of Jehoshaphat, Elisha, as the successor
of Elijah, was summoned to foretell the issue of the
war. On seeing Jehoram, the prophet said to him,
"Were it not out of consideration for King Jehoshaphat, I would not look at thee. Go thou to the prophets of thy father and thy mother." He nevertheless prophesied a favorable result. Mesa, king of
Moab, who was awaiting the attack of the allies on
the southern border of his kingdom, was overcome
by force of numbers, and fled to the mountain fortress of Kir-Haraseth (Kir-Moab, Kerek). The land
of Moab was laid waste, although Mesa was not subjugated. Not long after, on the death of Jehoshaphat, Edom also fell away from Judah. Edom had
not acted quite fairly in the combined attack on
Moab, and appears to have come to a friendly understanding with Mesa after the withdrawal of the
allies. It seemed as if the close friendship and intermarriage with the house of Omri was destined to
bring nothing but misfortune on the house of David.
Joram (Jehoram), the son of Jehoshaphat, the name-
sake of his royal brother-in-law of Israel (894–888),
was so intimately connected with the royal house of
Israel that he introduced idolatrous practices into his
own country. There can be no question but that his
wife Athaliah was the cause of this, for she, like her
mother Jezebel, was fanatically attached to the disgraceful rites connected with the worship of Baal.

At length the fate impending over the house of
Omri was to be fulfilled, and the house of David was
destined to be entangled in its meshes, woven by
Elisha. A change of dynasty had occurred in Da-

mascus, where Ben-hadad II., the same king who had
warred with Ahab, had been suffocated by his confidential servant Hazael, who seized the throne. Hazael
was desirous of regaining the conquered portions of
the kingdom of the Ten Tribes, which had been lost
by Ben-hadad. He first directed his attacks against
the tribes on the other side of the Jordan. Jehoram
of Israel repaired with his army to Ramoth-Gilead, in
order to defend that important fortress. The contest
for the citadel seems to have been a severe one, and
Jehoram was wounded by an arrow. In consequence
he went to Jezreel to have his wound attended to,
and left one of his captains, named Jehu, as commander of the defence. One day a disciple of the
prophets came to Jehu as a messenger from Elisha,
and after leading him from the council of warriors to
a distant room, where he appointed him the executor
of divine justice on the house of Omri, he disappeared as suddenly as he had come. When Jehu
returned to the council, they observed a change in
his manner, and eagerly asked him what the disciple
of the prophets had announced to him. Jehu at first
did not wish to reply, but at last he disclosed to
them that at Elisha's instance he had been anointed
king over the Ten Tribes. The chiefs of the army
did him homage. Improvising a throne by spreading
their purple garments on the highest steps of the
palace, amid trumpet blasts they shouted, "Long
live King Jehu." Having been acknowledged king
by the army, Jehu proceeded without delay to carry
out his design. He blockaded all the roads leading
from Ramoth-Gilead to Jezreel, so that the news
might not spread. He then led forth a part of the
army, crossed the Jordan, and rode in haste to Jezreel, where Jehoram still lay ill from the effects of his
wound. The king recognised Jehu from afar, by his
rapid driving, and as the messenger whom he had
sent out to meet him failed to return, he foreboded
evil. Jehoram therefore ordered his chariot that he

might see what had brought Jehu to Jezreel in such hot haste. Ahaziah, the king of Judah (who had shortly before this succeeded to the throne of his father Joram, 888), accompanied his uncle. They met Jehu in the field of Naboth, the victim of the judicial murder which Jezebel had brought about. When Jehoram saw that Jehu had come with hostile intentions, he turned to flee, but an arrow from Jehu's hand struck him, and he sank down lifeless in his chariot. Jehu ordered his follower Bidkar to cast the body into the field of Naboth, reminding him how they had been witnesses of the prophetic threat which Elijah had uttered against Ahab in that very field, and of the execution of which he was now the instrument. Ahaziah fell on the same day at the hands of Jehu's followers.

The destruction of the house of Ahab was imminent, and no one arose in its defence. Jehu entered Jezreel unmolested; the queen-mother, Jezebel, richly decked out, came to the palace window, and called, "How goes it, thou regicide, thou Zimri?" Jehu commanded the eunuchs of the palace to throw her into the street, and they obeyed. The body of the queen who had done so much harm was trampled down by the horses, and her blood spurted on the wall of the palace and over the horses. Naboth was not yet, however, fully avenged by the death of the son and the grandmother. There were still sons, grandsons, and relations of Jehoram, about seventy in number, who lived in Samaria, where they were trained and educated by the most respected men. To these men Jehu sent a message that they should appoint one of the royal family as king. They, however, knew that this charge was not to be taken seriously, and preferred to submit to the man who had already killed two kings. Jehu then ordered them to come with the "heads" to Jezreel, and thereupon they came with the heads of Ahab's descendants. Jehu placed the heads in two rows on the city gates, and the next morning he explained to the inhabitants of the city that, while he had only conspired against Jehoram, destiny had fulfilled the words of Elijah concerning the house of Ahab. Jehu combined cunning with determination; he had all the officers who had brought him his victims executed as murderers. There being now no survivor of the royal house, Jehu took possession of the throne, and the inhabitants of Jezreel paid him homage.

In order to gain the hearts of the nation, he made preparations to exterminate the worship of Baal in Samaria. On his road thither he met with Jonadab, who had adopted the Nazarite mode of life as introduced by Elijah. Together with Jonadab, Jehu went to Samaria, where he assembled the priests of Baal on a certain day. While pretending to join in their rites, he placed armed men inside and outside the temple of Baal, and went there accompanied by Jonadab. Hardly had the sacrifice been offered, when all the priests fell as victims. The soldiers killed all those inside the temple, and those who fled were cut down by the men stationed outside. The soldiers then rushed in, burnt the images, destroyed the altar, the columns, and also the temple, and converted the whole into a dunghill. Throughout the country Jehu destroyed the public monuments of the hideous idol-worship, for he professed to be a follower of Elijah, and zealous in the cause of Jehovah. In Jerusalem alone the worship of Baal continued, or rather it was fanatically upheld there by Athaliah, who was in every way the worthy daughter of her mother.

CHAPTER XI.

THE HOUSE OF DAVID AND THE JEHUIDES.

Athaliah's rule—Early years of Joash—Proclamation of Joash by Jehoiada—Athaliah slain—Religious Revival—Elisha—Repairing of the Temple—Death of Jehoiada and of his Son—Invasion of Israel by Hazael—Jehoahaz—Murder of Joash, King of Judah— Jehoash, King of Israel—Defeat of the Aramæans—Amaziah— Conquest of Edom--Death of Elisha—Amaziah defeated by Jehoash—Jeroboam II.—Death of Amaziah.

887—805 B. C. E.

IT is a striking fact that Israelitish women, the appointed priestesses of chastity and morality, displayed a special inclination for the immoral worship of Baal and Astarte. Maachah, the queen-mother in Judah, established an altar in Jerusalem for the worship of idols; Jezebel had erected one in Samaria, and now Athaliah followed the same course in Jerusalem. Yet, this was not Athaliah's sole nor her greatest sin. The daughter of Jezebel greatly surpassed her mother in cruelty. The victims of Jezebel had been prophets, staunch adherents of the ancestral law,—at all events, persons whom she considered as her enemies. Athaliah, however, shed the blood of her own relations, and did not hesitate to destroy the family of her husband and her son. No sooner had she received tidings of the death of her son Ahaziah, than she ordered the soldiers devoted to her cause to execute all the surviving members of the house of David in Jerusalem. Only the youngest of the princes, Joash, who was not quite one year old, was saved from sharing the fate of his brothers by the special intervention of Jehoshebah. What did Jezebel's bloodthirsty daughter expect to accomplish by this massacre? Was her wickedness the outcome of an ambitious scheme to gain possession of the throne, to the exclusion of all rivals? Or did Athaliah, herself a firm believer in the worship of Baal, desire to establish and diffuse this worship throughout Jerusalem and Judah, and was it in pursuance of that design that she destroyed the remnant of the house of David, in order to have her hands unfettered? Did she hope to succeed where her mother had failed, and by establishing idolatrous practices in Jerusalem, to give new fervour to the Phœnician worship?

Whatever motive actuated the worthy daughter of Ahab and Jezebel, Athaliah reduced the Judæans to so complete a subservience to her will that no one dared oppose her evil courses. The nation and the priests bowed before her. Even the high priest, Jehoiada, who was connected with the royal house, kept silence. At the very time when Jehu was destroying those emblems of idolatry in Samaria, there was erected in Jerusalem an image of Baal, with altars and pointed pillars, and a high priest, named Mattan, with a number of subordinate priests, was appointed and installed. Did Athaliah leave the temple on Mount Moriah untouched and undesecrated? It appears that she, less consistent in her daring and more timid than later sovereigns, did not venture to introduce an image of Baal into the sanctuary which Solomon had erected, but merely inhibited its use for divine services. The Carians, mercenary troops employed by Athaliah, and the old royal body-guard were placed at the entrance of the Temple, to keep off the people. For this purpose, they were divided into three bodies, which by turns guarded the Temple from Sabbath to Sabbath. For six years (887–881) Athaliah governed the political and religious affairs of the nation, the more aristocratic of the Jewish families probably being of her party. Only the nearest relative of the royal family, the high priest Jehoiada, remained true to the ancient teachings and to the house of David. His wife, Jehoshebah, was a daughter of King Jehoram of Judah, and the sister of the king Ahaziah who had been slain by Jehu.

When Athaliah was ruthlessly killing the last remnants of the house of David, Jehoshebah rescued the youngest child of her brother from the massacre, and brought him and his nurse into the chamber in the Temple where the Levites slept. Here she secreted the royal infant for a considerable time, and reared him for his country. Athaliah troubled herself but little as to what was happening in the deserted Temple, and the Aaronites and Levites, who remained faithful to Jehoiada, betrayed nothing. His very youth aroused their interest in the last descendant of the house of David. During the six years while Athaliah was ruling with absolute power in Jerusalem, Jehoiada did not remain idle, but entered into friendly relations with the chiefs of the Carians and the guards, gradually revealing the fact that a youthful prince was still in existence, to whom the throne of Judah by right belonged. He found them well disposed towards the royal house, and opposed to the usurper Athaliah. When he had convinced himself of their sympathy with his views, he led them to the Temple, and showed them Joash, who was then seven years of age. The soldiers having recognised in him the rightful heir to the throne, probably by his resemblance to the family of David, Jehoiada demanded that the chiefs take the oath of fealty to the child. With their assistance he could hope to effect a revolution, and to restore the royal line. The chiefs could reckon on the blind obedience of their followers, and, accordingly, the plan of action was decided on, as well as the date for its execution. One Sabbath a division of the Carians then on guard went to their posts, whilst two-thirds occupied the entrance of the Temple. They had all received strict orders to kill any one who should cross the

boundaries of the Temple courts with hostile intentions. As the prince was now secure from all attacks,
Jehoiada also permitted the populace to enter the
Temple courts. At a thrilling moment, when the
Carians and guards stood with drawn swords, and
whilst the chiefs held the weapons used by David,
the high priest led the child Joash from the room in
which he had been concealed, put the crown on his
head, anointed him as king, and made him mount
the pillar-like throne which had been brought into the
courts of the Temple for the king's use. Amid
trumpet blasts and clashing of arms, the people
clapped their hands, and cried "Long live King
Joash."

Not until the noise from the Temple reached
Athaliah's palace was she roused from the indifference and security which a belief in the fidelity of her
paid troops had encouraged in her. She hurriedly
repaired to the Temple, accompanied by a few attendants. There, to her terror, she beheld a young
child with a crown on his head, surrounded by her
troops, who were protecting him, and by a crowd of
people shouting with delight. She found herself
betrayed, rent her clothes, and cried, "Conspiracy,
conspiracy!" Some of her captains immediately
seized her, led her by a circuitous path out of the
Temple courts to the eastern gates of the palace, and
there killed her. Thus the last grandchild of the house
of Omri perished as disgracefully as her mother had
done. The close connection of Israel with Tyre had
brought no happiness to either kingdom. The
mother and the daughter, Jezebel and Athaliah,
resembled their goddess Astarte—"the authoress of
destruction, death, and ruin." Ahab's daughter does
not appear to have had many adherents in Jerusalem
—in the hour of death she found no partisans. Her
priests of Baal were powerless to help her, for they
themselves perished, the victims of the nation's
wrath. Jehoiada, having planned and effected the

great revolution, now endeavoured to take precau-
tions against a repetition of similar misfortunes in
Jerusalem.   He utilised the joyous and enthusiastic
sentiments of the youthful king and the nation to
remove all traces of the worship of Baal, and to
arouse in all minds a faithful dependence on the God
of their ancestors.   He demanded of the king and
the whole assembly a solemn promise to remain
henceforth a people of God, to serve Him faithfully,
and to worship no idol.   The promise, which was
uttered aloud by the king and the nation, was sealed
by a covenant.   The inhabitants of Jerusalem poured
into the temple of Baal, which had been erected by
Athaliah, destroyed the altars, trampled on the images and all objects connected with idol-worship.
The nation itself undertook to protect its own religion.   It was not till after the covenant had been
ratified both by the young king and the nation, that
Joash, triumphantly escorted by the guards, the soldiers, and the multitude, was led from the Temple
Mount into the palace, where he was placed on the
throne of his fathers.   Jerusalem was in a state of
joyful excitement.   The adherents of the late queen
kept quiet, and did not dare damp the general
enthusiasm.

It is remarkable that in the political and religious
revolutions which followed each other in quick succession in Samaria and Jerusalem, Elisha's helping hand
was not felt.   He had commissioned one of his disciples to anoint Jehu as the avenger of the crimes of
Omri's house, but he himself remained in the background, not even presenting himself at the overthrow
of Baal.   He does not appear to have had any intercourse with King Jehu, and still less did Elijah's chief
disciple take any part in the fall of Athaliah and the
overthrow of idolatry in Jerusalem.   He seems to
have occupied himself chiefly with the instruction of
prophetic disciples, in order to keep alive the religious ardour which Elijah had kindled.   Elisha, how-

ever, was not, like his teacher, universally recognised
as leader.   He was reproached for not wearing long
flowing hair, and thus creating the impression that he
laid less stress on the Nazarite mode of life.   Sons of
prophetic disciples at Bethel jeered at him, and called
him "Bald-head."   Elisha also differed from his
master in associating with his fellow-men, instead of
passing his life in solitude as Elijah had done.   It is
true, that as long as the Omrides were in power, he
remained on Mount Carmel, whence he came, accompanied by his disciple Gehazi, to visit the prophetic
schools in the Jordanic territories.   But later on, he
made Samaria his dwelling-place, and was known
under the title of the "Prophet of Samaria."   Through
his friendly intercourse with men, he exercised a
lasting influence on them, and imbued them with his
beliefs.   Men of note sought him to obtain his advice,
and the people generally visited him on Sabbaths and
New Moons.   It was only in the kingdom of Judah
and in Jerusalem that Elisha did not appear.   Why
did he avoid this territory?   Or, why have no records
of his relations with it been preserved?   Was he not
of the same disposition as the high priest Jehoiada,
and had they not both the same end in view?   It
seems that the violent prophetic measures of Elijah
and Elisha were not much appreciated in Jerusalem.
Elijah had built an altar on Carmel, and had there
offered up sacrifices; but though he did so in the
name of the same God whose temple was in Jerusalem, his conduct was doubtless not countenanced
by the priesthood; it was contrary to the law.   And
Elisha would hardly have been a welcome guest in
Jerusalem.

There, attention was concentrated on the sanctuary
and the law from the moment when Jehoiada had
shown himself their strict guardian.   The Temple had
suffered injury under Athaliah.   Not only had the
golden covering of the cedar wood been in part
destroyed, but entire blocks had been violently pulled

out of the walls.   It was therefore an important matter for the young king Joash, at the beginning of his
reign, to repair these damages, and Jehoiada impressed
on him the necessity of this undertaking.   The means,
however, were wanting.   Whatever treasure might
have been in the Temple—the accumulated offerings of former kings or of pious donors—had, without doubt, been transferred by Athaliah to the house
of Baal.   The king therefore commanded the priests
to collect money for effecting the necessary repairs,
and bade them engage in this work with as much
energy as though it were their own affair.   Every
Aaronite was to obtain contributions from his ac-
quaintances, and out of the sums thus collected the
expenses of repairing the Temple were to be defrayed.
Whether it was that the moneys received were insufficient, or that the priests used them for their own purposes, the repairs were for a long time not attempted.
At length the king ordered the high priest Jehoiada
(864) to enlist the interest of the nation in the work
on hand.   A chest with a slit in it was placed in the
courtyard of the Temple, and into that chest all whom
piety or generosity influenced might place a free-will
offering, each according to his means, or he might
give his contribution to the priests, who would deposit
it in the chest.   The gifts were liberal, and proved
sufficient to procure materials, and to pay the masons
and carpenters.   Jehoiada raised the position of the
high priest, which until then, even under the best
kings, had been a subordinate one, to an equality with
that of royalty.   Had not the high priest, through his
wisdom and energy, saved the kingdom?   Would not
the last descendant of the house of David have been
destroyed, if Jehoiada had not rescued him from the
bloodthirsty Athaliah?   He could justly claim that the
high priest should henceforth have an important voice
in all matters of state.   Jehoiada used his influence
to secure due respect for the law, and to avoid a recurrence of the deplorable period of apostasy.   But

strife between the royal power and that of the priests was inevitable, for the former, from its very nature, was dependent on personal disposition, whilst the latter was based on established laws. During the lifetime of Jehoiada, to whom Joash owed everything, the contest did not break out. Joash may have been prompted by gratitude and respect to submit to the orders of the high priest, and when Jehoiada died, he paid him the honour of burial in the royal mausoleum in the city of David.

After Jehoiada's death, however, a contest arose between his son and successor Zachariah and the king, which cost the former his life. The details have not reached us; it has only been stated that at Joash's command some princes of Judah stoned the son of Jehoiada in the Temple courts, and that the young high priest, in his dying moments, exclaimed, " May God take account of this and avenge it !"

In every other respect, the overthrow of the house of Omri, which had caused so many differences and quarrels in Samaria and Jerusalem, had resulted in the internal peace of both kingdoms. The present condition was tolerable, except that private altars still existed in the kingdom of Judah, and that the God of Israel was still worshipped under the form of a bull in the kingdom of the Ten Tribes. The worship of Baal was, however, banished from both kingdoms.

From without, both lands were harassed by enemies. Jehu, the bold chief of horsemen, who had destroyed the house of Omri in Jezreel and Samaria, did not display the same energy against powerful foreign enemies. Hazael, the Aramæan regicide, who was daring in warlike undertakings and eager for conquest, attacked the land of Israel with his troops, took the citadels by storm, burnt the houses, and spared neither children nor women. He also conquered the towns on the other side of the Jordan. The entire district of Manasseh, Gad, and Reuben, from the mountains of Bashan to the Arnon, was

snatched from the kingdom of the Ten Tribes. Many
of the inhabitants were crushed to death under iron
ploughshares; the survivors were reduced to a state
of semi-bondage. Jehu was not in a position to hold
his ground against Hazael, perhaps because he also
met with opposition from the king of Tyre, whose
relatives and allies he had slain.

Matters fared still worse under his son Jehoahaz
(859–845). The land had been so hard pressed by
Hazael and his son Ben-hadad, and the Israelites had
been so reduced in strength, that their available
forces consisted of but 10,000 infantry, fifty horse-
soldiers, and ten war-chariots. From time to time
the Aramæans made inroads, carried off booty and
captured prisoners, whom they treated and sold as
slaves. Jehoahaz appears to have concluded a disgraceful peace with the conqueror, to whose troops
he granted free passage through his lands. Thereupon Hazael overran the land of the Philistines with
his warriors, and besieged and conquered the town
of Gath. He then intended to advance against Jerusalem, but Joash submitted without a stroke and
bought peace. Either popular discontent was aroused
by his cowardice, or he had in other ways caused
disaffection; at all events, several nobles of Judah
conspired against him, and two of them, Jozachar
and Jehozabad, killed him in a house where he
chanced to be staying.

Joash, king of Israel (845–830), at last succeeded
in gradually reducing the preponderance of the Aramæan kingdom. Probably this was owing to the fact
that the neighbouring kings of the Hittites (who
dwelt on the Euphrates), as well as the king of
Egypt, envious of the power of Damascus, took
hostile positions towards Ben-hadad III. The latter,
in order to weaken or destroy the kingdom of the
Ten Tribes, laid close siege to the capital, Samaria,
until all food was consumed, and the distress was so
great that the head of an ass was sold for eighty

shekels, and a load of dung, for fuel, for five shekels.
Few of the war-horses survived, and these were so
emaciated that they were incapacitated for service.
The famine drove two women to such extremities
that they determined to kill and eat their children.
The Aramæans, however, unexpectedly raised the
siege and hurried away, leaving their tents, horses,
asses, valuables and provisions behind them. The
king, to whom this discovery was communicated by
some half-starved lepers, was once more encouraged.
He gave battle to Ben-hadad on three occasions, and
defeated him in each combat. The king of Damascus
saw himself compelled to make peace with the king
of Israel, and to restore the towns which his father
Hazael had taken from the territory of the Ten
Tribes on the east side of the Jordan.

The weakening of Syria of Damascus had a favourable effect on the fortunes of Judah under king
Amaziah (843–816). Damascus had accorded its
protection to the petty commonwealths of Moab,
Ammon, and Edom, which stood in hostile relations
to Israel and Judah. Ben-hadad's humiliation set
free Amaziah's hands, and enabled him to reconquer
the former possessions of the house of David. The
small territory of Edom had freed itself from vassalage about half a century before. One of the Edomite
kings had built a new capital on an eminence of
Mount Seir. On chalk and porphyry rocks, it rose
at a height of 4000 feet above the sea-level. A
pathway led up to it from the valley below. In this
mountain city (Petra), fifteen miles south of the Dead
Sea, the Idumæans hoped to remain secure from all
attacks. Edom said proudly, " Who shall bring me
down to the ground?" Amaziah had the courage
to attack the Idumæans in their mountain fastnesses.
A battle was fought in the salt valley, not far from
the Dead Sea, where Amaziah caused great destruction among the enemy, the survivors taking to flight,
and leaving their fortress at his mercy. Having cap-

tured it, he, for some unknown reason, changed its name to that of a Judæan city, "Jokthel." Doubtless rich booty followed the successful campaign, for Edom was a country rich not only in flocks, but also in metals. Amaziah was not a little proud of his victory. But his pride led to his own ruin, and to the misfortune of his people.

A peaceable understanding existed between Jehu and his successors, and the kingdom of Judah. Although no such formal alliance as between the Omrides and Jehoshaphat had been concluded between them, yet they had a common interest in keeping down the adherents of the Baal-worship.

Both kings, Jehoash (Joash) of Israel and Amaziah of Judah, were devoted to the ancient law. When executing judgment against the murderers of his father, Amaziah, contrary to the barbarous customs of his time, spared their sons—an act of leniency which must not be underestimated. Most probably the high priest, or some other representative of the Law, had impressed on him that the religion of Israel forbids the infliction of suffering upon children for the sins of their fathers, or upon fathers for the sins of their children.

In Israel, Jehoash evinced deep respect for the prophet Elisha, and followed his counsel in all important matters. When, after more than fifty years of activity (900–840), Elisha lay on his death-bed, the king visited the prophet, lamented his approaching end, and called him the father and guardian of Israel. After Elisha's death, the king ordered Gehazi (Elisha's constant follower) to recount all the important deeds which the prophet had performed; and when the Shunamite woman, whom Gehazi mentioned in connection with the prophet's work, appeared before the king, accusing a man who, during her absence, had taken unlawful possession of her house and field: the mere fact that Elisha had once been interested in her, sufficed to induce the king to order her immediate reinstatement. Great, indeed, must have been the prophet's personal sway over his contemporaries, since the king submitted to his guidance. Elisha also gained a great triumph for the Law of God, though without any effort on his part. A prominent Gentile, the Syrian general Naaman, who was the inferior only of the king in the Aramæan country, voluntarily renounced the impious worship of Baal and Astarte, and acknowledged the God of Israel, because Elisha's ministry produced in him the conviction that only in Israel the true God was worshipped. He even carried with him earth from the land of Israel to Damascus, in order to erect his private altar, as it were, on holy ground.

Meanwhile, although the desire existed in both kingdoms to free themselves from foreign influences, and to remain true to themselves, internal differences had already taken such deep root that it was impossible for them to pursue the same road. After the return of Amaziah from his conquest of the Edomites, he conceived the bold idea of proceeding with his army against the kingdom of the Ten Tribes, in order to re-conquer it. As a pretext, he appears to have demanded the daughter of the king of Israel as a bride for his son, intending to regard a refusal as a justification for war. Jehoash satirically replied, " The thorn-bush once said to the cedar of Lebanon. ' Give thy daughter as a wife to my son'; thereupon the wild beasts of the Lebanon came forth, and trod down the thorn-bush. Because thou hast conquered Edom, thy heart grows proud. Guard thine honour, and remain at home. Why wilt thou plunge thyself into misfortune, that Judah may fall with thee ? " But Amaziah refused to yield, and sent his army to the borders of the kingdom of Israel. Jehoash, encouraged by the victory he had just obtained over the Aramæans, went forth to meet him. A battle was fought on the frontier at Beth-Shemesh, where the men of Judah sustained a considerable defeat, and fled.   Amaziah himself was taken prisoner by the king of Israel.

One must consider it an unusual act of leniency that Jehoash did not abuse his brilliant victory, and that he did not even actively follow it up.   Could he not dethrone the captive Amaziah, declare the house of David to be extinct, and merge the kingdom of Judah into his own realm?   This, however, he did not do, but contented himself with destroying the walls of Jerusalem, and ransacking the town, the palace, and the Temple.   Jerusalem, which since then has been the scene of repeated devastations, was, for the first time since its foundation, captured and partly destroyed by a king of Israel.   Jehoash magnanimously set the captured monarch at liberty, but demanded hostages.   The moderation displayed by Jehoash was no doubt due to the influence of the prophet Elisha or his disciples.   After the death of Jehoash (830), Amaziah reigned for fifteen years, but was not very successful in his undertakings.   The power and extent of the Ephraimite kingdom, on the other hand, increased so rapidly that it seemed as though the times of David were about to return. Jeroboam II possessed greater military abilities than any of those who had preceded him since the division of the kingdom, and fortune befriended him.   He enjoyed a very long reign (830–769), during which he was enabled to fight many battles, and achieve various conquests.   He appears first of all to have turned his arms against the Aramæans.   They were the worst enemies of the kingdom of the Ten Tribes, and had kept up continuous attacks against it since the time of Ahab.   The boundary of the kingdom of Israel extended from the road which led to Hamath, as far as the southeast river, which empties itself into the Red Sea.   A prophet of this time, Jonah, the son of Amittai, from the town of Gath-Hepher, had encouraged Jeroboam to make war against the Aramæans. The king also seems to have conquered the district

of Moab, and to have annexed it to the kingdom of
the Ten Tribes.

Amaziah's efforts, meanwhile, were impeded by the
humiliation he had had to undergo. Jerusalem having been deprived of its fortifications, Amaziah could
not undertake any war, and was well content to be
left unmolested. He had promised not to repair the
walls, and he had been obliged to leave hostages in
the Israelitish capital as pledges of his good faith.
The nobles and the nation in general had ample
reason for discontent. Amaziah had injured the
country by his presumption. It was through his
rashness that Jerusalem was left defenceless against
every hostile attack. The hostages, these vouchers
for the continuance of his humiliation, doubtless
belonged to the most respected families, and their
forced exile helped to nourish the discontent of the
nobles, which finally culminated in a conspiracy. A
violent conflict arose in Jerusalem, the people either
siding with the conspirators, or taking no part in the
contest. Amaziah was helpless, and sought safety
in flight. The conspirators, however, followed him
to Lachish (about fifteen hours' journey southwest of
Jerusalem, where he had taken refuge), and there
killed him. He was the third king of the house of
David who had fallen by the sword, and the second
who had fallen at the hands of conspirators.

After the death of Amaziah, Jerusalem and the
kingdom of Judah experienced still greater misfortunes. The princes of Judah, who had dethroned
and killed the king, do not appear to have resigned
the reins of government which they had seized.
Amaziah's only surviving son, Azariah (called also
Uzziah), was a child of four or five years of age, and
the land was surrounded by enemies. Advantage was
taken of this helpless condition of the country by the
Idumæans, who had been beaten and disgraced by
Amaziah. They commenced an attack on the kingdom of Judah, and Egypt again espoused their cause,

as it had done in the times of Rehoboam. Sanguinary battles ensued, and the Idumæans took many
prisoners. They pressed on to Jerusalem, where the
breaches in the walls had not yet been repaired, and
carried off numbers of captives. There are no further
particulars known of the attack of the Idumæans.
Some domains seem to have been separated from
Judah, and annexed to Edom and Egypt respectively.
The rude warriors exchanged Judæan boys and girls
for wine and prostitutes, and their new masters, chiefly
Philistines, in turn sold them to the Ionians, who at
that time vied with the Phœnicians in the pursuit of
slave-trading. The Tyrians, forgetful of their long-
standing alliance with the house of David, behaved
in no friendlier manner. This was the first dispersion
of Judæans to distant lands, whither the Ionians
had sold them as slaves. It was probably these
Jewish slaves who brought the first germs of higher
morals and culture to the Western nations. Amongst
the prisoners were many noble youths and beautiful
maidens of Jerusalem, who, owing to their home
influences, and their knowledge of the eventful history
of their nation, carried with them a store of ideas,
which they came to appreciate more now than they
ever had done at home.

CHAPTER XII.

Condition of Judah—The Earthquake and the Famine—Uzziah's Rule
—Overthrow of Neighbouring Powers—Fortification of Jerusalem—Navigation of the Red Sea—Jeroboam's Prosperity—The
Sons of the Prophets—Amos—Prophetic Eloquence—Joel's Prophecies—Hosea foretells Ultimate Peace—Denunciation of Uzziah—Zechariah, Shallum, Menahem—Last Years of Uzziah—
Contest between the King and the High Priest—Uzziah usurps
the Priestly Functions—Uzziah's Illness.

805—758 B. C. E.

AFTER the violent death of Amaziah, the kingdom of
Judah or house of Jacob had become so excessively
weakened, partly through internal dissensions and
partly through foreign warfare, that it was a by-word
among the nations. A contemporary prophet called
it "the crumbling house of David," and oftentimes
repeated, "Who will raise Jacob, seeing that he is so
small?" And yet from out of this weakness and
abasement Judah once more rose to such power that
it inspired the neighbouring peoples with fear. First
the internal dissensions had to be set at rest. The
entire nation of Judah rose up against the nobles
that had committed regicide a second time and created confusion. The young prince Azariah, or Uzziah, was made king. This king—who was only
seventeen years old, and who, like his contemporary,
King Jeroboam, enjoyed a long reign—possessed
energy, determination and caution, which enabled
him to restore the crumbling house of David. His
first care was to transport the corpse of his father
from Lachish, where it had been buried, to Jerusalem, where it was interred with the remains of the
other kings of the house of David. Whether Uzziah

punished the murderers of his father cannot be ascertained. He then proceeded to heal the wounds of his country, but the task was a difficult one, for he not only had to contend with enemies within the state itself and among the neighbouring nations, but also against untoward circumstances. The very forces of nature seemed to have conspired against the land, which was devastated by a succession of calamities calculated to reduce the staunchest heart to despair and apathy. In the first place, an earthquake occurred in Uzziah's time, which terrified the inhabitants of Palestine, who were unused to such occurrences. The people took to flight, shrieking with terror, expecting every moment to be engulfed in an abyss beneath the quivering earth. The phenomena accompanying the earthquake increased their terror. The sun was hidden by a sudden, thick fog, which wrapped everything in darkness, and the lightning flashes which, from time time, illuminated it, added to the prevailing terror. The moon and stars appeared to have lost their light. The sea, stirred up in its depths, roared and thundered, and its deafening sound was heard far off. The terrors of the earthquake were intensified when the people recalled the fact that a prophet, belonging to the kingdom of the Ten Tribes, had predicted the event two years before. The fulfilment of this awful prophecy filled all hearts with consternation; the end of the world seemed at hand.

Hardly had this terror subsided when a fresh misfortune broke upon them. The periodical falls of rain failed, no dew quickened the fields, a prolonged drought parched all vegetation, the springs dried up, a scorching sun transformed the meadows and pasture lands into a desert, man and cattle thirsted for refreshment and food, whilst wild beasts wandered panting about in the forest thickets. Inhabitants of cities in which the water-supply was exhausted set out for the nearest place, hoping to find a supply there, but were unable to satisfy their thirst. The drought, affecting extended areas of land, reached also the lava districts of Hauran in northeastern Palestine, which are not unfrequently infested with swarms of locusts. In search of nourishment, these locusts now flew across the Jordan to the kingdom of the Ten Tribes, and devoured all that had not been withered by the dry rot. In heavy swarms which obscured the sun, they flew onward, and suddenly the vines, fig and pomegranate trees, the palms and the apple-trees were laid bare. These devastations by the locusts continued throughout several years.

In the land of Judah, which had been brought to the verge of destruction by the reverses of war, the consternation was deep. It seemed as though God had deserted His heritage, people, country and Temple, and had given them over to degradation and ruin. Public mourning and pilgrimages were instituted in order to avert the evil. The prophet Joel, the son of Pethuel, exhorted the people publicly in these days of trouble, and was largely instrumental in raising their sinking courage. His stirring exhortations could not help leaving a deep impression. Their effect was especially felt when the destruction caused by the drought and the locusts ceased. Once more field and garden began to burst into blossom, the brooks and cisterns were filled, and scarcity was at an end. The young king immediately availed himself of this auspicious change, in order to chastise the enemies of Judah. He first turned his arms against the Idumæans, who had laid his land waste. He defeated them, possibly because they were no longer aided by the Egyptians, and reduced Edom to subjection. The town of Elath, on the shore of the Red Sea, he re-annexed to Judah, and the maritime trade with Arabia and Ophir (India) could thus be renewed. The Maonites or Minites, who occupied a small territory in Idumæa, around the city of Maon (Maan), were subjugated by Uzziah, and compelled to pay tribute. He punished the Philistines for their hostile attitude towards Judæa during his minority, when they had delivered over the Judæan refugees and emigrants to the Idumæans. He conquered the towns of Gath, Ashdod, Jabneh, which lay nearest to the land of Judah, and razed their walls. In other portions of Philistia, which he annexed to his own territory, he erected fortified cities.

He especially devoted himself to the task of fortifying Jerusalem, which, owing to the destruction of 400 yards of the northern wall at the time of the war between his father and Jehoash of Israel, could offer no resistance to an invading enemy. Uzziah, therefore, had the northern wall rebuilt, and undoubtedly rendered it safer than before against attacks. He must have established friendly relations with Jeroboam II., or he would not have been able to commence the fortifications without risking a war. Uzziah had three towers built, each 150 yards in height, at the corner gate in the north, at the gate leading to the valley of Hinnom in the south, and at the gate Hananel; on the gates and on the parapets of the walls were placed machines (Hishbonoth), by means of which heavy stones could be hurled to great distances. Uzziah, in general, displayed great energy in making warlike preparations, the warriors being provided with shields, armour and spears. He also employed cavalry and war-chariots, like those brought from Egypt in Solomon's time.

Uzziah appears, in all respects, to have taken Solomon's kingdom as his model. The navigation of the Red Sea, from the harbour of Ailat, which Solomon had obtained from the Idumæans, was again resumed, and great vessels (ships of Tarshish) were fitted out for the purpose. Altogether, Uzziah attained a position of predominance over the neighbouring nations.

The kingdom of the Ten Tribes, at the same time, became possessed of great power under Jeroboam

II., who was as warlike as Uzziah. In the latter part of his long reign he was engaged in continual warfare with the Syrians. He conquered the capital, Damascus, and pressed victoriously to the city of Hamath, which also fell before him. The nationalities which inhabited the district from Lebanon to the Euphrates, and which till then had paid allegiance to the kingdom of Damascus, became tributary to the king of Israel in consequence of these victories. Jeroboam had no longer any rival in his vicinity to contest the supreme power with him. The Phœnicians had become considerably weakened through dissensions between the city of Tyre and the descendants of King Ethbaal. During Jeroboam's government a civil war appears to have broken out in Tyre, in consequence of which the whole of Phœnicia lost the influential position which it had been occupying for a considerable time. The rich booty of war, and, perhaps, the renewed impulse to trade, brought wealth to the entire country of Samaria. Not only the king, but even the nobles and the wealthy classes, lived in luxury surpassing that of Solomon's time. King Jeroboam possessed a winter and a summer palace. Houses of broad-stone, adorned with ivory and furnished with ivory seats, became very common. In contemplating the increase of power in the two kingdoms, one might have been tempted to believe that the times of Solomon were not yet over, and that no change had occurred, except that two kings were ruling instead of one—that no breach had ever taken place, or that the wounds once inflicted had been healed. Jeroboam and Uzziah appear to have lived on terms of perfect peace with one another. Israelites were permitted to make pilgrimages to Beersheba. No doubt some of them also visited the Temple in Jerusalem. But it was only the last glimmer of a politically happy period. The corruption which prosperity helped to develop in the kingdom of Judah, and still more conspicuously in the kingdom of the Ten Tribes, soon put an end to these happy days, and hastened the decadence of both states.

In the latter, the bull-worship was not only continued in Bethel and Dan, but even assumed greater proportions, when additional images of the bull were erected in Samaria and in Gilgal. Jeroboam appears to have elevated Bethel to the rank of a capital. Here the chief sanctuary was established. A sort of high priest, named Amaziah, ministered there, and appears to have been very jealous of his office. Unlike the Aaronites in Judah, he enjoyed a rich prebend in the possession of fields around Bethel. Either this perverted form of worship was not yet low enough to satisfy the cravings of its devotees, or the voluptuousness consequent upon the accession of wealth may have demanded new departures; at all events, the hideous worship of Baal and the immoral cult of Astarte were again introduced. It is extraordinary that this idolatry, which had been extirpated with so much energy by Jehu, was again promoted, and received fresh encouragement under his grandson. The idolatry thus newly re-introduced brought in its train every species of wickedness and corruption. In order to gratify the senses, all thoughts were bent on acquiring riches. The wealthy made usury their business, and pursued their debtors with such severity as to make slaves of their impoverished debtors or their children. Usurious trade in corn was especially prevalent. In years of famine the rich opened their granaries, and sold the necessaries of life on credit, not always without employing false weights and measures; and when the poor were unable to return what had been lent to them, they heartlessly took their clothes or even their persons in pledge. When these unfortunates uttered their complaint against such injustice in the national assemblies, they found no ear to listen; for the judges were either themselves among the evil-doers, or had been bribed and made deaf to the voice of justice. The treasures thus extorted were wasted by their owners in daily revelry. The contemporary prophet Amos pictures in gloomy colours the debauched life of the rich and noble Israelites residing in the capitals in Jeroboam's time.[1] The wives of the nobles followed the bad examples of their husbands, and urged them to be hard-hearted to the poor, demanding of them, "Bring, bring, and let us drink."

The people itself could not, however, be so much influenced by the moral depravity of the nobles as to allow it to obtain full sway. Morality, justice and pure worship of God still had followers, who protested more and more strongly against the vices practised by the great, and who, though in humble positions, knew how to obtain a hearing. Although almost a century had passed since the prophet Elijah, with flowing hair, declaimed against the sins of Ahab and Jezebel, the prophetic societies which he had founded still existed, and acted according to his spirit and with his energy. The young, who are generally readier to receive ideal impressions, felt a disgust at the increasing moral ruin which came on them, and assembled round the prophetic disciples in Bethel, Gilgal and Jericho. The generation which Elisha had reared and taught adopted the external symbols of prophecy, pursuing the same abstentious mode of life, and wearing long-flowing hair; but they did not stop at such outward signs, but raised their voices against the religious errors, against luxury and immorality. Sons became the moral judges of their fathers. Youths gave up drinking wine, whilst the men revelled in the drinking places. The youthful troop of prophets took the place of the warning voice of conscience. In the presence of king and nobles, they preached in the public assemblies against the worship of Baal, against immorality and the

---

[1] Amos vi. 4–6.

heartlessness of the great. Did their numbers shield
them from persecution, or were there amongst the
ranks of the prophets sons of the great, against whom
it was impossible to proceed with severity? Or was
King Jeroboam more patient than the accursed Jezebel, who had slaughtered the prophets' disciples by
hundreds? Or did he disregard and ignore their
words? In any case, it is noteworthy that the zealous
youths remained unharmed. The revellers merely
compelled them to drink wine and forbade them to
preach; they derided the moral reformers who exposed their wrongdoings, but they did not persecute
them.

One of the prophets in the kingdom of the Ten
Tribes made use of this freedom of speech; he was
the first of a succession of prophets who combined
great and poetic thought with evenly flowing rhythm
of diction, and made kings and grandees as well as
the people wince under their incisive words of truth.
It was Amos of Tekoa. Amos did not belong to the
prophetic guild, he was no prophetic disciple, and
probably neither wore a garment of haircloth, like
Elijah, nor let his hair grow long, but was a simple
herdsman and planter of sycamores. Whilst tending
his herds, the prophetic spirit came mightily upon
him, and he could not refrain from appearing in
public. " God spake to him, and in him, how should
he not prophesy?" The prophetic spirit urged him
to repair to Bethel, and there, in the temporary capital of King Jeroboam II., he declaimed against the
perversions and vices of the nobles, and opened
their eyes to the consequences of their evil deeds.
That a countryman, clad in shepherd's garb, dared
speak publicly, could not help creating sensation in
Bethel. A high degree of culture must have prevailed in those days in Samaria, when a shepherd was
able to speak in beautiful, rhythmic utterances, and
was understood, or at least expected to be understood, by the people. The speeches of Amos and

those of his successors combine the eloquence and comprehensibility of prose with the metre and the rhythm of poetry. Metaphors and imagery lend additional solemnity to their diction. It is therefore difficult to decide whether these utterances should be classed as prose or as poetry. In place of a more suitable description, they may be designated as beautifully formed poetic eloquence. The orations of Amos, however, did not fail to betray his station. He used similes taken from his shepherd life. They showed that, while tending his flocks, he often listened to the roaring of the lion, and studied the stars in his night-watches. But these peculiarities only lent a special charm to his speeches. Amos came to Bethel before the earthquake occurred, and he predicted the event in words of prophetic foresight. The earthquake thereupon followed, with all its accompanying terrors, and carried desolation everywhere. The subsequent plagues of drought, sterility, and locusts afflicted the kingdom of the Ten Tribes equally with the kingdom of Judah. Amos, and with him all right-minded people, expected that these visitations would effect a reform, putting an end to the hideous excesses of the wealthy and their cruel oppression and persecution of the poor. But no improvement took place, and Amos inveighed against the impenitent sinners in the severest terms. He reproved the men who ridiculed his prophetic utterances. He denounced those who, relying on their power or their piety or their nobility of descent, felt themselves unassailable. (Amos v. 4–15, vi. 1–8.)

Against such daring speeches, directed even against the royal house, the high priest of Bethel, Amaziah, felt it his duty to take measures. Either from indifference or out of respect for the prophet, King Jeroboam seems hitherto to have allowed him unlimited sway; but even now, when Amaziah called his attention to the prophet's dangerous upbraidings, he appears to have remained unmoved. At all events, the prophet was not interfered with, except that the high priest, probably in the king's name, said to him, "Go thou, haste to Judah; eat thy bread and prophesy there, but in Bethel thou mayest not remain, for it is the sanctuary of the king, and the capital of the kingdom." Amos did not permit himself to be interrupted in his preaching further than to say, "I am no prophet and no prophetic disciple, but only a shepherd and planter; but the Lord spake unto me, 'Go, prophesy unto my people Israel.'" In the strongest language, he concluded with a threat of punishment. It is noteworthy that he did not protest against the evil deeds in Judah with the same energy, but rather displayed a certain leniency towards the kingdom governed by the house of David. He entered into no particulars concerning the sins which were rife there, but only spoke of them in general terms. He predicted a happy future for the kingdom of Judah, while predicting woe to Israel.

"Behold, the eyes of the Lord God are upon the sinful kingdom, and I will destroy it from off the face of the earth ; saving that I will not utterly destroy the house of Jacob, saith the Lord."

When contemplating in his prophetic vision the new plagues which would descend upon the land, he interceded with prayer in behalf of Judah, exclaiming : "Lord God, cease, I beseech thee; how shall Jacob rise, since he is so small?" (Amos vii. 2, 5.)

The state of weakness into which Judah had fallen since the death of Amaziah, and from which it had not yet recovered in the first years of Uzziah's reign, filled the prophet Amos with compassion. He did not wish to discourage the nation and the court still further, but prophesied the future reunion of the tribes under the house of David.

At this time another prophet arose in Jerusalem, named Joel, the son of Pethuel. Most of the prophets were of obscure origin, and returned to obscurity without leaving a trace of their individuality, which was entirely merged in their deeds or works. Joel appeared at a time when all minds had been terrified and driven into a condition of despair bordering on stupor, by the repeated attacks of the Idumæans and neighbouring nations, and the subsequent plagues of earthquake, drought and locusts. The inhabitants of Jerusalem and the country were wearing themselves away in long fasts and lamentations; they tore their garments as a sign of mourning, and assembled around the Temple with cries and supplications to avert Divine anger, and the priests were equally despondent. Joel, therefore, had a different task from that of Amos; not to censure and blame the people was his mission, but to raise and cheer up the despondent, and to arouse those whom despair had stupefied. He did not openly denounce, but merely hinted at the sins and errors of the nation, alluding to the drunkards now left without wine, pointing to the external repentance which contented itself with torn garments and left the heart untouched, and scorning the popular notion that the Deity could not be appeased without sacrifices. Joel had to exert the whole power of his eloquence in order to convince the nation that God's mercy had not departed from them, that Zion was yet His holy mountain; that He would not deliver up His people to disgrace ; that He was long-suffering and full of mercy, and would relieve them from their misfortunes without their burnt-offerings and fasts.

Joel's oratorical power was, perhaps, even greater than that of Amos. His highly coloured description of the ravages of the locusts and the accompanying calamities is a stirring picture; the reader feels himself to be an eye-witness. The extant production of Joel's prophetic eloquence, with its rhythm and metre and even a certain strophic structure, also occupies the middle between poetry and prose. The only speech of his which has been preserved is divided into two halves; in the one half he describes the misfortunes of the nation, blames their perverted ideas, and points out wherein their conversion must consist; and in the other, he seeks to fill their hearts with a joyous hope for the future. Joel endeavoured to carry his trembling, wailing and despondent hearers, who had collected on the Temple Mount, beyond the narrow boundaries of their present sorrow to a higher view of life. He told them that God had sent the plagues as forerunners of a time full of earnestness and awe, of a day great and fearful, destined to purify them and lead to a higher moral order. The sorrows of the present would pass away and be forgotten. Then the great day of the Lord would dawn.

Joel also predicted political changes, when the enslaved Jews of Judah and Jerusalem, whom Philistines and Tyrians had sold to the slave-trading Ionians, who again on their part had scattered them far and wide, should again return. The peoples who had committed acts of cruelty would be severely punished in the Valley of Justice (Emek Jehoshaphat), where God would pronounce judgment on all nations. Then Egypt and Idumæa would become deserts, because they had shed the innocent blood of the Judæans; but Judah and Jerusalem would be inhabited throughout all generations. Then a higher moral order would begin, and all creatures would be filled with the divine spirit of prophecy.

" And it shall come to pass afterwards that I will pour out my spirit upon all flesh; and your sons and your daughters shall prophesy, your old men shall dream dreams, your young men shall see visions. And also upon the servants and upon the handmaids in those days will I pour out my spirit." (JOEL iii. 1–2.)

The wish which has been attributed to Moses (Numbers xi. 29) will, according to Joel's prophecy, be realized at some future time. Not only Israelites born in the land, but also the strangers, who lived as slaves in their families, would have a share in this kingdom of God, and would become worthy of the gift of prophecy. Thus the prophetic vision began to roam beyond the national barriers.

Hosea, son of Beeri, the third prophet of Jeroboam's and Uzziah's times, spoke yet more decidedly against the kingdom of the Ten Tribes, and in favour of the house of Jacob. Nothing is known of his life and actions; we are not even told in which kingdom he delivered his speeches. It is, however, probable that the scene of his activity was Bethel or Samaria. Whilst Amos made moral corruption the main object of his rebuke and scorn, Hosea declaimed against the religious defection of the kingdom of the Ten Tribes, which had returned to the worship of Baal. He did not possess the wealth of expression nor the metrical evenness of his two contemporaries. His eloquence comes nearer the form of common prose; it is more amplified, more fluent, but also more artificial; it likes the interweaving of allegorical names, in which Hosea probably followed the style of the prophetic school from which he appears to have come. He started from one simile, which he applied in a twofold manner. He represented the introduction of the Baal worship in the Ten Tribes as the conduct of a faithless wife, and compared the future return of the people to God, which he predicted, to the return to the path of duty of a repentant and abashed adulteress. This his theme he premised with an introduction. In a prophetic vision, he said, he received the command to take to himself an adulterous wife. Following this command, he married a woman of evil repute, who bore him three children—a son, Jezreel, a daughter, whom he called "Unloved" (Lo-Ruchamah), and a second son, named "Not-My-Nation" (Lo-Ammi). The prophet explained these metaphorical names; thus, Jezreel meant two things—in the first place, that God would visit on the house of Jehu the blood that their forefather had shed in Jezreel; and further, Jezreel denoted that God would

destroy the armies of Israel in the Valley of Jezreel.
The name of the daughter meant that God would
no longer care for the house of Israel; and, lastly,
the name of the second son denoted that the God of
Israel had deserted the nation, and would no longer
be its God.　After this introduction and its interpretation, the prophet began his address:

> "Contend with your mother, contend,
> For she is not my wife,
> And I am not her husband;
> Let her put away her prostitution from her face,
> And her adulteries from her bosom." (HOSEA ii. 4-6.)

Then the prophet depicts the entire extent of the
faithlessness of the house of Israel,—that adulteress
who pursues her lover (Baal), in the belief that her
riches and her plenty had come from him, forgetting that God had endowed her with the corn and
wine, the silver and gold which she was wasting on
the idol Baal; God would therefore deprive her of
everything, and not leave her even sufficient clothes
to cover her body.　In her need she would be overcome by repentance, and say, "I will return to my
first love, for then it was better with me than now."
The prophet then pictures the return of the faithless
wife, who would remorsefully recognise the whole
extent of her past wickedness, and, turning to her
husband, would call him "My husband," for the
name "lord" (Baal) would have become hateful to
her. (Hosea ii.)

Reconciled with his betrothed (the nation), the Lord
would again show mercy to her, as in the days of the
exodus from Egypt; from the desert he would again
lead her to her land, and she would once more sing
psalms of praise as in the time of her youth, and in
the days when she went forth from Egypt. The
renewed covenant between her God and her would
shield her from the wild beasts, and bow and sword
and war would be no more. Jezreel, the ominous name,
would receive an auspicious meaning (*planted in the*

land)*;* the "Unloved" would be once more the "Beloved," and "Not-My-Nation" would again become "My-Nation" and would acknowledge his God.

In unrolling a glowing picture of the future of the Ten Tribes, Hosea did not desire to mislead his hearers into the belief that such a time was close at hand. In a second oration, which has probably not been fully preserved, he predicts that many unhappy days would intervene before the return of the Ten Tribes and their expiation. This speech he also introduced with the account of a vision. God had commanded him again to take a much-beloved, yet faithless wife. She was not to bear him children, but he was to keep himself apart from her, nor permit her to associate with other men. This vision denoted that, though God loved the Israelitish nation, she had, forgetting all ties of honour and duty, given her love to other gods. And it denoted further, that the sons of Israel would remain long without a king or a prince, without an altar or columns, without an ephod, as well as without house-gods (Teraphim); till at last, purified by severe trials, she would return to her God—in the latter days. Hosea prophesied the total destruction of the kingdom of the Ten Tribes. On the other hand, he laid even more stress than his contemporaries on the continuance of the house of David and the kingdom of Judah, at the same time reproaching King Uzziah for the importance which he attached to his warlike preparations.

Corruption in the one kingdom and misfortunes in the other brought from the hidden depths the precious ore of prophetic eloquence, which was destined to obtain wide-reaching influence. The sins of Ahab and Jezebel aroused Elijah; the evil deeds of Jeroboam II. and his nobles drew Amos away from his flocks, and brought Hosea out of his quiet life into publicity, to communicate in a fascinating form the thoughts which possessed their souls. Their fears and hopes, their thoughts and convictions, became thenceforth the common property of the many whom they inspired and ennobled. Anxiously listening disciples of the prophet imprinted these prophetic lessons on their memories or recorded them in writing. They formed the first pages of that prophetic literature, which was destined to stir up the indolent nations of the earth. By picturing, though only in dim outlines, the prospect of a better future, the prophetic wizards, Amos, Hosea and Joel, have insured the permanence of the nation from which they sprung; for a nation which looks confidently forward to a happy future is safe against destruction, and does not permit itself to be crushed by the most terrible trials of the present. One of these prophets—Joel or Hosea—pictured an ideal of the future, to which the noblest minds have clung, and to which they still hold fast. (Isaiah ii. 2–4.)

That grand picture of everlasting peace—to be founded on the teachings of Israel—which will transform the deadly instruments of war into implements of life-giving labour, excels all works of art that will ever charm the eyes and hearts of mankind. The Israelitish prophets have predicted that this high morality of the nations of the earth will be the outcome of the law which will go forth to them from Zion.

The hostile attitude which the two prophets of the kingdom of Israel assumed towards the house of Jehu was not without effect. Just as Elisha and his disciples raised up an enemy against the Omris, so were the attempts against the last of the Jehuides probably the outcome of Amos's and Hosea's fiery opposition.

Jeroboam II. died in peace, at an advanced age and after a long and happy reign, but no sooner had his son Zechariah ascended the throne (769), than a conspiracy was formed against him. The ringleader was Shallum, son of Jabesh, who killed the fourth descendant of Jehu in Ibleam. Zechariah reigned only a few months. His murderer, following the example set by Jehu in dealing with the house of Ahab, destroyed the house of Jeroboam II., sparing neither women nor children. Shallum then went to Samaria in order to take possession of the throne and kingdom, but he maintained his position only one month. A conspiracy was also instituted against him by Menahem, the son of Gadi, a former inhabitant of the capital Tirzah. He proceeded towards Samaria, and was admitted into the capital without difficulty. He killed Shallum (768), but no doubt met with greater opposition than he expected. Although the capital opened its gates to him, other towns did not immediately submit. The town of Tiphsah (Tapuach) shut its doors against him. Menahem, however, was more daring than his predecessor, and united with his courage the utmost hardness of heart. He laid siege to the rebellious city, and, having compelled it to surrender, he executed the entire population—men, women, and children, not even sparing pregnant women. After this massacre he proceeded to Samaria, where he seized upon the throne of the Jehuides. A chief who displayed cruelty such as this could hardly expect to win all hearts. Menahem appears to have abolished the worship of Baal. The worship of the bull, however, was still continued. During his reign the fate of the Ten Tribes was influenced by a powerful kingdom which was destined to put an end to the house of Israel.

If the better elements of that house might have felt inclined to follow the intimations of the prophet, and turn to the house of Judah for remedy, they met here with conditions equally repulsive. Internal dissensions broke out under Uzziah, which, it appears, were purposely ignored. Uzziah's aim was wholly and solely directed to military affairs—the acquisition of bows, shields, and spears. Spiritual interests were far from his mind, or perhaps were even distasteful to him. To the Aaronides he undoubtedly gave frequent offence, the former harmony between royalty and priesthood having received a severe shock in the latter days of his grandfather Joash. Any endeavour on the part of the king to extend his sway over the Temple would have met with the opposition of the anointed high priests, whose authority rested on claims equal to those of the descendants of David. It is certain that in the latter years of Uzziah's government conflicts arose between him and the high priest Azariah, similar to those between King Joash and Zechariah. In order to deprive the high priest of his prestige, Uzziah took a bold step. He entered the sanctuary and began to light the incense-burner on the golden altar, an act which was the especial privilege and duty of the high priest. The indignation of the Aaronides ran high. The high priest, Azariah, who together with eighty priests hastened after the king into the sanctuary, angrily reproved him, saying, " It is not for thee, O Uzziah, to bring incense, but only for the anointed priest of Aaron's family. Leave the sanctuary: thou art guilty of desecration, and it will not be for thy honour from the Lord."

What followed is wrapt in obscurity. Uzziah in the latter years of his reign was attacked by leprosy, and had to be kept in a special house for the rest of his days. The nation considered this illness as a divine punishment for his daring to perform the rites of the priesthood.

In this contest between the sacerdotal and royal houses the former was triumphant, for it possessed the law as its weapon, and this was of greater avail than the sword. But another spiritual power was soon to enter the contest against the priesthood.

CHAPTER XIII.

THE DOWNFALL OF THE KINGDOM OF THE TEN TRIBES; THE
HOUSE OF DAVID, AND THE INTERVENTION OF
THE ASSYRIANS.

King Menahem—The Babylonians and the Assyrians—Pekah—
Jotham's reign—Isaiah of Jerusalem—His style and influence—
His first public address—Later speeches—Their immediate and
permanent effect—His disciples—Their characteristics—Zechariah—His prophecies.

758—740 B. C. E.

WHILE Uzziah was compelled by his disease to pass
his last years in solitude, his youthful son Jotham
managed the affairs of the kingdom. In the kingdom of the Ten Tribes, Menahem, the cruel usurper
(768–758), was probably ruling with an iron hand.
Both kingdoms continued in the same grooves, uncon-
scious of the fact that in the distant horizon storm-
laden clouds were gathering which would discharge
themselves on them with fearful effect. From the
north, from the districts of the Euphrates and Tigris,
heavy trials were approaching for the people of both
kingdoms.

No sooner had the Assyrians extended their territory in the north, east and west, than they turned
their attention to the south. They intended, in the
first place, to gain possession of the sea-coast of the
Phœnicians, and thus obtain control over the wealth
of that commercial nation. The next point in view
was Egypt, the wealth and renown of which attracted
their ambition. For the first time an Assyrian army
appeared on Israelitish ground, when King Pul
invaded Samaria. King Menahem did not dare
summon his forces against the mighty Assyrian hosts.
The internal confusion must have crippled his powers
to such an extent that he could not think of resist-

ance. The curse of the regicide rested heavily on his head, but it pressed with equal, if not greater, severity on his nation. Menahem was hated by his people, for the cruel means by which he had obtained possession of the throne were ever fresh in their memories, and the friends of the murdered king nursed this hostile feeling. When Pul arrived on Israelitish ground, it appears that the enemies of Menahem suggested to the invader the advisability of dethroning the king. Menahem, meanwhile, betook himself to the Assyrian conqueror, and promised him a large sum of money on condition that his government was left secure. Pul accepted the money and retired from the country, carrying his booty and prisoners with him. Menahem did not draw the money from his own treasury, but forced wealthy individuals to provide it. Each one had to pay what was at that time a heavy sum, viz., 50 shekels.

Thus came the beginning of the end, and the fate which Amos had clearly predicted half a century before, appeared to be in process of realisation. He had said that a distant nation would carry off the Israelites to a foreign land beyond Damascus. The Israelites were in fact carried off to the region of the Tigris, or to some other division of the large Assyrian kingdom. The power of the kingdom of the Ten Tribes, however, remained to all appearance unbroken. It still numbered 60,000 wealthy men, who could pay large sums of tribute money. Menahem still had his cavalry, his war materials, and the fortresses on which he thought he could place dependence. But, unknown to him, old age (as one of the prophets had rightly designated the national decadence) had now crept over the people. Menahem probably introduced the Assyrian mode of worship. One characteristic feature of this consisted in the adoration of Mylitta, the goddess of love, and the duties of her creed included the renunciation of virtue and the adoption of an immoral life. This innovation, added to the already existing internal dissensions, gradually sapped the foundations of the state. When the cruel Menahem died, and his son Pekahiah succeeded (757), the latter was able to retain the throne for scarcely two years. His own charioteer, Pekah, the son of Remaliah, headed a conspiracy against him, killed him in his palace in Samaria (756), and placed himself on the vacant throne. The mode of this regicide, the seventh which had occurred since the commencement of the kingdom of the Ten Tribes, is wrapped in darkness; it seems, however, that Pekah had to remove two other competitors before he could himself ascend the throne of Samaria.

The son of Remaliah, the last king but one in Israel (755–736), was an inconsiderate and ruthless man, who oppressed the country to an even greater extent than his predecessors. He was characterised as a faithless shepherd, " who deserted his flock, who sought not the missing ones, who healed not the wounded, who tended not the sick, and who even devoured the flesh of the healthy." In order to protect himself against the attacks of the Assyrians, he joined an alliance which the neighbouring princes had formed in order to resist the encroachments of the Assyrians. The plan probably originated in Damascus, which now once more owned a king, named Rezin, and which would be the first to suffer from the Assyrian conqueror. Judah was also drawn in. Uzziah, the king, having died in the leper's house, his son Jotham, who had ruled for many years as viceroy, assumed the title of king (754–740). Jotham had no very striking qualities. He was neither ambitious nor statesmanlike, but he kept in the grooves in which his father had moved. Civic peace seems to have remained undisturbed; there is at least no account of any conflict between him and the high priest. The material condition of the country also remained the same as under Uzziah. There were the squadrons of cavalry, the war chariots, the ships of Tarshish which navigated the Red Sea, and wealth and splendour. Jotham also strengthened the fortifications of Jerusalem. He maintained friendly relations with the kingdom of the Ten Tribes, or rather with their king, Pekah, and there seems to have been a very intimate connection between the two sovereigns. This friendship, however, as well as the rise of an ambitious nobility in Judah, exerted an injurious influence on the morals of the people, the evil being especially strong in the capital. Through circumstances which cannot now be traced, some of the noble families had attained a height of power that exalted them almost to equality with the king. The princes of Judah led the councils, decided the most important affairs of state, usurped the powers of justice, and so thoroughly obscured the dignity of the house of David, that but a mere shadow of its authority remained. There existed a junior branch of the royal family, the house of Nathan, from which the superintendent of the palace seems always to have been chosen. This high official ruled court and attendants alike, and gradually attained to such power and influence, that he was considered the actual regent. He was known by the title of Manager of the Court (Sochen).

Other evils arose out of these abuses. The princes of Judah sought to enrich themselves by all possible means, and to extend their territories by obtaining possession of the pasture lands, vineyards, and meadows of the country people. Things seem to have come to such a pass that the nobles and elders employed slaves, or the poor whom they had reduced to slavery, to cultivate their vast estates. They did not hesitate to make serfs of the children of those poor who were unable to pay their debts, and force them to tread the mill. To this cruel injustice, they soon added the vices of debauchery. They arose early in the morning and had recourse to the wine-cup, and till late at night they inflamed their

blood with wine. At such entertainments they had
the noisy music of flutes, trumpets, harps, and lutes.
This was an innocent amusement compared with the
excesses resulting therefrom. But the severe morality
enjoined by the Sinaitic law was hostile to dissipation.
As long as this law held sway, the love of licentious
pleasures could not be fully gratified. But this re-
striction disappeared, when Judah entered into connection with the kingdom of the Ten Tribes. Here,
and especially in the capital Samaria, the greatest
excesses wore, so to say, a sacred character, forming,
as they did, a constituent part of the Baal worship.
Here there were temple priestesses in numbers;
sacrifices were offered on the summits of the mountains and hills, whilst vice held its orgies in the shade
of the oaks and terebinths. So great had been its
progress, that Israelitish daughters unblushingly followed the example of their fathers. Wine and depravity had so vitiated the minds of the great, that
they consulted blocks of wood and sticks as oracles
concerning the future. From these nobles of the
kingdom of the Ten Tribes,—"the drunkards of
Ephraim,"—the princes of Judah learnt how to follow
their evil desires without restraint. Divine service
in the Temple of Jerusalem was, it is true, officially
recognised; but this did not prevent the princes
from following their own mode of worship privately.
The brotherly fusion of Israel and Judah chiefly resulted in making idolatry, dissipation, intoxication,
pride, and scorn of what was right, the common
character of both kingdoms.

However, depraved as the Israelitish and Judæan
nobles had become, there existed a safeguard which
prevented depravity from becoming an established
institution of law. In Israel, injustice could never
pass as public justice. Here there were men who
loudly declaimed against the mockery of justice, and
the degradation of the poor; men who defended justice and morality as the only right course; men who

supported the weak against the mighty. Just at this period of degradation, while Jotham ruled in Judah and Pekah in Israel, several God-inspired men arose, who spoke with words of fire against the vices of the nobility. These men were the third generation of great prophets who succeeded Amos, Joel, and Hosea, as these had followed Elijah and Elisha.

The most important amongst them was Isaiah, son of Amoz, from Jerusalem. With his contemporary prophets, Zechariah, Hosea II., and Micah II., he shared the courage which calls vice and crime by their right names, and which mercilessly brands the guilty. But he surpassed them and all his predecessors in depth of thought, beauty of rhythm, exaltation of poetical expression, in the accuracy of his similes, and in the clearness of his prophetic vision. Isaiah's eloquence combined simplicity with beauty of speech, conciseness with intelligibility, biting irony with an inspiring flow of language. Of his private life but little is known. His wife was also gifted with prophetic insight. He wore the usual prophet's dress—a garment of goat's hair. Like Elijah, he considered his prophetic task as the vocation of his life. His energies were entirely directed to exposing wickedness, to warning and exhorting the nation, and to holding before it the ideal of a future, to attain which it must strive with heart and soul. He gave his sons symbolical names, indicative of future events, to serve as signs and types. For more than forty years (755–710) he pursued his prophetic ministration with untiring zeal and unshaken courage. In critical moments, when all—great and small, kings and princes—despaired, his confidence never deserted him, but aroused the hope and courage of his people.

Isaiah first appeared in the year of king Uzziah's death (755), when he was about thirty-three years of age. He announced to the nation (probably on the Temple Mount) the vision which he had been vouchsafed. and his election as a prophet. Isaiah's first speech was a short, simple communication of this vision, the deep meaning of which could not be misunderstood.   He related that he had seen in a dream Jehovah Zebaoth on a high and exalted throne, surrounded by the winged seraphim.   One seraph after another cried, " Holy, holy, holy is Jehovah Zebaoth," with such thrilling voices that the very supports of the Temple trembled :

"Then I said, Woe is me, for I am undone ; I am a man of unclean lips, and I dwell in the midst of a people of unclean lips, for mine eyes have seen the King, the Lord of Hosts.

"Then flew one of the seraphim unto me, having a live coal in his hand, which he had taken with the tongs off the altar, and he touched therewith upon my mouth, and said, Lo, this hath touched thy lips ; thine iniquity is taken away, and thy sin is purged."

In his first speech, Isaiah had but lightly touched on the sins of the nobles, only intimating that they were not alive to pure influences.   In another speech, which has been preserved, he went into greater detail, and more especially held up a mirror to the princes of Judah wherein they might see their folly and sin. He described the ideal destiny of the people of Israel, of the Law which had been entrusted to it, and of the Temple which was to be its visible representation, and he chose for his purpose the ever-memorable words of an older prophet :

"For from Zion shall the law go forth, and the word of the Lord from Jerusalem."

In this speech Isaiah touched the root of the evil which had produced that state of religious demoralisation and heartless injustice which he denounced. It was pleasure-seeking and wantonness, encouraged by the women, to satisfy whom the men were continually urged to commit depredations, and to pillage and enslave their weaker neighbours.   With surprising force the prophet describes the love of display of the daughters of Zion.   Leaving for a moment this sad picture, the speaker attunes a cheery, hope-inspiring strain :—

" The Lord will create upon every dwelling-place of Mount Zion, and upon her assemblies, a cloud and smoke by day and the brightness of a flaming fire by night. For upon all the glory shall be a covering. There shall be a tabernacle for a shade in the daytime from the heat, and for refuge, and for a covert from tempest and from rain."

It may be questioned whether this masterly speech, perfect though it was in subject and form, made any impression for the moment. At all events it led to no lasting improvement, for Isaiah and contemporary prophets had still often to preach against the same errors and the same sins. The nobles could not easily be converted; they scorned and scoffed at the threats of an awful future. But Isaiah's powerful words have not been spoken in vain ; they have influenced people to whom they were not addressed ; they have been heard in distant lands, among distant nations, and in remote days. Isaiah did not content himself with inveighing against sin; he depicted a moral ideal, through the realisation of which men would find happiness and contentment. "The king shall rule with justice, and cause the princes to govern according to right." "The king shall not judge after the sight of his eyes, and shall not decide after the hearing of his ears." Isaiah treated with great contempt the hypocrisy which praises God with the lips whilst the heart is far from Him. He scorned still more the offering of sacrifices combined with baseness of thought and wickedness of deed. (Isaiah xxix. 13; i. 11–14.)

Isaiah appears to have used other means besides soul-stirring sermons, in order to heal the moral and religious ills of Judah. Adopting the measures of Elijah and Samuel, he assembled around himself those who shared his principles, or instructed young men and imbued them with his spirit. From among those who had suffered from the injustice and tyranny of the nobles of Judah, he drew into his circle the thoughtful and susceptible, who became at once his disciples and his children. He did not instil into them impatient and impetuous zeal, but he impressed on them the virtues of gentleness, patience, and entire resignation to God. The members of the circle which he had collected around him were called the " gentle ones," or " the sufferers of the land" (Anavim, Anve-Arez). They were mostly either of poor family, or impoverished through the depredations of the nobles. They called themselves or were called " the poor " (Dallim, Ebionim). From Isaiah they learnt not to complain of poverty and spoliation, but to bear suffering and wrong with faith in God and His dispensations. These " gentle ones" formed a special community, to which they devoted all their heart and mind, and to which Isaiah and his successors looked forward as the national core and substance. They were expected to regenerate and purify the entire people. These poor Anavim were to become the popular models of virtue. The light shed by these great prophets cast beneficent rays around; germs of thought, which lay hidden in the teachings of Sinai, came to light, and the spiritual rulership of the nation became established through them. Isaiah, therefore, forms a turning point in the national history of the people of Israel, as Samuel and, in a lesser degree, Elijah had done before him. Isaiah's prophetic view was not confined to his nation and country; it passed beyond these boundaries to the two great states of Egypt and Assyria, which, like great cloud-masses, were soon to cast their electric flashes over Israel and Judah.

Another prophet, named Zechariah, son of Berechiah, rose up against the continued perversions of the times. This prophet's oratory could not compare with the fiery and graceful eloquence of his contemporary, Isaiah. He is wanting in power and continuity; he does not let thought follow thought in logical sequence, but passes without any perspicuous connection from one subject to another. The language of Zechariah, too, is poetically tinted and not without symmetry, but it lacks the scansion and other forms of poetry. Zechariah frequently employs the metaphor of shepherd and flock, which he applies to the relation between king and people. He unrolls the picture of a glorious future, in order to lift the people up above the dispiriting present. He predicts that the neighbouring nations, who were hostile to Israel, —the Aramæans, Tyrians, and even the Philistines— would acknowledge the God of Israel, and would be accepted as His children, when they have laid aside their evil deeds and their false pride. He also prophesies that God would make peace between the house of Judah and the house of Ephraim, and that He would bring back their exiles. Even though He had dispersed them amongst the nations, they would remember Him in their banishment, and return to Him with their children. The pride of Assyria would be humbled, the Egyptian rod be stayed. This declaration closed with the prospect that of the entire nation only a third should survive; but even this remnant would have to pass through the refining crucible of trials in order to become worthy of its mission as the people of God. Zechariah made special allusions to Pekah, king of Israel, as the "false shepherd," who had treated his flock more ruthlessly than his predecessors. He relates how God appointed a shepherd over His people, and gave him two staves—one named "Mercy," and the other "Concord." But the nation had rejected God, and therefore it had been rejected by God, who broke the staff of mercy, and annulled the covenant He had made with all the tribes of Israel; and now He would break the second staff, the "staff of Concord," to annul the friendship between the tribes of Israel and Judah. God had placed over them a foolish shepherd. who did not seek for the lambs that are lost—

who did not heal the wounded, and who devoured the flesh of the healthy ones. The nation, it is true, deserved no better guide; nevertheless, the shepherd who had thus deserted his flock would surely incur the chastisement of God.

CHAPTER XIV.

THE END OF THE KINGDOM OF THE TEN TRIBES, AND THE HOUSE OF DAVID.

The Reign of Ahaz—His Character—Alliance between Pekah and Rezin—Tiglath-Pileser and Assyria—Ahaz seeks Assyrian Aid—Isaiah's Opposition—Defeat of Pekah and Rezin—Introduction of Assyrian Worship—Human Sacrifices—The Second Micah—Samaria after Pekah's Death—Assyria and Egypt—Hoshea—Samaria taken by Shalmaneser—The Exile—Hezekiah—His Early Measures—His Weakness of Character—Isaiah's Efforts to Restrain Hezekiah from War with Assyria—Arrangements for the Defence—Change of Policy—Isaiah Predicts the Deliverance—Micah—Rabshakeh's Embassy—Hezekiah's Defiance—His Illness and Recovery—The Destruction of Sennacherib's Army—Merodach-baladan—Hezekiah's Rule—The Psalmists—Death of Hezekiah.

739—696 B. C. E.

THE bond of union which connected Judah and Israel, under Uzziah and Jotham, was snapped asunder on the death of the latter, and dissensions filled all minds. The cause of this can only be conjectured. The new king of Judah, Ahaz (739–725), who ascended the throne in his twenty-fifth year, was a weakling, with confused ideas, and by no means equal to his dangerous position. Important political complications occurred during his reign, in the meshes of which he became hopelessly entangled. Shortly after his accession to the throne he had to decide a question of great import, namely, whether or not to join the alliance formed by Pekah of Israel, Rezin, king of Damascus, and other less important confederates. This alliance was formed to meet a twofold danger. On the one side was Egypt, which had become powerful under King Sabako, and on the other side Assyria, which was also governed by a king ambitious of conquest, whose strong hand had reduced to subjection the refractory tributary states.

After the death of King Pul, the last descendant of the royal house of the Derketades, an energetic king ascended the throne of Assyria, who not only reunited the crumbling kingdom, but gave it still greater power and extent; this was Tiglath-Pileser. After capturing and destroying the fortresses of Mesopotamia, he turned towards the countries westward from the Euphrates and in the neighbourhood of Lebanon. He wished to complete the annexation of the kingdoms which Pul had subjugated. In order to oppose the Assyrian conqueror, Rezin, king of Aram-Damascus, formed an offensive and defensive alliance with Pekah, and was desirous of securing the co-operation of Ahaz. When the latter refused to join them, the two kings, united, it appears, with the Philistines and other neighbouring nations, prepared an attack upon Judah.

The report of this plan occasioned great alarm in the house of David, and Ahaz then had recourse to a fatal step. He sent secret messengers to the Assyrian king, Tiglath-Pileser, and asked him for help against his enemies. At the same time he offered himself as a vassal, and his land as an Assyrian province. This step might bring him momentary help, but could only endanger the whole future.

Isaiah, with his prophetic insight, looked far into the future, and warned the king against acting rashly. Accompanied by his son Shear Jashub, he went to Ahaz, to the spot near the lake where he was supervising the work of fortification. He first tried to reassure the king in clear, yet eloquent language (Isaiah vii. 3–9). He then pointed out the evils which would result from an alliance with the Assyrian king (Ib. 17–25). From the near future, however, Isaiah's prophetic vision turned to more distant days. He sees the land, overrun by the Assyrian army, turned into a field of thorns and thistles, and dwells particularly on the devastation of the mountains covered with noble vineyards, which had become the cause of revelry and dissipation. Only the pasture lands were to remain, and every man would have to content himself with a young bull and two sheep; but the land would once more flow with milk and honey, sufficient for the needs of the remnant of the nation (Shear-Jashub).

Isaiah then reverted to the present time. He related how instructions had come to him to write in large letters in popular writ, "Quick booty, hasty plunder" (Maher Shalal, Chash Baz). He was to take the priest Uriah and the prophet Zechariah, the son of Berachiah, as witnesses to confirm his prophecy. Furthermore, when his wife, the prophetess, had borne to him a son, he had, in prophetic inspiration, bestowed on him the significant name of Maher-Shalal-Chash-Baz, as a sign of the foreboding, "Before the new-born son of the prophet shall have knowledge to call Father and Mother, the land of Damascus and the possessions of Samaria will be carried off by the king of Assyria." Isaiah then declaimed against the traitorous party which was secretly allied with the enemy (Ib. viii. 5–8).

Ahaz, however, remained deaf to all these predictions. He had more confidence in Tiglath-Pileser than in the God of Israel, and thus fate took its course. No sooner did the news reach the Assyrian king that various nations and princes had formed an alliance against him, than he invaded their lands. Rezin consequently had to raise the siege of Jerusalem, and hurry to the defence of his country. Pekah also had to think of his own safety, and Jerusalem was for the moment safe from both of the hostile kings.

The latter could no longer avert the consequences of the steps they had taken. Tiglath-Pileser first besieged Damascus, captured it, took Rezin prisoner, and slew him. From Damascus the victor proceeded against the kingdom of the Ten Tribes, conquered the fastnesses of the mountain lands and of the maritime as well as the Jordanic districts. Pekah does not appear even to have attempted any opposition, but to have submitted without resistance. Tiglath-Pileser therefore spared his life, but he carried off the inhabitants of the northern cities and those of the other side of the Jordan as prisoners (738). He distributed them in various districts of the great Assyrian empire. Thus the kingdom of Israel was deprived of half its land and half its inhabitants. Its boundary on the north barely reached Mount Tabor, and this remnant became an appendage to the Assyrian kingdom, bound to pay a yearly tribute and gifts of allegiance. Great, no doubt, was the discontent felt against Pekah, who had incurred these misfortunes through his cowardice; he was the foolish shepherd who had deserted his flock. This discontent ended in a conspiracy against him. Hoshea, the son of Elah, headed the plot, and killed Pekah (736), after he had ruled for two decades, and brought down misfortunes on his country.

An important change also occurred at this period in the kingdom of Judah. Ahaz, in his timidity, had made himself the vassal of the king of Assyria, and had, therefore, to pay homage to Tiglath-Pileser. Instead of feeling humiliated, he was seized with admiration for the Assyrian customs, and determined to imitate them in his own country. He introduced the worship of the sun and stars in Jerusalem. The image of the sun-god was erected probably at the entrance of the Temple, and horses and chariots were dedicated to him. Ahaz outvied the king of Israel in idolatry. Other Assyrian influences made themselves felt in Judah. The Assyrian language, which closely resembles that of the Aramæans, was spoken by the courtiers to facilitate communication with their sovereign lord. Ahaz went beyond all bounds in his love of imitation. Once, when a misfortune befell him, he determined to sacrifice his own son in honour of Moloch, this cruel rite being part of the Assyrian creed. In the beautiful vale of Hinnom, or Ben Hinnom, at the southern extension of the valley of Kidron, where the spring of Siloah and other brooklets produce a magnificent vegetation, a fire-altar was erected. There, Ahaz, regardless of the heart-rending lamentations of his son, sacrificed the innocent child.

The example of Ahaz was, as a matter of course, not without influence on others. The nobles of Judah, who had a decided preference for all that was foreign, because it allowed full sway to their passions, gladly welcomed this adoption of Assyrian customs. Favoured by the weakness of King Ahaz, they could indulge in sensual pleasures, and continue their acts of injustice towards the nation. The priests were also infected by the bad example. From motives either of selfishness or of fear, they passed over with silence, and even favoured the evil deeds of the king and the nobles. They preached for hire according to the wishes of the mighty nobles. One of these depraved priests appears to have asserted that the sacrifice of the first-born was not displeasing to the God of Israel, but that such offerings were acceptable to Him. The law of Moses which commanded the first-born to be sanctified to the Lord, was explained as an order to surrender them to the fire. Happily, there yet remained representatives of the ancient law in its purity, who raised their voices in powerful and eloquent protest against these crimes and depravities. A younger prophet of that time laid his finger on the gaping wound, and not only called the degeneracy by the right name, but also pointed out the source whence it had arisen. The second Micah of Moresheth, probably one of the disciples of Isaiah, shared with him the arduous task of appealing to the hearts of the sinners, and of making clear to them the indispensable results of their evil-doings. He probably took up his dwelling-place in Jerusalem, but knowing the feelings prevalent in the country places and villages, he paid more attention to them that did the other prophets.

In a speech uttered in the time of King Ahaz, Micah laid bare the prevalent religious and moral evils, and especially declaimed against human sacrifices (Micah vi.). Notwithstanding all this, the evil spread further, and also attacked the healthy portions of the nation. False prophets, speaking in the name of the Lord, arose, who advocated crimes and vices in order to flatter the men in power. These false prophets spoke with eloquence—they pretended to have had visions; they employed the prophetic mode of speech, and by these means brought about a terrible confusion of ideas. The nation was bewildered, and knew not which to believe—its critics and censors, or its adulators and encomiasts. These evil days under King Ahaz were even more baneful than the six years of Athalia's government; they witnessed a king trampling the ancient law under foot, and introducing idolatry with its concomitant immorality and contempt of justice, nobles allowing their passions untrammelled license, and false prophets daring to speak in defence of those misdeeds, while the prophets of truth and justice were proscribed.

But in the meantime political events took their course and gave rise to fresh complications. In the kingdom of Samaria, which since its separation from the eastern and northern districts, could no longer be called the kingdom of the Ten Tribes, wrongdoing and short-sightedness continued to prevail. The wounds inflicted by the Assyrians had not crushed the pride and selfishness of those in power. Defying the misery of the present, they said: "Dwellings of brick have fallen in; we will erect buildings of stone. Sycamores have been hewn down; well, let us plant cedars instead." In their drunken carousals the Ephraimitish nobles failed to perceive that the defeats which their country had suffered, unless followed by a manly revival of energies, were only the prelude to their complete destruction. In addition to this short-sightedness, or perhaps in consequence of it, anarchy set in. After Pekah's death at the hands of Hoshea, the ringleader of the conspirators, nine years elapsed, during which no king could maintain himself in power. Hoshea appears at first to have refused the crown of thorns, and there was no one else who could lay claim to sovereignty. From the time of Pul's interference with the Lebanon affairs and the destruction of the Aramæan kingdom by Tiglath-Pileser, war between Egypt and Assyria had become inevitable. The two empires, on the Nile and on the Tigris, watched each other suspiciously, and prepared themselves for the final contest, through diplomatic movements and counter-movements, in which each endeavoured to strengthen itself and weaken the enemy by the acquisition of allies.

Meanwhile the doom of Samaria was ripe for fulfilment. Was it from a knowledge of their weakness, or only a thoughtless whim, that her nobles finally recognised Hoshea the son of Elah, the murderer of King Pekah, as their king? This last king of Samaria (727-719) was better, or rather less bad than his predecessors. He was also warlike; yet he was unable to avert the impending destruction. He appears to have secretly entered into connections with Egypt, which continually duped him with false promises. At this time a warrior-king of Assyria, Shalmaneser, proceeded against Elulai, king of Tyre and Phœnicia, and subdued him. The Tyrian kingdom was not able to offer any resistance. On this occasion Shalmaneser directed his plans also against Samaria. Hoshea did not await his coming, but went to meet him, offering surrender and gifts of allegiance. But no sooner had the Assyrian king withdrawn than conspiracies were organised against him. Hoshea commenced the secession by withdrawing the yearly tribute, and Phœnicia followed suit.

Shalmaneser thereupon collected his troops, and crossing the Euphrates and Lebanon, proceeded first against the Phœnicians. At his approach, the nations lost all hope of liberty. The Phœnician towns of Zidon, Acre, and even the ancient capital of Tyre, surrendered, probably without attempting resistance. From Acre, Shalmaneser advanced to the Samaritan kingdom by way of the plain of Jezreel. The inhabitants of the Israelitish towns either submitted to the mighty king or fled to the capital. Hoshea, undaunted by all these defections, continued his opposition, though, as it appears, the expected or promised help from Egypt was withheld. The capital, Samaria, which lay on a hill-top, could, if properly intrenched, hold out for some time. Meanwhile, Hoshea and the inhabitants of Samaria hoped for some unlooked-for event which might compel Shalmaneser to retreat. The walls, towers, and battlements of Samaria were therefore fortified, and rendered capable of defence; provisions and water supplies were also collected, and all the preparations needed for the defence of a besieged city were made. But the Assyrians were masters in the art of attacking and capturing fortified cities. The attack and the defence must have been carried on with great energy and endurance, for the siege of Samaria lasted nearly three years (from the summer of 721 till the summer of 719). But all the exertions, the courage and the patience of the besieged proved fruitless. The capital of the kingdom of the Ten Tribes, after an existence of two hundred years, was taken by storm. The last king of that state, Hoshea, though he was probably caught fighting, was mercifully treated by his conqueror. He was stripped of his dignities, and kept in prison for the rest of his life. No pen has noted how many thousands perished in this last contest of the kingdom of Israel, or how many were carried off into banishment.   So estranged was that kingdom, from those who recorded the memorials of the Israelitish nation, that they devoted but few words to its decline.   No lament resounded, as though the sad fate of the nation was a matter of indifference to the poets.   The prediction of the prophets had been fulfilled.   Ephraim was no more; the idols of Dan, Samaria, and other cities, wandered away to Nineveh, and prisoners in thousands were carried off and dispersed.   They were sent to colonise the thinly-populated territories—the position of which is not precisely known—in Halah and Habor, on the river Gozan, and in the towns of mountainous Media. The kingdom of the Ten Tribes, or Israel, had existed for two centuries and a half; twenty kings had ruled over it; but in one day it disappeared, leaving no trace behind.   Alienated from the source of its existence through the obstinacy of Ephraim, which disregarded the Law and its influences on national morality, liberty and political strength, it had fallen into idolatry and its attendant vices.   The country vomited out the Ten Tribes, as it had vomited out the Canaanitish tribes.   What has become of them?   They have been looked for and believed to have been discovered in the distant East as well as the far West.   Cheats and dreamers have claimed to be descended from them.   But there can be no doubt that the Ten Tribes have been irretrievably lost among the nations.   A few of them, such as agriculturists, vine-dressers, and shepherds may have remained in the country, and some, especially such as lived near the borders of Judah, may have taken refuge in that country.

Thus the diseased limb, which had infected and paralyzed the entire body of the nation, was cut off and rendered harmless.   The tribe of Ephraim, which on its first entry into the country had caused national disintegration through its selfishness, and which later on, owing to its haughtiness and self-seeking, brought on the weakening and final destruction of a kingdom once occupying the position of an empire, was now lamenting in exile. " Thou hast chastised me, and I was chastised as an untamed calf. I was ashamed, yea, I am confounded, because I bear the disgrace of my youth." (Jeremiah xxxi. 17, 18.) The body of the nation seemed to be healthier and more at ease after the removal of its unruly member. The tribes of Judah and Benjamin, with their dependencies of Simeon and Levi, which, since the downfall of the Ten Tribes, formed the people of Israel, or the "remnant of Israel," now rose to new power and developed fresh splendour. The destruction of Samaria, stunning as it was in its immediate effect on the remnant of the nation, served also a salutary purpose, inasmuch as, for the moment at least, it induced the people to put aside the follies and sins which had contributed also to their degeneration and weakness. The people and the nobles were now no longer deaf to the exhortations of the prophets; Isaiah's prediction to erring Samaria— that " the crown of pride on the head of the fat valley of the drunkards of Ephraim would be as an early ripe fig which is hastily devoured," (Isaiah xxviii. 1-4)— being fulfilled, they could no longer refuse him a hearing. How little was wanting, and Jerusalem had shared the fate of Samaria! Its existence depended on a whim of the Assyrian conqueror. In Jerusalem the fear of national overthrow begot humility, and a desire to listen to the words of those who would lead them in the right path.

Fortunately a king now occupied the throne, the like of whom had not been known since the time of David. Hezekiah (724–696), the son of Ahaz, was the very opposite of his father. His gentle, poetical soul was filled with an ideal, which he beheld in his people's own law, in its ancient statutes and traditions. With the same eagerness with which his father had paid homage to foreign usages, Hezekiah was intent on the restoration of pristine Judæan morals, and the purification of religious conceptions and institutions. He accepted the Torah as the guide of his own life and of that of his nation. His were not only the virtues of justice, generosity and high-mindedness, but also those distinctions of character, which as a rule are foreign to crowned heads, gentleness, modesty, and humility, adorned him. He possessed that deep piety and pure fear of God which are as rarely met with as artistic perfection or military genius.

Did the prophets early recognise this nobility of soul and heart in the young prince? Or did their power of vision enable them to foresee the accession of a king on David's throne who would adorn it? Or was it through their early teaching and guidance that he grew up to become the ideal king that he was? Nevertheless it is a fact that two prophets predicted great and promising things of Hezekiah while he was still in his boyhood.

During Ahaz's misrule, the prophets and that circle of "the Gentle" who composed the kernel and heart of the nation of Israel, turned their attention to the young prince, from whom they expected the restoration of the golden age enjoyed during the glorious days of David. Hezekiah had witnessed the sins of his father with pain, and bore testimony to the aversion he felt for them immediately after his father's death, inasmuch as he did not bury him in the hereditary sepulchre of the house of David, but in a specially prepared tomb. Hezekiah expressed his convictions in a psalm composed on his accession to the throne, which may be considered a manifesto. (Ps. ci.)

Hezekiah's reign, rich as it was in the manifestation of great virtues, in events of great import and in poetical creations, might have become a golden age had it not been that his wishes and plans were opposed by a barrier which he found it impossible to break down. Royalty had long ceased to have

sole power in Judah. The overseer or superintendent of the palace (Sochen) had full power over the
army and the officers of the court. He kept the
king like a prisoner in his own apartments. In
Hezekiah's time, the superintendent Shebna behaved
as though he were the possessor of the throne and
of sovereign power. In the beginning of his reign,
however, the courtiers and those who were in office
as judges or otherwise, not knowing his character or
force of will, gave the young king free scope. During
this time Hezekiah could carry his good resolves
into effect, and in part introduce innovations, such
as removing the idols, restoring the unity of worship, and dismissing the most unworthy of the
courtiers from the palace and filling their places
with more deserving men.

But it was no slight task to remove the accumulated
evils of idolatry and long-continued immorality. The
Temple was deserted, and the country was filled with
idols and altars. Hezekiah reopened the sanctuary,
and restored it to its former dignity. In order to root
out the evils of idolatry, he ordained that altars should
be no longer erected on the mountains and heights,
not even for the worship of the God of Israel, but that
all who felt a desire to show Him honour should
repair to Jerusalem. This precaution appeared to
many as a hardship and an infringement on ancient
customs. But Hezekiah felt that he dared not
spare local predilections if he wished to ensure a
purification of the popular religion. When the
spring festival approached, he commanded that the
paschal lamb, which had hitherto been sacrificed on
private altars, should be offered in the sanctuary at
Jerusalem only. He, however, postponed the celebration of the feast from the usual month to the one
following, probably because the season was not
sufficiently advanced. Meanwhile the courtiers did
not mean to leave the king to his own devices in his
government. The inspector of the palace—Shebna—

appears to have gradually wrested all power from him. Hezekiah was a poet, an idealist, weak and yielding, and possessed of but little firmness of will. Men with such a disposition can easily be led, and even kings will submit to a strong mind. Shalmaneser's invasion of Tyre and Samaria, which occurred in the first year of Hezekiah's reign, naturally aroused great alarm and fear at Jerusalem and at the court. It was necessary to take a firm decision—either to join the allies, or to offer the Assyrian monarch pledges of loyalty. Hezekiah, from his peculiar character and mode of thought, was wavering as to the course he should take. Was it honourable to desert his fellow-tribesmen, who were bleeding to death under the three years' invasion of Samaria, and who, if conquered, could only have a most dismal fate? On the other hand, was it prudent to expose himself to the anger of the great monarch? Hezekiah was perhaps glad that Shebna and his ministers relieved him of the trouble of deciding.

In consequence of this want of harmony amongst the highest authorities of the country, Hezekiah's government appears full of contrasts—high-mindedness and meanness, moral improvement and degradation, pure faith in God and dependence on foreign aid; the king an ideal of justice, and his capital full of murderers. Not even in effecting the banishment of idolatry was Hezekiah successful. The nobles retained their silver and golden idols, and worshipped the handiwork of man; in their gardens remained the statues of Astarte under the thickly-laden terebinth trees, planted for idolatrous purposes. This internal double policy, due to the powerlessness of the king and the obstinacy of the palace inspector and the nobles, exercised a bad influence on the foreign relations of the government. The Judæan statesmen, after the fall of Samaria, followed a course of politics which would have been more wise and more honourable if it had been resolved upon earlier. They adopted the plan of breaking with Assyria and uniting themselves with Egypt. They took the same measures that Samaria had pursued a decade ago. They courted the aid of Egypt in order to obtain, if not an army, yet a sufficient number of horses to resist Assyria. The plan of rebelling against the sovereign power of Assyria was naturally developed in secret, for the premature report of their intentions might have led to great misfortunes. But, however secret their undertakings, the Judæan statesmen could not keep them concealed from public notice. They could not escape Isaiah's prophetic vision, and he exerted all his eloquence, in order, if possible, to prevent their rash proceedings. His most glorious, most thrilling speeches were made at this time of public anxiety. All the weapons of prophetic oratory—description of the threatening evils, scorn of the blindness of the leaders, and exhortations and cheering prospects for the future—all these he employed in order to win his obstinate countrymen from their undertakings. The most beautiful figures and most striking metaphors, the most touching thoughts dropped from his lips in powerful eloquence. Isaiah's advice was that Judah should remain neutral in the hot contest which was about to break out between Assyria and Egypt.

Meanwhile matters took their course regardless of Isaiah's exhortations and advice. King Hezekiah (for all steps were taken in his name) gave up his allegiance to the Assyrians; at least, he no longer sent tributary offerings to Nineveh, and the only result which could be expected followed. King Sennacherib collected a large army, with the intention of making an onslaught upon Judah as well as upon Egypt. Having subdued the intermediate lands of Aram, Phœnicia, Samaria and Philistia, the road to Egypt was paved and the obstacles in the way of direct attack removed. Judah prepared for defence. Her generals, feeling themselves too weak for open warfare, determined to occupy the mountain fastnesses, and hoped to check the progress of the Assyrian troops until the arrival of their Egyptian allies. Jerusalem was fortified with especial care. The weak parts of the wall were repaired, the wall itself raised, and those houses which had been built too near the wall in consequence of the extension of the city, were pulled down. Around the old fortifications of the town of David (Zion) and the lower town (Millo) a new outer wall, strengthened by towers, was erected. The upper lake, which was fed by the spring of Gihon, was closed up, and its water was conducted into the town by means of a subterranean canal. The aqueduct was also pulled down, in order to cut off the water supply of the enemy, and thus to make a protracted siege infeasible. The armoury, "the House of the Forest of Lebanon," was provided with instruments of warfare.

Shebna, the lieutenant and inspector of the palace, appears to have been the moving spirit in all these arrangements. Both he and the princes of Judah, with their adherents, were of good courage, and without fear expected the advance of the Assyrians. In fact, excessive wantonness ruled in Jerusalem; the evenings were spent in feasting; people ate and drank and made merry. As though impatient of the arrival of the enemy, they ascended the roofs of the houses in order to espy them. Isaiah could not allow such folly and daring to pass unreproved. In an exhortation, every word of which was of crushing force, he portrayed to the nation, or rather to the nobles, their thoughtless confidence (Isaiah xxii. 1–14).—Turning towards Shebna, he exclaimed " What hast thou here? and whom hast thou here that thou hast hewn out for thyself a sepulchre? . . . Behold, the Lord will thrust thee about with a mighty throw, O man! . . . thou, disgrace of the house of thy lord!" (Ib. 16–25).

This speech of Isaiah's, directed as it was against the most powerful man in Jerusalem, could not but have created a great sensation. It surely roused King Hezekiah from his contemplative and passive attitude, for soon after this we find Eliakim, son of Hilkiah, occupying the post which Shebna had so long maintained. This new superintendent of the palace acted according to the advice of Isaiah, and Hezekiah, through his means, appears to have been drawn into an active interest in public affairs. Shebna's fall initiated a change for the better. What had been done could not, however, be undone. The Assyrian monarch Sennacherib, filled with anger at Hezekiah's rebellion, was already on his way to Judah in order to devastate it. A part of his army, having crossed the Jordan, proceeded to the interior of the country. All fortified towns that lay on the way were taken by storm and destroyed, and the inhabitants fled weeping to the capital. The roads were laid desolate, no traveller could cross the country, for the enemy respected no man. The bravest lost courage whilst the enemy came ever nearer to the capital; their daring was changed to despair. Every thought of resistance was abandoned. But when all despaired, the prophet Isaiah remained steadfast, and inspired the faint-hearted with courage. In one of the open places of Jerusalem he delivered another of those orations, sublime in thought and perfect in form, such as have never flowed from other lips than his (Isaiah x. 5—xi. 10). He predicted to Assyria the frustration of her plans, and unrolled before Israel a glorious future which was to follow their deliverance from the threatening enemy. The scattered would return from the lands of their dispersion; the exiles of the Ten Tribes would be re-united with Judah; jealousy and enmity would appear no more; the miracles of the time of the Exodus from Egypt would be repeated, and the nation once more raise its voice in inspired hymns.

What marvellous strength of mind, what all-conquering faith in God, in the ultimate victory of justice and the realisation of the ideal of everlasting peace, amidst the terror, devastation, and despair, and the deathlike gloom of the present!

Sennacherib had marched his troops (then proceeding to the attack on Egypt) through the Philistine lowland southward without turning towards Jerusalem, while he himself put up his headquarters at Lachish, which was one of the most important of the provincial cities of Judah. He had no reason to besiege the town of Jerusalem, fortified as it was by nature and human art. When the country was completely conquered, the capital would be forced to surrender of itself. If this plan had succeeded, Jerusalem would have suffered a fate similar to that of Samaria, and the few remaining tribes would have been carried off into captivity and scattered abroad, to be irretrievably lost amongst the various nationalities. In spite of this hopeless prospect, Isaiah held firm to the prediction that Judah would not fall. It would suffer under the dominion of Sennacherib, but these very sufferings would tend to the reformation of a part of the nation, if not of the whole of it.

Isaiah was not the only prophet who, at this day of oppression and imminent destruction, held aloft the banner of hope, and predicted a glorious future for Israel, in which all the nations of the earth would take part. Micah spoke in a similar strain, though his speeches were not so artistic or striking. But amidst the din of battle he spoke yet more decidedly than Isaiah of the everlasting peace of the world, and thus endeavoured to raise the fallen hopes of Jerusalem (Micah iv.–v.).

The actual present, however, formed a striking contrast to Isaiah's and Micah's high-soaring predictions of a most brilliant and noble future. King Hezekiah, seeing the distress of Jerusalem resulting from the subjection and devastation of the country, sent messengers to Sennacherib in Lachish, to ask pardon for his rebellion and give assurances of his submission. The Assyrian king demanded in the first place the immense sum of 300 khikars (talents) of silver, and 30 khikars of gold. Hezekiah succeeded in collecting this sum, but he did it with a heavy heart, for he found himself obliged to remove the golden ornaments which adorned the temple. When Sennacherib had received this sum, he demanded more—unconditional surrender. In order to add weight to his demand, he sent a division of his army to Jerusalem. This detachment was stationed to the north-east of the city on the way to the upper lake, and made preparations for a siege. Before beginning it, however, the Assyrians summoned King Hezekiah to an interview. Rab-shakeh, one of the Assyrian officials, representing Sennacherib, spoke with as much disdain as if the conquest of Jerusalem were as easy as robbing a bird's nest. The Judæan warriors stationed on the outer wall waited with great anxiety for the result of the interview. In order to daunt their courage, Rab-shakeh uttered his bold and daring speech in the Hebrew or Judæan tongue, in order that the listeners might understand him. When Hezekiah's officers requested Rab-shakeh to address them rather in the Aramæan language, he replied that he desired to speak in their own language, so that the warriors on the outer wall might understand him, and be disabused of Hezekiah's delusion. In order to win them to his side, Rab-shakeh called aloud to them that they should not be persuaded by Hezekiah into the belief that God would save them. Were the gods of those countries subdued by the Assyrians able to save their people? Nor had the God of Israel been able even to rescue Samaria from the king of Assyria. Rab-shakeh openly demanded of the Judæan warriors that they should desert their king and acknowledge Sennacherib, and he would then lead them into a land as fruitful as that of Judah.   The people and the warriors silently listened to those words.   But when they became known in Jerusalem, they spread fear and consternation amongst all classes of the inhabitants.   Hezekiah, therefore, appointed a fast and a penitent procession to the Temple, to which he himself repaired in mourning garments.   Isaiah made use of this opportunity in order to appeal to the blinded princes of Judah, whose danger could not wean them from sin, and to impress on them that mere outward piety, such as sacrifices and fasts, was of no avail (Isaiah i.).   The address he gave could not but have a crushing effect.   Safety and rescue, said the prophet, could only be brought about by a thorough moral regeneration ; but how could this be effected in a moment?   Rab-shakeh insisted on a decision, and the troops as well as the nation were disheartened.   What if, in order to save their lives they opened the gates and admitted the enemy?   All eyes were, therefore, turned on the prophet Isaiah.   The king sent the highest dignitaries and the elders of the priests to him, that he might pray in behalf of the unworthy nation, and speak a word of comfort to the remnant of the people that was crowded together in Jerusalem.   Isaiah's message was brief but reassuring.   He exhorted the king to throw off his terror of the scornful victor, and predicted that Sennacherib, scared by some report, would raise the siege and return to his own country. This announcement appears to have pacified not only the king, but also the terror-stricken nation. Hezekiah then sent to Rab-shakeh a reply for which the latter was unprepared.   He refused to surrender. How exasperated the great sovereign must have been when Rab-shakeh reported to him the decision of Hezekiah!   A petty prince, who had nothing left to him but his capital, had dared defy him!   He immediately sent a messenger with a letter to Hezekiah, in which he gave utterance to his contempt for the little state and for the God in whom Hezekiah trusted.   He enumerated therein the fortresses which had been subdued by the Assyrians: " Have their gods been able to save them, and dost thou hope that confidence in thy God will save thee ? "

The reply to this blasphemous epistle was dictated by Isaiah.   In it he predicted that Sennacherib would return to his country in abject defeat, for God was not willing to give up the city.   Before Rab-shakeh could bring the answer to Sennacherib, a change had already taken place.   Tirhakah, the Ethiopian king of Egypt, who desired to prevent the advance of the Assyrians, went to meet them with a large army.   Hearing of the advance of the Egyptian and Ethiopian troops, Sennacherib left his encampment in Lachish, collected his scattered forces, and proceeded southward as far as the Egyptian frontier town, Pelusium, which he besieged.

Hezekiah's despair at Sennacherib's blasphemous letter was calmed by Isaiah's prediction that the land would indeed suffer want in this and in the coming year, but after this it would once more regain its fertility; ' yea, the remnant of Judah would again strike its root downward, and bear fruit upward, and this revival would proceed from Jerusalem ; but Sennacherib would not be permitted to direct even an arrow against Jerusalem.'   Whilst the king and the nobles who believed in Isaiah's prophecy, gave themselves up to hope, looking upon the departure of the besieging troops from before Jerusalem as the beginning of the realisation of the prophetic prediction, an event occurred which roused fresh terror in Jerusalem.   Hezekiah was afflicted with a virulent tumour, and was in such imminent danger that even Isaiah advised him to put his house in order and arrange for the succession, as he would not recover from his sickness.   The death of the king, without heirs, in this stormy time, would have been a signal for disunion among the princes of Judah, and would have occasioned a civil war in the distressed capital. The nation was strongly attached to its gentle and noble king He was the very breath of its life ; and the prospect of losing him made him doubly dear to the inhabitants of Jerusalem.   At this sorrowful prediction, Hezekiah, lying on his sick bed, turned his face to the wall, and tearfully prayed to God.   Then Isaiah announced to him that his prayers had been heard, that God would send him health, and that on the third day he would repair to the Temple.   By the application of soft figs the ulcer disappeared, and he became well again.   On his recovery the king composed a heartfelt psalm of praise, which was probably sung in the Temple.   (Isaiah xxxviii. 10–20.)

The recovery of the king caused great rejoicing in Jerusalem; but it was not unmixed.   Doubt and anxiety were still felt in the capital so long as Sennacherib's contest with Egypt remained unended. If he were victorious, the thrones of Judah and David would be lost.   How long this war and the siege of Pelusium lasted is not certain.   Suddenly the joyful news reached Jerusalem that Sennacherib with the remainder of his army was returning in hot haste to his country (711).   What had happened to the numerous host?   Nothing definite was known, and the scene of action lay far away.   In Jerusalem it was related that a devouring pestilence or the Angel of Death had destroyed the entire Assyrian host, 185,000 men.   In Egypt, the priests related that a numberless swarm of field-mice had gnawed to pieces the quivers, bows, and trappings of the army till they were useless, and that the soldiers, deprived of their weapons, were obliged to take to flight.   Whatever may have caused the destruction of the mighty host of Sennacherib, his contemporaries appear to have considered it as a miracle, and as a punishment sent to the Assyrian king for his pride and blasphemy. In Jerusalem the joy following on anxiety was increased by the fact that the prophet had repeatedly and, from the very commencement of the attack, predicted that the Assyrians would not cast one arrow against Jerusalem, and that Sennacherib would return on the way by which he had come without having effected his intentions.

The exultation over their deliverance found vent in the hymns—beautiful in form and thought—which were composed by the Korahite Levites, and sung in the Temple. (Psalms xlvi. and lxxvi.)

Thus Jerusalem was delivered from the Assyrians. Isaiah's prediction that "Assur's yoke shall be removed from the shoulder of Judah" was fulfilled to the letter. The inhabitants of the country, part of whom had been shut up in the capital, and part of whom had fled for refuge to the neighbouring hollows and caves, now returned to their homes, and tilled the land in safety. All fear of the frowning eye of the Assyrian king having passed away, the Judæans, whose territory was but small, could now seek out other dwelling places where they could settle down and spread. Hezekiah's thoughts were not directed towards war; his was the mission of a prince of peace. It appears that the neighbouring people, indeed, called on him as an arbiter in their disputes, and that fugitives and persecuted men sought protection with him. Although Judah could not be said to boast of victories under Hezekiah, it yet attained to an important position amongst the nations.

After the defeat of Sennacherib, a king from distant parts endeavoured to form an alliance with Judah. The king of Babylon, Merodach-baladan (Mardo-kempad), son of Baladan (721–710), sent an embassy with letters and presents to Hezekiah, ostensibly under the pretext of congratulating him on his recovery, but doubtless in order to form an alliance with him against their common foe. Hezekiah being naturally gratified at this sign of respect from a distant land, received the Babylonian embassy with the customary honours, and showed them his treasures. This manifestation of joy and pride displeased Isaiah, who prophesied injury to Judah from the land with which it was forming a treaty. The king received the reproof of the prophet with humility.

The fifteen years of Hezekiah's reign after the downfall of the Assyrian kingdom was a golden age for the inner development of the remnant of Israel. They could dwell without disturbance under their vines and fig-trees. As in the days of David and Solomon, strangers immigrated into the happy region of Judah, where they were kindly received, and where they attached themselves to the people of Israel. The poor and the sorrow-stricken, the mourner and the outcast were the objects of the king's special care. He could now put into execution his heartfelt desire 'to have the faithful of the land, the God-fearing and the true, to dwell with him in his palace.' The disciples of Isaiah, imbued as they were with their master's spirit, were the friends and advisers of Hezekiah, and were called " Hezekiah's people."

The second part of Hezekiah's reign was altogether a time of happy inspiration for the poet. The fairest blossoms of psalmody flourished at this period. Besides songs of thanksgiving and holy hymns which flowed from the lips of the Levites, probably written for use in the Temple, half-secular songs were dedicated in love and praise to King Hezekiah. On the occasion of his marriage with a beautiful maiden, whose charms had touched the king's heart, one of the Korahites composed a love-song. The two kinds of poetry, the peculiar property of the Hebrew people, which the literature of no other nation has paralleled, the poetical and rhythmical expression of prophetic eloquence and the psalm, reached their culmination under Hezekiah. The Proverbs, that third branch of Hebrew poetry, were not only collected, but also amplified by the poets of Hezekiah's time.

Hezekiah ruled in quiet and peace until the end of his days. The defeat of Sennacherib had been so complete that he could not think of undertaking another expedition against Judah. Great joy was felt when Sennacherib, who had hurled such proud and blasphemous utterances at Israel's God and nation, was murdered by his own sons, Adrammelech and (Nergal-) Sharezer, in the temple of one of the Assyrian gods. Nothing is known of the last days of Hezekiah (696). He was the last king whose remains were interred in the royal mausoleum. The people, who were strongly attached to him, gave him a magnificent burial. It appears that he left an only son named Manasseh, whom his wife, Hephzi-bah, had borne to him after the close of the Assyrian war.

CHAPTER XV.

THE LAST KINGS OF JUDAH.

Manasseh—Fanatical Hatred of Hezekiah's Policy.—Assyrian Worship Introduced—The Anavim—Persecution of the Prophets—Esarhaddon—The Colonisation of Samaria—Amon—Josiah—Huldah and Zephaniah—Affairs in Assyria—Regeneration of Judah under Josiah—Repairing of the Temple—Jeremiah—The Book of Deuteronomy—Josiah's Passover—Battle at Megiddo.

695—608 B. C. E.

It was not destined that the Judæan nation should enjoy uninterrupted happiness for even a few generations. Its strength was tried by rapid changes from prosperity to misfortune. Close upon the power and unity of the second half of Hezekiah's reign came weakness and disintegration; quiet and peace were followed by wild disturbances, and the spring-time of mental culture by a destructive drought. It is true that no disasters of a political nature disturbed the country under the rule of Hezekiah's successor, and what perils threatened the land from abroad, soon passed over. But at home, unfortunate circumstances arose which brought about a schism, and thus led to lasting weakness. What can be worse for a commonwealth than jealousy and hatred among its members, and the antipathy of the rural population to the capital? Such feelings arose under the government of Hezekiah's son, who, to the injury of the land, reigned for more than half a century (695–641). Manasseh's youth was in part the cause of this disaffection.

Under the sway of a boy of twelve, whose government lies in the hands of his servants, ambition, avarice, and even worse passions are apt to rule, unless those in power are men of great moral worth, whose patriotism surpasses their self-love. The princes of the house of Judah had not, however, attained to this moral height. They were, in fact, filled with resentment at the neglect which they had suffered during Hezekiah's reign, and only anxious to regain their former position, by removing the intruders and satisfying their vengeance. Courtiers and officers now came into power who seemed to find their chief occupation in reversing everything which had been introduced under Hezekiah. The order of things established by this king, whether it be defined as a restoration or an innovation, rested on the ancient Israelitish doctrines of the unity of God, of His incorporeality, of a rejection of all idolatry, and on a centralised worship.

It was the aim of the fanatics who stood at the head of the government to overturn this system. An idolatrous faction was formed, which was not only influenced by force of habit, love of imitation, or misdirected religious feeling, but also by passionate hatred of all that appertained to the ancient Israelitish customs, and love for all that was foreign. At the head of this party were the princes, under whose influence and care the young king was placed. Not long after Manasseh's accession to the throne, the nobles, who acted in the king's name, proceeded with the innovations which they had planned. Their first step was to proclaim lawful the use of high altars, which Hezekiah had so strongly reprobated. They then introduced the wild orgies of idolatry into Jerusalem and the Temple. Not only the ancient Canaanitish, but also the Assyrian and Babylonian modes of worship became customary at the Temple, as if in scorn of the God of Israel. In the courts of the Temple, altars were erected to Baal and Astarte, and smaller altars on the roofs of houses in honour of the five planets. In the court of the Temple, a large image (Ssemel), probably of the Assyrian goddess Mylitta, was erected, as if to give offence to the God of Israel.

More pernicious even than this wild medley of idolatry in itself, were its influences on morality. The profligate temple-servants and priestesses (Kedeshoth) of Astarte were provided with cells, where they led a wild and dissolute life. The pyre (Tôpheth) was once more raised in the beautiful vale of Ben-Hinnom, where tender children were cast into the fire as offerings to Moloch to avert calamity. Everything was done to cause the memory of the God of Israel to fall into oblivion. The faction of idolaters persuaded themselves and others that God had become powerless, and that He could neither bring them good nor bad fortune. The desire of imitation had no mean share in this religious and moral perversion. Habit and compulsion exercised on the disaffected soon spread the evil, which proceeded from the court and the prince till it extended over the whole land. The priests of the family of Aaron were probably at first unwilling to participate in this secession from the God of Israel. Idolatrous priests (Khemarim) were therefore brought into the country, who, as in the days of Jezebel and Athaliah, were permitted to take part in the service of the Temple. Nor were false prophets wanting to lend their voices to these abominations. What cause, however bad, if enjoying the favour of the great, has not found eloquent tongues to shield, justify, or even recommend it as the only true and good one? This state of things, if unopposed, would have led to the utter oblivion of all the past, and to the destruction of the nation which was to bring blessings to the entire human race.

Happily there existed in Jerusalem a strong party who respected the law so despised and scoffed at by the court faction. These formed a striking contrast to the representatives of idolatry, and were determined to seal their convictions even with their blood. These " disciples of the Lord," whom Isaiah had taught and educated as his own children, were the

long-suffering Anavim, small in numbers and low in
rank, whose determination, however, rendered them
a strong power.   They may be called the Anavites
or prophetic party; they called themselves " the community of the upright " (*Sod Jescharim w' Edah*).
This community was subjected to many hard trials
through the change under Manasseh.   The least of
their troubles was that the men whom Hezekiah had
placed as judges and officers of state were turned
out of their positions by the court party, and that
Aaronides, of the family of Zadok the high-priest,
who refused to take part in the idolatrous worship,
were dismissed from the Temple, and deprived of
their incomes from sacrifices and gifts.   Prophets
raised their voices in denunciation of these crimes,
and other members of this community manifested
their horror at the daring of the court party; but
Manasseh and the princes of Judah did not stop short
of any crime, and, like the abhorred Jezebel, drowned
the voices of the prophets in blood.   The prophetic
utterances of this period have not been preserved ;
the zealous men of God had no time to write them
down.   A violent death overtook them before they
could seize the pencil, or they were obliged to hide
their thoughts in veiled language.   As though these
sad times were doomed to be forgotten, the historians have noted down but little of public interest.
An event of great import to Judæa occurred during
Manasseh's reign, and the books of history have
given but slight or no account of it.

One of the sons of Sennacherib, whose parricidal
act destroyed the proud conqueror in the temple,
had placed himself on the tottering throne of Nineveh.
He also died a violent death at the hand of his
brother Esarhaddon.   Esarhaddon (680–668) utilised
the confusion and civil war which had broken out
in Babylonia, to reduce that old mother-country to a
mere dependence on Assyria.   Thus strengthened
Esarhaddon commenced a war with Egypt, the con-

quest of which his father had been obliged to relinquish. Some of his generals appear to have landed on the Judæan coast, in order to effect Manasseh's subjection by means of threats. Manasseh went to him to secure a fair peace, but, as is related, he was made a captive, and led in chains to Babylon. It was a bad omen for the house of David, which had become faithless to its origin, and had shown a blind love of the stranger.

Sennacherib's son is supposed to have sent the prisoners of the countries he had subdued, such as Babylon, Cuthah, Sepharvaim, and Hamath, to Samaria in order to colonise it. This event, which, at the time, seemed without significance to Judæa, was destined to be important in the future. These exiles, who were called Cuthæans, from their origin, and Samaritans, from their dwelling-places, gradually adopted Israelitish customs, probably from the small remnant of Israelites who remained after the destruction of the kingdom of the Ten Tribes. The Cuthæans made pilgrimages to the holy places of Bethel, where Israelitish priests performed the service. They, however, continued to worship idols, and some of them sacrificed human beings.

Manasseh himself was delivered from captivity, and sent back to his country by Esarhaddon or his successor; but his character had not improved. Idolatrous worship and the unfortunate conditions brought about by immorality and cruel persecution lasted until his death. When he died (641), he was not buried in the city of David, as his predecessors had been, but in the garden of Uzza, attached to the royal palace in the suburb of Millo. He had himself selected this spot for his tomb, and had thereby tacitly acknowledged himself unworthy to rest in the grave of his forefather David.

He was succeeded by his eldest son Amon (640–639), who, although older than his father had been at his accession, yet appears to have had no more

aptitude for reigning than his predecessor. The idolatrous aberrations, which had brought with them con
sequences so injurious to morality in his father's reign,
continued under his rule, but, unlike his father, he
does not appear to have persecuted the prophet
party. However, he reigned for so short a time that
but little is known of him, his deeds or sentiments.
His servants—that is to say, the captain of the palace
and the chief courtiers around him—conspired against
him, and killed him in his own palace (639). The
nation appears to have loved Amon, for the people
rose in rebellion against the conspirators, killed
them, and placed Amon's son Josiah, who was eight
years of age, on the throne (638–608). This change
of rule was not immediately felt. The nobles and
princes of Judah continued to govern in the name of
the king during his minority, and maintained the
innovations of Manasseh, which they sought to establish firmly.

But the number of 'the sufferers of the land,' who
clung to the precepts of the God of Israel, increased
daily, and these formed themselves into an active body.
From this circle various prophets arose under Josiah.
They lent their words of fire to the promulgation of
the pure doctrines of God, and opened their lips in the
cause of right, and endeavoured to bring about a
better state of things. A prophetess named Huldah
also arose at this time, and her counsel, like that
of Deborah, was much sought after. Zephaniah
was the eldest of the later prophets. He was descended from a respected family in Jerusalem, whose
forefathers were known as far back as the fourth
generation. He openly declaimed against the weakness, the moral degradation, and the idolatrous
ways of his contemporaries, particularly of the
nobles and princes, who took pride in the imitation
of all foreign customs. Like the older prophets,
Amos and Joel, he predicted the advent of " a terrible
day of the Lord, a day of darkness and obscurity."

In his prophecies concerning other nations, he especially predicted the total destruction of the proud city of Nineveh.

At this time commenced the gradual decadence of Assyria's power. The nations which had remained faithful to Assyria now separated themselves from the last but one of the Assyrian kings (Samuges?), or were compelled by the Medes to renounce their allegiance. The second king of Media, Phraortes (Fravartch), subdued nation after nation, including the Persians, and in conjunction with these he undertook a campaign against Nineveh. The Assyrians, though deserted by their allies, were yet sufficiently strong and warlike to effect the defeat of the Median host (635), when Phraortes was killed. But his son Cyaxares, who was even more daring and adventurous than his father, hastened to avenge the latter, collected a large army, which he divided according to the armour of the various bodies, attacked Assyria, defeated its army, and advanced upon Nineveh (634). But an invasion of Media by countless hordes of Scythians forced him to raise the siege of the Assyrian capital. Unable to cope with them in battle, he bought release at the price of an enormous tribute. The Assyrians were compelled to follow a like course. Turning westward, the Scythians reached Phœnicia, and, advancing along the coast of Philistia, soon stood threatening before the gates of Egypt. Here King Psammetich met them with rich gifts, and through earnest entreaties prevailed upon them to desist from their intended invasion. Thereupon a great number of them went to the north, while others threw themselves on Asia Minor. A number of them remained in Philistia, overran the country, and burnt the temple of Mylitta, the Assyrian goddess of debauchery. The Scythians swarmed from Philistia into the neighbouring country of Judæa, ravaged the land, carried off the cattle, and burnt the cities and villages. They appear, however, not to have entered Jerusalem.   No doubt the youthful king Josiah, with the steward of his palace, went to meet them, and induced them by the surrender of treasures to spare the capital.

This time of terror, when reports of the destruction of towns and the cruel murder of men were constantly reaching the ears of the people, made a deep impression on the inhabitants of Judah.   Where the predictions of the prophets had fallen upon deaf ears, their actual fulfilment proved the folly of idolatrous worship.   Had the gods of Assyria, Babylon, Phœnicia, or Philistia been able to save their people from the violent attack of the Scythians?   A change of sentiment now came over the inhabitants of Jerusalem, and the soul of King Josiah was deeply touched.   He was gentle, pious, and susceptible by nature ; only from habit had he devoted himself to the follies of idolatry, without entirely yielding to the malpractices of the times.   The significant occurrences now taking place showed him that he and his nation were wandering in crooked paths. He did not venture, however, when he had come to this conclusion, to cast out from the capital of his kingdom the idol-worship which had been introduced during his grandfather's reign, half a century before.   He did not dare arouse the princes of Judah, who held the reins of power, and who were strongly attached to idolatry.   This would have required heroic decision, and Josiah could not bring himself to act with the required strength of purpose.   It was, therefore, necessary for some one to urge him to action, and to the assertion of his royal power over those who surrounded him.   The prophetic party undertook the work of inducing Josiah to return to the service of God, and to put aside all foreign worship.   However he only took measures calculated to rescue the holy Temple of the Lord from its deserted state and the decay into which it was falling.   The walls, halls and outbuildings of the Temple were cracking, and threatened to fall, and the decorations had been disfigured. Josiah took measures to prevent at least this outward decay. He recalled the exiled priests and Levites to the service of the Temple (627), and commanded them to collect contributions for the renovation of the Temple. At their head he placed the high-priest Hilkiah, whose house had not been polluted by the impurities of idol-worship. But whence were the means to be derived? The love of the rich for their Temple had grown so cold, or the nation had become so impoverished through the pillage of the Scythians that it was impossible to reckon on freewill offerings like those in the times of King Joash. Thus it became necessary actually to go begging for gifts in order to be able to repair the sanctuary. Levitic emissaries went through the city and country, from house to house, asking for contributions. Meanwhile, though King Josiah was thus actively working for the Temple, he was wanting in firmness in stamping out the errors of idolatry. A number of the nobles, it is true, had formally returned to their ancient creed, but only inasmuch as they swore by Jehovah, while they continued to worship idols. Other influences were needed to impress Josiah before he could summon heart to act. From two sides came the force which induced him to take a final step. On the one hand the impulse came from one of the prophets, who, from early youth, had spoken in powerful and irresistible language, and on the other, from a book which had revealed to the king the unmanliness of indecision. These two combined to bring about a better state of things in an extended circle, and also to lend fresh interest and a halo of poetry to the ancient law. The youth was the prophet Jeremiah, and the book that of Deuteronomy. Jeremijahu (Jeremiah), son of Hilkiah (born between 645 and 640, died between 580 and 570), came from the little town of Anathoth, in the tribe of Benjamin. He was not poor, though by no means enjoying great wealth. His uncle Shallum and the latter's son Hanameel (his mother's relations) possessed landed property in Anathoth.

Jeremiah's soul was rich and pure, like a clear mirror or a deep well-spring. Endowed with a gentle disposition and inclined to melancholy, the religious and moral condition of his surroundings had made a sad impression on him, even in his earliest youth. All that was false, perverse, and unworthy was repulsive to him, and filled him with sorrow. From the time that he began his work, his countrymen, the priests of Anathoth, persecuted him with such burning hate that it is impossible to think that they could have determined the bent of his mind. Undoubtedly, however, the writings of the elder prophets exercised an influence over his disposition and ideas. His spirit became so imbued with their teachings that he used their thoughts, expressions, and words as his own. This study of the written prophetic legacies gave his mind its tendency, and filled him with exalted ideas of God, of the moral order in the events of humanity, of the importance of Israel's past and its significance in the future, and taught him to hate what was low. Following the divine call, he entered upon his prophetic mission, and afterwards initiated others, either in Anathoth or in Jerusalem. The description of his own initiation (Jer. ch. i.) can bear no comparison with the simplicity and depth with which Isaiah introduced himself as a prophet. The times demanded a different kind of eloquence. Moral degradation had strongly affected the nation, and ruin was sure to come, unless help were soon at hand. Nor did Jeremiah, like former prophets, speak to a small cultured circle, but to great popular assemblages, to the princes as well as to the inhabitants of Jerusalem and the people of Judah. On them figures of speech would have been wasted ; it was necessary to speak clearly, and to the purpose, in order that the words might have effect, and so Jeremiah spoke chiefly in simple prose, only occasionally weaving into his speech the flowers of rhetoric. The threats of punishment and announcements of salvation of his predecessors, with the exception of Isaiah, were mostly vague and indefinite, and on this account the scornful inhabitants of Jerusalem had cast them to the winds. Jeremiah had to counteract the effects of such scornful disregard of prophetic announcements. He was endowed with greater prophetic gifts than any of his predecessors— even than Isaiah. He prophesied in the first instance from year to year; later on, when the tragic fate neared its fulfilment, he predicted from month to month occurrences that were to come to pass, and his prophetic visions were realised with marvellous accuracy. He did not see the future in the uncertain light of dreams, but in broad daylight, with open eyes, while in communion with the outer world. Therefore he did not speak in enigmas, did not make hidden allusions, but called things by their true names.

Upon this pure prophetic spirit had been put the heavy task of rousing the perverse nation, which had been going astray for nearly half a century, just at the time when the king was rousing himself from the lethargy into which he had drifted.

No sooner had Jeremiah received his call than his diffidence and gentleness disappeared. He describes the sensations which the prophetic spirit awoke in him (Jeremiah xxiii. 29):

"Is not my word like as a fire? saith the Lord: and like a hammer that shivereth the rock?"

His first speech of burning eloquence was directed against the nation's falling away from its traditions, against idolatry and its abominations. In it he not only hurled his crushing words against the perverted idol-worship, but also against the frequent recurrence of bloodshed (Jeremiah ii.).

Words like these from so young a speaker could
not fail to make an impression.   Some of the noble
families turned away from their immoral course,
and returned to the God worshipped by Jeremiah
and the other prophets.   The family of Shaphan,
which occupied a high position, joined the prophet's
party, and defended it with fervour.   King Josiah
meanwhile devoted himself earnestly to the restoration of the ruined Temple.   He commissioned (621)
three of his chief officers—Shaphan, Maasseiah, the
governor of the city, and Joah, the chancellor—to
summon the high-priest to surrender the funds collected under his supervision, that they might be employed in the purchase of building materials and the
pay of the workingmen.   When Hilkiah gave up the
sum, he also handed a large roll to Shaphan, saying,
"I have found the book of the law in the Temple."
Shaphan read the roll, and was so struck by its
contents that he informed the king of the discovery
that had been made.   This book exercised a wonderful influence.   The Book of the Law which the high-
priest Hilkiah gave to Shaphan to hand to the king
was the last testament of the prophet Moses, which,
before his death, he recommended to the earnest consideration of his people.   It has an historical introduction and an historical epilogue, leading the historical
record up to and beyond the death of Moses.   Laws
are generally cold, stern, and hard, and with threatening gesture they say, " Thou shalt, or shalt not, or
heavy punishment will overtake thee."   The law-book
found in the time of Josiah is not couched in such
terms.   It exhorts, warns, and actually entreats that
this or that may be done or left undone.   It uses
the language of a loving father, whose son, standing
before a great goal, is warned not to lose the bright
future before him through his own fault, and thus
become an object of scorn and a disgrace.   A pleasant
breeze is wafted from this book of Deuteronomy.
As though with a garland of flowers, the laws (Miz-

voth), statutes (Chukkim), and ordinances (Mish-patim) are surrounded with historical reminiscences and heartfelt admonitions, couched in sublime and poetic language.

The book also contains a peculiar hymn, said to have been composed by Moses.   In this hymn it is stated that the nation, in consequence of its prosperity, would turn away to false gods, and a depraved nation would be called to punish it.   Then it would see that its chosen gods could not avail it, and that God alone, who had so wonderfully guided it, could kill and make alive, could wound and heal, and that He would avenge it, and purify the stained land. Terrible are the punishments inscribed in this roll for disobeying the laws.   The veil is snatched away from the future, and the terrible disasters shown which await the people and the king, if they con-tinue in their present course.   All the plagues which could bring humanity to despair are vividly described in this picture.   On the one hand are sterility, starvation, drought and pestilence; humil-iation and persecution, oppressive slavery and dis-grace on the other, till physical and spiritual sufferings would end in heart-breaking, madness and idiocy.

This peculiar book of the law, with its convincing exhortations and its gloomy prospect, which the priest Hilkiah had found and read to Shaphan, was carried by the latter in haste to King Josiah, to whom he read passages out of it.   Terrified and shaken by the threats of punishment, and conscience-stricken for hav-ing hitherto permitted trespasses so plainly depicted in the newly-discovered book, the king in his grief tore his garments.   He sent for the high-priest Hilkiah to counsel him.   On his suggestion, King Josiah sent him and some of his officers to the prophetess Huldah, wife of Shallum, the overseer of the ward-robe, one of the royal officers.   She announced to the king that the impending misfortune should not descend on him and his people in his own days, as he had repented of his former ways.

Comforted as to the fate of his people during his own reign, King Josiah pursued the task of regeneration with great energy. He took the newly-discovered book of the law as his guiding principle, and was far more severe and thorough than Hezekiah in the uprooting of idolatry. He first summoned all the elders of the people from the capital and the country, as also the entire population of the capital, the priests and prophets, and even the humble hewers of wood and drawers of water of the Temple, and had the contents of the law-book read to them. He himself stood during the reading on a stand which had been erected for the king in the Temple. For the first time the entire nation of Judah was informed of its duties, its expectations and prospects in obeying or disobeying the laws. The king proposed to form a covenant by which all present should bind themselves to carry out with heart and soul the laws and ordinances which had been read to them. Then the words were loudly proclaimed, "May all those be cursed who shall depart from this law," and all present said "Amen." The king commanded the high-priest Hilkiah, the priests of the second order, who had to watch over the Temple, and the Levitical guardians of the Temple gates, to cleanse it from the various forms of idol-worship. Thus the disgraceful figure of Astarte, the altars and cells of the prostitutes, also all articles belonging to the worship of Baal and Astarte, the sun-horses at the entrance of the Temple, and lastly the altars for the worship of the stars were all removed, crushed and burnt in the vale of Kidron, and the ashes cast over the graves of the dead. The altar in the vale of Hinnom, where children were sacrificed, was desecrated by order of the king. All the chief altars throughout the country were destroyed. This purification extended as far as Bethel, where the Cuthæans, who had settled in the place, and the remnant of Israel still had their sanctuaries, and as far as those towns which had formerly be longed to Samaria. The priests of the idols and altars were deposed, those of Levitical descent were obliged to remain in Jerusalem, where they could be kept under supervision, and where, though not allowed to offer sacrifices, they received their share of the tithes of the descendants of Aaron. The foreign priests were all removed, and probably sent out of the country. Josiah made a cruel exception of the Israelitish priests in Bethel, who had continued the worship of the bull, which had been introduced by Jeroboam, and had caused the degradation of the nation. These priests were killed on the altars, and the latter were desecrated by human remains. The king determined to make a striking example of Bethel, the spot where the negation and neglect of God's ancient law had originated. The less guilty descendants had in this case, as in many others, to atone for their more guilty forefathers. The king himself commenced the desecration of the idolatrous altar at Bethel. He cleared away the various idol-worships which had taken root and flourished at different times on Jewish ground, and he thus acted according to the precepts contained in the Book of Deuteronomy.

In the spring of the same year (621) Josiah summoned the entire nation to celebrate the feast of Passover in Jerusalem, according to the ordinances of the Law, and the nation willingly obeyed his mandate, having sworn to act according to the Law. This festival—celebrated for the first time by the mass of the nation—was rendered especially solemn by inspiring psalms, sung and accompanied by the Levites. One psalm, which was apparently sung on that occasion, has been preserved. The choir of Levitical singers exhorted the Aaronites to praise the God of Jacob, reminded them of the persecutions they had undergone, of the deliverance from Egypt, and of the revelation at Sinai, and also admonished them to keep away from

strange gods.   They alluded to the exile of a part
of the nation, and prophesied happy days for those
who observed the Sinaitic law.   (Psalm lxxxi.)   Josiah's energetic action against idolatry appeared so
important an event to the faithful portion of the people that the prophets dated a new epoch from that
time.   The abominations of idolatry, with its terrible
effects, which had so demoralised the nation for
seven decades, had suddenly disappeared, owing to
the zeal of the king.   Social conditions were also
improved.   Josiah insisted on the enfranchisement of
Hebrew slaves who had been six years in slavery, in
accordance with the law which he had chosen as his
guide.   He also appointed unbiassed judges, who
should secure justice to the poor and the helpless
against the powerful.   Historical accounts assert of
Josiah that no king before him ever returned so
sincerely to God, and carried out the law of Moses
so strictly.   In fact, Josiah appears also to have
exerted himself energetically in political matters;
he had the courage to assert his independence even
against Egypt.

At the outset of his prophetic career Jeremiah had
announced a period of universal ruin and devastation, to be followed by a new constitution of things.
This change began in the last years of Josiah's
reign.   The empire of Assyria, which had subjected
so many nations to its yoke, was to be delivered over
to total destruction, and in its place new empires
were to arise.   Media and Babylon, the nearest dependencies of Nineveh, avenged the crimes of which
that city had been guilty in its proud treatment of
its adherents.   The adventurous Nabopolassar, of
Babylon (625–605), had broken the last tie which
bound his country to Assyria, and had made himself
independent.   Egypt also endeavoured to take advantage of the increasing weakness of Assyria.
Here a daring king named Necho (Nekos, Nekaii),
son of Psammetich, had ascended the throne, and

strove to restore Egypt's former power. Necho assembled a great army, with the intention of conquering the district of the Lebanon as far as the Euphrates, and of humiliating Assyria. He took the fortified Philistine city of Gaza by storm, and advancing along the slope on the coast of the Mediterranean Sea, he purposed reaching the Jordan by the plain of Jezreel. Josiah, however, opposed his advance through this territory, which had formerly been in the possession of the Israelites. Hardly had Necho and his army reached the middle of the plain of Jezreel, than the army of Judah barred his way at Megiddo. The Egyptian king, it is said, assured Josiah that his campaign was not directed against the land of Judah, but against more distant territories. Notwithstanding this, Josiah compelled him to do battle. The result was disastrous to the king of Judah, for his army was beaten, and he himself was dangerously wounded (608). His attendants hastily brought their beloved king to Jerusalem, and on his arrival there he breathed his last. When he was interred in the new mausoleum, men and women wept bitterly, and exclaimed, "Oh, king! oh, glory!" From year to year, on the anniversary of the day on which this last excellent king of the house of David had sunk pierced by arrows, a lamentation was sung, composed by Jeremiah for the occasion. No king was more sincerely mourned than Josiah. The unfortunate battle of Megiddo in the plain of Jezreel was the turning point in the history of Judah.

CHAPTER XVI.

END OF THE KINGDOM OF JUDAH.

Effects of Josiah's Foreign Policy—Jehoahaz—Jehoiakim—Egyptian Idolatry introduced—The Prophets—Uriah the Son of She-maiah—Jeremiah's renewed Labours—Fall of Assyria—Nebu-chadnezzar—Baruch reads Jeremiah's Scroll—Submission of Jehoiakim—His Rebellion and Death—Jehoiachin—Zedekiah—Siege of Jerusalem by Nebuchadnezzar—The Siege raised owing to the Intervention of Egypt—Defeat of the Egyptians—Renewal of the Siege—Capture of Jerusalem—Zedekiah in Babylon—Destruction of the Capital—Jeremiah's Lamentations.

608—586 B. C. E.

JOSIAH had expected to secure the independence of Judah, by calling a halt to the interference of Egypt in the affairs of other lands, but this policy led to the subjection of his own people to Egypt. In Jerusalem, where the king's death was bitterly mourned, no further steps were taken till the election of a new king had been decided on. Josiah had left three sons; the first-born was Eliakim, and the two younger sons, Shallum and Mattaniah. The father appears to have named Shallum, the son of his favourite wife, as his successor. In order to do honour to their deeply-mourned king, the people confirmed Josiah's choice, though Shallum was two years younger than Eliakim. On his accession he, according to custom, took a different name—that of Jehoahaz.

Matters had, however, come to such a pass that the will of the nation could no longer establish their king firmly, nor could the holy oil render his person sacred: the decisive word lay with another power. The king of Egypt, to whom the country had become subject by the victory at Megiddo, had decided other-wise. Apparently without troubling himself about

Judæa, Necho had reached the district of the Euphrates by forced marches; had obtained possession of the territories of Aram or Syria, belonging to Assyria, and had taken up his residence in Riblah.   Jehoahaz repaired thither to meet Necho, to have his election confirmed by him, and at the same time to receive the land of Judæa from him as a tributary state. But the newly-elected king found no favour in the eyes of the Egyptian sovereign, who caused him to be put into chains and carried off to Egypt.   He then named Eliakim king of Judah.   Jehoahaz had only reigned three months.

Eliakim, or, as he was called after his accession, Jehoiakim (607–596), had to perform an unpleasant duty at the very commencement of his reign. Necho had imposed on the land a heavy and humiliating tribute of 100 khikars of silver and one khikar of gold, as a punishment to Josiah for having hindered his march through the country.   There was no treasure at that time in the palace or the Temple. Jehoiakim, therefore, taxed all the wealthy according to their wealth, and caused these imposts to be forcibly collected by his servants.   Added to this humiliation there arose another evil.   The moral and religious improvement brought about by Josiah was, according to the predictions contained in the law lately discovered, to bring happier times in its wake, and now the people found themselves sorely disappointed.   The God fearing king had fallen on the battle-field, and had been brought back dying to the capital; the flower of the Israelitish army had been cut down, a royal prince lay in fetters, and the country had fallen into disgraceful bondage.

This change occasioned a turn in the tide of opinion; a relapse set in.   The nation, including the more enlightened amongst them, began to doubt the power of God, who had not fulfilled, or could not fulfil, the promises He had made to them.   They cherished the delusion that by resuming the foreign idolatrous practices which had existed during so long a period under Manasseh, they would better their fortunes. They therefore returned to their evil ways, erected altars and high places on every hill and under every green tree. In Judah there were as many gods as there were towns. They paid special homage to the Egyptian goddess Neïth, the Queen of Heaven, who was most zealously adored in Sais, the capital of King Necho; for had not this goddess assisted the Egyptian king in the victory he had obtained? Images of gold and silver, of wood and stone, were again erected in the houses. The Temple itself was, as in Manasseh's time, once more desecrated by hideous idols. The most disgraceful feature of the change was that the sacrifice of children again prevailed, as in the days of Ahaz and Manasseh. In the beautiful Valley of Hinnom an altar was again erected, and moaning children were ruthlessly offered up to Moloch, the first-born especially being selected for the sacrifice.

These idolatrous and immoral practices were accompanied by the vices and crimes of debauchery, adultery, oppression of strangers, widows and orphans, by corruption of justice, untruth, dishonesty, usury and cruelty towards impecunious debtors, and murder. There was certainly a class which upheld the law, and which regretted the horrors of these crimes. But amongst the masses who gave themselves up to the aberrations of idolatry and immorality, it was difficult for those who desired better things to give practical effect to their views. False prophets advocated wrong-doing and crime. King Jehoiakim, although he did not actually encourage the revival of idolatry, permitted it, and either from weakness, or from sympathy with them, did nothing to check the moral decadence. The stern warnings of the prophets were unheeded by the king, his monitors being persecuted or slain.

The prophets of God had a heavy task in this time of degeneracy; they had to be prepared for persecution and ill-treatment. But they paid little heed to the dangers they incurred; they felt impelled to oppose fearlessly the moral and religious ruin which was impending. At no period did there arise so many prophets as in the last two decades before the destruction of the Jewish kingdom. They addressed the nation, the princes, and the king almost daily, at every opportunity; they warned, roused and threatened them, and prophesied their destruction, if the prevailing wickedness did not cease. The names of only four of these prophets have been preserved: Jeremiah, Uriah, Habakkuk, and Ezekiel. But the prophecies of others, who fought the battle against idolatry, have remained, though their names have not been recorded.

Of Uriah, son of Shemaiah, from the Forest City (Kirjath-Jearim), nothing is known, except his tragical death. At the commencement of the reign of King Jehoiakim (between 607–604) he had prophesied the destruction of Jerusalem and of the whole land, if the people did not give up their evil ways. When Jehoiakim was informed of this prophecy of evil, he dispatched messengers to seize and kill its author. Meanwhile Uriah, having been secretly warned of his danger, fled to Egypt. Jehoiakim, however, was so enraged against him, that he sent one of his nobles to Egypt to demand his surrender. He was brought back to Jerusalem and beheaded, his body being cast on the burial-place of the common people. This murder of the prophet, instead of intimidating Jeremiah, seems to have confirmed him in his energetic action. With the accession of Jehoiakim and the relapse of the nation into its former state of sin, he began anew his work as a prophet, which had been in abeyance during the reign of Josiah. Jeremiah now, for the first time, comprehended the meaning of

the words which had been addressed to him as a
disciple in the first hours of his prophetic calling.
"I have made thee a fortified city, and an iron
pillar, and brazen walls against the whole land,
against the kings of Judah, against the princes
thereof, against the priests thereof, and against
the people of the land." He was to remain firm
and unmoved, and to meet fearlessly the impending
persecutions. Acting on this idea, he prepared
to announce the inevitable destruction, though his
tender heart bled, and he often had to seek fresh
courage in order that he might not grow faint in his task
of prophesying evil. Jeremiah, meanwhile, had grown
to man's estate; but he took no wife. He could not
devote himself to household joys whilst the shadow
of approaching troubles darkened his soul. He
went forth alone and in sadness. He could take no
part in convivial pleasures, because the sins of the
nation crushed in him all feelings of gladness.

Through one of his first addresses in Jehoiakim's
reign he drew on himself the hatred of all zealous
idolaters, and especially of the priests and false
prophets. When the populace, at one of the festivals, had assembled to offer up sacrifices, he called
to them,

"Thus saith the Lord God of Hosts : Amend your ways and your
doings, and I will cause you to dwell in this place. . . . Is this
house, which is called by my name, to be a den of robbers ? Behold
even I have seen it, saith the Lord. . . . And now, because ye
have done all these works, saith the Lord, and I spake unto you,
rising up early and speaking, but ye heard not, and I called you and
ye answered not, therefore will I do unto this house, which is called
by my name, wherein ye trust, and unto the place which I gave to you
and your fathers, as I have done unto Shiloh." (JEREM. ch. vii.)

Hardly had Jeremiah finished these words when
the priests and false prophets seized him, and said,
" Thou shalt die—as thou hast prophesied that this
Temple will become as that of Shiloh." A tumult
arose in the courts of the Temple, and some of the
bystanders supported Jeremiah. This tumult induced

some of the princes to repair from the palace to the Temple—amongst these was Ahikam, son of Shaphan—and others who belonged to the prophet's party. The princes immediately formed a court of justice at one of the gates of the Temple, and heard the accusation and the defence. The priests and the false prophets said, " This man deserves death, for he has prophesied destruction to the city and the Temple." A few of the elders spoke in favour of Jeremiah. Then the princes said to the angry priests and the false prophets, " This man does not deserve death, for he has spoken to us in the name of our God." Through the exertions of his friends, and especially of Ahikam, Jeremiah was set free for the time. But the hatred of the priests and the false prophets towards him raged the more fiercely, and they watched for an opportunity to attack him.

Meanwhile the doom of the Assyrian empire had been fulfilled. It fell ignominiously, through the united exertions of Cyaxares of Media and Nabopolassar of Babylon. Nineveh, the giant city, fell after a long siege (605). The last king of Assyria, Sardanapalus, burnt himself in his citadel. In consequence of the downfall of Assyria, important changes occurred on the central scene of passing events. Media became the chief heir of the Assyrian possessions—Cyaxares took the lion's share, and gave to his ally, Nabopolassar, Babylonia, Elymais, and the privilege of conquering the countries on the western side of the Euphrates. King Nabopolassar did not long survive his victory. He was succeeded by Nebuchadnezzar—a great warrior (604-561), and a wise, far-seeing statesman. He was by no means cruel, and only punished his enemies as severely as was necessary to render them harmless. Nebuchadnezzar strengthened his now enlarged kingdom internally, erected gigantic buildings, and established a system of navigation by means of canals. He then undertook a more extensive expedition of conquest. Aramæan Assyria, or Syria, which was split up into small districts, was subdued without much opposition.   Next Phœnicia fell, and its king, Ithobal (Ethbaal) II., also became Nebuchadnezzar's vassal.

The mighty conqueror then offered Jehoiakim the alternative to pay him allegiance or to be crushed. On the other hand, the king of Egypt counselled him to resist firmly, and promised that he would send help.   Judah fell into a condition similar to that in the days of Hezekiah, and became the battle-field for the contest between two great powers.   A policy had to be resolved on, but whilst awaiting aid from Egypt, or a miracle, Jehoiakim and his counsellors delayed coming to a decision from day to day.

Amidst the general alarm a fast was proclaimed; in the ninth month, in the winter of 600, the whole nation was summoned to Jerusalem, and there it entreated the Lord to avert the impending evil from the land.   The nation, in great excitement and fear as to what the future might bring on it, crowded to the Temple as though it would find security there.   Jeremiah meanwhile commanded his faithful disciple, Baruch, to write down the prophetic exhortation which he had uttered some years before, and in which he had predicted that Judah herself, as well as all the nations around her, would be reduced to subjection to the young Chaldæan empire.   After Baruch had inscribed this address on a roll, Jeremiah commanded him to read it in front of the Temple, in the presence of all the inhabitants of the capital and the entire country.   The prophet himself was from some cause prevented from being present, and therefore Baruch was to represent him.   Baruch, though not without hesitation, undertook this task.   In an open hall, in the upper court of the Temple, he read the contents of the scroll to the whole nation.   The address made a deep impression on the people, confronted as they were with the impending danger of an attack from Nebuchadnezzar's army, which now lay but a short distance from Jerusalem. A young man, Michaiah, son of Gemariah, hastened to the princes who had assembled in one of the halls of the palace, and there, agitated as he was, he communicated to them what he had heard. The alarmed princes invited Baruch to read again, in their presence, Jeremiah's scroll. Each word fell heavily on their hearts, and they were seized with terror. They, therefore, determined to inform the king of what they had heard, hoping that he, too, would be moved and convinced that he must give up all opposition to Nebuchadnezzar. For a moment they hoped for the best, when Jehoiakim commanded that the scroll be brought and read to him. But as each leaf was read, it was, by the king's order, handed to him, and he threw it into the fire. The princes witnessed this act of defiance with dismay, and entreated the king not to draw down destruction on them. He, however, paid no heed to them, and continued to throw the pages into the fire until the whole scroll was consumed. Jehoiakim then issued an order that the prophet of evil and his disciple be sought, in order that they might be killed as Uriah had been. Happily, the anxious princes had previously made arrangements to save Jeremiah and Baruch by hiding them in a secure place.

It was, doubtless, a day of intense excitement for Jerusalem. The entire nation that had assembled for the fast departed without having gained its end. The reading of the scroll had, however, one effect: it brought about a division in the council of the princes. Those who were convinced by Jeremiah's prophecies, and had been instrumental in saving him, were determined to submit to Nebuchadnezzar. Amongst them was the Keeper of the Lists (Sopher), Elishama, who directed the war arrangements. He and other men of note being opposed to war, Jehoiakim could not undertake war, or his throne might be endangered. He therefore made peace with Nebuchadnezzar, paid the tribute imposed, promised him military aid, and assumed all the duties which in those days were imposed on a vassal. This was the commencement of the Chaldæan vassalage of Judah (600). Jeremiah, it appears, could now leave his hiding-place. Incensed as the king was against him, he dared not touch a hair of his head, for the princes who had saved him continued to protect him.

Jehoiakim, however, bore the Chaldæan yoke with great reluctance; he could no longer give reins to his passion. The king of Egypt, no doubt, continued to urge Jehoiakim to rebel against Nebuchadnezzar. When, therefore, Ethbaal II. of Phœnicia withdrew his allegiance (598), Jehoiakim, with incomprehensible blindness, likewise refused to pay tribute, and allied himself with Egypt, and probably also with Phœnicia. Nebuchadnezzar, consequently, had to collect all his forces against Phœnicia. He commenced the siege of Tyre, which lasted thirteen years. He was, therefore, for the time being, prevented from chastising the rebellious king of Judah, and the latter might flatter himself with the belief that he had lastingly secured his independence. But though Nebuchadnezzar could not send a great army out against him, he nevertheless distressed the country by predatory inroads. Idumæan, Moabitish and Ammonitish hordes also overran the land and devastated it. At this critical period, Jehoiakim died (697). His successor was his young son Jehoiachin (Jeconiah, shortened into Coniah), or rather the reins of government were taken in hand by his mother, Nehushta. Jehoiachin also cherished the idea that he could oppose Nebuchadnezzar, and, therefore, did not pay him homage. He also continued to practise the horrors of idolatry and immorality as his father had done. But this blindness of Jehoiachin and his mother lasted only a short time.

Nebuchadnezzar at length was enabled to withdraw, from the siege of Tyre, a great portion of his army, with which he proceeded against Egypt. This Chaldæan army easily subdued the entire country south of Phœnicia as far as the Egyptian river (Rhinokolura). The whole of Judah was also taken, with the exception of a few fortified towns in the south. Those who fell into the hands of the enemy were made prisoners. Notwithstanding this, Jehoiachin continued his opposition, thinking himself safe behind the thick walls of Jerusalem, relying besides on the support of Egypt in the event of a siege.

Nebuchadnezzar, therefore, sent some of his generals to besiege Jerusalem. Jehoiachin had no time to think of repentance, for the besiegers were gaining on him, and the distress in the city was great. He therefore commenced to arrange conditions of surrender with the generals, when Nebuchadnezzar came to the camp, and was entreated by the king, the queen-mother and her court, to be merciful. The victor, however, showed no mercy, but imposed hard conditions. Jehoiachin had to relinquish his throne, and go, together with his mother, his wives, his kindred, and eunuchs, into exile in Babylonia. He had occupied the throne of David for only one hundred days. It was surprising that Nebuchadnezzar spared his life, and indeed, that he refrained altogether from bloodshed. He only banished ten thousand of the warriors and the inhabitants of Jerusalem, taken indiscriminately from the various families that lived in the capital, and transplanted them to Babylonia. Among them he also carried off a thousand mechanics who were skilled in forging arms and building fortifications. Of the Judæans who lived in the country he also took three thousand and twenty-three to Babylon as prisoners. That Nebuchadnezzar took possession of the treasures of the palace and the Temple was not an act of especial violence, but was justified by the military laws of those days. But he left the commonwealth intact, spared the city and its walls, and left the Temple uninjured. The first foreign conqueror Jerusalem had had after an existence of five hundred years showed greater mercy than many of the conquerors of later ages.

Nebuchadnezzar likewise refrained from disestablishing David's throne, and placed on it the youngest son of Josiah, Mattaniah, who called himself Zedekiah. He was of a gentle, unwarlike and pliable character. The Babylonian conqueror thought that these qualities would be guarantees of peace and submission. In order, however, to make sure of Zedekiah's loyalty, Nebuchadnezzar entered into a solemn treaty with him, and bound him by an oath of fealty. The land of Judah was of extreme importance to him as a bulwark against Egypt, in the subjection of which he was continually engaged. For this reason he had sent into banishment the noble families and the princes of Judah, thus removing the daring and foolhardy men who might urge the king to ambitious schemes and rebellion. His object was to render Judah a weak, insignificant and dependent state, deriving its strength from him.

Judah might, in fact, have continued to exist as a modest appendage of Babylon. It would soon have recovered from the severe blows inflicted on it. Though the banishment of so many noble families, the flower of the army and of the nation, was a severe blow; and though the capital and the country were filled with sorrow in consequence of their subjection, the remnant of the people nevertheless recovered themselves with wonderful rapidity, and again attained to a prosperous condition.

The nobles, however, were not satisfied with their modest condition; they wished for wider spheres of activity. It was the curse of the country during the last century that the nobles of the capital not only governed the people, but also the court. The kings

were but of little account, for, in imitation of the custom
of kings like Sardanapalus, they lived in the harem of
their palaces, and occupied their time with trifles.
These nobles could now the more easily assert themselves, as their king, Zedekiah, was swayed by a most
unkinglike weakness and indolence, and had not the
courage to withstand them.   He was, however, personally well-disposed.   He does not seem to have particularly favoured idolatry, but rather to have lamented
the national evils when they were brought under
his notice, and to have given ear to the prophets.
But he did not possess the power to oppose the
nobles and their actions.   Zedekiah may have intended to remain faithful to the oath of fealty which
he had taken to his liege lord Nebuchadnezzar; but
he had not the strength of will to adhere to his reso-
lution.   Rebellious schemes were secretly formed,
which he, in the seclusion of his palace, did not find
out, or, if cognisant of them, was incapable of opposing.   This weakness on the part of the king, and
foolhardiness on the part of the nobles, led to the fall
of Judah.   The nobles appear to have been seized with
madness.   Suggestions were made, in various quarters, of rebelling against Nebuchadnezzar.   Egypt, ever
false and deceitful, was continually goading the Judæans on by making brilliant promises of alliance which
it seldom kept.   On the other side, King Ethbaal of
Tyre urged upon Judah and the neighbouring
countries a war against Nebuchadnezzar.   And by
a third party, Judah was urged to revolt against
Babylon, namely, by the banished Judæans, who
stood in constant communication with their native
land by letters and messengers.   They clamoured
for war, because they cherished the vague hope that
Nebuchadnezzar's army would be defeated, and they
would, in one way or another, regain their freedom
and return to their country   In the fourth year of
Zedekiah's reign (593), the ambassadors from the
countries which were simultaneously urging Zedekiah

to break his word and faith, arrived in Jerusalem: from Edom, Moab, Ammon, Tyre, and Zidon. They employed all the artifices of eloquence, and made promises and suggestions in order to bring the wavering monarch to a decision. Judah might have felt proud to be thus sought after and courted, to be considered, indeed, as the centre of political events.

It is not known what reply Zedekiah sent through the ambassadors. His weak character surely made a definite decision an impossibility. Jeremiah opposed the universal frenzy, and it required no little courage on his part to do so. His prophetic spirit perceived that Nebuchadnezzar was destined to hurry through a course of victories, and to subjugate many nations to his sceptre. He, therefore, warned King Zedekiah, the nation and the priests, not to give themselves up to flattering hopes, but to submit to the Babylonian rule, or they would be crushed by the mighty conqueror. Jeremiah considered it as his prophetic calling to warn the deluded exiles in Babylon. He directed a message to them, telling them:

"Build ye houses and dwell in them; and plant gardens and eat the fruit of them; take ye wives and beget sons and daughters, and take wives for your sons, and give your daughters to husbands, that they may bear sons and daughters; and multiply ye there and be not diminished. And seek ye the peace of the city whither I have caused you to be carried away captive, and pray unto the Lord for it: for in the peace thereof shall ye have peace. For thus saith the Lord of Hosts, the God of Israel: Let not your prophets that be in the midst of you, and your diviners deceive you, neither hearken ye to your dreams which ye cause to be dreamed. For they prophesy falsely to you in my name: I have not sent them, saith the Lord. For thus saith the Lord, After seventy years be accomplished for Babylon, I will visit you, and perform my good word toward you, in causing you to return to this place." (JEREMIAH xxix. 4–8.)

But Zedekiah could not long resist the distracting voices of the false prophets, the pressure from without, from Egypt and the neighbouring countries, and the impetuosity of Judah's ambitious nobles. He permitted himself to be carried along with the stream, refused to pay the tribute to Nebuchadnezzar, and thus, unmindful of his oath, renounced Judah's allegiance to Babylonia (591). Thus the die was cast which was to decide the future of the nation. Nebuchadnezzar, who for some time, however, remained passive, proceeded with his army to chastise the rebellious people like disobedient slaves. It appears that the surrounding nations who had urged the revolt were the first to submit. Judah was left entirely dependent on the assistance of Egypt, but even Egypt was afraid to deal an effective blow. It was, therefore, easy for Nebuchadnezzar to subdue the land of Judah and even to occupy its fortresses In the south-west only, Lachish and Azeka offered opposition. The Chaldæan army, however, left them unmolested, and proceeded against Jerusalem on the 10th day of the 10th month (at the end of 588, or the beginning of 587). The capital of Judah had meanwhile been fortified, and supplied with provisions and water for a long siege, but the inhabitants of the country, having, at the approach of the enemy, fled into the city with their children and herds, had increased the number of consumers. Zedekiah or his palace-officers, courtiers, and nobles having refused to obey the summons to surrender, Nebuchadnezzar commenced a regular siege. The men of Jerusalem must have defended themselves bravely, for the siege lasted, with little interruption, for nearly a year and a half (from January, 587, to June, 586). The leader of the besieged party was a eunuch in the service of King Zedekiah. The king himself played a passive part. He was neither commander of the troops, nor leader of the movement. His irresolution and weakness were clearly shown in this time of trouble.

The siege of Jerusalem had made the task of Jeremiah a painful one. Though prevented by his advanced age from taking part in the defence and the war, yet his patriotism and his sympathy with the people impelled him to inspire the warriors with courage. His prophetic calling and power of foresight, on the other hand, compelled him to announce that the contest was in vain, and that the destruction of the city was decreed, on account of the blood which had been shed and the sins which had been committed. Freedom of speech could not at this period be denied him, as his name as a true prophet had been established by the events which had occurred. The nations of the north had set up their throne at the gates of Jerusalem, and had prepared a great chastisement.

When the siege of Jerusalem had lasted nearly a year, during which there had been many engagements with varying success, a change suddenly took place. King Apries (Hophra) of Egypt at length determined to fulfil his oft-repeated promise, and sent an army against Nebuchadnezzar. This Egyptian army must have been a mighty one, for the Chaldæans, hearing of its approach, raised the siege of Jerusalem, and marched to oppose it (February or March, 586). The joy in Jerusalem was unbounded; as the gates were at length opened, after being so long closed, the inhabitants hurried out to enjoy a sense of freedom. Hardly had the terrors of the siege abated, when many of the nobility and the opulent returned to their former wickedness. The slaves who had been recently released were, notwithstanding a solemn covenant and oath, compelled to return to their former bondage and former degradation. Jeremiah was deeply angered at this cruelty and selfishness; he delivered a scathing address to the nobles and the king, in which he reproached them with their perjury, and announced that the Chaldæans would return and capture Jerusalem; and that fire, war, hunger, and pestilence would rage amongst the people.

The princes of Judah had been greatly incensed against Jeremiah for his former opposition; but his last address excited a deadly hatred against him. As he was one day leaving the city to go to his birth-place, Anathoth, he was seized by a sentinel under the pretext that he was deserting to the Chaldæans. In spite of his assurance that he had no thought of flight, he was delivered up to the princes. Glad of an opportunity to revenge themselves on him, they treated him as a traitor and spy, beat him, and put him into a cistern (Adar, 586) in the house of Jonathan, the Keeper of the Lists (Sopher), a hard, heartless man who was made his jailor. In this narrow, dirty, unhealthy place Jeremiah remained for many days.

The frenzied joy did not last long in Jerusalem. The Chaldæan army, which had marched against the Egyptian forces, under Apries, utterly routed the enemy and put them to flight. The power of Egypt was broken, and Judah was now again left entirely to its own resources. The Chaldæans returned to the siege of Jerusalem, and surrounded it more closely than before, so as to bring the siege to a speedy end. The courage of those who were shut up in the capital now began to fail. Many, anxious for their own safety, left the besieged city at unguarded places, and went over to the Chaldæans, or fled to Egypt. King Zedekiah himself was fearful about the result, and saw too late that he had been guilty of folly in attempting to cope with the Babylonian power, without the support of a liberty-loving people.

Not alone had the war killed off many, but famine and pestilence now increased the number of deaths. The number of warriors continued to decrease, and at last so few remained that they were unable to defend the walls. At length the last hour of Jerusalem struck, of that city which even the heathen had considered impregnable. On the 9th of Tamuz (June, 586) there was no more bread in the city, and in consequence of the utter exhaustion of the garrison, the Chaldæans succeeded in making a wide breach in the wall, by which they penetrated into the city. Nebuchadnezzar was not present; he was at Riblah, in Syria. His generals and the elders of the Magi proceeded to the very heart of Jerusalem unmolested, in order to pass judgment on the inhabitants. The Chaldæan warriors probably met with no opposition, as the inhabitants, enfeebled by famine, could scarcely drag themselves along. They overran all parts of the city, killing youths and men who appeared capable of resistance, making prisoners of others and loading them with chains. The barbarous soldiers, rendered savage by the long siege, violated women and maidens irrespective of age. They also entered the Temple and massacred the Aaronides and prophets who had sought safety in the Sanctuary, amidst cries of rage, as if they wished to wage war with the God of Israel. The Chaldæans were accompanied by many of the neighbouring nations, the Philistines, Idumæans, and Moabites, who had joined Nebuchadnezzar. They stole the treasures and desecrated the Sanctuary.

Zedekiah, with the remnant of the defenders, meanwhile succeeded in escaping at night through the royal gardens and by a subterranean passage in the north-eastern part of the city. He sought in haste to reach the Jordan, but Chaldæan horsemen hurried after the fugitives, and blocked their way in the narrow passes. Weakened as they were, crawling along rather than walking, they could be easily overtaken and made captive. In the city, the only dignitaries whom the troops found were the High Priest (Seraiah), the Captain of the Temple (Zephaniah), the Eunuch who had conducted the war, the Keeper of the Lists (Sopher), the confidants of the king, the door-keepers, and about sixty others. They were all taken to Riblah, and there beheaded at Nebuchadnezzar's command. No one could remain in Jerusalem or its neighbourhood, as the air was rendered pestilential by the numerous corpses which lay unburied. Amongst the prisoners was the prophet Jeremiah. He was found in the court Mattara, in the king's palace, and the Chaldæan soldiers, believing him to be a servant of the palace, made him prisoner.

His disciple Baruch no doubt shared his fate. The generals appointed Gedaliah, a Judæan of noble birth, son of Ahikam, of the family of Shaphan, as overseer of the prisoners and fugitives.

The last hope left the unfortunate remnant of the nation when the news reached them that the king was captured. Zedekiah and his followers were overtaken near Jericho by the Chaldæan horsemen. The warriors who were with him scattered at the approach of the enemy, and crossed the Jordan or took refuge in some hiding-place, but Zedekiah, his sons, and some of his nobles were taken prisoners by the Chaldæans, and led to Riblah, before Nebuchadnezzar. The latter poured out all his justified anger on the king for his faithlessness and perjury, and the punishment he decreed upon him was terrible. Nebuchadnezzar caused all the sons and relations of Zedekiah to be executed before his eyes, and then had him blinded. Deprived of his sight and loaded with chains, he was taken to Babylon. He did not long survive his sufferings.

What was to be done with the city of Jerusalem? She had become a charnel-house, but was still standing. The generals who had captured her had no instructions as to her fate. Nebuchadnezzar himself appears at first to have been undecided about it, but at last he sent Nebuzaradan, the chief of his guard, with orders to destroy the city. The Idumæan nobles, filled with hate, immediately sought to make him complete the destruction without mercy (Psalm cxxxvii 7). Nebuzaradan gave orders to raze the walls, to burn the Temple, palace, and all the beautiful houses, and this order was conscientiously fulfilled (10th Ab—August, 586). The treasures still remaining in the Temple, the artistically worked brazen pillars, the molten sea, the lavers of brass, the gold and silver bowls and the musical instruments, were all broken to pieces or conveyed to Babylon.

Jerusalem had become a heap of ruins, the Temple-mount a wilderness, but not one of the great capitals which fell from the height of glory into the dust has been so honoured in its destruction as Jerusalem. Poetry recorded her mournful fate in lamentations, psalms and prayers, in such touching tones that every tender heart must feel compassion with her even at this day. Poetry has wound about her head a martyr's crown, which has become transformed into a halo.

Jeremiah and probably two or three other poets composed four lamentations corresponding to the four stages of the trouble which befell the city. The first lamentation was written immediately after the capture of Jerusalem. The city still stood, the walls, palaces, and Temple were not yet destroyed, but it was deprived of its inhabitants and its joys. This lamentation chiefly deplores the friendlessness of Jerusalem; her greatest sorrow lies in the faithlessness of her allies, who now delight in her fall. The second lamentation deplores the destruction of the city and its walls, and especially the fall of the Sanctuary. The third lamentation bemoans the destruction of all that was noble by the lingering famine, and the despair which fell upon the survivors on the capture of the king. The fourth lamentation describes the utter desolation of Jerusalem after its complete destruction by the enemy.

CHAPTER XVII.

THE CONSEQUENCES OF THE DESTRUCTION.

The National Decay—The Fugitives—Enmity of the Idumæans—Johanan, Son of Kareah—The Lamentation—Nebuchadnezzar appoints Gedaliah as Governor—Jeremiah Encourages the People—Mizpah—Ishmael Murders Gedaliah—The Flight to Egypt—Jeremiah's Counsel Disregarded—Depopulation of Judah—The Idumæans make Settlements in the Country—Obadiah—Condition of the Judæans in Egypt—Defeat of Hophra—Egypt under Amasis—Jeremiah's Last Days.

586—572 B. C. E.

ABOUT a thousand years had passed since the tribes of Israel had so courageously and hopefully crossed the Jordan under their brave leader, and half that interval had elapsed since the first two kings of the house of David had raised the nation to a commanding position. After such a career, what an ending! The greater part of the Ten Tribes had been scattered for more than a century in unknown countries. Of the remaining tribes, composing the kingdom of Judah, the greater part had been destroyed by war, famine and pestilence; a small number had been led away into captivity, and an insignificant few had emigrated to Egypt or fled elsewhere, or lived in their own country, in constant terror of the fate which the victors might have reserved for them. Manifold enemies, in fact, let loose their anger against these few, in order to bring about their destruction, as if not a single Israelite was to survive in his own country.

The remainder of the soldiers, who had fled at night with Zedekiah from the conquered capital, had dispersed at the approach of the Chaldæan pursuers. A handful, under the command of one of the princes of the blood royal, Ishmael, son of Nethaniah, had escaped across the Jordan, and had found shelter with Baalis, the king of the Ammonites. The rest had preferred to flee to Egypt, whither several families had already emigrated, because they hoped to receive the protection of Hophra, who was an ally of their country. But in order to reach it they had to cross Idumæan territory, and here a fierce, unrelenting enemy awaited them. The Idumæans, mindful of their old hatred, untouched by the brotherly kindliness of Judah, and not contented with the fall of Jerusalem and with the booty they had acquired, carried their enmity so far as to post a guard on the borders of their land for the purpose of killing the fugitive Israelites or delivering them up to the Chaldæans, with whom they wished to ingratiate themselves. It was not only dislike, but also policy which prompted Edom to behave with cruelty to the miserable fugitives. They hoped to obtain possession of the entire territory which had so long been in the hands of the people of Israel. The Idumæans loudly exclaimed, " Both the nations and both the kingdoms will belong to us " (Ezekiel xxxv. 10). The Philistines also, and all the neighbouring nations displayed hatred and malice, and but few of the Israelitish fugitives found refuge in the Phœnician cities. Phœnicia was too far from Judæa, and before the fugitives could reach it they were overtaken and made prisoners by the Chaldæans.

The greater number of the chiefs and soldiers who had fled from Jerusalem with Zedekiah preferred to remain in their own counrty. They clung to the ground on which they had been born as though they could not separate themselves from it. At their head was Johanan, son of Kareah. But they had to seek hiding-places in order to escape from the Chaldæans. They hid in the clefts, grottoes and caves of the mountains, or among the ruins of the fallen cities, and doubtless made raids from their hiding-places in order to obtain provisions, or to attack straggling Chaldæans

and their adherents.   These Judæans were often
obliged to seek the means for sustaining their miserable existence at the peril of their lives.   If they were
caught they were condemned to an ignominious
death or subjected to disgraceful treatment.   The
nobles of advanced age were hanged; the young
were condemned to carry mills from one place to
another, and to do other slavish work.   A psalmist,
who was one of the sufferers from the woes of
this desperate condition, composed a heart-rending
lamentation, the short verses of which sound like
sobs and tears (Lamentations, ch. v.).   For a short
time it seemed as if this miserable condition of
the scattered people, this destructive war against
the fugitives, would come to an end.   Nebuchadnezzar did not wish Judah to be annihilated; he
determined to let the insignificant community remain
in the land, though he did not wish a native or even
a foreign king to be at their head.   He therefore
determined to appoint Gedaliah, the son of Ahikam,
as governor over them; his capital was to be at
Mizpah, which is an hour and a half's journey to the
north-east of Jerusalem.

Nebuchadnezzar could not have made a better
choice.   Gedaliah was a man in every way fitted for
the difficult post; he was gentle and peace-loving,
having been to a certain extent the disciple of the
prophet Jeremiah, of whom his father Ahikam had
been the friend and protector.   In order to heal the
still bleeding wounds, a gentle hand was wanted,
that of a man capable of complete self-devotion and
abnegation.   Gedaliah was, perhaps, too gentle, or he
relied too much on the grateful feelings of men.   Nebuzaradan entrusted to him the more harmless of the
prisoners, the daughters of King Zedekiah and many
women and children; he also placed under him the
husbandmen, in all, not much above a thousand persons.   Nebuchadnezzar also desired that the prophet
Jeremiah should assist Gedaliah; he therefore ordered

Nebuzaradan to behave considerately towards Jere-miah, and to grant all his wishes.

Nebuzaradan proceeded from Jerusalem to Ramah (in the vicinity of which was the tomb of Rachel), in order to decide which of the prisoners and deserters should remain in their country, and which should be banished to Babylon. Here he released Jeremiah from the chains with which he, like the other prisoners, had been bound, and offered him the choice of emigrating to Babylon, where he would be kindly treated, or of selecting any other dwelling-place; but he advised him to go to Gedaliah, at Mizpah.

Jeremiah, who had justly bewailed the lot which fell to him, of being selected to see the full measure of misery, was now forced to behold the pitiful sight of the captives at Ramah being led in fetters to Babylon. Heart-rending were the cries of the unfortunate men, women, and children, who were being dragged away from their fatherland; Jeremiah endeavoured to comfort them (Jerem. xxxi. 14, seq.).

With a heavy heart Jeremiah, attended by his disciple Baruch, prepared to visit Gedaliah in Mizpah. He had not much hope of effecting good results among the small remnant of the ignorant common people, seeing that for forty years he had striven in vain amongst the nobles and educated classes. How-ever, he determined to cast his lot with theirs. Neb-uchadnezzar thought so well of Jeremiah that he sent him gifts and money. His presence in Gedaliah's immediate vicinity inspired those who had remained in the country with greater confidence in the future. The governor had announced that all those fugitives who would collect around him would remain un-molested and at peace in the cities, and be permitted to cultivate their fields. Gradually the scattered tribes from Moab and the neighbouring countries who did not feel at ease in the places where they had settled, joined Gedaliah, and made peace with him; that is to say, they bound themselves to be faithful subjects of the Chaldæan king.

They cultivated the land, and not only grew corn, but also vines and figs; the soil yielded its fruits again, and as the population was small, the farmers, gardeners and vine-dressers received larger shares of the land, and succeeded in obtaining rich harvests. Several towns arose out of the ruins; in Mizpah, Gedaliah erected a sanctuary, as Jerusalem and the Temple on the Mount were destroyed and had become haunts for jackals.

Mizpah thus became a centre of importance and a holy place. The half-Israelitish, half-heathen colony of the Cuthæans of Shechem, Shiloh and Samaria, recognised this sanctuary, and made pilgrimages thither, offering sacrifices and incense.

"The remnant of Judah" over whom Gedaliah had been placed was reminded of its dependence on a Chaldæan ruler by the presence of the Chaldæan garrison. The latter not only kept watch over the nation, but also over the governor, in order that they might not engage in conspiracies. But considering the circumstances and the fearful misfortunes which had befallen the country, this state of things was endurable, or at least more favourable than the people could have expected; they were, at any rate, in their own country. The military chiefs, who were weary of their adventurous lives in the mountains and deserts, and of their contests with the wild animals that infested the land and the yet wilder Chaldæans, and who had relied on their swords and on delusive hopes, now determined to submit to Gedaliah. Johanan, son of Koreah, and his associates, laid down their weapons, cultivated the fields, and built up cities upon the ruins which until now had served them as hiding-places.

The last to make peace was the leader Ishmael, son of Nethaniah. Ishmael was a cunning and unprincipled man, and an evil spirit seems to have accompanied him to Mizpah, to disturb the comparatively favourable condition of the remnant of Judah.

It is true that he made peace with Gedaliah and the
Chaldæans, and promised submission; but in his
heart he cherished anger and rage against both.
Baalis, the king of Ammon, who had been opposed
to the growth and development of a Judæan colony
under Chaldæan protection, now instigated Ishmael
to a crime which was to put an end to it. The
remaining captains, and especially Johanan, the son
of Koreah, received private intelligence of Ishmael's
treacherous intentions towards Gedaliah. They
informed Gedaliah of the matter, placed themselves
at his disposal, and entreated permission to put an
end to the malefactor; but Gedaliah placed no faith
in their warning. This confidence, whether it owed
its cause to a feeling of power or of weakness, was
destined to prove fatal to him and to the newly-
organised community.

It was about four years after the destruction
of Jerusalem and the gathering of the scattered
Judæans around their governor, that Ishmael, with
ten followers, displaying great friendliness to Gedaliah, arrived in Mizpah to celebrate a festival. Gedaliah invited them to a banquet, and whilst the assembly, perhaps under the influence of wine, anticipated
no evil, Ishmael and his followers drew their swords
and killed the governor, the Chaldæans and all men
present who were capable of bearing arms. The
remaining people in Mizpah, old men, women, children, and eunuchs, he placed under the guard of his
people, in order that his crime might not become
known. Ishmael and his ten followers then carried
off into captivity the inhabitants of Mizpah, for the
most part women and children, among them the
daughters of King Zedekiah, as also the venerable
prophet Jeremiah and his disciple Baruch, taking
them across the Jordan to the Ammonites.

However, secretly though he had performed his evil
deeds, they could not long remain unknown. Johanan and the other chiefs had received information of

what had happened, and were not a little indignant at being deprived of their protector, and cast back into the uncertainties of an adventurous existence. They hurriedly armed themselves to punish the crime as it deserved. The murderers were met at their first halting-place, at the lake of Gibeon, by Johanan and the others, who prepared to do battle with them. At sight of the pursuers the prisoners hurried to join them. It appears that a fray ensued, in which two of Ishmael's followers were killed. He, however, escaped, with eight men, crossed the Jordan, and returned to the land of Ammon. His nefarious design, nevertheless, had succeeded; with the death of Gedaliah the Jewish commonwealth was broken up.

The survivors were at a loss how to act. They feared to remain in their country, as it was easy to foresee that Nebuchadnezzar would not leave the death of the Chaldæans unavenged, even if he overlooked the murder of Gedaliah, and would punish them as accessories. Even had this fear been groundless, how could they remain in the country without a leader to control the unruly elements? Their first thought was to emigrate to Egypt. The chiefs, with Johanan at their head, therefore directed their steps southwards. As they gradually became calmer, the question arose whether it might not be more advisable to remain in the land of their fathers than to travel, on a venture, into a foreign country. It appears that the idea first suggested itself to Baruch, and that it was received with favour by some of the chiefs, whilst others were opposed to it. Owing to this difference of opinion concerning the plan on which the weal and woe of so many depended, the leaders determined to leave the decision to Jeremiah. He was to pray to God, and entreat Him for a prophetic direction as to the course they should adopt, calling on God to witness that they would abide by his word.

Ten days Jeremiah wrestled in prayer that his spirit might be illumined by the true prophetic light. During this time the feelings of the leaders had changed, and they had all determined on emigration. When Jeremiah called together the chiefs and all the people, and informed them that the prophetic spirit had revealed to him that they should remain in the land without fear, he saw from their looks that they rejected this decision. He therefore added the threat that, if they insisted on emigration, the sword which they feared would the more surely reach them; that none of them would ever again behold his fatherland, and that they would all perish through manifold plagues, in Egypt. Hardly had Jeremiah ended his address, when Jezaniah and Johanan called to him, "Thou proclaimest lies in the name of God; not He has inspired thee with these words, but thy disciple Baruch." Without further consideration the leaders proceeded on the way towards Egypt, and the entire multitude had perforce to follow them.

Jeremiah and Baruch also had to join the rest, for they could do nothing in their deserted country. Thus they wandered as far as the Egyptian town of Taphnai (Tachpanches). They were kindly received by King Hophra, who was sufficiently grateful to show hospitality towards those whom his persuasions had brought to their present misery. There they met with older Judæan emigrants. Thus, more than a thousand years after the Exodus, the sons of Jacob returned to Egypt, but under what changed circumstances! At that time they had been powerful shepherd tribes, narrow in their views it is true, but unsullied and strong, with hearts swelling with hope. Their descendants, on the contrary, with sore hearts and disturbed minds, were too much estranged from their principles to find solace and tranquillity in their God and their nationality, yet not sufficiently changed to merge them-

selves into the other races and disappear amongst
them. Like all unwilling emigrants, they were
buoyed up by false hopes, and watched every political movement which might bring them an opportunity to return to their country, there to live in their
former independence.

Meanwhile, Judæa was almost completely depopulated. Nebuchadnezzar was not inclined to treat
the occurrences at Mizpah, the murder of Gedaliah
and the Chaldæans with him, with indifference. He
probably saw that it had been an error to permit a
weak Judæan community to exist, dependent solely
on one man. He, therefore, once more sent out the
leader of his guards, in order to take revenge on the
remaining Judæans. Nebuzaradan, as a matter of
course, found none of the leaders, nor any man of
importance; none but the remaining agriculturists,
gardeners, and vine-dressers. These, with their
wives and children, being seven hundred and forty-
five persons in all, the last remnant of the population
of Judæa, were led to Babylonia (582) into captivity.
This was the third banishment since Jehoiachin.
The innocent, on this occasion also, had to suffer for
the guilty. There is no historical record as to what
became of Ishmael and his fellow-conspirators. Gedaliah's name, on the other hand, remained in the memory of the survivors, on account of his violent death.
The anniversary of his murder was observed in Babylonia as a fast day. Nebuchadnezzar, after Gedaliah's
death, determined to leave no Judæan in the country,
and Judæa remained depopulated and deserted. A
later prophet laments over its utter desertion: "The
holy cities have become a waste, Zion a wilderness,
Jerusalem a desolation" (Isaiah lxiv. 9).

Thus the punishment which the prophets had predicted was fulfilled. The soil of Judah could now
rest, and celebrate the Sabbatical years which had
been neglected so long. In the south the Idumæans
had appropriated some stretches of Judæan territory

on their borders (with or without permission from the Babylonian king), and had extended their possessions as far as the slope (Shephela) of the Mediterranean Sea. The exiles therefore felt a bitter hatred against the Idumæans, who, in addition to plundering Jerusalem, and giving up the fugitives, had now seized on the land of their heritage. Two prophets, who had escaped from the massacre and the desolation, and lived amongst the exiles, gave vivid expression to this deplorable feeling—Obadiah and an anonymous prophet. Both prophesied evil against Edom, as a retribution for its conduct towards the kindred nation, the Jews, and towards Jerusalem.

Although the Judæans were everywhere coldly received, and their own country had become, to a certain extent, the property of their enemies, the refugees in Egypt still nursed the hope that they would soon return to their fatherland, and again inhabit it. Warlike happenings strengthened this hope, but the venerable prophet Jeremiah endeavoured to dispel their illusions. His heart prompted him to speak severely to the Egyptian Judæans, because, unchastened by misfortunes, they had once more devoted themselves to the worship of the goddess Neith. Despite their infatuation with strange gods, they yet, in their incomprehensible blindness, clung to the name of Jehovah, and swore by Him. Jeremiah, for the last time before descending to his grave, desired to tell them that, owing to their unconquerable folly, they would never return to their fatherland. He therefore summoned the Judæans of Migdol, Taphnai, Memphis, and Sais (?) to a general meeting at Taphnai. He still possessed sufficient influence to ensure their obeying his summons. He put the case before them in plain language. Their idolatrous practices, however, were so dear to their hearts that they openly boasted of them, and told the prophet that they would not relinquish them. The women were particularly aggressive: "The oath which we have taken, to offer up incense and wine to the queen of heaven, shall be kept, as we and our fathers were formerly accustomed to do in the cities of Judæa and in the streets of Jerusalem. At that time we had bread in plenty, we were happy, and saw no evil. Since we have left off making sacrifices to the queen of heaven we have been in want, and our people have perished by the sword or through hunger." Jeremiah thus answered their blasphemy: "Fulfil your oaths; all the men of Judah will surely die in the land of Egypt; only a few fugitives from the sword shall return from Egypt into the land of Judah. They shall learn whose word shall endure—mine or theirs." As a sign, he predicted that King Hophra, on whom they depended, would fall into the hands of his enemy, as Zedekiah had fallen into the hands of Nebuchadnezzar. The announcement that Hophra would meet with a disastrous end was fulfilled. In a warlike expedition against Cyrene, his army was defeated, and his warriors, jealous of the Carians and Ionians, whom he favoured, rebelled against him. An Egyptian of low caste, Amasis (Amosis), placed himself at the head of the rebels, conquered Hophra, dethroned him, and caused him to be strangled (571–70). This new Pharaoh, who was very careful to attract to himself the Egyptians and also to win the Greeks over to his side, took no interest in those Judæans who had settled in Egypt. They were neglected, and their dream of returning to their fatherland through the help of Egypt was dispelled. Jeremiah seems to have lived to see this change.

His tender heart must have become still sadder in his old age, as he had not succeeded in "bringing forth the precious from the vile." The few Judæans who were around him in Egypt remained firm in their folly and hardness of heart. But Jeremiah had not toiled in vain. The seed which he had sown grew up plentifully on another ground, where it was carefully tended by his fellow-prophets. His office, not only to destroy, but to rebuild and plant anew, was carried on in another place. His disciple Baruch, son of Neriah, appears to have left the exiles in Egypt for those in Babylon, after the death of the prophet of Anathoth.

CHAPTER XVIII.

THE BABYLONIAN EXILE.

Nebuchadnezzar's treatment of the Exiles—The Exiles obtain grants
of land—Evil-Merodach favours Jehoiachin—Number of the
Judæan Exiles—Ezekiel's captivity in the first period of the Exile
—Moral change of the People—Baruch collects Jeremiah's Pro-
phecies and compiles the Histories—The Mourners of Zion—
Proselytes—The Pious and the Worldly—The Poetry of the
Time—Psalms and Book of Job—Nabonad's Persecutions—The
Martyrs and the Prophets of the Exile—The Babylonian Isaiah
—Cyrus captures Babylon—The Return under Zerubbabel.

572—537 B. C. E.

Was it chance, or was it a special design, that
the Judæans, who were banished to Babylonia, were
humanely and kindly treated by the conqueror Nebuchadnezzar? Is there, in fact, in the history of
nations, and in the chain of events, such a thing as
chance? Can we affirm positively that the condition
and state of mankind would have been quite unlike
what they now are, if this or that circumstance had
accidentally not occurred? Can we believe that,
whilst firm and unalterable laws govern all things in
the kingdom of nature, the history of nations should
be the result of mere caprice? Nebuchadnezzar's
clemency to the people of Judah was of great importance in the historical development of that nation. The preservation of the exiles, reduced by
much misery to a mere handful, was mainly due to
this kindness. Nebuchadnezzar was not like those
ruthless conquerors of earlier and later days, who
took pleasure in wanton destruction. The desire to
build up and to create was as dear to his heart
as conquest. He wished to make the newly
established Chaldæan kingdom great, populous
and rich. His capital, Babylon, was to surpass the

now ruined Nineveh. He built a wall round his city, which was nine miles in circumference, and he added a new town to the old one, on the eastern side of the river Euphrates. The conquered people, taken forcibly from their own homes, were transplanted into this new city, whilst domiciles were given to many Judæan captives in the capital itself, those in particular being favoured who had freely accepted Nebuchadnezzar's rule. In fact, so generous was his treatment that entire families and communities from the cities of Judæa and Benjamin, with their kindred and their slaves, had the privilege of remaining together. They were free, and their rights and customs were respected. The families transplanted from Jerusalem—such as the princes of the royal house (the sons of David), the descendants of Joab or the family of Pahath-Moab, the family of Parosh and others, formed each a special league, and were allowed to govern themselves after the manner of their family traditions. Even the slaves of the Temple (the Nethinim) and the slaves of the state, who had followed their masters into exile, lived grouped together according to their own pleasure.

Most probably the exiles received land and dwelling-places in return for those which they had forfeited in their own country. The land divided amongst them was cultivated by themselves or by their servants. They not only possessed slaves, but also horses, mules, camels, and asses. As long as they paid the tax on their lands and, perhaps, also a poll-tax, and obeyed the laws of the king, they were permitted to enjoy their independence. They probably clung to each other and their common national memories the more closely, as, like most exiles, they fondly cherished the hope that their return to their own country would surely be brought about by some unforeseen event. One other circumstance greatly helped them. In the Chaldæan kingdom the Aramaic language predominated, and as it was cognate with Hebrew, the exiles learnt it easily, and soon made themselves understood by the inhabitants.   Even in those days the Judæans possessed peculiar facility for acquiring foreign languages.   The position of the Judæans in Babylonia after the death of Nebuchadnezzar (561) was still more favourable.

Nebuchadnezzar's son and successor, Evil-Merodach (Illorodamos) was utterly unlike his father. He was not courageous, nor did he love warfare, and he paid little attention to the business of the state.   Judæan youths, from the royal house of David, were to be found at his court as eunuchs. How often have these guardians of the harem, these servants of their master's whims, become in turn masters of their master.   The king Evil-Merodach appears to have been under the influence of a Judæan favourite, who induced him to release the captive king Jehoiachin, who had been imprisoned for thirty-seven years.   The Babylonian monarch clothed him in royal garments, invited him to the royal table, and supplied his wants most generously.   When Evil-Merodach held his court with unusual pomp, and assembled all the great men of the kingdom about him, he raised a throne for Jehoiachin higher than the thrones of the other conquered kings.   He wished all the world to know that the former king of Judæa was his particular favourite.

This generosity of Evil-Merodach must have extended in some degree to Jehoiachin's fellow-prisoners, for to many of them greater freedom was given, whilst others, who had been kept in the strictest captivity on account of their enmity to Nebuchadnezzar, were released.   In fact, it is possible that Evil-Merodach might have been persuaded to allow the exiles to return home, with Jehoiachin as king of Judæa, had not his own death intervened.   After a short reign of two years, he was murdered by his brother-in-law, Neriglissar (560).   The dream of returning to their own country, in which some Babylonian Judæans had indulged, was thus dispelled. They were soon to learn the hardships of captivity.

One of the many prophecies of the Hebrew seers —namely, that only a small part of the people should be saved—had been fulfilled. Insignificant indeed was the remnant. Of the four millions of souls which the children of Israel numbered in the reign of King David, only about a hundred thousand remained. Millions had fallen victims to the sword, famine, and pestilence, or had disappeared and been lost in foreign lands. But there was another side to the prophecies, which had not yet been realised. The greater number of the Judæan exiles, particularly those belonging to the most distinguished families, unchastened by the crushing blow which had befallen their nation and their country, persisted in their obstinacy and hardness of heart. The idolatrous practices to which they had been addicted in their own country, they continued in Babylon. It was difficult indeed to root out the passion for idolatry from the hearts of the people. The heads of the families, or elders, who laid claim to a kind of authority over all the other exiles, were as cruel and as extortionate in Babylonia as they had been in Palestine. Regardless of those beneath them, they did not try to better their condition. They chose the best and most fruitful portions of the lands assigned to them, leaving the worst to their subordinates.

Ezekiel, the son of Buzi, the first prophet of the captivity (born about 620, died about 570) directed his prophetic ardour against the folly and obstinacy of the exiles. Gifted with simple, yet fiery and impressive eloquence, with a sweet and impassioned voice, and fully conscious of the highest ideal of religion and morality that the Judæans were capable of attaining, he spoke with courage and energy to his fellow-exiles. At first they treated him roughly (actually fettering him upon one occasion), but at last he gained their attention, and they would gather round him when he prophesied.

The elders had often entreated him to foretell the end of that terrible war whilst it was raging in and about Jerusalem, but he had been silent. Why should he repeat for the hundredth time that the city, the nation, and the Temple were to be inevitably destroyed? But when a fugitive announced to him that the threatened misfortune had become a reality, he broke silence. Ezekiel first addressed himself to the conscienceless and heartless elders, who were leading a comfortable existence in captivity, whilst they were ill-treating their unfortunate brethren. (Ezekiel, ch. xxxiv.) But also in another direction, he had to combat a false idea prevailing amongst the exiles. Like the rest of the prophets, Ezekiel had foretold with absolute certainty the ultimate return of the Judæans to Palestine, but also their return to a purer state of morality. Many of the captives, however, in consequence of their repeated misfortunes, began to despair of the new birth of the nation, and looked upon it as a mere dream. They said, " Our bones are dried up, and our hope is lost: we are quite cut off." The greatest of all evils is for a nation to despair of its future and to give up every hope. Ezekiel considered it a most important duty to banish this gloom from the hearts of his people. In a beautiful simile—that of the dry bones restored to life—he placed before them a picture of their new birth.

But there was another group of exiles who despaired of the restoration of the Judæan people. They felt themselves utterly crushed by their sins. For centuries the nation had tempted the anger of its God by idolatry and other misdeeds. These sins could not be undone, but must meet with their inevitable result—the death of the sinner. These unfortunate people exclaimed, " If our transgressions and our sins be upon us, and we pine away in them, how then should we live?" But the prophet Ezekiel also combated this gloomy belief, that sin and its punishment were inseparably connected, and that crime must necessarily lead to the death of the sinner. In eloquent words, he laid before the people his consolatory doctrine of the efficacy of repentance.

Often and in varied terms Ezekiel spoke of the future deliverance of the exiles, and painted it in ideal colours. So deeply was this prophet of the exile impressed with the certainty of a return to the old order of things in his own country, that he actually devised a plan for the building of a new Temple, and for the ordering of divine service and of the priesthood. Ezekiel was far from thinking that such a brilliant and glorious future was near at hand. The ideas, the feelings, and the actions which he daily observed in the exiles were not of a kind to justify such a hope. But he and other holy men helped to make a small beginning. Not long after the death of Ezekiel and Jeremiah, an unexpected change for the better commenced. The captivity which, notwithstanding the kind treatment at the hands of Nebuchadnezzar and his son, was attended with much suffering, but more especially the influence of their peculiar literature led to a change in the disposition of the people. In the very midst of the idolatrous abominations of the kingdoms of Ephraim and Judah, the flowers of a higher morality had blossomed. "The Spirit of God had dwelt amidst the uncleanliness of the people." The sublime thoughts of the prophets and the psalmists, awakened during the course of centuries, had not vanished into thin air with speech and song, but had taken root in some hearts, and had been preserved in writing. The priests of the sons of Zadok, who had never been idolatrous, had brought with them into captivity the Torah (the Pentateuch); the disciples of the prophets had brought the eloquent words of their teachers; the Levites had brought the sublime

Psalms; the wise men, a treasure of excellent sayings; the learned had preserved the historical books. Treasures, indeed, had been lost, but one treasure remained which could not be stolen, and this the exiles had taken with them into a strange land. A rich, brilliant, and manifold literature had been carried into exile with them, and it became a power that taught, ennobled, and rejuvenated. These writings were replete with wonders. Had not the prophecy been realised to the letter, that the land of Israel would spew forth its people on account of their folly and their crimes, just as it had thrust out the Canaanites? Had not the menacing words of the prophets come to pass in a most fearful manner? Jeremiah had prophesied daily, in unambiguous words, the destruction of the nation, the city, and the Temple. Ezekiel had foretold the terrible war and subsequent misery, and his words had been fulfilled; and earlier still, Isaiah, Hosea, Amos, and even Moses had warned the people that exile and destruction would follow upon the transgression of the Law. Yet in spite of all their terrible misery, the people were not entirely annihilated. A remnant existed, small indeed, and homeless, but this remnant had found favour in the eyes of the conquerors. It was clear that even in the land of their foes, God had not entirely rejected them; He did not " utterly abhor them, to destroy them and break His covenant with them."

Another miracle took place before their own eyes. A part of the descendants of the Ten Tribes, scattered for more than a century in the Assyrian provinces, and looked upon as lost, had asserted their nationality. Though long separated by jealousy and artfully whetted hate, they approached their suffering brethren with cordial affection. Those Israelites who had dwelt in the capital of Nineveh had, without doubt, left that doomed city at the destruction of the Assyrian empire, and had fled to Babylonia, the neighbouring kingdom. Thus the words of the prophets were again fulfilled, "Israel and Judah shall dwell together in brotherly love."

Those who were able to read eagerly studied the rescued manuscripts, and anxiously sought instruction and consolation in their pages. The prophecies and words of Jeremiah were especially studied, their pathetic and elegiac tone being peculiarly adapted to men living in exile. Jeremiah's writings, which had probably been brought by Baruch from Egypt, became a popular book. The effect which the living words, fresh from the prophet's own lips, had failed to produce was accomplished by the written letter. The spirit of the prophets passed into the souls of their readers, filled them with hopes and ideals, and prepared them for a change of mind.

In order to make the conversion a lasting one, the spiritual leaders of the people chose a new method of instruction. One of them, probably Baruch, wrote (about 555) a comprehensive historical work for his readers, relating the events from the creation of the world and the commencement of Israel as a nation down to the time when Jehoiachin was released from his prison, and loaded with marks of the royal favour. This collection embraced the Torah (Law), the Book of Joshua, the histories of the Judges, of Samuel, Saul and David. To these Baruch added his own redaction of the history of the Kings from Solomon to Jehoiachin, whose downfall he himself had witnessed. He gave his own colouring to these events, in order to demonstrate that the decline of the kingdom, from the death of Solomon, was owing to the apostasy of the king and the people.

The historical work that Baruch compiled has no equal. It is simple, yet rich in matter and instructive, unaffected yet artistic; but above all things it is vivid and impressive. It was the second national work of the Babylonian exiles, and they not only read it with interest, but took it to heart, and listened to its lessons. Levitical scribes applied themselves to copying it. This literature gave a new heart to the people, and breathed a new spirit into them. What Ezekiel had commenced, Jeremiah's disciple, Baruch, continued.

Influenced by the study of these writings, the exiles began to devote themselves to self-examination. This was followed by contrition for their constant disobedience and idolatry. Those who were moved to penitence by the consciousness of their great sins longed to wash away the bitter past in tears of repentance. They acknowledged that all the misfortunes that had befallen them were well deserved, for just as " the Lord of Hosts had purposed to do unto them according to their ways and according to their doings, so had He dealt with them." Many atoned sincerely; four days in the year were set apart, at first by a few, and later on by a large number of exiles, as days of mourning. These occasions were the anniversaries of Nebuchadnezzar's siege of Jerusalem in the tenth month, of the conquest of Jerusalem in the fourth month, of the destruction of Jerusalem in the fifth month, and of Gedaliah's assassination in the seventh month. At these times it became customary for the people to fast and lament, wear garments of mourning, sit in ashes and bow their heads in deep contrition. These days of mourning heralded the people's awakening; they were signs of repentance, and the first institution of national anniversaries after the captivity. This keen feeling of remorse gave birth to a new kind of psalm, which we may call the Penitential Psalm. Those who had forsaken their evil ways in turn converted others; former sinners showed other evil-doers the way to God. The number of the faithful, " those who were eager for God's word," those " who sought after God," thus gradually increased. Naturally, the Patient Sufferers (Anavim) formed the nucleus of this new party. They mourned the destruction of

Jerusalem and its former glory; they were "contrite in heart," and "meek in spirit." They bore outward signs of mourning, and called themselves "the mourners of Zion." With them were associated members of noble families, who held some office or dignity at the Babylonian court. All their thoughts dwelt upon Jerusalem. They loved the stones of the Holy City, and longed to see its very ruins, lying in the dust. (Psalm cxx. 14-15.) The Levite, who, in the name of his companions in captivity, described so poetically this faithful remembrance of Jerusalem, gave utterance, in the 137th Psalm, to the sentiments of "the mourners of Zion."

While praying for deliverance or confessing their sins, the mourners turned their faces towards Jerusalem, as if the place where the Temple had once stood were still holy, and as if only thence a merciful answer to their supplications were to be expected. As those "eager for God's word" would not offer up sacrifices in a strange land, they accustomed themselves to look upon prayer as a substitute for sacrifice. Three times a day, a number of persons forming a congregation met for this purpose. The House of Prayer took the place of the Temple. It was probably the penitential psalms and the psalms of mourning that were sung in these houses of prayer, and were composed for them.

The enthusiasm for Jerusalem, for the deliverance from captivity, and for the Law, was fanned to a brighter flame by the astounding fact that some of the heathen population accepted the doctrines of the exiles, and entered into their covenant. Only the enthusiasm of the exiles could have effected this wonderful phenomenon. Zeal of a self-sacrificing, self-forgetting nature is a magic power which kindles enthusiasm. It was comparatively easy, by contrasting the Judæan doctrine of one sublime, spiritual God with the childish image-worship of the Chaldæans, to make the latter appear ridiculous. The Judæan, fully conscious of the majesty of his God, could ill restrain his derision, or withhold a smile of contempt at the sight of a Babylonian workman carving an image out of wood, praying to it for help in adversity, and then kindling with the rest of the material a fire, at which he warmed himself, or over which he baked his bread and cooked his meat. In this way many who heard of the great name of the God of Israel forsook their own false belief, and associated themselves with a people that professed a totally different religion. These newly-won proselytes, after their conversion, kept the Sabbath, obeyed the statutes, and even submitted to the rite of circumcision. This, the first achievement of the exiles during the Captivity, exercised a reflex influence upon the Judæans. They began to love their God and their Law with far greater fervour, as soon as they discovered that heathens had been won to their side. This regeneration was effected before two decades had elapsed since the death of the prophets Jeremiah and Ezekiel.

The now accessible literature, the Torah and the Prophets, was a rejuvenating fountain, refreshing the spirit and softening the heart. However, this new spirit, by which the nation was inspired, had to be tried and tested, and the hour of probation was at hand.

Some of the most distinguished families amongst the Judæans adhered to their old abominations, and in addition adopted many of the errors of their heathen neighbours. The giant capital Babylon and the vast Chaldæan empire exercised a magical charm over those "who stood highest" among the exiles, tempting them into imitating the Chaldæan customs, opening a wide horizon before them, and giving them the opportunity of developing their talents. The products of the soil and the artistic fabrics of Babylonia, which were eagerly sought after and largely exported, formed the staples of a flourishing commerce. Thus the former merchants of Judah were able, not only to continue their calling, but to follow it more actively. They undertook frequent journeys for the purpose of buying and selling, and began to accumulate great riches. In a luxurious country wealth produces luxury. The rich Judæans imitated the effeminate life of the Babylonians, and even began to profess their idolatrous beliefs. To ensure the success of their commercial undertakings, they prepared a table with food for the god of Good Fortune (Gad), and filled the pitcher of wine for the goddess of Fate (Meni). So completely did the wealthy exiles identify themselves with the Babylonians, that they entirely forgot Judah and Jerusalem, which until lately had been the goal of their desires. They could not bear to think of their return; they wished to be Babylonians, and looked with contempt upon the fanatical lovers of their own land. The two rival parties, which hated each other, were represented, on the one hand, by men of zeal and piety, and on the other, by men of worldliness and self-indulgence. The earnest-minded Judæans, who were full of fervour for their cause, attempted to influence their brethren, whose religious views and conduct were so widely opposed to their own. To this effort we are indebted for a new poetical literature which almost excelled the old. The last twenty years of the Captivity were more productive even than the times of Hezekiah. The men of genius, disciples of Jeremiah and Ezekiel, who had so thoroughly absorbed the spirit of their literature that their own souls were brought into harmony with it, now produced fruitful thoughts of their own, clothed in elegant forms. An apparently inexhaustible fountain of poetry flowed once more in a strange land, in the very midst of the sufferings of captivity. The Hebrew language, so lovingly fostered by the exiles in their Aramaic home, was the language of their poetic works. New psalms, maxims of wisdom, and prophetical discourses followed each other in rapid succession. A poet of that time collected a number of proverbs, written at a much earlier date, and in the prefatory chapters which he affixed to them he gave a true picture of the age. He was an acute observer of human failings and their consequences, and his work is an eloquent exposition of practical ethics. If he could but bring the worldly-minded to listen to his teaching, he argued, they might be induced to abandon their evil ways. The leading idea of this poet is that the beginning of wisdom is the fear of God, and the fear of God, the safeguard against corruption; sin is folly, and causes the death of the sinner; even the prosperity of fools kills them, and their happiness destroys them.—But what reward is there in store for the pious or the wise who suffer?

To this question our poet, like the psalmists of the exiled congregation, had no other answer than that " The just will inhabit the land again, and the pious shall dwell in it once more." But if this sufficed for the God-fearing people and the mourners of Zion, it was not sufficient to comfort and satisfy the weak in faith, still less could it alter the feelings of those who had forgotten the Holy Mountain, and whose hearts clave to Babylonia. For it was evident that the sinners enjoyed prosperity, and that those who feared God and remained true to their ideals were often unhappy and unfortunate. This discord in the moral order of the world demanded a satisfactory explanation. Doubts arose as to the justice of God, and as to the truth of the teachings of the fathers, and these misgivings were bitterly felt by the Babylonian Judæan community.

A poet undertook the solution of these distressing questions, and he created a work of art which is ranked among the most perfect ever conceived by a human mind. This unknown author composed the book of Job, a work which was to dispel the gloomy thoughts of his contemporaries. Like the psalms and the proverbs, it also was intended to convey instruction, but its method was different. In a solemn but most interesting conversation between friends, the question that kept the Babylonian community in painful suspense was to be decided. This dialogue is not carried on in a dry and pedantic way ; the author has made it singularly attractive in form, expression, and poetical diction. The story of the patient Job, fascinating from beginning to end, is the groundwork of the dialogue. The arrangement of the poem is artistic throughout; the ideas that the author wished to make clear are allotted to different speakers. Each person in the dialogue has a distinct character and remains true to it. In this way the dialogue is lively, and the thoughts therein developed command attention.

Meanwhile events took place in Babylonia and Asia Minor that were to decide the fate of the exiles. Neriglissar, the successor of their protector, Evil-Merodach, was dead, and had left a minor to succeed him. But this young prince was killed by the Babylonian nobles, one of whom, named Nabonad, seized the throne (555). A few years previous to that date, a Persian warrior, the hero Cyrus, had dethroned the Median king Astyages, taken possession of his kingdom with its capital, Ecbatana, and subdued the provinces belonging to it.

The pious and the enthusiasts among the Babylonian Judæans did not fail to recognise in these events favourable signs for themselves. They appear to have entreated Nabonad to free them from captivity, and permit them to return to Judæa. They must have been encouraged to hope for the realisation of their wishes by the fact that Merbal, a noble Phœnician exile of the royal house, had been permitted by Nabonad to return to and rule over his own country, and after his death, his brother Hiram was allowed to succeed him. It was not improbable, therefore, that Nabonad would confer the same favour upon his Judæan subjects. Shealtiel, the son of King Jehoiachin, probably urged this request upon the usurper, and doubtless the Judæan favourites at the Babylonian court warmly espoused his cause. But Nabonad was as loth to let the exiles leave his country as Pharaoh had been of old to dismiss the Israelites from Egypt. This frustration of their hope, or rather this discrimination against them, enkindled in the patriotic exiles a burning hatred of Babylonia and its monarch. The old wounds burst open anew. Babylon was loathed as Edom had been in former ages. Such violent hatred was probably not controlled, but found expression in speech and action. The speedy downfall of this sinful country, teeming with idolatry and immorality, seemed certain to the Judæans. They followed with intense interest the warlike progress of the hero Cyrus, because they foresaw that a conflict was imminent between the Medo-Persian empire and Babylonia. Cyrus had directed his weapons against the Lydian kingdom of Crœsus, who had made an offensive and defensive alliance with Nabonad of Babylonia, and Amasis, king of Egypt. Well aware that they, in turn, would be attacked, these monarchs tried to gain strength by alliance. But this served only to incite the Persian conqueror to destroy the sooner the independence of Babylonia. Did any of the Judæan favourites at the Babylonian court, or any of the converted heathens open secret negotiations with Cyrus? The kindness shown later on to the Judæans by the Persian warrior, and their persecution by Nabonad, lead to the supposition that such was the case.

Nabonad's persecutions were first directed against the patriotic and pious exiles; severe punishments were decreed against them, which were cruelly put into execution. It seemed as if the staunchest of the nation were to be proved and tried, as Job had been, by suffering. Upon some, heavy labour was imposed, from which even the aged were not exempt. Others were shut up in dungeons, or were whipped, beaten, and insulted. Those who dared speak of their speedy deliverance through Cyrus were doomed to a martyr's death, to which they submitted fearlessly.

A contemporary prophet, who witnessed the persecution, or, perhaps, was one of its victims, described it in harrowing words. Considering the sufferers as the wards of the people, he speaks of their terrible anguish as being that of the entire national body:

"He is despised and rejected of men, a man of sorrows, and acquainted with grief. . . . . He was oppressed, although he was submissive, yet he opened not his mouth; he is brought as a lamb to the slaughter; and as a sheep before her shearers is dumb, so he openeth not his mouth. Through prison and through judicial punishment was he taken away." (ISAIAH liii. 3, 7.)

The suffering of the Judæans in Babylonia, at that time, closely resembled the persecution of their ancestors in Egypt. But there was this difference: in Egypt all Israelites alike were subjected to slavery and forced labour in the fields and on buildings, whilst in Babylonia the dungeon and death awaited those exiles only who refused to abjure their nationality and their religion. Psalm cii., composed at this time, pictures the sombre mood of one of these victims of persecution, relieved, however, by the hope of future deliverance. The Judæans who were threatened with imprisonment and torture followed the victories of Cyrus with anxious interest. Several prophets now appeared, who announced, to the consolation of the sufferers, the downfall of Babylon, and the speedy deliverance of the exiles. Two of them have left us prophecies that are unsurpassed; indeed, one of those writers manifested so boundless a wealth of eloquence and poetry, that his works rank among the most beautiful in literature. When Cyrus at length commenced the long-planned siege of Babylon, and the anxious expectations of the exiles had grown harrowing, this prophet, with his gift of glowing eloquence, uplifted and instructed his people.

If the perfection of a work of art consists in the fact that the ideas and the language are in true harmony with each other, and that the latter makes the abstruse thought clear and intelligible, then the speech or series of speeches of this prophet, whom, in ignorance of his real name, we call the second, or the Babylonian Isaiah, form an oratorical work of art without a parallel. Here are combined richness of thought, beauty of form, persuasive power and touching softness, poetic fervour and true simplicity, and all this is expressed in such noble language and warm colouring that, although intended for the period only in which they were composed, they will be understood and appreciated in all time.

The Babylonian Isaiah wished to comfort his suffering Judæan brethren, and, at the same time, to give them a high aim. The suffering Jewish tribe as well as all those who have minds to comprehend and hearts to feel, whatever their race and language may be, can find in this prophet the solution of a problem, the correctness of which history has proven. He showed how a nation can be small yet great, wretched and hunted to death yet immortal, at one and the same moment a despised slave and a noble exemplar. Who was this prophet, at once a great thinker and a great poet? He says not a word about himself, and there are no records of his life. The collectors of the prophetical writings, finding that in eloquence and sublimity his words resembled those of Isaiah, added them to the prophecies of the older seer, and included them in the same scroll.

No one could console the sorrowing Judæan community with such sympathy, or encourage it with such ardour as the Prophet of the Captivity. His words are like balm upon a burning wound, or like a gentle breeze upon a fevered brow.

"Comfort ye," he begins, "comfort ye, comfort ye my people, saith your God. Speak ye to the heart of Jerusalem, and cry unto her, that her warfare is accomplished, that her iniquity is pardoned; for she hath received of the Lord's hand double for all her sins." (ISAIAH xl.)

The exhausted and despairing community was described by this prophet as a wife and mother who had been rejected, and robbed of her children on account of her sins, but who still is dear to her husband as the beloved of his youth. This deserted one he calls " Jerusalem," the emblem of all that was tender to his soul. He exclaims to the forlorn mother:

"Awake, awake, stand up, O Jerusalem, which hast drunk at the hand of the Lord the cup of his fury. Thou hast drunken the dregs of the cup of trembling and wrung them out.
" There is none to guide her among all the sons whom she hath brought forth, neither is there any that taketh her by the hand, of all the sons that she has brought up. , ... O thou afflicted, tossed with tempest, and not comforted, behold I will lay thy stones with fair colours, and lay thy foundations with sapphires, and I will make thy windows of agates, and thy gates of carbuncles, and all thy borders of precious stones, and all thy children shall be taught of the Lord, and great shall be the peace of thy children. . . . .
" As one whom his mother comforteth, so will I comfort you, and ye shall be comforted in Jerusalem."

But where is this consolation to be found? Not in the hope of vain, worldly glory, not in might and power, but in an all-embracing salvation. This prophet of the Captivity was the first who clearly grasped and demonstrated that a creed of general salvation was promised through Abraham to future generations. The past was to be forgotten and forgiven; a new social order was to spring up; heaven and earth were to be re-created. All people from all the ends of the earth would be included in this universal salvation, and every knee would bend and every tongue swear homage to the God adored by Israel. It was for this purpose that Abraham had been called from a distant land, and that his descendants had been chosen before their birth. God had created the people of Israel to be His servant among nations, His messenger to all people, His apostle from the beginning of the world.

The prophet describes this apostolic people in

poetry of such transcendental beauty that it becomes an ideal. And is there any mission sublimer than that of being the vanguard of the nations in the path of righteousness and salvation? Was Israel not to be proud of having been chosen for such a duty? The prophet goes on to say how this ideal nation was to realise its apostolic mission:

"Behold my servant, whom I uphold, mine elect, in whom my soul delighteth; I have put my spirit upon him, he shall bring forth judgment to the Gentiles. He shall not cry, nor lift up, nor cause his voice to be heard in the street. A bruised reed shall he not break, and the smoking flax shall he not quench; he shall bring forth judgment into truth." (ISAIAH xlii. 1-4.)

The Law of God was thus to be universally acknowledged, and the messenger of God was to bring about this acknowledgment by his own example, in spite of scorn, contempt, and persecution. This, Israel's recognised mission, the prophet of the Captivity explained briefly, in words supposed to be spoken by the nation itself (Isaiah xlix. 1-6). He taught that martyrdom, bravely encountered and borne with gentle resignation, would ensure victory to the law of righteousness, which Israel, if true to its ideals, was to promulgate. The leading conception that runs through Isaiah's poetical monologue was thus expressed by the prophet in the short but effective verse:

"For mine house shall be called an house of prayer for all peoples." (ISAIAH lvi. 7.)

The fall of the Babylonian empire, with its absurd and immoral idolatry, and the deliverance of the Judæan community were to be the first steps in this great work of universal salvation. The fall of Babylon seemed indeed inevitable to the prophet, so that he spoke of it as of an accomplished fact, and not as a subject of prophetic vision.

He apostrophized Babylon in a satirical song of masterly perfection (Is. xlvii.); he derided the astrological science by which the Babylonian sages boasted that they could raise the veil from the future; he treated the coarse idolatry of the Chaldæans with more bitter irony than any of his predecessors had done. He foretold the siege of the city by Cyrus, and declared that the Persian conqueror would give freedom to the Judæan and Israelitish exiles; that they would return to their country and rebuild Jerusalem and the Temple. The prophet laid great stress upon these predictions, declaring that in their realisation Divine Providence would be manifest. Cyrus was but an instrument of God for furthering the deliverance of Judah and the salvation of the world.

For the sake of the exiles, the wonders of the exodus from Egypt would be renewed, every mountain and hill would be made level, springs would gush forth in the wilderness, and the desert would become a blooming garden. The exiles would raise Jerusalem from its ruins, and live in their beloved city in peace and comfort. But in spite of his reverence for Jerusalem, the prophet declared that the Divine Being was too great to be pictured as dwelling within a temple, however spacious it might be, but that each human heart should be a temple dedicated to God.

"Thus says the Lord: The heaven is my throne, and the earth is my footstool: where is the house that ye build unto me; and where is the place of my rest? For all these things hath mine hand made, saith the Lord; but to this man will I look, to him that is poor and of a contrite spirit and trembleth at my word." (ISAIAH lxvi. 1.)

The exiles, purged and truly pious, adopted this thought, and embodied it in Solomon's prayer:

"Behold, the heaven of heavens contain Thee not; how much less a temple." (I KINGS viii. 27.)

Unfortunately, in spite of the beautiful words of the prophet of the Captivity, the servant of God declined to accept this apostolic work, and remained blind and deaf. Instead of making the Law of God beloved, he made it contemptible, and became contemptible himself.

The ideal and the real being thus at variance with each other, the prophet felt that his mission was to preach, to exhort, to denounce and to arouse. The Judæan community in the Captivity was now more than ever divided into two camps : on the one side were the pious and patriotic ; on the other, the worldly and the callous. The former, who had become timid and despondent from continued persecution and suffering, dared not come forward at this anxious time to oppose their persecutors ; they were oppressed by the sorrowful thought that God had forsaken His people and had forgotten them, whilst their enemies called out mockingly, " Let the Lord be glorified and we will see your joy." (Isaiah lxvi. 5.) Now the aim of the great unknown prophet was to encourage the one class to action, and to move the other to penitence and improvement. He announced that God's salvation was at hand, and that if the worldly and selfish persisted in their evil ways, they would reap the punishment of their sins, whilst the pious would be rewarded with undimmed happiness. He finally depicted the coming deliverance and the return, when all the scattered of Judah and Israel would assemble on the holy mount of Jerusalem.

The king Nabonad and the Babylonian people probably felt less anxiety about the result of the war between Persia and Babylon than did the Judæan exiles. For the Judæans were alternating between the highest hopes and the most desponding fears; the preservation or the downfall of the Jewish race hung upon the issue of this war. The Babylonians, on the contrary, looked with indifference, it might be said, upon all of Cyrus's preparations. But one night, when they were dancing and carousing at one of their orgies, a large and powerful army appeared before the bastions of the city. The Babylonians were utterly unprepared for resistance, and when day broke, Babylon was filled with the enemy. Thus, as the prophet had foretold, the city of Babylon fell (539), but the king and the people escaped their predicted doom. Cyrus was a humane conqueror.

The disgusting idolatry of the Babylonians was uprooted when their city was taken. The religion of the victorious Persians and Medes was pure in comparison with that of the Babylonians. They worshipped only two or three gods, and abhorred the image-worship of the Babylonians, and perhaps destroyed their idols.

The fall of Babylon cured the Judæan community radically and for all time of idolatry. For the exiles saw that those highly honoured images were now lying in the dust, that Bel was on his knees, that Nebo was humbled, and that Merodach had fallen. The destruction of Babylon completed the regeneration of the Judæan people, and their hard hearts became softened. From that time all, even the worldly-minded and the sinners, clung to their God. For, had they not learned how His word, spoken by the mouth of His prophets, had been fulfilled? The sufferers and the mourners of Zion were no longer objects of hatred and contempt, but were, on the contrary, treated with veneration, and placed at the head of the community.

No sooner had Babylon fallen than the pious and patriotic party took steps towards realising the predicted deliverance and return of the exiles. Cyrus, having taken possession of the throne and of the palace, declared himself king of Babylonia and the successor of her former monarchs, dating his reign from the fall of Babylon (B.C. 538). The servants of the palace, who had crouched and trembled before Nabonad, now became servants of Cyrus. Amongst them were also eunuchs of the royal family of Judæa, who had remained true to their faith. They as well as some converted heathens, who had joined the Judæan community, tried to obtain from Cyrus the freedom of their fellow-

believers.   In this they were probably aided by Zerubbabel, the grandson of King Jehoiachin.   Those
Judæans who had been imprisoned on account of the
devotion with which they clung to their faith were
set free at once.   But Cyrus went still further, for
he permitted the Judæans to return to their own
country, rebuild Jerusalem, and restore the Temple.
Together with Babylon, all the provinces conquered
by Nebuchadnezzar, westward from the Euphrates
to the Mediterranean sea, and southward from Lebanon and Phœnicia to the confines of Egypt, fell
beneath Cyrus's sway.   Judæa, therefore, belonged
to the Persian kingdom.   But what reasons could
have been given to the mighty conqueror for the bold
request that he should allow the Judæans to have an
independent government?   And what could have
induced Cyrus to grant this request so generously ?
Was it the gratification of a momentary caprice, or
indifference to a strip of land, of which he probably
knew not even the name, and of whose historical
importance he was certainly ignorant?   Or had one
of the Judæan eunuchs, as was afterwards related,
described to the Persian conqueror how a Judæan
prophet had foretold his victories, and had prophesied that he would let a banished people return
to their home?   Or was he so deeply impressed by
the faith of the Judæans, for which they had borne so
much suffering, that he was induced to favour its
adherents?   The true reason for his decision is unknown, but Cyrus not only granted permission to the
Judæans to return to their country, but he restored
to the exiles the sacred vessels belonging to the
Temple, which Nebuchadnezzar had seized and placed
as trophies of victory in the temple of Bel.

As soon as the permission for the return had been
granted, a group of men undertook the organisation
of the returning exiles.   The leadership was entrusted
to two men of about the same age, and of distinguished
lineage, Zerubbabel, called in Babylon Sheshbazzar,

the son of Shealtiel, and grandson of king Jehoiachin, hence a scion of David's house, and Joshua, the son of Jehozedek, and grandson of the last high-priest Seraiah. They were joined by ten men, so that they formed a company of twelve, representing, to a certain extent, the twelve tribes. Cyrus invested Zerubbabel with the office of governor or regent (Pechah) of the province which the exiles were to re-occupy, the appointment being in reality a stepping-stone to royal honours. All the Judæans who were to return to their own country addressed themselves to these leaders.

Compared with those who had once gone out of Egypt, the number of those who now returned was very small, but still there were more than might have been expected, 42,360 men, women and children, counting from the age of twelve. The greater number belonged to the two tribes of Judah and Benjamin; there were a few Aaronides and Levites. Besides, the march was joined by some from the other tribes and from other nations, who acknowledged the God of Israel (Gerim, Proselytes).

The joy of those who were preparing for the exodus from Babylon and the return to the Holy Land was overpowering. To be permitted to tread the soil of their own country, and to rebuild and restore the sanctuary seemed a sweet dream to them. The event caused great sensation amongst other nations; it was discussed, and considered as a miracle, which the God of Israel had wrought on behalf of His people. A poem faithfully reproduces the sentiments that inspired the exiles:

"When the Lord turned again the captivity of Zion, we were like them that dream.

"Then was our mouth filled with laughter, and our tongue with singing; then said they among the nations, The Lord hath done great things for them.

"The Lord hath done great things for us, whereof we are glad." (Ps. cxxvi.)

As the patriots were preparing to make use of

their freedom to return to Jerusalem, one of their poets, in Psalm xxiv., bade them reflect whether they were worthy of this boon. For only the righteous and those who sought the Lord were to assemble upon God's ground. But who would dare take on himself the right to pronounce judgment?

CHAPTER XIX.

THE RETURN FROM BABYLON, THE NEW COMMUNITY IN JUDÆA, EZRA AND NEHEMIAH.

The Journey to Jerusalem—The Samaritans—Commencement of the Rebuilding of the Temple—Interruption of the Work—Darius —Haggai and Zechariah—Completion of the Temple—Contest between Zerubbabel and Joshua—Intermarriage with Heathens —The Judæans in Babylonia—Ezra visits Jerusalem—Dissolution of the Heathen Marriages—The Book of Ruth—Attacks by Sanballat—Nehemiah—His Arrival in Jerusalem—Fortification of the Capital—Sanballat's Intrigues against Nehemiah—Enslavement of the Poor—Nehemiah's Protest—Repopulation of the Capital— The Genealogies—The Reading of the Law—The Feast of Tabernacles—The Great Assembly—The Consecration—Departure of Nehemiah—Action of Eliashib—Withholding the Tithes —Malachi, the Last of the Prophets—Nehemiah's Second Visit to Jerusalem—His measures.

537—420 B. C. E.

AFTER forty-nine years of exile, in the same month (Nisan) in which their ancestors had departed from Egypt some eight or nine centuries before, the Judæans now left the land of Babylonia. It was the spring of the year (537) when they marched forth to take possession of their dearly-beloved home, of the much longed-for Jerusalem. It was a significant moment, carrying thousands of years in its bosom. Not like trembling slaves, just freed from their chains, did they go forth, but full of gladness, their hearts beating high with lofty hopes and swelling with enthusiasm. Singers, with stringed instruments and cymbals, accompanied them on their way, and they uttered new songs of praise, beginning and ending with the words:

"Give thanks unto the Lord, for He is good, for His mercy endureth for ever."

Those Judæans who remained in Babylonia—and they were not a few—rich merchants and landed proprietors—evinced their sympathy for their brethren by escorting them part of the way, and by presenting them with rich gifts for the new buildings in their own country.   Cyrus sent an escort of a thousand mounted soldiers to defend the Judæans from the attacks of predatory tribes upon the way, and also to ensure their being able to take possession of Judæa.   The prophecy but lately spoken was now to be realised:

"In joy shall ye depart, and in peace shall ye be led home." (ISAIAH lv. 12.)

In peace and in safety the travellers completed the six hundred miles from Babylonia to Judæa, protected by the Persian escort.   The exodus from Babylonia, unlike the one from Egypt, has left no reminiscences; it seemed needless to record the various halting-places, as, in all probability, no noteworthy incident occurred on the way.

"God led them by the right path, and brought them to the place of their longing."   (PSALM cvii. 7, 30.)

When the travellers approached the land of their passionate desire, after a march of four or five months, their joy must have been overwhelming.   The prophecies that had been uttered, the hopes they had cherished, the visions they had indulged in were realised. Meanwhile their happiness was not undimmed.   The Holy City, the chief object of their longing, was desolate.   A great part of the country was inhabited by strangers; in the north were the Samaritans, or Cuthæans, in the south, the Idumæans.   But these races were soon obliged to give place to the descendants of Judah, who, with the tribe of Benjamin, returned to their ancient dwelling-places.   The beginning of the new Judæan commonwealth was indeed humble and small.   The people could not occupy the whole of the country which had once constituted the kingdom of Judah.   A population of 40,000 was not numerous enough to settle a large territory. The colony was thus compelled to group itself round the capital at Jerusalem. This concentration of forces was, in some respects, advantageous, inasmuch as the whole population, being thus brought near to the capital, could take part in all its affairs. But, though the extremely confined territory of the new colony, and the small number of members in the community were calculated to depress the lofty hopes that their prophets in Babylonia had awakened, and fill the arrivals with gloom, unexpected circumstances arose to reinspire them with energy. From many countries to the east, west, south, and north, from Egypt, Phœnicia, and even from the Greek coasts and islands, whither they had gone of their own free will or had been sold as slaves, Judæan exiles streamed back to crowd like children around their resurrected mother, Jerusalem. These new Jewish arrivals were accompanied by large numbers of strangers, both "great and small," illustrious and obscure, who collected round them. They were received with rejoicing, for they all acknowledged the God of Israel, and were ready to follow His laws. These new proselytes not only added strength to the young community, but also inspired the settlers with greater self-reliance, who, with their own eyes, saw the words of the prophets fulfilled.

At the approach of the seventh month, in which, according to law and custom, various festivals occur, the elders of the families among all classes in Jerusalem assembled, and, marching under the command of their two leaders, the governor Zerubbabel and the high-priest Joshua, they proceeded to perform the first act of reconstruction—they erected an altar of stone. This altar was to be the nucleus of the Temple, the building of which was, for the present, impossible.

While the altar was dedicated with joyous and solemn ceremonies, the leaders were making preparations for the erection of this great and important edifice, which was to be the spiritual centre of the new commonwealth. The rich gifts which they had brought with them enabled them to hire labourers and artisans, and, as in the days of King Solomon, cedar trees were procured from Lebanon; stone was brought from the mountains, and after enough had been quarried and shaped, steps were taken to lay the foundations of the Sanctuary. Not only Zerubbabel and Joshua, but also the heads of families, and a large number of the people were present at this ceremony, which was performed with great solemnity. The Aaronides again appeared in their priestly garments, sounding their trumpets; the Levites of the house of Asaph chanted songs of praise, thanking the Lord whose mercy endures for ever; and the people burst forth into a loud transport of joy. Yet there mingled with the jubilant notes the voice of regret that the new Temple was smaller and less magnificent than the old.

Jerusalem, so long mourned and wept over, began to rise from her ruins. The joyful enthusiasm called forth by the re-building of the city was, however, soon to be damped; the honeymoon of the young commonwealth waned rapidly, and anxious cares began to disturb its peace. Close to the boundaries of Judæa lived the mixed tribe of Samaritans or Cuthæans. These people had in part accepted the doctrines taught them by an Israelitish priest at Bethel, but they had also retained many of their own idolatrous practices. Quite unexpectedly, some of the Samaritan chiefs came to Jerusalem, with the request that they might be allowed to help in re-building the Temple, and also that they be received into the Judæan community. This seemed so important a matter to the Judæans, that a council was convoked to discuss the subject. The decision was against the Samaritans. Zerubbabel informed the Samaritan chiefs that their people neither would nor could be permitted to join in the re-building of the Temple. This decision was of great import for the entire future of the new commonwealth. From that day the Samaritans began to develop a hostile spirit against the Judæans, which seemed to show that they had been less anxious to take part in the temple-service than to injure the community and to obstruct the re-building of the Temple. On the one hand, they tried to make those Judæans with whom they came in contact lukewarm towards the project of building the Temple, and, on the other, they persuaded Persian officials to interfere with its execution, so that the work ceased for fully fifteen years. Again the Jews found themselves suffering evils similar to those which they had experienced after their first entry into Canaan. The neighbouring tribes envied them their strip of land, —on all sides they encountered hostility. They were powerless to defend themselves, for they lacked the means for carrying on war.

In these untoward circumstances the members of the community gave their first thought to themselves, and not to the general welfare. The richest and most distinguished persons built large and splendid houses, using, it seems, the building materials designed for the Temple. Bad harvests, drought, and hail disappointed the hopes of the agriculturists. Much was sown and little reaped; there was hardly sufficient to satisfy the hunger of the people, and to clothe them, and "whoever earned money put it into a purse full of holes." Still worse was the moral deterioration caused by this physical distress. The people did not relapse into idolatry; they were radically cured of that evil; but selfishness gained the upper hand, and the members of the community often treated one another most harshly. This state of things contrasted sadly with the new-born hopes of the people, and damped the courage of some even of the nobler spirits.

The death of Cambyses (521) and the succession

of Darius, the third Persian king (521–485), led to a change favourable to Judæa. Darius, differing from his predecessor, was, like Cyrus, a mild and generous ruler. An apocryphal tradition tells us that Zerubbabel went to Persia and there found favour in the eyes of Darius on account of his wisdom. As a proof of his favour, Darius sent Zerubbabel back to Jerusalem with permission to rebuild the Temple at the king's expense. But, in reality, the task was not so easily accomplished. When the death of Cambyses put an end to the wars which had been disturbing the peace of neighbouring provinces, Zerubbabel and Joshua intended doubtless to proceed with the building. But the people, that is to say, the heads of families, exclaimed: "The time has not yet come to rebuild the Temple." It required the fiery enthusiasm of the prophets Haggai and Zechariah to set the work in motion. These prophets harangued the people frequently during several successive months (from Elul to Kislev 520), encouraging and rebuking and, at the same time, prophesying a glorious future At last they roused the people to recommence their work. In four years (519–516) the building was finished, and the Sanctuary was consecrated, amid great rejoicing, just before the Feast of Passover.

Seventy years had passed since the destruction of the Temple of Solomon by Nebuchadnezzar, when the entire nation assembled at Jerusalem for the consecration of the second Temple, henceforth to be the centre and loadstar of the community. Three weeks later the Feast of Passover was celebrated by the whole congregation of Israel, as well as by those who had in sincerity joined its faith. However, although the young community was imbued with the spirit of the Law and of the prophets, and although the people anxiously strove for unity, there arose differences of opinion not easy to smooth over, and liable to produce friction. The people had two leaders: Zerubbabel, of the royal house of David, and Joshua, the high-priest, of Aaronide descent. One was at the head of the secular, the other, of the spiritual power. It was impossible to prevent the one power from occasionally encroaching upon the jurisdiction of the other. A circumstance in Zerubbabel's favour was the people's allegiance to the royal house of David, and he was a living reminder of a glorious past, and a pledge for an equally brilliant future, as foretold by the prophets. The prophet Haggai had called him the chosen favourite of God, His precious Signet-ring. But this in itself was an obstacle. It gave the enemies of the Judæans the opportunity to charge the community with the purpose of proclaiming him as the successor of David to the throne. On the other hand, the prophet Zechariah had proclaimed that the high-priest Joshua should wear the crown, ascend the throne, and effect the realisation of the Messianic hopes. In this way he gave the preference to the high-priest, producing tension and divisions. Peace could only be restored by the withdrawal of one of the two leaders: their joint rule could not fail to be the occasion of excitement and irritation. A choice had to be made between the two, and Zerubbabel was obliged to give way, the high-priest being more necessary than the king's son. It is probable that Zerubbabel left Jerusalem and returned to Babylon, and thus the house of David retreated into the background.

After Zerubbabel's withdrawal, the leadership of the community was put into the hands of the high-priest Joshua, and after his death into those of his son Jehoiakim. Was this change a desirable one? True, no evil is reported of the first two high-priests, nor do they seem to have done anything specially praiseworthy towards uplifting and strengthening the community. The supreme command over the people does not seem to have been given to the high-priest, but to have been vested in a governor or administrator (Pechah), appointed over Judæa either by the Persian kings or by the satraps of Syria and Phœnicia. This official does not appear to have lived in Jerusalem, but to have visited the city from time to time, where, seated on a throne, he heard and decided disputes, but not infrequently rather caused dissensions and aggravated existing bad feelings, in order to raise complaints against the Judæans. For, as some Judæans nourished the hope, held out by the prophets, that Judah might yet become a mighty power, to whom kings and nations would bow, the suspicion that the people were plotting a defection from Persia was not removed with the retirement of Zerubbabel. Accusations on that ground commenced directly after the death of Darius, in the reign of his successor, Xerxes (Ahasuerus, 485–464). The enemies of the Judæans, particularly the Samaritans, did not fail to draw the governor's attention to the disloyalty of the Judæans, and thus caused unfavourable decrees to be issued against them at court. Added to this, the successive governors tried to oppress the landowners by excessive demands. The position of the Judæans in their own country, which they had entered with such buoyant hope, grew worse and worse in the second and third generations.

In order to free themselves, on the one side at least, from these constant troubles, the most distinguished Judæan families took a step that led in the end to mischievous complications. They approached the neighbouring peoples, or received the advances of the latter, in a friendly spirit, and as a proof of the sincerity of their feelings, they began to form connections by marriage. As in the days when the Israelites first occupied the land of Canaan, in the time of the Judges, the necessity for friendly intercourse with neighbouring tribes led to mixed marriages, so during the second occupation of Palestine by the Israelites, similar relations led to similar results. But the circumstances

differed, inasmuch as the Canaanites, Hittites, and
other original dwellers in the land practised abominable idolatry, and infected the Israelites with their
vicious customs, while the new neighbours of the
Judæan commonwealth, particularly the Samaritans,
had given up idolatry, and were longing earnestly
and sincerely to take part in the divine service at Jerusalem. They were, in fact, proselytes to the religion
of Judæa; and were they always to be sternly
repulsed? The principal Judæan families determined to admit the foreigners into the community,
and the high-priest, of that time, either Jehoiakim
or his son Eliashib, was ready to carry these wishes
into effect. Marriages were therefore contracted
with the Samaritans and other neighbouring people,
and even some members of the family of the high-
priest formed such connections.

The leader of the Samaritans at that time was
Sanballat, a man of undaunted strength of will and
energy of action, clever, cunning, audacious and per-
severing. He was an honest proselyte, who believed
in the God of Israel, and desired to worship in His
Temple; but he determined, as it were, to take by
storm the kingdom of Heaven. If he were not
allowed a part in it voluntarily, he would seize it by
force or by cunning.

But not only the Samaritans, also the Moabites
and the Ammonites were among the people anxious to maintain friendly relations with the Judæans.
Tobiah, the leader of the Ammonites, was doubly
allied to Judæan families. He had married a daughter
of the noble family of Arach, and a distinguished
man, Meshullam, the son of Berechiah, had given his
daughter in marriage to Tobiah's son. But mixed
marriages with Ammonites and Moabites were spe-
cifically prohibited by the Law, until the tenth generation after conversion.

The leaders of the Judæan community, the high-
priest and others, who were not quite prepared to

violate the law, doubtless eased their consciences by some mild interpretation of the text. But not all were so pliable. A small number of the noblest families had kept themselves pure from mixed marriages, which they deplored as an infraction of the law and as a cause of deterioration of the Judæan race. More especially the singers, who were the cultivators and preservers of the Hebrew language and of its ancient, venerated literature, kept themselves clear of mixed marriages. They may have raised their voices against the pliability of their co-religionists, against this blending with the stranger, but, as they were in the minority, their voices were not heeded. But when a leading authority appeared in Jerusalem from the land of exile, the minority cried out loudly against what had taken place, and a complete reaction followed, from which disagreeable complications necessarily ensued.

It is but rarely the case that historical reformations are made with such suddenness that the contemporary witnesses of the change are themselves affected by it, and are reminded at every turn that old things have passed away, and that a new order has arisen. In general the people who live during an important historical crisis are not aware of the changes occurring in themselves, in their opinions, their customs, and even in their language. Such a change, imperceptible at first, but complete and effectual, took place in the Judæans during the first half of the fifth century. This transformation did not proceed from the community of Judæa, but from those who remained in the land of exile; it soon, however, penetrated to the mother-country, and impressed its stamp upon her.

In Babylonia, the land of the captivity, there had remained a considerable number of the descendants of the exiles, either from material considerations, or for other reasons. But they had been touched by the unbounded enthusiasm of their co-religionists, and they had shown their sympathy by rich gifts and fervent wishes. The Babylonian Judæans laid great stress upon maintaining their own peculiarities and their own nationality. They kept themselves apart from all their neighbours, married only members of their own nation, and were guided by the inherited Law as their rule of life. Their absence from the mother-country served but to make them obey the more strictly the behests of the Law, which thus formed the bond of union that bound them together as members of one community. They could not offer sacrifices, nor keep the observances connected with the Temple service, but all the more scrupulously did they cling to those customs that were independent of the sanctuary, such as the Sabbath, the Holy Days, circumcision, and the dietary laws. Without doubt they had houses of prayer, where they assembled at stated times. Even the Hebrew tongue they cultivated to such an extent at least that it could not become a strange language to them, although they employed the Aramaic or Chaldaic in their intercourse with their neighbours and among themselves. They obtained a correct knowledge of the Hebrew from the scriptures which they had brought with them, and which they made the object of careful study. They gave particular heed to that portion of these scriptures to which, heretofore, little or only occasional attention had been paid, namely the Pentateuch, with its code of laws and observances. During the time of the captivity, the writings of the prophets had chiefly been read, because they possessed the greater power of consolation. But as soon as it was necessary to give reality to the hopes and sentiments which the prophets roused and nursed, and to stamp life with a peculiar religious and moral character, the Book of the Law was sought out and consulted. The Torah, or Law, so long neglected in its own home, now received due honour and attention on a foreign soil. The Sabbath, for instance, was kept far less strictly in Jerusalem than in the Babylonian-Persian community. This ardour for the exact carrying out of the Law and its observances found its embodiment in Ezra, who was the cause of that momentous change in the history of the nation which endowed it with a new character. He did not stand alone, however, but found many who were in accord with him.

This man, who was the creator of the new religious and social order of things, seemed, by reason of his birth, specially called to kindle unwonted enthusiasm for the Torah; for he was a descendant of high-priests. It was his ancestor Hilkiah who had found the book of Deuteronomy in the Temple, and, by giving it to King Josiah, brought about great changes. He was also the great-grandson of that high-priest, Seraiah, who was slain by the command of Nebuchadnezzar, and whose sons carried the Book of the Law to Babylon. Ezra had, therefore, the opportunity of occupying himself with the study of this book. But he gave it more attention than either his ancestors or his relatives had done. After he had read and studied it with care, he determined that it should not remain a mere dead letter, but that it should be realised in the daily life of the people. He began by applying it to himself, carefully obeying the laws regarding dress, diet, and particularly those bearing upon the festivals. Then he assumed the post of teacher to his brethren; he expounded the Law, brought it nearer to their understanding, and urged them to follow it in every detail. The Law was to him an emanation of the Deity, revealed to Israel by Moses; he placed it higher, infinitely higher, than the writings of the other prophets, for the first prophet and law-giver was the greatest of all. Convinced of the Divine inspiration of the Law of Moses, and glowing with zeal to make its authority paramount, he found no difficulty in infusing his own belief and his own zeal into the Judæans of Babylonia and Persia. He soon acquired an honoured position amongst them, his word gained authority, and he was more eagerly listened to than the prophets had been. Ezra may have known that the Law was but negligently followed in Judæa, and he thought that, by visiting that country, he might awaken in his fellow-believers a perception of its true worth. Or he may have been impelled by a strong impulse to settle in Jerusalem, in order to comply with the religious duties pertaining to the Temple and the sacrifices. As soon as he had determined upon the journey, he invited those members of his faith who might be willing to join him. The number that responded was a considerable one, including over 1,600 men, together with women and children, of distinguished families, who had remained in the land of captivity. Amongst them was a great-grandson of Zerubbabel, a descendant of the house of David. Those who could not take part in the emigration gave Ezra rich gifts of gold, silver, and precious vessels for the Temple. It is an astonishing circumstance that King Artaxerxes (Longimanus) also sent presents for the sanctuary in Jerusalem, and that many Persian nobles followed his example. It is evident that at this time the God of Israel had many earnest worshippers amongst the Persians and other nations, and that from "sunrise to sunset His name was glorified and reverenced among the peoples." Not only did Artaxerxes grant Ezra permission to journey with his brethren to Jerusalem, but he also gave him letters to the satraps of the countries through which he passed, and to the authorities of Palestine. He would also have sent an escort to protect the travellers from hostile tribes, but Ezra declined it, assuring the king that the God to whom they prayed would protect them.

The arrival of Ezra with his numerous companions must have caused much surprise in Jerusalem (459–458). They came provided with letters from the king, laden with gifts, and imbued with enthusiastic feelings. Without doubt, Ezra's name as an instructor and expounder of the Law had already penetrated as far as Judæa, and he was received with every mark of consideration. No sooner had he assumed the ecclesiastical function, than the men of strong convictions who condemned intermarriages with the surrounding peoples brought their complaints before him. Ezra was dismayed when he heard of these occurrences. The representatives of the people and of the Temple had, in contempt of the Law, connected themselves with the heathen. Ezra held this to be a terrible sin. For the Judæan or Israelitish race was in his eyes a holy one, and suffered desecration by mingling with foreign tribes, even though they had abjured idolatry. According to Ezra's reading of the Law, heathens who had accepted the Law might enter into the community; they were, however, not to be put upon a footing of equality with Israelites by birth, but were to live as a group apart. The Gibeonites, in former days the slaves of the Temple, who had accepted the Israelitish doctrines more than a thousand years before, were still kept distinct, and were not permitted to intermarry with the Israelites; and in Ezra's opinion, the new proselytes from the heathen nations were to be treated in a similar manner. The connection with them ought not to be of an intimate character; such was Ezra's opinion, based, not on ancestral pride, but on religious and social grounds. Some dim presentiment warned him that the reception of proselytes or half-proselytes into the community—of such elements as had not been tried and proved in the furnace of suffering, as the seed of Abraham had been—would give undue preponderance to the foreign element, and would destroy all the moral and religious advantages which the Judæans had acquired. This fear seized upon his whole soul; he rent his clothes, plucked the hair from his head and beard, and refusing all nourishment, sat until the afternoon, sorrowing and desolate because of this danger which threatened the life of the nation. Then he entered the court of the Temple, and throwing himself upon his knees, he poured forth a confession full of deep contrition, lamenting that the people had not improved by their bitter experiences, but had relapsed into their former evil ways. This keenly-felt penitence, uttered amid sobs and tears, powerfully affected the bystanders, men, women and children, who had been attracted by the sight of the kneeling sage. They burst into passionate weeping, as if their tears could obliterate the dark pages in their history. One of those present, Shechaniah, touched by sympathy, uttered a weighty suggestion: " Let us make a covenant to put away all the strange wives, and such as are born of them." Ezra seized upon the idea at once; he rose and demanded that the heads of the families, who were present on that occasion, swear before the Sanctuary, and by their God, that they would repudiate their foreign wives and their children. That moment was to decide the fate of the Judæan people. Ezra, and those who thought as he did, raised a wall of separation between the Judæans and the rest of the world. But this exclusiveness was not strictly in agreement with the letter of the Law, for Ezra himself, with all his knowledge, was not able to point out any passage in the Torah, implying that mixed marriages were forbidden when contracted with those who acknowledged the God of Israel.

Such members of the community as, in a moment of enthusiasm, had taken this vow, were now obliged to keep it. With bleeding hearts they separated themselves from their wives, the daughters of neighbouring tribes, and repudiated their own children. The sons and relations of the high-priest were forced to set an example to the rest. Those of the elders of the people who were the most ardent disciples of the Law formed a kind of senate. They issued a proclamation throughout Judah, commanding all who had been guilty of contracting mixed marriages, to appear within three days in Jerusalem, on pain of excommunication. A special court of enquiry was instituted for this one question. Ezra himself selected the members who were to make the needful researches to discover whether the Judæans had really repudiated their wives. So thoroughly was the work of this court of enquiry carried on, that all those who were living in the towns of Judæa separated themselves from their wives and children, as the inhabitants of Jerusalem had done. Still there were some who, influenced by family feelings, made some show of resistance.

The severity with which this separation from all neighbouring tribes, Samaritans and others, had been effected led naturally to grave results. The raising of this wall of separation by Ezra and his party against those who were truly anxious to belong to the community caused much bitterness. They were to be separated for ever from the Deity they had chosen, and excluded from the Sanctuary in Jerusalem to which they had belonged. The decree of separation sent to them changed their friendly relations towards the Judæans to enmity. Hatred which arises from despised affection is always most bitter. The grief of the wives deserted by their husbands, and the sight of children disowned by their fathers could not fail to awaken and to increase the animosity of those who were closely related to them. Unfortunately for the Judæans, Sanballat and Tobiah, two forceful and able men, were at the head of the party excluded from the community. Tobiah, the Ammonite, was related to several Judæan families. They had both accepted the Judæan teaching, and now they were both repulsed. Henceforth they assumed a hostile position towards Judæa; they were determined, by force or by intrigues, to maintain their right of worshipping in the Temple and sharing in the faith of Israel. At first they probably took steps to restore their peaceful intercourse with the Judæans, and urged them to revoke their cruel decision. In Jerusalem, as well as in the provinces, there was a party which strongly disapproved of Ezra's stern action. The well-informed among these differed with Ezra on the illegality of marriages with women who had, at all events outwardly, accepted the Law. Was Ezra's severity justifiable? Did not the historical records contain many instances of Israelites having married foreign wives? Such questions must have been constantly put at that time.

A charming literary production, written probably at that date, echoes the opinions of the gentler members of the community. The poetical author of the Book of Ruth relates, apparently without a purpose, the simple idyllic story of a distinguished family of Bethlehem which had migrated to Moab, where the two sons married Moabitish wives; but he touches at the same time upon the burning question of the day. Ruth, the Moabitess, the widow of one of the sons, is described as saying to her mother-in-law, " Entreat me not to leave thee, or to return from following after thee: for whither thou goest I will go, and where thou lodgest I will lodge: thy people shall be my people, and thy God, my God: where thou diest will I die, and there will I be buried; the Lord do so to me, and more also, if aught but death part thee and me." And the Moabitess kept her word faithfully. Upon her marriage with Boaz, the people exclaim: " The Lord make the woman that is come into thine house like Rachel and like Leah, which two did build the house of Israel." The son born to Ruth was the ancestor of David, the great king of Israel. The several incidents of this exquisite story are most delicately and artistically developed. But the author meant to place two facts before his readers, namely, that the royal house of Israel sprang from a Moabitess, and that the Moabitess, after having connected herself closely with the people of Israel and acknowledged their God, gave proof of such virtues as grace a daughter of Israel: chastity, refinement of feeling, and cheerful self-sacrifice. The reference in this tale to the all-absorbing question of the day was too pointed to be passed over unnoticed. Among those unfortunate wives who had been, or who were to be repudiated by their husbands, might there not be some who resembled Ruth? And the children born of foreign women, but having Judæan fathers,—were they to be looked down upon as heathens? If so, then not even the house of David, the royal family, whose ancestor had married a Moabitess, belonged to the Judæan nation!

But none of these representations were of avail. Ezra and the reigning senate in Jerusalem insisted sternly upon the exclusion from the community of all people who could not claim Judaic descent, and who were, therefore, not of " the holy seed." The failure of all conciliatory measures resulted in hostilities, which lasted for several years (457–444). Ezra was, unfortunately, not a man of action; he could only pray and arouse the feelings of others, but he could not prevent many Judæan families from secretly abetting his opponents. On the other hand, Sanballat and his followers were men of decided character, full of virulent hatred towards their adversaries, and they took every opportunity of harassing their enemies. At last they even attacked Jerusalem.

What could have inspired them with such boldness, knowing as they did that Ezra was favoured by the Persian court, and that Judæan favourites possessed great influence over Artaxerxes? Did they, perhaps, count upon the fickleness of the Persian king? Or were they emboldened by the revolt of Megabyzus, satrap of Syria, to whom both Judæa and Samaria were subordinate? And while the Syrians vanquished one Persian army after another, were they encouraged to commence hostilities on their own account and to aim at the heart of their enemy? But, no matter what it was that induced Sanballat and his followers to take warlike steps against Jerusalem, they were entirely successful. They were able to raise an army, whilst their opponents in Jerusalem were mostly ignorant of the use of arms. The result was that Sanballat and his followers made breaches in the walls of the city, burned the wooden gates, and destroyed many of the buildings, so that Jerusalem again resembled a heap of ruins. They, however, spared the Temple, for it was sacred in their eyes also; but it was nevertheless abandoned, and most of the inhabitants, having lost the protection of the city walls, left Jerusalem, and established themselves in other places, wherever they could find shelter.

The Aaronides and Levites, deprived of their income from gifts and tithes, left the Temple and sought other means of subsistence. The commonwealth of Judæa, after barely a century's existence, was passing through sad times. Many noble families made peace with their neighbours, took back their repudiated wives, and contracted new connections with the stranger. They pledged themselves by a reciprocal vow of constancy to respect these new ties. For a short time it seemed as if Ezra's great work were frustrated, and as if the life of the commonwealth were endangered. How little was lacking to effect a complete dissolution!

The religious zeal kindled by Ezra was, however, too ardent to be so easily extinguished. Some of the Judæans, maddened by grief at the destruction and desolation of Jerusalem, hurried to the Persian court to seek aid. They counted upon the aid of Nehemiah, the Judæan cup-bearer of Artaxerxes. Hananiah, a kinsman of Nehemiah, and an eye-witness of the sad occurrences, gave him a harrowing description of the sad state of the Judæans and of the fall of the Holy City. Nehemiah was struck with dismay at these tidings. He belonged to the zealous party in

Persia, and was, if possible, more exacting than Ezra. Jerusalem, the Holy City, had always presented itself to his imagination as especially protected by God, and surrounded by a fiery wall, which permitted no enemy to approach with impunity. And now it had been humbled and put to shame, like any earthly city. But he did not allow his grief to master him; he was a man of vigorous action and great ingenuity. At court he had learned the art of governing, and knew that a firm will could control both men and circumstances. He instantly determined upon going to Jerusalem, to put an end to this miserable state of things. But how could he leave Persia, seeing that he was bound to the court by his office? The great favour that Artaxerxes always showed him chained him to the place, and removed all prospects of a journey to Jerusalem.

Full of tact, Nehemiah refrained from entreating Artaxerxes to give him leave to start upon his journey, until a favourable opportunity should occur. But the grief that was gnawing at his heart soon showed itself in his face, and clouded his usually cheerful countenance. One day, when he was pouring out wine for the king and queen, his sad expression attracted their attention, and Artaxerxes questioned him as to its cause. He instantly made use of the opportunity, and answered, "Why should not my countenance be sad, when the city, the place of my father's sepulchre, lieth waste, and the gates thereof are consumed with fire?" He then expressed his earnest desire to the king. Artaxerxes at once granted his every wish, permitting him to undertake the journey, to rebuild the city walls, and to restore order in the unsettled State. The king gave him letters to the various royal officials, directing them to lay no obstacles in his way, and to deliver to him timber for building purposes. He even appointed an escort of soldiers to accompany Nehemiah, and named him governor of Judæa. The king made but one condition, namely, that his stay in Jerusalem was not to be permanent, but that he must return to the Persian court at the expiration of a given time.

A new chapter in the history of the commonwealth commences with Nehemiah's journey to Jerusalem, or rather this event completes the chapter begun by Ezra. Nehemiah left the city of Susa with a large retinue, accompanied by an armed escort. As he travelled through the former dominion of the Ten Tribes, he presented his credentials to the various officials, and thus Sanballat and Tobiah were apprised of the object of his journey, and naturally felt that they were on the eve of a war. It was disappointing to them to see that a Judæan, the favourite of Artaxerxes, one who would devote himself to the protection of his persecuted brethren, had been appointed governor of the land.

When Nehemiah arrived in Jerusalem, he secluded himself for three days. He wished, first of all, to become acquainted with the scene of his duties, and with the people with whom he would come into contact. Meanwhile, he devoted himself to the establishment of a kind of court, for he possessed a princely fortune, and he made a princely display. He kept the reason of his sojourn secret, and did not even divulge it to the leaders of the community, for he did not trust them. One night he rode forth secretly to examine the extent of the injury sustained by the walls, and to devise a plan for repairing them. He then summoned the leading men of the community, and announced, to their amazement, that King Artaxerxes had given him complete power, not only to rebuild the walls, but to govern the country, and that it was his intention to wipe out the disgrace and misery that had fallen upon them. He found the assembled Judæans ready, heart and soul, to help him. Even those who had intermarried with the strangers, and were on a friendly footing with them, evinced their approbation. But Nehemiah had imposed a heavy task upon himself. He was to reorganise a disjointed commonwealth, whose members, through fear, weakness, selfishness, and a variety of motives, had not sufficient courage to face real danger. Nehemiah's first care was to fortify Jerusalem; he himself superintended the work of building the fortifications, and made it less arduous by a careful division of labour. But the task of rebuilding was necessarily a tedious one. The repudiated proselytes, headed by Sanballat and Tobiah, whose every hope of alliance with the Judæans had been cut off by Nehemiah's words, "Ye shall have no portion, no right, no memorial in Jerusalem," manifested as much zeal in disturbing the work, as he did in accomplishing it. They artfully tried to make the Persians suspect Nehemiah of treason, and of having conceived the ambitious scheme of making himself king of Judæa. Then they endeavoured to discourage the workmen by deriding them, and by declaring that the walls were weak enough for a jackal to break through them. When the walls had risen to half their destined height, the enemy secretly determined upon an attack. Nehemiah, however, had armed some of his own people, as well as some of the leading members of the community, and placed them on guard. Every workman had a sword girt upon his side; every carrier bore his burden in one hand and his weapon in the other. In order to hasten the completion of the walls, the work was carried on continuously from dawn to sunset, while a part of the force stood on guard, day and night, within the city. Nehemiah himself was always on the spot, accompanied by a trumpeter. At the blast of his trumpet, the scattered workingmen were instructed to assemble around him.

But instead of resuming the attack upon the walls, Sanballat busied himself with devising intrigues against Nehemiah. He gave out that as soon as Jerusalem was fortified, Nehemiah would cause himself to be proclaimed king of the Judæans, and would revolt against Persia. The more credulous began to feel alarmed, and to think of withdrawing from the work, so as not to be regarded by the Persians in the light of accomplices. Furthermore, the heads of those families who were related to the enemy were in active treasonable correspondence with Tobiah. But all these intrigues were of no avail, and Nehemiah completed the work with such energy as to compel the unwilling admiration of the foe. From that time Sanballat and his followers appear to have given up their fruitless attempts to annoy Nehemiah, or to hinder his work.

But within the community itself, Nehemiah had to fight no less severe a battle. Many of the most distinguished families who were apparently loyal, not only entertained secret communications with the enemy, but also were oppressing the poor in a most heartless manner. When, in the days of scarcity, the poor borrowed money from the rich in order to pay taxes to the king, or obtained grain for their own consumption, they had given as security their fields, their vineyards, their olive groves, their own houses, and sometimes even their own children; and if the debts were not repaid, the creditors would retain the land as their own property, and keep the children as slaves. As the complaints of those who had been thus cruelly treated rose louder and more frequently to the ears of Nehemiah, he determined to call these heartless men to account. He summoned a great assembly, and spoke severely against this form of heartlessness, which was specially condemned by the Law.

" We, the Judæans of Persia," he exclaimed, " have, according to the best of our ability, redeemed our brethren, the Judæans that were sold unto the heathen. And will ye even sell your brethren so that they will be sold again unto us? " he added ironically. So deep was the respect enjoyed by Nehemiah, so

weighty his opinion, and so ready were even the great
and the rich to hearken to the admonitions of the
Law, that they promised forthwith not only to release
the enslaved persons, but also to restore the houses,
fields and gardens to their owners and to cancel their
debts.   Nehemiah made use of this favourable mood
to administer an oath to the rich, binding them to
carry out their promises.

This was an important victory gained by the Law,
through its representative, Nehemiah, over selfishness.
He indeed excelled all others in the example of self-
denial which he set to them.   Not only did he
refuse the revenues due to him, but he advanced money
and grain to the poor, and if they were unable to
repay it, he relinquished the loans.   His relatives and
servants behaved in the same generous and unselfish
manner.

In this way Nehemiah overcame all difficulties, and
brought order into the community.   The people hung
upon his words, and the leading men yielded him
obedience.   But when the walls of the city were rebuilt
and the gates replaced, it appeared that the Levitical
gatekeepers, and in fact all the Levites were missing.
They had migrated after the destruction of the city,
into other parts of the country, because they received
no tithes.   Altogether, the city was but thinly populated, and many houses were destroyed or deserted.
Jerusalem therefore had to be peopled again, and
the Temple furnished anew with attendants.

It seems that Nehemiah caused a proclamation to
be issued to all those who had deserted Jerusalem in
the time of its insecurity, and to those who had originally settled in the provincial towns, inviting them
to take up their permanent abode in the capital.
Many of the noble families at once offered to do this.
But as the number of these was too small to repeople
Jerusalem, it was determined that the tenth part
of the population of the rural districts be called
upon to migrate to the capital, and that they be

selected by lot. Nehemiah, however, did not think
every one worthy of becoming a citizen of the Holy
City, least of all those born of mixed marriages.
He carefully went through the register of Judæans
who had returned from Babylonia, examining the
pedigree of each separate family. He conducted the
matter with great rigour. Three families, consisting
of six hundred and forty-two persons, who could not
prove that they were descended from Israelites, were
not admitted, and three Aaronide families, who were
unable to produce the record of their lineage, were
temporarily deprived of the dignity of the priesthood.

As soon as Nehemiah had fortified Jerusalem, and
found means to provide a population for it, giving
the community a centre and forming the people
into a compact body, he sought to breathe into this
body the living soul of the Law. But for this purpose he required the aid of the scribes. Ezra, who
had been thrown into the background by the great
activity of Nehemiah, now re-appeared upon the
scene. On the festival celebrated on the first day of
the seventh month, Ezra assembled all the people,
even those who dwelt in the country. " They gathered themselves together as one man into the open
place which is before the Water-gate in Jerusalem."
Here an elevated stand of wood was erected, upon
which Ezra stood to read the Law. Everything
was calculated to produce a solemn and imposing
effect. The assembly was a numerous one; it
consisted not only of men, but also of women, and
of children who were old enough to understand
what they heard. When Ezra unrolled the Book of
the Law, all the people arose, and when he opened
the services by reciting a blessing, they lifted up
their hands, responding, in a loud voice, Amen.
Then Ezra began to read a section of the Torah
with an impressive voice, and all present listened
intently. There were some, indeed, unable to follow
the reading, but the Levites added a short and clear

explanation, so that even the most ignorant could understand. The people were deeply moved by what they heard, and burst into tears. Probably they heard for the first time that portion of Deuteronomy in which are announced the fearful punishments consequent upon disregard of the Law; and the conscience-stricken people felt themselves unworthy of the Divine love, and were overwhelmed with grief. Some time elapsed before Ezra and the priests could restore tranquillity to the excited multitude. But at length they were quieted, and proceeded to celebrate the festival in an exalted mood. It was the first time that the people had taken the Book of the Law into their hearts, and that they had felt it to be an integral part of their existence, and themselves to be its guardians.

The change which had begun during the time of the Babylonian exile was now completed. What the prophets had commenced, the scribes ended. It is remarkable that so important an assembly should have met, not in the Temple itself, but in its immediate vicinity, and that the high-priest should have taken no part in it. The Sanctuary, with the altar and the vessels for sacrifice, was, to a certain extent, thrown into the background. Though a priest, Ezra unconsciously led the way to a separation between the Law and the Temple, that is to say, the subordination of the priesthood to the Scriptures. The people became so enamoured of the Law, for which they had cared but little previously, that they were anxious to hear more of it. The heads of the community, whose ancestors had obstinately rejected the teaching of the prophets, and had seemed utterly incapable of reformation, repaired to Ezra, on the next day, and begged of him to continue his reading of the Pentateuch. Ezra thereupon read the portion concerning the festivals that were to be celebrated during the seventh month. In obedience to the injunctions contained therein, the leading men caused heralds to

proclaim that all the people were to bring branches
of olive trees, myrtles, and palms from the neighbouring mountains, for the erection of huts or booths.
The people executed this order with alacrity, and celebrated the Festival of Tabernacles in a brighter mood
than they had ever done before. During the eight
days of this festival a portion of the Law was read
daily, and from that time the reading of the Law
became a permanent feature in the Divine service.
Ezra and Nehemiah were anxious to avail themselves
of this religious fervour in a way to influence those
who still lived with their foreign wives to repudiate
them of their own free will. For this purpose a penitential day was appointed. All the people appeared
fasting, in mourning, and with ashes upon their heads.
The portion of the Law forbidding intermarriage with
Ammonites and Moabites was read and expounded.
Then a general acknowledgment of sin, in the name
of the people, was recited by the Levites. The desired effect was obtained; the Israelites separated
from their foreign wives, and sundered their connection with the Samaritans and all of doubtful descent.

Ezra and Nehemiah now induced them to make a
solemn covenant that they would in future respect the
teaching of the Law, and not relapse into their old
errors and shortcomings. From that day forward the
whole community was to live according to the Law of
Moses. Men, women, and children, the Temple servants, and even the proselytes, who clung faithfully to
the Judæans, took the oath that was required of them.
They swore not to give their daughters in marriage to
foreigners, and not to marry daughters of foreign
tribes. This matter was looked upon by Ezra and
Nehemiah as one of peculiar importance, and, therefore, the first place was given to it. They also swore to
observe the Sabbath and the holidays, to let the fields
lie fallow every seventh year, and, during that year,
to remit all debts. Furthermore, every individual
who had attained his majority was to pay annually

one-third of a shekel towards the maintenance of the Temple, to bring the first produce of the fields and the orchards to the Sanctuary, to provide wood for the altar, and to contribute the tithes for the maintenance of the priests and the Levites.

The obligations assumed by the people were inscribed upon a scroll, which was signed by the heads of the families, and sealed.   Nehemiah's name stood first upon the list, followed by the signatures of about eighty-five prominent men.   According to one account, one hundred and twenty names were subscribed.   This important gathering of Judæans was called the Great Assembly (Keneseth ha-gedolah). Nehemiah had indeed accomplished much in a short time.   He had not only restored the decayed commonwealth, and assured its stability by fortifying the capital, but he had also endowed the people with the Law, and had induced them to live in harmony with its requirements.

Nehemiah appears designedly to have contrived the gathering of large popular assemblies in order to make a deep impression on those present.   He convened the people a second time, to consecrate the walls of the city.   As at the former ceremony, women and children were in the congregation. In order to impart a joyful character to these solemnities, he invited a number of Levites who were skilled in music and song to come to Jerusalem. Two divisions of the people, starting from the same point, marched, in opposite directions, round the walls, and met in the Temple.   At the head of each division, a choir of Levites sang hymns of praise, each being accompanied by a band of musicians. Ezra followed one choir, and Nehemiah the other, each of them heading an immense concourse of people.   In this way the two processions passed slowly round the walls of the city.   Far into the distance sounded the joyous notes of the cymbals, harps and trumpets, whilst the songs bursting from the lips of the Levites echoed again and again from the mountains. After the day of mourning and atone-ment followed a day of universal joy and gladness. This festival of dedication, we are told, lasted eight days, and took place two years and four months after the commencement of Nehemiah's work (442).

In order to establish the community to whom he had given new life, Nehemiah sought able, worthy and conscientious officers. It seems that it was he who divided the country into small districts (Pelech), and placed over each an officer to manage its affairs and to maintain order. To the north of the Temple, Nehemiah built a citadel, which he fortified strongly, so that in case of necessity it might prove a defence for the Sanctuary; this fortress was called Birah. He appointed a faithful and God-fearing man, Hana-niah, as commander. His colleague in the work of regeneration, the scribe Ezra, was made guardian of the Temple. The chief thing he had in view was the full restoration of the Temple-worship. If the sacri-ficial services were not again to be interrupted, pro-vision must be made for the maintenance of the Aaronides and Levites. The landowners had, it is true, bound themselves most solemnly to pay the imposts to the former, and the tithes to the latter, but Nehemiah, not content with the mere promise, required the delivery of the supplies to be constantly watched. The Levites were sent into the country at harvest time, to collect their tithes, and to bring them back to Jerusalem. In order to secure an even distribution of the tithes, a tenth of which was in turn due to the Aaronides, and of those gifts which belonged to the latter exclusively, Nehemiah built large granaries, where all contributions were to be stored, and whither those entitled thereto were to repair to have their due shares assigned to them by special officials.

Not only did Nehemiah provide for the re-popula-tion of the deserted city of Jerusalem, but he also sought means to furnish the new inhabitants with suitable dwellings. At his own cost he erected houses for the poorest of the nation, and tried to supply all wants in the same way. Thus he built up a new state, upon which he laid but one obligation, that it should abide strictly by the Law. For twelve years he was governor of Judah (from 444 to 432); he was then obliged to return to the court of Artaxerxes, where he still enjoyed great favour with the king. He departed with the hope that the work he had accomplished might be blessed with lasting security and glory.

But no sooner had Nehemiah left than a counter-current set in that could be traced to the influence of the high-priest Eliashib. The first retrograde step was taken when Eliashib held friendly communication with the Samaritans and the offspring of mixed marriages, in violation of the decision of the Great Assembly. As an earnest of this friendship, a member of the priest's household, named Manasseh, married Nicaso, a daughter of Sanballat. Others, who had been secretly dissatisfied with Nehemiah's strict line of separation, now followed the example of the priestly house. An entire change took place. Tobiah, the second great enemy of Nehemiah, was allowed to return unmolested to Jerusalem, and a large court in the outer Temple was actually assigned to him.

This sudden change, which allowed what had recently been strictly forbidden, produced a general disintegration. The people as a body was so outraged by the actions of the high-priest and his party that it openly showed its contempt for them. The landowners, moreover, left off paying tithes and imposts for the support of the priesthood, and thus the innocent Levites also lost their income. To avoid starvation they were compelled to leave the Temple and the city. The contributions for the sacrificial services ceased, and to prevent the altar from being entirely neglected, the priests in charge offered up diseased, lame, blind or unsightly animals. Many Judæans were so utterly disgusted at the behaviour of the priests that they turned their backs upon the Sanctuary and the affairs of the community, pursuing their own interests, and this not rarely at the expense of justice, and of all that they had sworn to uphold. When this class grew prosperous, the truly pious people, who were struggling with poverty, became utterly confused in their ideas of right and wrong, and exclaimed: "It is vain to serve God: and what profit is it that we have kept His charge?" "Every one that doeth evil is good in the sight of the Lord, and He delighteth in them."

But worse than all else was the discord which prevailed in the Judæan community, and which even divided families. What could be pronounced right and lawful? The father did not agree with the son; the one accepted the stern practice, the other the lax, and thus disputes arose in each household. To counteract these lamentable occurrences, the more pious, who would not allow themselves to be shaken in their convictions, met and discussed a plan of action. They turned with hope and longing towards Nehemiah, who was still at the court of Artaxerxes. If he would but return to Jerusalem, he could, with one blow, put an end to this miserable state of confusion, and restore peace, unity, and strength to the city. At this auspicious moment a God-fearing man suddenly appeared on the scene. He belonged to the party that was incensed at the behaviour of the high-priest and his followers, and he undertook to chastise the wicked, and to reanimate the waning courage of the good. This man, full of vigour, and moved by the prophetic spirit, was Malachi, the last of the prophets. Worthily did he close the long list of godly men who had succeeded each other for four centuries. Malachi announced to his dejected and despairing brethren the speedy arrival of the

Messenger of the Covenant, whom many delighted in, and who would bring better days with him. The prophet counselled the people not to omit paying the tithes on account of the evil-doing of some of the priests, but to bring them all, as in former days, into the store-houses.

Malachi, like the early prophets, proclaimed that in the distant future a great and awful day would dawn, when the difference between the pious and the wicked would be made clear. Before the coming of that last day God would send His prophet Elijah, and he would reconcile the father to the son. He bade them remember and take to heart the Law of Moses, with its statutes and its judgments, which had been given to them on Mount Horeb. With these words, the voice of prophecy was hushed.

The written Law, which had been made accessible to many through the zeal of Ezra, and which had found a body of exponents, rendered the continuance of prophetic utterances unnecessary. The scribe took the place of the seer, and the reading of the Law, either to large assemblies or in houses of prayer, was substituted for prophetic revelation.

Did Nehemiah at the court of Persia have any idea of the yearning for his presence that existed at this very moment in Jerusalem? Had he any knowledge that Malachi's belief in better days rested upon the hope of his return? It is impossible to say, but, at all events, he suddenly re-appeared in Jerusalem, between the years 430 and 424, having again obtained the king's permission to return to his spiritual home, and soon after his arrival he became, in the words of the prophet, " like a refiner's fire, and like the fuller's lye." He cleansed the community of its impure elements. He began by expelling the Ammonite Tobiah from the place which had been given to him by his priestly relative, Eliashib, and by dismissing the latter from his office. He then assembled the heads of the community, and reproached them bitterly with having caused the Levites to desert the Temple, by neglecting to collect the tithes. A summons from Nehemiah was enough to induce the landed proprietors to perform their neglected duties, and to cause the Levites to return to their service in the Temple. The charge of the collected tithes and their just distribution he placed under the care of four conscientious Judæans, —some of his devoted followers. He restored the divine service to its former solemnity, and dismissed the unworthy priests. A most important work in the eyes of Nehemiah was the dissolution of the mixed marriages which had again been contracted. Here he came in direct conflict with the high-priestly house. Manasseh, a son or relation of the high-priest Joiada refused to separate himself from his Samaritan wife, Nicaso, Sanballat's daughter, and Nehemiah possessed sufficient firmness to banish him from the country. Many other Aaronides and Judæans who would not obey Nehemiah's commands were also sent into exile. After peace and order had been restored in the capital, Nehemiah tried to abolish the abuses which had found their way into the provinces. Wherever Judæans lived in close proximity to foreign tribes, such as the Ashdodites, Ammonites, Moabites, or Samaritans, mixed marriages had led to almost entire ignorance of the Hebrew tongue, for the children of these marriages generally spoke the language of their mothers. This aroused Nehemiah's anger, and stimulated his energy. He remonstrated with the Judæan fathers, he even cursed them, and finally caused the refractory to be punished. By such persistent activity he was able to accomplish the dissolution of the mixed marriages, and the preservation of the Hebrew tongue.

Nehemiah next introduced the strict observance of the Sabbath, which had been but negligently observed hitherto. The Law had certainly forbidden all labour on that day, but it had not defined what really was to be considered as labour.   At all events, the Judæ-ans who lived in the provinces were ignorant on that point, for on the Sabbath they pressed the wine, loaded their beasts of burden with corn, grapes, figs, and drove them to market into the city of Jerusalem.   As soon as Nehemiah discovered that the Sabbath was treated like an ordinary week-day, he assembled the country people, and explained that they were sinning against God's Law, and they listened to him, and followed his injunctions.   But he had a more diffi-cult task in abolishing an old-established custom. Tyrian merchants were in the habit of appearing in Jerusalem on the Sabbath-day, bringing fish fresh from the sea, and they found ready customers.   But Nehemiah ordered that henceforth all the gates should be closed on the Sabbath eve, so that no mer-chant could enter the city.   These ordinances were strictly enforced, and from that time the Sabbath was rigorously observed.

The strict observance of the Law, enjoined by Ezra, was insisted upon by Nehemiah; he built the wall of separation between Judæans and Gentiles so securely, that it was impossible to break through it.   The Judæans who were discontented with this separation and the severity of the Law were obliged to leave the Judæan community, and form a sect of their own.   Nehemiah himself probably lived to see the formation of the first sect among Jews, and as he himself might virtually be held responsible for it, he thought it necessary to justify his proceedings, and to set forth his own meritorious part in raising the fallen community.   He composed a kind of memoir, in which he related what he had achieved in his first and second visits to Jerusalem.   At intervals he inserted the prayer that God would remember him for what he had done for the people and for his services in behalf of the Sanctuary and its preserva-tion.   It was a kind of self-justification written in his old age, and his name has remained eternally in the remembrance of a grateful people. To him and to Ezra, the creators of that spiritual current which has since attained an irresistible force in the Jewish world, grateful posterity has attributed all beneficial institutions whose origin is unknown.

CHAPTER XX.

THE SOPHERIC AGE.

Enmity of the Samaritans against the Judæans—The Temple on Mount Gerizim—The High-Priest Manasseh—The mixed language of the Samaritans—Their veneration for the Law of Moses—Judaism loses its national meaning—The Jubilee and Sabbatical Year—Almsgiving—The Council of Seventy—The Assyrian Characters—The Schools and the Sopherim—Observance of the Ceremonies—The Prayers—The Future Life—The Judæans under Artaxerxes II. and III.—Their Banishment to the Caspian Sea—Johanan and Joshua contend for the office of High-Priest—Bagoas—The Writings of the Period—The Greeks and Macedonians—Alexander the Great and the Judæans—Judæa accounted a Province of Cœlesyria—Struggles between Alexander's Successors—Capture of Jerusalem by Ptolemy—Judæa added to the Lagidean-Egyptian Kingdom—The Judæan Colonies in Egypt and Syria and the Greek Colonies in Palestine.

420—300 B. C. E.

HATRED which arises from rejected love is stronger and more vehement than enmity resulting from inexplicable antipathy, jealousy, or disagreement. Sanballat, as well as his Samaritan followers and companions, out of preference for the God of Israel, had struggled to be received into the Judæan community. The virulence of their enmity against Nehemiah, who had raised the commonwealth from its declining state, was in reality an impetuous offer of love, by which they hoped to secure an intimate connection with Judæa. But as they were repulsed again and again, this yearning love changed into burning hatred. When Sanballat, who thought he had attained his aim by his connection with the high-priest's family, learned of the insult shown him in the banishment of his son-in-law Manasseh, because of that priest's marriage with his daughter, the measure of his wrath was full. He cunningly conceived the plan of disorganising the Judæan community, by the help of its own members. What if he were to raise a temple to the God of Israel, to contest the supremacy of the one at Jerusalem? There were among his followers priests of the descendants of Aaron, who could legally conduct the service, as prescribed in the Torah, in the projected sanctuary. The dignity of high-priest could fitly be assumed by his son-in-law Manasseh, and the other Aaronides who had been expelled from the Temple could officiate with him. Everything appeared favourable to his design. Both his desire of worshipping the God of Israel, and his ambition to be at the head of a separate community, could easily be satisfied at the same time.

On the summit of the fruitful Mount Gerizim, at the foot of the city of Shechem, in the very heart of the land of Palestine, Sanballat built his Temple, probably after the death of Artaxerxes (about 420).

The Aaronides who had been expelled from Jerusalem, and who were well versed in all the tenets of the Law, had selected this site because they knew that, according to the Book of Deuteronomy, the blessings were to be pronounced upon the followers of the Law of Moses from that mount. But the Samaritans gave to the old words a new interpretation. They called, and still call to this day, Mount Gerizim "the Mount of Blessings," as if blessing and salvation proceeded from the mount itself. Even the town of Shechem they called "Blessing" (Mabrachta). Sanballat, or the priests of this temple of Gerizim, declared that the mixed race of the Samaritans were not descendants of the exiles placed in that country by an Assyrian king, but that, on the contrary, they were true Israelites, a remnant of the Ten Tribes, or of the tribes of Joseph and Ephraim. There may indeed have been amongst them some descendants of the families who, after the destruction of the kingdom of the Ten Tribes, clung to Samaria; but that the numerous Cuthæans who

gathered round Sanballat, together with the Ammonites and the Arabians, were descendants of
Joseph and Ephraim and Israelites, was one of those
ingenious and audacious fictions which, by their very
exaggeration, stagger even those who are thoroughly
convinced of their falsehood. Their language, however, betrayed their mixed origin; it was a con-
glomeration of Aramaic and other foreign elements,
so that it is to this day impossible to define its origin
satisfactorily.

But the venture was a successful one. The Samaritans had their temple, around which they
gathered; they had priests from the house of Aaron;
they impudently opposed their Hargerizim, as they
called their holy mount, to Mount Moriah; they
interpreted the Book of the Law to suit themselves,
making it appear that God had designed Mount
Gerizim as a site for a sanctuary, and they proudly
called themselves Israelites. Sanballat and his followers, intent upon attracting a great many Judæans
to their community, tempted them with the offer of
houses and land, and in every way helped to support
them. Those who had been guilty of crime in Judæa
or Jerusalem, and feared punishment were received
with open arms by the Samaritans. Out of such
elements a new semi-Judæan community or sect was
formed. Their home was in the somewhat limited
district of Samaria, the centre of which was either the
city that gave its name to the province, or the town of
Shechem. The members of the new community became an active, vigorous, intelligent people, as if
Sanballat, the founder, had infused his spirit into
them. In spite of its diminutive size, this sect has
continued until the present day. The existence of
the Samaritans, as a community, may really be considered a signal victory of the Judæan faith, for it
was their religion alone that kept so mixed a people
together; it became the loadstar of their lives, and to
it they remained faithful, in spite of adversity and

disaster. The Samaritans treated the Torah, brought to them by exiled priests, with as much reverence as the Judæans did, and regulated their religious and social life according to its requirements. But, in spite of this community of essential principles, the Judæans were not delighted with this accession to the ranks of their faith. This first Judæan sect caused them as much sorrow as those which, at a later period, grew up among them. The Samaritans were not only their most bitter foes, but actually denied to them the right of existence as a community. They declared that they alone were the descendants of Israel, disputing the sanctity of Jerusalem and its Temple, and affirming that everything established by the Judæan people was a mere counterfeit of the old Israelitish customs. The Samaritans were ever on the alert to introduce into their own country such improvements as were carried into effect in Judæa, though, had it been in their power, they would have destroyed the nation which was their model. On the part of the Judæans, the hatred against their Samaritan neighbours was equally great. They spoke of them as "the foolish people who lived in Shechem." The enmity between Jerusalem and Samaria that existed in the time of the two kingdoms blazed up anew; it no longer bore a political, but a religious character, and was therefore the more violent and intense.

The existence of the Samaritan sect had, however, a stimulating effect upon the Judæans: as the latter continually came into collision with their opponents, and were obliged to listen to doctrines in the highest degree distasteful to them, they were forced to a careful study of the essence of their own belief. The Samaritans helped them to acquire self-knowledge. What was it that distinguished them, not only from the heathen world, but also from those neighbours who worshipped the one God, and acknowledged as authoritative the same Revelation?

It was the thought that they possessed a peculiar creed, and the conception of "Judaism" gained clearness in their minds. Judaism no longer meant a *nationality*, but a religious *conviction*. The name " Judæan" lost its racial meaning, and was applied to any adherent of the Jewish faith, be he a descendant of Judah or Benjamin, an Aaronide or a Levite. The two fundamental principles of this faith were the acknowledgment of the one God, and of the Torah, in which God reveals himself through the mediation of Moses.

The reverence and love with which the Sacred Book came to be regarded after the days of Ezra and Nehemiah were as deep as had been the general indifference to it in earlier times. "A wise man trusts the Law, and the Law is as true to him as the words of the truth-giving Urim and Thummim." The Torah was looked upon as the quintessence of all wisdom, and was honoured as such. Hebrew poetry, still full of life, glorified it with enthusiastic praise. It followed naturally that the Torah became the fundamental law of the little state or commonwealth of Judah. Before a Judæan undertook or desisted from any action, he would ask whether his course was in conformity with the Law. Slavery ceased to exist; even if a Judæan wished to sell himself as a slave he could not find a buyer. Therefore the year of Jubilee, intended as a year of release of slaves, became a superfluous institution. On the other hand, the Sabbatical year was strictly kept. The debts of the poor were then cancelled, and the fields lay fallow. Probably the Judæan favourites at the Persian court had already demanded that, in the Sabbatical year, the taxes upon the produce of the fields be remitted. The poor were looked after with great solicitude, for the Pentateuch demanded that there should be no needy in the land. Alms-giving was looked upon in this new order of things as the exercise of the highest virtue. In every town,

members of the Judæan community were appointed
to devote themselves to the care of the poor. The
constant denunciations by the prophets and psalmists
of the hard-heartedness displayed towards the poor
and the helpless were no longer justified. Justice
was admirably administered, and so conscientiously
was the law executed that the Judæan law-officers
might have been held up as models to the rest of
the world. Twice a week, on Mondays and Thurs-
days, the market days, public courts of justice were
held in all large towns.

It was most natural that, as the life of the community was regulated according to the commands of
the Torah, the spiritual leaders of the people should
devise a supreme court of justice, possessing the
power to make and interpret laws. They were
but carrying out the words of Deuteronomy, in
which was enjoined the establishment of a superior
court of justice, where a final decision in doubtful
cases could be given. The question now arose as
to the number of members to constitute this court.
Seventy elders had shared with Moses the great
burden of his duties, the representatives of the
seventy chief families of the children of Israel. It
was therefore decided that the supreme tribunal
and high court of justice should number seventy
elders. This peculiar institution, which lasted until
the destruction of the Judæan commonwealth, which
became the strict guardian of the Law, and at times
rose to great political importance, was doubtless
called into life at this period. At no other time
could it have arisen. Thus the great assembly which
Nehemiah had originally summoned, merely for the
purpose of accepting the obligations of the Torah,
developed into a permanent council for settling all
religious and social questions. The seventy members
of the supreme council were probably chosen from
various great families. The high-priest, whether
he was worthy of the dignity or not, was placed

at their head. The president was called "father of the tribunal" (Ab Beth-din). As soon as the council was formed, it proceeded to carry into effect what Ezra and Nehemiah had begun, namely, the application of Judaism or the Law to the life and customs of the people. This supreme council brought about a complete revolution.

All the changes which we notice two hundred years later in the Judæan commonwealth were its work; the new regulations which tradition assigns to Ezra, and which were known under the name of Sopheric regulations (Dibre Sopherim) were the creations of this body. It laid a sure foundation for the edifice that was to last thousands of years. During this period it was that regular readings from the Law were instituted; on every Sabbath and on every Holy Day a portion from the Pentateuch was to be read to the assembled congregation. Twice a week, when the country people came from the villages to market in the neighbouring towns, or to appeal at the courts of justice, some verses of the Pentateuch, however few, were to be read publicly. At first only the learned did the public reading, but gradually as it came to be looked upon as a great honour to belong to the learned class, every one was anxious to be called upon to do duty as a reader. But the characters in which the Torah was written were an obstacle in the way of overcoming illiteracy. The text of the Torah was written in an antique script with Phœnician or old Babylonian characters, which could be deciphered only by practised scribes. For the Judæans in Persia, even more than for the Judæans in Palestine, the Torah was a book with seven seals. It was therefore necessary to transform the old-fashioned characters of the Hebrew Scriptures (Khetab Ibrith) into others, which were familiar to the inhabitants of the land between the Euphrates and the Tigris, and which the Judæans of Palestine and of the Persian provinces used also for the ordinary purposes of every-day life. In order to distinguish it from the old writing, the new style was called the Assyrian (Khetab Ashurith), because it had arisen in one of the Assyrian provinces. The Samaritans, animated by a spirit of contradiction, retained the old Hebrew characters for their Pentateuch, only in order to be able to reproach their opponents with having introduced a forbidden innovation and falsified the Torah. Until the present day, their holy writ exists in these old-fashioned characters, and it is a closed book even to most of their priests.

Owing to the regular reading of the Law and to its accessibility, there arose among the Judæans an intellectual activity which gradually gave a peculiar character to the whole nation. The Torah became their spiritual and intellectual property, and their own inner sanctuary. At this time there sprang up another important institution, namely, schools for young men, where the text of the Law was taught, and love for its teachings and principles cultivated. The intellectual leaders of the people continually enjoined on the rising generation, "Bring up a great many disciples." And what they enjoined so strenuously on others they themselves must have zealously laboured to perform. One of these religious schools (Beth-Waad) was established in Jerusalem. The teachers were called scribes (Sopherim) or wise men; the disciples, pupils of the wise (Talmide Chachamim). The wise men or scribes had a twofold activity: on the one hand, to explain the Torah, and on the other, to make the laws applicable both to individual and communal life. This supplementary interpretation was called "exposition" (Midrash); it was not arbitrary, but rested upon certain rules laid down for the proper interpretation of the Law. The supreme council and the houses of learning worked together, and one completed the other.

The result was a most important mental development, which impressed upon the descendants of the patriarchs a new characteristic so strongly as to make it seem second nature in them : the impulse to investigate, to interpret, and to tax their ingenuity in order to discover some new and hidden meaning either in the word or the substance. The supreme council, the source of these institutions and this new movement, did not confine itself to the interpretation of the existing laws, and to their application to daily life, but it also drew up its own code of laws, which were to regulate, to stimulate and to strengthen the religious and social life of the people. There was an old maxim of great repute in Judæa: "Make a fence about the Law." By this maxim the teacher of the Law was directed to forbid certain things in themselves permissible, which, however, touched too closely upon the forbidden points, or might be confounded with them. This method of guarding against any possible infringement of the Law, by means of a " fence " (Seyag), had its justification in the careless, unsettled habits of those early days. It was absolutely necessary that the mass of the people, who were wholly uneducated, should accustom themselves to the performance of the precepts and duties enjoined by the Law.

An entire set of laws, made for the purpose of preventing the violation of the commands of the Torah, belong to the Sopheric age. For instance, the degrees of relationship considered unlawful for matrimony were increased in number; to prevent the violation of chastity, men were forbidden to hold private interviews with married women in solitary places. The loose way in which the Sabbath was observed in Nehemiah's age was replaced by an extraordinarily rigid observance of the Sabbath. In order to prevent any possible violation of the Sabbath or of the festival days, all work was to cease before sunset on the preceding evening, and an official was appointed to proclaim, by the blast of a horn, the proper hour for repose. But the Sabbath day and the festivals were intended to create a feeling of both devotion and exaltation in the observers of the Law, and to banish from their memory the cares and the troubles of the working days. It was partly to express this that it became a custom in those days to drink a goblet of wine at the coming in and at the going out of the festivals, and to pronounce a blessing upon them, at their commencement declaring that these days are holy, and sanctified by God (Kiddush), and at their close, that they have a peculiar significance in contradistinction to the working days (Habdalah). By laws such as these, which were not permitted to remain a dead letter, the Sabbath acquired a holy character.

The first evening of the Paschal feast, falling in the spring time, was also invested with peculiar importance. It was intended to arouse every year and to keep alive a grateful remembrance of the deliverance from Egypt, and the consciousness of being in possession of precious freedom. It became either a law or a custom to drink four glasses of wine upon this festival of rejoicing, and even the poorest managed to obtain the draught "that rejoices the heart." On the eve of the Passover, the members of each family, with their most intimate friends, gathered round the table, not to indulge in a luxurious meal, but to thank and praise the God of their fathers; they ate bitter herbs, broke unleavened bread, tasted some of the paschal lamb in commemoration of their freedom, and drank the four goblets of wine to celebrate this bright festival with a cheerful heart. Gradually the custom arose for several families to celebrate the Paschal eve in common, the whole assembly (Chaburah) to partake of the lamb, amid the singing of psalms. The Paschal eve became in time a delightful family festival.

The prayers prescribed on Sopheric authority had no hard and fast form, but the line of thought which they were to contain was, in general, laid down. The form of prayer used in the Temple became the model of the services in all prayer-houses, or houses of gathering (Beth-ha-Keneseth).   Divine service was performed at early morning in a court of the Temple, and commenced with one or more specially selected psalms of praise and thanksgiving.   At the conclusion of the psalms, the whole congregation exclaimed : "Praise be to the God of Israel, who alone doeth wonders, and praised be the glory of His name for ever and ever, and may His glory fill the whole earth"; upon which followed a prayer of thanksgiving for the light of the sun, which God had given to the whole world, and for the light of the Law, which He had given to Israel.   This was suc-ceeded by the reading of several portions from the Torah, the Ten Commandments and the Schema : " Hear, O Israel, the Lord our God, the Lord is one," to which the whole congregation responded : "Blessed be the name of the glory of His kingdom for ever and ever."   The principal prayer, the Tephillah, was composed of six short parts : a thanksgiving that God had chosen the children of Israel as His ser-vants ; an acknowledgment of the Divine Power, as shown in nature, by the life-giving rain, and as manifested in man, by the future resurrection of the dead ; an acknowledgment of the holiness of God ; a supplication for the accomplishment of all prayers and for the acceptance of sacrifice; a thanksgiving for the preservation of life, and finally a prayer for peace, following the blessing of the priest.   In the afternoon and evening, the congregation assembled again for prayer, but the service was short, as the Psalms and chapters of the Law were omitted.

On the Sabbath and festive days, the morning service was not materially different, except that a particular prayer was interpolated, in which special mention was made of the sanctity of the day, and a longer portion from the Torah was read at its close. In time a portion from the prophets, especially a chapter bearing upon the character of the day, was read. The opposition in which the Judæans stood to the Samaritans prompted this reading from the prophets. For the Samaritans who denied the sanctity of the Temple and of Jerusalem, rejected the prophetical writings, because they contained constant allusions to the holy city and the chosen sanctuary. So much the more necessary did it appear to the upholders of Judaism to publish these writings. In consequence of this regulation, the words of the prophets who had but rarely been listened to while they lived, were now read in every Judæan house of prayer, and though they were but partially understood by the greater number of the congregation, nevertheless they became mighty levers to arouse the enthusiasm of the nation. As these readings ended the morning service, they were called "the conclusion" (Haphtarah). It thus became necessary to make an authoritative collection of the prophetic writings, and to decide which of the books were to be excluded, and which adopted. This choice was probably made by the legislative body of the Sopheric age. The collection embraced the four historical books, Joshua, Judges, Samuel, and Kings, which were called the Earlier Prophets; then came three books, great in interest, bearing the names of the prophets Isaiah, Jeremiah, and Ezekiel; and lastly the twelve minor prophets, Hosea, Amos, Joel, Obadiah, Jonah, Micah, Nahum, Habakkuk, Zephaniah, Haggai, Zachariah, and Malachi, these twelve, in conjunction with the three greater, being styled the Later Prophets. These works were all recognised as Holy Writ, but were placed next to the Torah, as of secondary degree of holiness.

In this way the divine service of the Sopheric age was constructed; it was simple and edifying; it contained nothing superfluous, disturbing or wearying, and it embodied the thought and spirit of those time-honoured treasures, the writings of the prophets and the psalmists. It contained only one foreign element, the belief in the resurrection of the dead on the last day. With this exception, everything was taken from the pure spring of the earliest teachings.

The inhabitants of the country towns introduced in their own congregations an exact copy of the divine service as it was conducted in Jerusalem. They needed no urging to this by mandatory enactments. Thus in each town, houses of prayer (Synagogues, Moäde-El) were established, in which was introduced the order of prayer which is the groundwork of the divine service of the present day. Besides the prayers, sacrifices were offered up according to the letter of the Law. These two forms of divine service were blended into one; they completed and helped one another. The spiritual service adapted itself to the sacrificial ceremonies; three times during the day, whilst the priests were offering up their sacrifices, the congregations assembled in the prayer-houses, whereas on the Sabbath and on festivals, when special sacrifices were offered up in the Temple (Korban Mussaph), the congregation assembled four times for prayer (Tephillath Mussaph). But even the sacrificial service could not shut out the living word; it had to grow, as it were, more spiritual, and it became customary to sing the Psalms at intervals between the offerings, because of the great influence which this sublime poetry possessed.

There was, however, one very prominent feature connected with the Temple and the sacrifices, which was opposed to the essentially spiritual tendency of the prophetic and psalmistic poetry. It was that which related to the laws concerning purity and impurity. The law of the Torah had certainly given very precise regulations on these matters; an unclean person could not bring offerings, or approach the sanctuary, or even taste consecrated food. There were many degrees of uncleanness, and the Law prescribed how unclean persons might be purified. The last act of purification always consisted in bathing in fresh running water. These laws would never have attained such far-reaching importance, involving every station in life, had it not been for the sojourn of the Judæans, during so many centuries, among the Persians, whose much more stringent purification laws were rigorously observed. The statutes concerning uncleanness, according to the Iranian Avesta of the Persians, whose priests were the Magi, were extremely strict, and the means adopted for purification revolting. Dwelling among the Magi, the Judæans absorbed much from them. The striking resemblance of many of their laws and customs to their own could not escape their observation, and they yielded to Magian influences.

The fundamental conception of the Deity, as of one incorporeal perfect God, was so firmly implanted in the heart of every Judæan, that no one would allow himself to be influenced by the conception of the Persian god of light, Ahura-Mazda (Ormuzd), however spiritual that conception might be. Their seers, full of penetration, speedily divined the error of the Iranian doctrine of acknowledging two great rival powers, the god of light and goodness, and the god of darkness and sin, Angro-Mainyus (Ahriman). They contrasted that doctrine with their own belief, that the God of Israel created light and darkness, good and evil. They denied that the world and mankind are being perpetually drawn in divergent directions by two rival powers, but are destined to live in peace and unity. The spiritual leaders of the Judæans in the Sopheric age expressed this belief in one of the morning prayers: "God is the Creator of light and of darkness, He has created peace and has made everything." But although the Judæans resisted any alteration in their conception of the Deity, still they could not prevent many of the ideas and customs of the Persians from gaining ground among the nation. They imagined that they were adding to the glory of God if, in imitation of the Iranians, they surrounded Him with myriads of obedient servants. The "messengers of God," whom we read of in the Bible as executors of His will, became, after the pattern of Persian beliefs, heavenly creatures, endowed with peculiar characteristics and special individuality. The people pictured to themselves the divine throne, surrounded by a countless throng of heavenly beings, or angels, awaiting a sign to do the bidding of God. "Thousand times thousands served Him, and myriad times myriads stood before Him." Like the Persians, the Judæans called the angels "the holy watchers" (Irin-Kadishin). The angels received special names: Michael, Gabriel, the strong, Raphael, the healer, Uriel or Suriel, Matatoron, and others.

As fancy had changed the Yazatas into angels, and given them a Hebrew character and Hebrew names, so also were the bad spirits, or Daevas, introduced among the Judæans. Satan was a copy of Angro-Mainyus, but he was not placed in juxtaposition to the God of Israel, for this would have been a denial of the fundamental doctrine of the Judæans. He, the Holy One, high and mighty and all-powerful, could not be limited, or in any way interfered with by one of His own creatures. Still the first step had been taken, and, in the course of time, Satan grew to be as strong and powerful as his Iranian prototype, and was endowed with a kingdom of darkness of his own, where he reigned as the supreme power of evil. Once created in the image of Angro-Mainyus, Satan had to be surrounded with a host of attendant demons or evil spirits (Shedim, Mazikim, Malache Chabalah). One demon, as an adaptation of the Iranian Daeva names, was called Ashmodai; another, by the name of Samael, was at the head of a troop of persecuting spirits. The angel of death (Malach-ham Maveth), lying in ambush, ready to seize upon men's lives, was endowed with a thousand eyes. These creatures of the imagination soon took firm hold of the Jewish

soul, and with them many usages resembling those
of the Magi invaded the Jewish religion ; and especially the laws of purification became more and
more rigorous.

It was also at that time that a new doctrine of retribution was developed in Judaism. According to the
Iranian doctrine, the universe was divided into two
great kingdoms ; that of light and that of darkness ;
the pure, or worshippers of Ahura-Mazda, were admitted into the region of light (Paradise), and the
wicked, the followers of Angro-Mainyus, into the kingdom of darkness (Hell). After death, the soul remained during three days near the body it had ten-
anted ; then, according to its life upon earth, it was
taken by the Yazatas to Paradise, or was drawn down
by the Daevas into Hell. This idea of retribution
after death was adopted by the Judæans. The Garden of Eden (Gan-Eden), where the story of the
Creation, placed the first human beings whilst they
lived in a state of innocence, was transformed into
Paradise, and the Valley of Hinnom (Ge-Hinnom), in
which, since the days of Ahaz, sacrifices of children
had been offered up, gave the name to the newly-
created Hell. In what way could such new beliefs
have crept into the Judæan faith? That is as little
capable of demonstration as is the way in which the
pores of the skin become impregnated with a disease
that has poisoned the atmosphere. However, these
views about angels and Satan with his attendant
spirits, about Paradise and Hell, never obtained the
dignity of fixed dogmas which it would be mortal
sin to doubt, but on the contrary, during that time,
and in all future time, their adoption or repudiation was
left to the discretion of the individual. Only one
belief emanating from the Iranian religion, that of
the resurrection of the dead, became part of the
spiritual life of the Judæans, until it grew at last
to be a binding dogma. The Magi had taught
and insisted upon this doctrine. They believed

that the re-awakening of the dead would take place at a future day, when Ahura-Mazda will have conquered and destroyed his rival, when the god of darkness will have to give up the bodies of the "pure men" which he has stolen. The Judaism of the Sopheric age adopted this hopeful and inspiriting doctrine all the more readily, as allusions to it existed in the Judaic writings. The prophets had constantly made references to the day of the last judgment, and the scribes, inferring that the resurrection of the dead was meant, made it an article of faith amongst their people, and in the daily prayer, praise was rendered to God for awakening the dead to life.

At a later day, when the Judæan nation was struggling with death, a seer, comforting the sufferers, said:—

"Many of those who are sleeping in dust will awake, some to eternal life, and some to disgrace and everlasting abhorrence." (DANIEL xii. 2.)

In this manner a peculiar doctrine of retaliation, with a brilliant picture of the future, or of the next world (Olam ha-Ba), was evolved. A magical world unfolded itself to the eye, intoxicating the believer. He saw the time come when all discords of life would change into harmony, when all disappointments would vanish, when the pious, the faithful, and the just, who had suffered so much upon earth, would rise from their graves and enter on eternal life in innocence and purity. Even the sinners who had erred only from frivolity and weakness would be purified by penitence in Hell, and would enjoy the pleasures of eternal life. But how was this resurrection to take place, and how was this beautiful new world to be organised? Imagination could not find an answer to such a question. Fervent faith and enthusiastic hope do not indulge in subtle inquiries; they are contented with giving the pious the comforting assurance that a just recompense is in store for them, in a future life, and thus assuaging the sorrows of an unhappy earthly existence. Although Judaism received the essence of this teaching from without, yet the power of enriching it, and of endowing it with the faculty of working immeasurable good came from within. The foreign origin of this belief becoming finally obliterated, it was considered as an original Judæan doctrine. Only the Samaritans objected, for a considerable time, to the belief in the resurrection and to the idea of a future life.

During this long period of nearly two hundred years, while the Judæan community established itself, and Judaism developed by the enlargement of its own doctrines and the adoption of foreign elements—from the death of Nehemiah to the destruction of the Persian kingdom—we do not find a single personage mentioned who assisted in that great work, which was to outlive and defy the storms of ages. Was it from excess of modesty that the spiritual leaders of the people, with whom the new order of things had originated, veiled themselves in obscurity, in order to eliminate from their work every vestige of individualism? Or is it the ingratitude of posterity that has effaced these names? Or, again, were the members of the Great Council not sufficiently gifted or remarkable to merit any particular distinction, and was the community indebted for its vigour, and Judaism for its growth and development, entirely to the zeal of a whole community, in which every individual will was completely absorbed? Whatever was the cause, the astonishing fact remains, that of these long stretches of time but few details have become known to us. Either no annals were kept of the events of those years, or they have been lost. It is true there were no very remarkable events to describe, the activity of the Judæan community being entirely restricted to its inward life; there was nothing which might have appeared of sufficient importance to be chronicled for posterity. There was indeed but little for the historian to write about: a stranger might perhaps have been struck by the changes which were gradually unfolding themselves, but to those who lived and worked in the community, what was there of a peculiar or extraordinary nature which might deserve to be perpetuated in history?

The Judæan people occupied themselves almost entirely with peaceful avocations; they understood but little of the use of arms; perhaps not even enough to preserve their own territories against the attacks of their neighbours. The prophet Ezekiel had described what the condition of the Jews would be after their return from captivity:

"In the latter years thou shalt come into the land that is turned away from the sword and is gathered out of many people against the mountains of Israel." (EZEK. xxxviii. 8.)

A peaceful, quiet existence naturally withdraws itself from curious observation. In the wars which were often raging on their borders, the Judæan people certainly took no part. Under Artaxerxes II., surnamed Mnemon (404–362), and under Artaxerxes III., surnamed Ochus (361–338), leaders of the discontented Egyptians, some of whom called themselves kings, endeavoured to free their country from the Persian yoke, and to restore it to its former independence. In order to be enabled to offer effectual resistance to the armies collected for the purpose of putting down these insurrections, the ephemeral kings of Egypt joined the Persian satraps of Phœnicia, to whom Judæa had also been allotted. Persian troops often passed along the Judæan coasts of the Mediterranean towards Egypt, or Egyptians towards Phœnicia, and Greek mercenaries, hired by either power, marched to and fro, and all this warlike array could be constantly observed by the Judæans from their mountain-tops. They did not always remain mere passive spectators; for, though they were not compelled to join the armies, they were certainly not exempt from various charges and tributes. The relations between the Judæans and the Persians was at the same time somewhat disturbed. The latter, influenced by foreign example, began to practise idolatry. The goddess of love, who, under the different names of Beltis, Mylitta, or Aphrodite, was constantly brought under the notice of the Persians, exercised a fascinating power over them. The victories they had achieved and the riches they had acquired, inclined them to sensual pleasures, and they were easily enthralled by the goddess, and induced to serve and worship her. As soon as they had adopted this new deity, they gave her a Persian name, Anahita, Anaitis, and included her in their mythology. Artaxerxes II. sanctioned her worship, and had images of her placed everywhere in his great kingdom, in the three principal cities, Babylon, Susa, and Ecbatana, as well as in Damascus, Sardes, and in all the towns of Persia and Bactria. Through this innovation the Persian religion sustained a double injury. A strange deity was admitted, and image-worship introduced. Thus the spiritual link which had bound the Persians to the followers of Judaism—their common abhorrence of idolatry—was broken. No longer was "pure incense" offered to the incorporeal God of the Judæans. Having compelled his own people to bow down to this newly adopted goddess of love, Artaxerxes tried, as it appears, to force her worship upon the Judæans; the latter were cruelly treated, in order to make them renounce their religion, but they chose the severest punishments, and even death itself, rather than abjure the faith of their fathers. It is related that after his war with the Egyptians and their king Tachos (361–360), Artaxerxes banished many Judæans from their country, and sent them to Hyrkania, on the shores of the Caspian Sea. If this account may be considered historical, the banishment of the Ju-

dæans must surely have been a mode of persecution
inflicted upon them on account of their fidelity to
their laws and their God; for it is hardly to be supposed that they took part in the revolt against
Persia, which was then spreading from Egypt to
Phœnicia. In Jerusalem there was much suffering
at that time, caused by one of those abject creatures,
who, owing to the growing degeneracy of the Persian
Court and increasing weakness of the kingdom,
raised themselves from the dust, and ruled both the
countries and the throne. This was the eunuch
Bagoas (Bagoses), who under Artaxerxes III. became
so powerful that he was able to set aside the king,
and fill the throne according to his own pleasure.
Before attaining this supreme position, Bagoas had
been the commander of the troops stationed in
Syria and Phœnicia, and he had taken advantage of
the opportunities thus offered him to acquire great
riches. He received bribes from Joshua, the ambitious son of the high-priest, who hoped thus to secure
that post for himself. Joshua had an elder brother,
Johanan, and both were sons of Joiada, one of
whose relations, having connected himself with Sanballat, had been banished from Jerusalem by Nehemiah, and subsequently had introduced the rival worship on Mount Gerizim. After the death of Joiada, the
younger son, trusting in the countenance of Bagoas,
came forward to seize the high-priest's diadem.
The elder brother was enraged at this presumption,
and a struggle, which ended in bloodshed, took place
between the two in the Temple itself. Johanan slew
Bagoas's protégé in the Sanctuary. A sad omen for
the future! Upon hearing what had occurred at
Jerusalem, the eunuch instantly proceeded thither,
not to avenge the death of Joshua, but, under the
pretext of meting out well-deserved punishment, to
extort money for himself. For each lamb that was
offered at the daily services in the Temple, the people
were ordered to pay 50 drachms as expiatory money,

and this sum was to be paid every morning before the sacrifice was performed. Bagoas also violated the law which forbade any layman's entering the Sanctuary, and when the priest, in accordance with the prohibitory decree, tried to prevent his entrance into the Temple, he asked, mockingly, if he was not so pure as the son of the high-priest, who had been murdered there?

The people paid the expiatory money for seven years, when, for some reason, they were freed from their burden. The disfavour into which the Judæan nation had fallen with the last Persian king was turned to account by their malevolent neighbours, the Samaritans, in order to injure them to their utmost power. They appear to have regained by force or cunning the border districts of Ramathaim, Apherema and Lydda, which they had formerly been obliged to quit. The Judæans were now reduced to a struggle for mere existence. Few and brief had been the glimpses of light which had brightened the annals of the Judæan community during the last two hundred years! This light had illumined the first enthusiastic days of the return from captivity during the reign of Darius, who showered favours upon them, and during the time of Nehemiah's presence and zealous activity at Jerusalem. With these exceptions, their lot had been oppression, poverty and pitiable helplessness. They appear to us in their sadness and misery to be ever asking with tearful, uplifted eyes, "Whence shall help come to us?" and traces of this helplessness and misery are visible in the writings that have come down from that period. While the exile lasted, the grief and the longing, which kept the captives in constant and breathless expectation, had brought forth the fairest blossoms of prophecy and poetry; but as soon as the excitement ceased, and hope became a reality, the mental and poetical activity began to sink. The later prophetical utterances, if beauty of form be considered, cannot bear comparison with those of the Captivity. The poetry of the Psalms became weak and full of repetitions, or else borrowed the bloom of older productions. The graceful idyl of the book of Ruth forms an exception in the literature of this period. Historical writings were, from causes easy to explain, completely neglected. Ezra and Nehemiah had given only a short and unpolished account of the occurrences they had witnessed. Quite at the end of this epoch, towards the close of the Persian dominion, it appears that a Levite compiled an historical work (Chronicles), narrating the events from the Creation down to his own time.

But during the life of the author of the annals, or shortly after he had finished his history, a new period dawned, which gave rise to fresh mental exertions among the Judæans, and brought forth proofs of their capacity and worth. This new period was ushered in by the Greeks. They wrought a thorough change in the manners, customs and thoughts of other nations, and materially raised the degree of civilisation among the various peoples then known in the world. However, the diffusion of this civilisation, which was the consequence of the acquisition of political power and widespread conquest, was owing, not to a purely Greek race, but to a mixed people of Greeks and Barbarians, namely, the Macedonians. The grace and charm of the Greeks have caused their faults to be leniently regarded by mankind, but they were not overlooked by the Ruler of the world, and their sins brought retributive punishment upon them. Advantage was easily taken of their mutual jealousies, their many foibles, their restless, unruly disposition, and Greece was apt to fall a prey to any ambitious leader who was an adept in the art of intoxicating flattery, lavish with his gold, and supported by martial force. Such was the case with Philip, king of Macedonia, who dazzled all with his cunning and his wealth, his valour and his army. All Greece lay at his feet. But even

now when the king proposed, as a satisfaction to
their national pride, that a war should be undertaken
against Persia, in which they might at once punish
the latter for inroads upon their country, and win
fame and booty for themselves, petty feelings of jealousy continued to exist among the people, and to prevent common action. Some of the States could not
be influenced, and refused to send delegates to the
assembly; whilst other States, or their representatives, had to be bribed to give their consent to the
proposed plan. Philip's project of war against
Persia was cut short by the hand of an assassin.
Then appeared his son, the great Alexander, who
was destined to remodel entirely the relations of the
various countries, and to draw the peaceful inhabitants of Judæa into the vortex of the great world
conflicts. New troubles and new trials were brought
upon the Judæan people by the convulsions felt
from one end of the known world to the other. A
Judæan seer compared Alexander to a leopard
endowed with the wings of an eagle. In two battles
he gave to the rotten Persian monarchy its death-
blow ; Asia Minor, Syria, and Phœnicia lay at his
feet, and kings and princes, attired in all their pomp,
did homage to the conqueror. Tyre and Gaza, the
one after a seven months', the other after a two
months' siege, were both taken (August and November, 332), and met with a cruel fate.

How did the insignificant dominion of Judæa fare
with the invincible hero before whom Egypt, the
proud land of the Pharaohs, had fallen humbly pros-
trate? The historical records of those times have
come down to us only in the form of legends, and
consequently give us no authentic account of the
passing events. It is scarcely credible that the Judæans were prevented from doing homage to Alexander through fear of incurring any guilt by breaking
their oath to their Persian rulers. They had never
taken such an oath of fealty, but even if they had,

after their treatment by the last Persian kings, they would not have felt much remorse in breaking it. There is no doubt that the story of Alexander's approach to Jerusalem, and the favours which he heaped upon the Judæans in consequence of a peculiar vision, rests upon a legend. The High Priest, so it is related, dressed in his holy garments, followed by a troop of priests and Levites, went forth to meet the youthful warrior, and produced so great and extraordinary an effect upon him, that his anger was at once changed into kindness and good will. The explanation given by Alexander to his followers was that the High Priest thus attired had appeared to him in a dream which he had had in Macedonia, and had promised him victory. According to one legend, it was the High Priest Jaddua, according to another, his grandson Simon, who produced this effect upon the Macedonian hero. In reality, the meeting between Alexander and the envoys of the Judæan community no doubt passed simply and naturally enough. The High Priest, perhaps Onias I., Jaddua's son and Simon's father, went forward, like the kings and princes of the land, with a suite of the elders, to do homage and swear allegiance to the conqueror. Alexander was a noble, generous conqueror, who punished cruelly only resistance to his will, but in no way interfered with the peculiar development, the customs, or religious rites of any nation under his sway. He did not force the Grecian faith on any nation, and the favour which he granted to other nations he certainly did not deny to the Judæans. They were only obliged to pay the Macedonian governor the same tax on their lands as the Persian satrap had received.

The first meeting of Greece and Judæa, both of which were, in different ways, to offer civilisation to the world, was of a friendly character, although the one appeared in all her glory and might, the other in her weakness and humility.—Judæa became part of a

province, which was bounded on the north by Mount
Taurus and Mount Lebanon, and on the south by
Egypt, and was called Hollow Syria (Cœlesyria), to
distinguish it from the Higher Syria, which lay in the
neighbourhood of the Euphrates. The governor of
this extensive province, which had formerly been
divided into many independent states, resided in Samaria, from which we may infer that it was a fortified
and populous town. Samaria, however, was indebted
for this preference or dangerous station to its situation in the centre of the province and in a fertile
region. Andromachos was the name of the governor
whom Alexander placed over the Cœlesyrians. Why
were the Samaritans displeased with this apparent distinction? Did they feel themselves hampered in their
movements by the presence of the Governor, or was
their anger roused by jealousy at the favour shown by
Alexander to the Judæans, whom they hated so bitterly? The violent resentment of the Samaritans, or
at least of their leaders, went so far that, heedless of
the consequences, they rose up against Andromachos,
seized him and consigned him to the flames (331).
Alexander's wrath, upon hearing of this act of atro-
city which had been committed upon one of his
generals, was as great as it was just. Had this small,
insignificant people dared defy one who had subdued all Egypt, the proud priests of which country
had prostrated themselves before him, proclaiming
his pre-eminence and his glory? Upon his return
from Egypt, while hastening to conquer Persia, he
hurried to Samaria to avenge the murder of Andromachos. The authors of the horrible deed were put
to death under cruel tortures, another governor called
Memnon was placed over Samaria, and the town was
filled with Macedonians. In various other ways,
Alexander appears to have mortified and humiliated
the Samaritans, and knowing that they were enemies
of the Judæans, he favoured the latter in order to
mark his displeasure towards the former. Several

border lands lying between Samaria and Judæa, which had often occasioned strife between the two peoples, he awarded to the Judæans, and likewise freed the latter from the burden of taxation during the Sabbatical year. This favour, of small importance to him who gave it, was a great boon to those who received it, and inflamed the hatred of the Samaritans against the Judæans; every gust of wind seemed to add new fuel to their enmity, which, however, as long as Alexander lived, they were obliged to conceal. His wonderfully rapid and victorious campaigns—as far as the Indus and the Caucasus—seemed to throw a spell over the world, and to paralyse all independent action. When he was not at war, peace reigned supreme, from Greece to India, and from Ethiopia to the shores of the Caspian sea. Alexander was the first conqueror who deemed it a wise policy to allow the peculiar customs of any conquered nation to be maintained; he insisted that respect should be shown to their various religious forms of worship. In Egypt he honoured Apis and Ammon, and in Babylonia the gods of Chaldæa. Thus he determined upon rebuilding the temple of the Babylonian idol Bel, which had been destroyed by Artaxerxes. To accomplish this, he ordered his soldiers to clear away the ruins which had accumulated over the foundations of the building. All obeyed with the exception of the Judæans who, either voluntarily or by compulsion, were serving in his army. They refused their help towards the reconstruction of the idolatrous temple. Naturally enough, their disobedience received severe chastisement from their superior officers, but they bore their punishment bravely, rather than comply with an order which demanded the transgression of one of the principal injunctions of their faith. When Alexander heard of this case of conscience and of the religious fortitude displayed by the Judæan soldiers, he was generous enough to grant them his pardon. But in that incident we may read an omen of the conflicts which were to take place between Judaism and Greekdom.

In the midst of his vast undertaking—that of uniting the whole world into one monarchy—the young hero died (323), leaving no lawful heir to his throne, no successor to his great mind. Confusion arose in all parts of the world, as well as among the armies of Alexander,—dire as if the laws of Nature had been upset, and the sequence of the morrow after to-day were no longer certain. Fearful battles, which resembled the wars of the Titans, ensued. Alexander's warriors, with the experience gained on a thousand battle-fields, would, had they only been united, have been capable of supporting the structure of the Macedonian kingdom; but, although they were not actually Greeks, and even looked down upon the latter, they resembled them in their spirit of insubordination, their want of discipline, and their passion for self-advancement, which greatly surpassed their zeal for the good of the State. Like the Greeks, they coveted power as a means to obtain luxuries and to enable them to indulge in licentious pleasures; in short, they had become adepts in corrupt practices.

The consequence of this state of things was the dissolution of the Macedonian kingdom and its division among the contending leaders. Ptolemy I. Soter, son of Lagos, reigned in Egypt. By means of a successful war he acquired Cœlesyria, together with Judæa. In 320, he demanded the surrender of Jerusalem, but its inhabitants refused to open their gates. On a Sabbath, however, he contrived to surprise the city, and, as the Judæans would not use weapons of defence on that day, he was able to seize the city and to make numerous prisoners, whom he carried away to Egypt. Many Samaritans shared their fate, probably because they had likewise attempted resistance. Both Judæans and Samaritans could have enjoyed happiness—at least, as much happiness as was possible in those hard, cruel times—had they remained subjects

of the Lagidian Ptolemy, who was the gentlest of the
warring successors of Alexander. He knew how
to recognise and appreciate merit, and when his own
interests were not at stake, he was just and merciful; but Ptolemy had no acknowledged right upon
Cœlesyria. His acquisition of those lands had not
been confirmed by the various regents of the Macedonian kingdom who followed each other in rapid
succession, and kept up the semblance of a united
government. Ptolemy roused the envy of the con-
federate captains, and in particular that of one of
his former allies and fellow-conspirators, Antigonus.
This bold soldier was endowed with inventive
genius and a fiery nature, and had resolved upon the
subjection of all his associates, in order to seize and
hold the whole kingdom of Macedonia in his own
strong hand. After many years of warlike preparations, a decisive battle at last took place between
Demetrius, the son of Antigonus, and Ptolemy, which
ended disastrously for the former. The battle of
Gaza, fought in the spring of 312, was a memorable
one, for from that event Seleucus, who had come as
a fugitive to Ptolemy, dated the beginning of his
power by introducing the new era called Seleucidæan, or Greek, which also came into use among
the Judæans, and was longest retained by them.
In consequence of the defeat at Gaza, Demetrius
was obliged to withdraw to the north, leaving
the whole country to the conqueror. Only a short
time elapsed, however, before Antigonus and his son,
having joined their forces, compelled Ptolemy to retreat to Egypt. He caused the fortified sea-coast
and inland cities, Acco, Joppa, Gaza, and Jerusalem
to be demolished, so that they might not become
places of defence to his enemies, and Judæa, with the
countries that belonged to Cœlesyria, remained in
this unguarded condition until, in the battle at Ipsus,
in Asia Minor (301), fought against the united armies
of Ptolemy, Lysimachus, Cassander, and Seleucus,

Antigonus lost at one blow both his glory and his life. The four generals divided the kingdom among themselves. Ptolemy received Egypt and the adjoining lands, and the greater part of Asia fell to Seleucus. Thus Judæa became a portion of the Ptolemæan or Lagidian kingdom, and its fate for a time was linked to that of the latter. The condition of the Judæans, however, underwent no material change. The tribute they had been obliged formerly to pay to the Persian monarch was now demanded by the Egypto-Macedonian court. The freedom and independence of their movements and actions were not more restricted than they had hitherto been ; on the contrary, their situation might be considered rather improved than otherwise.

In Judæa, the high-priest, who was answerable for the payment of taxes, was considered as the political chief, and was looked upon as a sacerdotal prince. Ptolemy I. was endowed with a gentle nature, and inclined to benefit his subjects. He had neither desire nor motive to oppress the Judæans. Alexandria, the seaport city founded by Alexander, and considered as the capital of his kingdom by the first Egypto-Macedonian monarch, acquired a large population, and it could only be a source of satisfaction to him to see Judæans from the neighbouring country establishing themselves there. Under Alexander, many Judæans had settled in that city, and, as this far-seeing hero had given equal rights of Macedonian citizenship to all comers, the first Judæan colony in Alexandria enjoyed perfect equality with the other inhabitants, and led a peaceful existence in the new land. A great number of Judæans took up their abode there during the disturbed state of their country, caused by the wars of Antigonus; they also received from Ptolemy protection and the enjoyment of equal laws and rights. And thus arose an Egypto-Judæan community, which was destined to fulfil a peculiar mission. In other places also Judæan colonies were formed. Assured of the good will of the Judæans, Ptolemy distributed them in various Egyptian cities and in Cyrene.

Seleucus, the founder of the Seleucidæan kingdom, the centre of which was situated in Persia, had in addition become possessed of the northern part of Syria, where he founded a new city, Antioch, which became his capital. In order to people this city, as well as other newly-built towns, he was obliged to bring inhabitants into them, and among these partly forced and partly willing settlers were many Judæans, to whom Seleucus gave the full rights of Macedonian citizenship. And, as Judæan colonies arose in the Græco-Macedonian countries, so also Greek colonies were formed upon Judæan ground. Along the Mediterranean coast new seaports were built, or old ones enlarged and embellished, and to these Grecian names were given.

CHAPTER XXI.

SIMON THE JUST AND HIS DESCENDANTS.

Condition of the Judæans under the Ptolemies—Simon effects Improvements—His Praises are sung by Sirach—His Doctrines—The Chasidim and the Nazarites—Simon's Children—Onias II. and the Revolt against Egypt—Joseph, son of Tobias—His Embassy to Alexandria—He is appointed Tax-collector—War between Antiochus the Great and Egypt—Defeat of Antiochus—Spread of Greek Manners in Judæa—Hyrcanus—The Song of Songs—Simon II.—Scopas despoils Jerusalem—The Contest between Antiochus and Rome—Continued Hellenisation of the Judæans—The Chasidim and the Hellenists—Jose ben Joezer and Jose ben Johanan—Onias III. and Simon—Heliodorus—Sirach's Book of Proverbs against the Errors of his Time.

300—175 B. C. E.

FOR more than a century after the death of Nehemiah, the inner life of the Judæan nation might have been likened to that of a caterpillar weaving the threads which enshroud it from the juices of its own body, while the world knew it as a martyr, bearing insult and humiliation alike in silence. During that period it had not produced any one man, who, by reason of his own strong individuality, had been able to bring into play the reserve force of the nation ; no one had arisen capable of pointing the way and arousing enthusiasm. The stimulus for development and improvement had always come from without, from the principal men of Persia or Babylonia. But now the people, in consequence of new political circumstances, were separated from their co-religionists of those lands. The Judæans of the Euphrates and the Tigris could no longer carry on active intercourse with their brethren in the mother-country. For the reigning dynasties, the Seleucidæ and the Ptolemies, looked upon each other with suspicion, and frequent visits of the Judæans from the provinces of the Seleucidæ to the Judæans of Jerusalem, would have been regarded with disfavour in Alexandria. Had the nation not been able to rally in its own country without extraneous help, it would have been lost; a people which cannot exist or improve of itself must sooner or later fall into insignificance. But the right man arose at the right time. He saved the Judæan community from its fall. This man was Simon the Just (about 300–270). In an age deficient in great men, he appears like a lofty and luxuriant tree in the midst of a barren country. Legendary lore has seized upon his name, and has added the marvellous to the historical. It is always a favourable testimony to an historical personage, and to the influence he wields over a large circle, when romance proclaims his praise. Authentic history does not tell us much of Simon I., still the few characteristics preserved to us portray him as a man of great distinction. He was, moreover, the one high-priest of the house of Joshua ben Jozedek, of whom there is anything laudatory to be related, and the one to restore the priesthood to honour. " He cared for his people to save it from falling." He rebuilt the walls of Jerusalem, which had been demolished by Ptolemy I., and he repaired the ravages of two centuries upon the Temple. He also carried out various measures for the safety and improvement of the capital. The supply of water from the several springs in the neighbourhood of Jerusalem is insufficient for ordinary purposes in dry seasons. The Temple, too, required water in copious quantities. To meet these requirements, Simon caused a large reservoir to be excavated below the Temple, which was fed by a subterranean canal, and brought a constant supply of fresh water from the springs of Etam. Thus there was no fear of drought, even in case of a siege. The poet, Joshua (Jesus) Sirach, who lived at a later date, gives us an enthusiastic description of Simon :—

"How was he distinguished in the midst of the people in his coming
out of the Sanctuary! He was as the morning star in the midst of
a cloud, and as the full moon in the vernal season.

"As the sun shining upon the temple of the Most High, and as the
rainbow giving light in the bright clouds.

"When he put on the robe of honour, and was clothed with the
garments of glory . . . . compassed with his brethren round about,
like palms around a cedar of Lebanon." (ECCLUS. l. 5–12.)

Not only was Simon the Just recognised in his
office of high-priest as head of the community and
of the Supreme Council, but he was also the chief
teacher in the house of learning. He inculcated
this maxim upon his disciples : " The world (*i. e.*, the
Judæan community) rests on three things, on the Law,
on Divine Service (in the Temple), and on Charity"
(Aboth i. 2). One may also ascribe to this remarkable man some share in the following saying of one
of his most distinguished pupils, Antigonus of
Soho, "Be not like those slaves, who serve their
master for their daily rations, but be rather like
the servants who faithfully serve their master without
expectation of reward." Although Simon the Just
attached great importance to the sacrificial rites,
still he disliked the excessive ceremonialism towards
which his generation was tending, nor did he conceal
his disapprobation. There were amongst the nation,
some over-pious people who took the vow of the
Nazarite to refrain from wine for a given time ; they
called themselves, or were called, the strictly pious,
Chasidim. When the term of their vows had expired,
they cut off their hair and went through all the ceremonies. Perhaps the excesses of the Greeks and
their Jewish followers, their numerous feasts and
orgies induced them to impose upon themselves this
Nazaritic abstention with its attendant rites. It is
certain that as the number of pleasure-seeking imitators of Greek habits increased in Judæa, so did also
that of the Chasidim. But Simon the Just was not
pleased with this exaggerated zeal, and took no part
in the sacrifices of the Nazarites.

Posterity has formed so exalted an opinion of Simon's character, that it designated his death as the end of an historical period of divine grace. In fact, sad and terrible events, brought about by his own descendants, and causing fresh trials to the Judæans, followed upon his death. Simon the Just left two children, a young son named Onias and a daughter. The latter was married to Tobiah, a somewhat distinguished man of priestly descent. Onias being too young to officiate as High Priest, a relative, named Manasseh, represented him during his minority. The rule of Onias II. became a turning-point in the history of the Judæans. The constant warfare carried on for years between the rival houses of the Seleucidæ and the Ptolemies affected the fate of Judæa.

When at last a treaty of peace was concluded (in 240), Cœlesyria and Judæa remained with Egypt, but the fourth king of the Seleucidæ, Antiochus Callinicos, instigated these provinces to revolt, and seems to have won over Onias II. to side with him. Onias refused to pay the annual tax of twenty talents to the Ptolemies. Although the sum was small, the payment was looked upon as a mark of submission, and its refusal gave great offence at the Egyptian court. Ptolemy II., after vainly demanding the tribute money, threatened to divide the province amongst various foreign colonists. He despatched one of his own favourites, Athenion, as special envoy to Jerusalem. The Judæans in alarm and despair entreated Onias to submit, but he resisted their prayers. When matters had come to this crisis, there suddenly appeared upon the scene a man, Joseph by name, of extraordinary strength of will and purpose. He was the nephew of Onias, and son of the Tobiah who had married the daughter of Simon the Just. Fascinating in his manners, clever, cunning, and unscrupulous, the son of Tobiah seemed born to govern. Unfortunately for himself,

Onias, the high-priest and ruler of the State, stood in his path. But now was the moment, as he thought, to remove the obstacle. As soon as Joseph was told of the arrival of the Ptolemaic envoy in Jerusalem, and of his threatening message, he hastened from his birth-place to that city, loaded his uncle Onias with reproaches for having led his people into danger, and finding the high-priest determined in his resistance, he offered to go himself to Alexandria, there to commence negotiations with the king of Egypt. As soon as Onias had empowered him to do so, Joseph assembled the people in the court of the Temple, soothed their excited feelings, and made them understand that they were to place entire confidence in his ability to avert the danger that threatened them. The whole assembly offered him their thanks, and made him leader of the people (about 230). From that moment, Joseph displayed so much decision that it was evident a plan had long been ripening in his brain. He was well aware of the weakness of the Greeks, and knew that they were not indifferent to flattery and to the luxuries of the table. So he prepared tempting banquets for Athenion, fascinating him by his charm of manner, making him costly presents, and assuring him that he might return to Egypt, secure of the tribute money, which he promised should be paid to the king. As soon as the envoy had left Jerusalem, Joseph entered into negotiations with some Samaritan friends, or money-lenders, to obtain a loan for his necessary expenses. In order to appear with dignity at the Egyptian court, he required splendid apparel, brilliant equipages, and money to defray the cost of his entertainments. Joseph had no means of his own, and in all Judæa there was no one who could advance him large sums of money. The people, at that time, supporting themselves by agriculture, and not being engaged in commerce, had had no opportunity of amassing wealth.

Furnished with the means of making a great display at court, Joseph hurried to Alexandria, where the envoy Athenion had already prepared a favourable reception for him. Ptolemy Euergetes was anxiously expecting him, and was not disappointed when he arrived. He was enchanted with Joseph's bearing and address, and invited him to be his guest at the royal table. The envoys from the Palestinean and Phœnician cities, who formerly had derided his simple appearance, now remarked with envy upon his presence at court. He soon gave them occasion not only to envy but also to hate him. For by a crafty stroke, he managed to obtain a position of great trust, that of head tax-gatherer of Cœlesyria and Phœnicia. The king gave him a force of two thousand soldiers, who were, if necessary, to lend their aid in the fulfilment of his duties, and Joseph became in reality the governor of all the districts that went by the name of Palestine. He was respected and feared as a favourite of the king, and he therefore did not hesitate to use extreme severity in levying taxes. In the cities of Gaza and Beth-Shean (Scythopolis), the Greek inhabitants ventured to load him with insults, and to offer resistance. In return he beheaded the noblest and richest of the citizens, and confiscated their possessions for the Egyptian crown. For twenty-two years, Joseph held the post of satrap, and spent that time in amassing extraordinary wealth and attaining great power.

After the death of Euergetes (223), his successor, Ptolemy VI., Philopator (222–206), retained him in office. He continued to act in the same heartless way, causing the following remark to be made in the presence of Philopator:—" Joseph is stripping the flesh from Syria, and is leaving only the bones."

At one time, his lucky star seemed to wane; for the Seleucidæan king, Antiochus, called by his flatterers The Great (223–187), attempted to wrest the province of Cœlesyria from Egypt (218). The commencement of the attack augured success. The Egyptian commanders were treacherous, they went over to the enemy, and betrayed the garrisons into their hands. Judæa and Jerusalem, under the control of Joseph, remained true to Egypt. But how long would they be able to resist an attack of the Seleucidæan army? And, if such an attack was made, which side should Joseph take? He must have lived through that time in the most painful anxiety. At last the decisive hour struck. In the spring of 217, Antiochus appeared on the sea-coast near Gaza. He was at the head of a large army, composed of various nationalities. His route lay to the south, towards Egypt. Meanwhile, Philopator had roused himself from his life of ease and self-indulgence, and was advancing to Raphia to meet his enemy. Antiochus, over-confident of success, sustained a severe defeat, and was obliged to return to Antioch, and give up the possession of Cœlesyria. All the cities and communities that had been under his rule outbade one another in flattery and adulation of the conqueror, Philopator. Joseph remained in his position of trust, and continued to be the favourite of the Egyptian king. Through him, and through his connection with the court life of Philopator, a complete change had taken place in the Judæan nation, hardly visible indeed in the provinces, but most striking in the capital.

By means of the immense riches that Joseph had accumulated, a veritable shower of gold fell upon the country; "he raised the people out of poverty and needy circumstances into ease and comfort." In order to collect the taxes of so many different towns, he was obliged to have responsible agents, and he preferred choosing them from amongst his own people. These agents enriched themselves in their own way, and bore themselves proudly. The consideration which Joseph enjoyed at the Egyptian court, his quickly-gained wealth, and the troop of soldiers always at his command, by whose help he held in check the people of various nationalities in Palestine, the remnant of the Philistines, the Phœnicians, Idumæans, and even the Greco-Macedonian colonists—all this had the effect not only of lending him and his surroundings a certain air of self-importance, but also of raising the people in general from the abject, submissive position they had occupied towards the neighbouring nations. The horizon of the Judæans, particularly of those who lived in Jerusalem, widened as they came into contact with the Greeks. Their taste became more refined, their dwellings more beautiful, and they began to introduce the art of painting. The Judæans of Alexandria, who had been for a century under Greek influence, and had, to a certain extent, become Hellenised, now brought their influence to bear upon their fellow-countrymen, but the simplicity of the Judæan habits and customs suffered in consequence.

A shower of gold not only fails to have a fructifying effect, it often causes desolation and ruin; and so it was in this case. The rich upstarts lost their balance; they attached undue importance to the possession of riches, and preferred money-making to every other occupation, but the most unfortunate feature was that they became blind admirers of the Greeks, whose extravagant habits and frivolous customs they soon acquired, to the deterioration of their own national virtues. The Greeks loved conviviality, gave public banquets, and indulged in most unruly merrymaking at their repasts. The Judæans imported the custom of dining in company, reclining on couches whilst they ate and drank, and indulging in wine, music, and song at their entertainments. All this was innocent enough; but unfortunately it led to more than merely making life brighter. Greek frivolity and extravagance drew their imitators rapidly into a vortex of dissipation.

Joseph was constantly at the court of Ptolemy

Philopator, when business took him to Alexandria. This court was a hot-bed of depravity. The days were spent in revelry, and the nights in shameless debauchery; the prevailing depravity led astray both the people and the army.

Philopator entertained the absurd belief that his ancestors were descended from the God of Wine, Dionysus (Bacchus); and he considered himself obliged to introduce bacchanalian revelries into his kingdom. Any one wishing to ingratiate himself with the king and his boon companions was forced to belong to the fraternity of Dionysus. Whenever Joseph was called to Alexandria, he enjoyed the doubtful honour of being invited to the king's orgies, and of being received by the followers of the God of Wine. It was at such a feast that he contracted a violent passion for one of those dissolute dancing-women who never failed to be present upon these occasions.

Jerusalem did not long remain untainted by this social impurity. Joseph, from friendship, let us suppose, for his royal patron, introduced Dionysian festivals into Judæa. At the turning-point of the year, when winter makes way for spring, when the vine bursts into blossom, and the wine in the barrels ferments a second time, then the Greeks held their great festival in honour of Dionysus: "the festival of the barrel-openings." Two days were devoted to intoxicating orgies, when friends interchanged pitchers of wine as presents. He who drank most was most honoured. This festival of the "barrel-opening" was now to be celebrated in much the same way in Judæa. But, in order to clothe this festival in a Judæan garb, the rich made it an occasion for dispensing alms to the poor. Revelry is always the attendant of excessive indulgence in wine. The rich Judæans soon copied the Greek customs, and, callous to the promptings of shame and honour, they introduced singers, dancers, and dissolute women at these festivals. A poetical writer raises a warning voice against the growing unchastity of the age:—

"Meet not with an harlot, lest thou fall into her snares. Use not much the company of the songstress, lest thou be taken with her attempts. . . . . Give not thy soul unto harlots, that thou lose not thine inheritance." (ECCLUS. ix. 3, seq.)

The love of art and beauty which Joseph introduced into Judæa did not compensate for this loss of chastity and morality. Even earnest men, under Greek influence, began to cast doubts upon their old traditional belief. They questioned whether the teachings of Judaism were correct and true throughout, whether God really demanded from man the denial of all self-gratification, and whether the Deity in any way concerned itself about the great universe and the small world of mankind.

The teachings of Epicurus, inculcating the impotence of the gods, and recommending self-indulgence to man, were well received by the degenerate Græco-Macedonians, and particularly by the upper circles of the Alexandrians. It was from that city that the poison spread to Judæa. In Jerusalem also doubters arose, who disregarded the teachings of Judaism. These doubts might have led to increased mental activity, had not discord been added to the corruption of manners. Feelings of jealousy sprang up between the seven sons of Joseph by his first marriage, and the youngest, Hyrcanus, the son of his second wife. The latter was distinguished in youth by his quick intellect, his ability, and his craftiness, characteristics that endeared him to his father. In the year 210, a son was born to the king Philopator. The different representatives of the cities of Cœlesyria were anxious to express, by presents and congratulations, their devotion to the Egyptian king. Joseph felt that he ought not to absent himself upon such an occasion. But his growing infirmities not allowing him to undertake such a journey, he asked one of his sons to represent him. Hyrcanus was the only one who felt equal to the task, and his brothers unanimously requested their father to accept his services. At the same time they suggested to their friends in Alexandria to put him out of the way. But Joseph's young son instantly gained favour at court. His extravagant gifts upon the great day of public congratulation—one hundred handsome slaves to the king, and one hundred beautiful female slaves to the queen, in the hands of each a gift of a talent—threw the presents of all others into the shade. His ready wit and adroit tongue soon made him a favoured guest at Philopator's table. He returned to Jerusalem filled with pride. But his perfidious brothers were lying in wait for him on the road, and determined to accomplish what the Alexandrians had failed to do. Hyrcanus and his companions defended themselves, and in the combat which ensued killed two of his brothers. His father received him sternly on account of his extravagance in Egypt, being perhaps also jealous of his extraordinary popularity. Hyrcanus dared not remain in Jerusalem, and probably returned to Alexandria.

Thus far, this discord was confined only to the family of Joseph, and seemed not to affect the people at large or the inhabitants of Jerusalem. No one could have imagined that the violent dissensions among the members of that house, and its Greek proclivities, would end by bringing misery upon the whole nation. The present seemed bright and sunny; prosperity was widespread in the land, and offered the means for beautifying life. The neighbouring peoples acknowledged the supremacy of the Judæan governor, and none ventured to attack the nation, or to treat it with contempt. Judæa had not known so peaceful a state of things since the age of Nehemiah.

It was, therefore, not unnatural that a poem in the

form of a love song should have appeared at that time, shedding a rosy flush over the age, and reflecting happy and joyous days.

A cloudless sky, green meadows, fragrant flowers, and, above all things, careless light-heartedness are mirrored in it, as though there were no more serious occupation in life than to wander over hills of myrrh, to repose among lilies, to whisper words of love, and to revel in the ecstasy of the moment. In this period of calm which preceded the storm, the "Song of Songs" (Shir-ha-shirim) was written. It was the offspring of untroubled, joyous days. In it the Hebrew language proved its capability of expressing tenderness and depth of sentiment, exquisite dialogue and picturesque poetry of nature. The author of this poem had seen the life of Greece, had felt the charm of its literature, and learned the cunning of its art. But beneath the veil of poetry he reprovingly pointed out the evils of the time.

In contrast to the impure and unchaste love of the Greek world, our poet's ideal is a shepherdess, Shulamit, the beautiful daughter of Aminadab. She bears in her heart a deep, ardent, unquenchable love for a shepherd who pastures his flock among the lilies, and with and through this love, she remains pure and innocent. Her beauty is enhanced by her grace of movement, by her soft voice and gentle speech. As her eyes are like the dove's, so is her heart full of dove-like innocence. In the flowery language of the most exquisite poetry, the author of the Song of Songs denounces the debauchery of the times, the lewdness of the public dancers and singers, the voluptuousness of town life, and the enervating effects of riotous living.

Joseph, the grandson of Simon the Just, died in the year 208, leaving his family torn by dissension. His office was to be transferred to one of his sons; but Hyrcanus, the youngest, being the only one known at the Egyptian court, and a favourite of the king, the preference was no doubt given to him.   This fired the hatred of his brothers. They assumed a hostile position towards him upon his arrival in Jerusalem, and as Hyrcanus had a large number of followers, civil war seemed imminent. The action of the high-priest, Simon II., who sided with the elder brothers, turned the scale, and Hyrcanus was again compelled to flee the city.   If he intended pleading his cause in Alexandria, as he probably did, he was disappointed, for he could obtain no hearing at the Egyptian court, as his patron Philopator had just died (206), and Egypt was a prey to disorder.

Two ambitious kings, tempted by the weakness of the house of Ptolemy, seized upon Egypt and her provinces, and divided them.   These were Antiochus the Great, of Syria, and Philip of Macedon.

Joseph's elder sons, or, as they were generally called, the Tobiades, out of hatred to their younger brother, Hyrcanus, determined to side with Antiochus against Egypt. They raised a Seleucidæan party. They are described as scoffers and reprobates, and, as matters went on, they showed themselves to be unprincipled men, who sacrificed their country's weal to their thirst for revenge and the gratification of their lusts.   They opened the gates of Jerusalem to the Syrian king, and did homage to him.   The adherents of the Ptolemies and of Hyrcanus yielded or were crushed.

Thus Judæa came under the rule of the Seleucidæan kings (203–202).   But an Ætolian commander of hired troops, Scopas, undertook to oppose the Syrian conqueror. He soon overran the Jordanic and trans-Jordanic territories, causing terror amongst the Tobiades and their followers. Desperately but in vain they struggled against their impending doom. Scopas took Jerusalem by storm, laid waste the city and the Temple, and put to the sword those who were pointed out as hostile to him. Numbers sought safety in flight

In order to secure the allegiance of the conquered people, Scopas left a contingent in the fortress of Baris or Acra. But the re-conquest of Judæa and Cœlesyria for the son of Ptolemy, the child Epiphanes, was not to be lasting. The Syrians now re-appeared on the scene. In the beautiful valley at the foot of Mount Hermon, near the mountain city of Panion, at the source of the Jordan, a terrible battle was fought, in which Scopas and his troops were entirely routed. Judæa once again became a prey to the horrors of war and internal dissensions; she resembled a storm-tossed ship, flung violently from side to side. Both parties inflicted unsparing blows on her.

Antiochus succeeded in re-conquering the greater part of the land, and then marched upon Jerusalem. The people, headed by the Synhedrin and the priests, came out to meet him, bringing provisions for his troops and elephants. But the Ætolian contingent still held the fortress of Acra. Antiochus or one of his commanders, with the help of the Judæans, undertook the siege of the fortress. The Seleucidæan king, it appears, greatly valued the friendship of the Judæans, for he gave orders to rebuild their ruined city and repair their Temple. They were treated with much consideration, and were allowed to govern themselves according to their own laws. None but Judæans had the right of entering the Temple; no impurities were suffered to pollute it, and no unclean animals were to be bred in Jerusalem.

Antiochus remained in undisputed possession of Cœlesyria, and therefore also of Judæa. But he cast a greedy eye upon Egypt and her neighbouring provinces, of whose conquest, since they were under the rule of a boy-king, he felt assured. But the Romans, free for action since the downfall of Carthage, formed a stumbling-block to his progress. Compelled to abandon his plans on Egypt, Antiochus conceived the idea of making war upon the Romans,

and after having conquered them, of seizing upon
Asia Minor and Greece and also Egypt. But his foolhardiness and over-confidence led to his humiliation. He suffered so crushing a defeat at the hands
of the Romans (190), that he was obliged to give up
his conquests in Greece and in a part of Asia Minor,
surrender the whole of his fleet, and pay 15,000
talents annually, for twelve years, to the victor. He
was constrained to send to Rome as hostage his
son, Antiochus Epiphanes, who was destined to leave
a bloody mark upon the annals of Judæan history.
Severe was the penalty that Antiochus paid for having over-estimated the strength of the Seleucidæans.
In order to be able to pay the heavy indemnity, the
Syrian kings robbed temples; this sacrilege made
them odious, and stirred up the hatred of the most
patient nationalities. Antiochus, surnamed the Great,
met his death through one of these acts of rapine
(187).

The sacrileges continued by his son became the
cause of the rise to new strength of the Judæan nation, as well as of the humiliation and decadence of
the Seleucidæan kingdom.

The disintegration of the Judæan community,
which began under Joseph's administration, increased
rapidly during the constant struggle between the
Seleucidæans and the Ptolemies for the possession
of Cœlesyria. The leaders of the two parties were
not particular as to the means they employed to
forward their own cause, or to injure that of their
antagonists. The friends of the Seleucidæans were
above all things determined to find allies amongst the
foreign nationalities in and around Judæa. The
Greeks living in Palestinean places, as well as the
native Gentiles, hated the Judæans, on account of
the humiliations they had suffered at the hands of
the tax-collector Joseph. There were other antago-
nistic races besides; the old names of the enemies
of the Judæans still existed, recalling the warlike

days of the Judges and of David's reign. The
Idumæans and the Philistines were in possession of
Judæan territory, and the former occupied even the
ancient city of Hebron. Both hated the Judæans,
and made them feel this hatred upon every occasion,
whilst in the north the Samaritans did the same.

The Judæan settlers in the provinces of the Seleucidæan kingdom looked up to the Græco-Macedonian
rulers, commanders and officers for protection from
their numerous foes. But in order to curry favour
with the Greeks, it was necessary to endeavour to
become like them in manners, customs and observances. As to Jerusalem, those who had Hellenised
themselves in outward appearance, determined upon
educating the Judæan youth according to the Greek
model. Thus they established races and contests in
wrestling. The richest and most distinguished among
the Judæans belonged to this Greek faction, amongst
others, Jesus (Joshua), the son of the high-priest, who
called himself Jason, and who was followed by many
Aaronides. The party was led by the Tobiades, or
sons and grandsons of Joseph the tax-collector. But
as Jewish law and custom were sternly opposed to
such innovations, and held in especial abhorrence
Greek shamelessness, these factions determined to
abolish the faith of the fathers, that the people might
be Hellenised without let or hindrance.

Complete incorporation with the pagan Greeks
was their aim. Of what use was the fence erected
by Ezra, Nehemiah, and the Synhedrin round Judaism? The Hellenists pulled down the fence, and
showed a desire to fell the primeval trees of the
forest too.

As has repeatedly occurred in the history of thinking nations, lack of moderation on the one side
brought forth exaggeration on the other. Those Judæans who saw with pain and rage the attempts of
the Hellenists grouped themselves into a party which
clung desperately to the Law and the customs of

their fathers, and cherished them as the apple of their eye. They were " the community of the pious," or Chasidim, a development of the Nazarites. Every religious custom was to them of inviolable sanctity. A more complete contrast than was presented by these two parties can hardly be imagined. They understood each other as little as if they had not been sons of the same tribe, people of the same nation. That which was the dearest wish of the Hellenists, the Chasidim condemned as a fearful sin; they called its authors " breakers of the Law," " trespassers of the Covenant." Again, what was dear and sacred to the Chasidim, the Hellenists looked upon as folly, and denounced as a hindrance to the welfare and stability of the community. Amongst the Chasidim there were two noted teachers of the Law, Josê, the son of Joëzer, of the town of Zereda, and Josê, the son of Johanan of Jerusalem, each of them the founder of a school. The one laid more stress upon the theoretical study of the Law, the other, upon the execution of its commands. Josê of Zereda taught his disciples: " Let your house be a place of assembly for the wise men; allow yourself to be covered with the dust of their feet; drink in their words greedily." Josê of Jerusalem, on the other hand, taught, " Let the door of your house be opened wide; let the poor be your guests, and do not converse with women."

Between the two widely opposed parties, the Hellenists and the Chasidim or Assidæans, the people took a middle course. They certainly took delight in the luxuries and refinements of life introduced by the Greeks, and did not care to have their pleasures narrowed by the severe Chasidim; at the same time they disapproved of the excesses of the Hellenists; they refused to break their connection with the past, or to have it obliterated through innovations. But the passionate warfare that existed between Hellenists and Chasidim, menacing with extinction one of the two parties, obliged the moderates to take sides with one or the other of them.

The pious, or patriots, were still supreme in their position of command in the community. At their head was Onias III., high-priest, son of Simon II. He is described as a man of excellent character. Though gentle by nature, he was an enemy to wrongdoing, zealous for the Law, a strong advocate of piety, and uncompromisingly opposed to Hellenistic practices. The Hellenists accordingly hated him fiercely. His principal enemies, besides the Tobiades, were three brothers, of a distinguished Benjamite family, who vied with each other in insolence—Simon, Onias called Menelaus, and Lysimachus. They hated the high-priest not only on account of his constant opposition to their innovations, but also on account of his alliance with Hyrcanus, who was still suffering from the persecutions of his brothers and their followers.

Hyrcanus was in great favour at the Egyptian court, and Ptolemy V. had given him the control over some trans-Jordanic territory. Armed troops were probably at his disposal to help him in the discharge of his duties. The Judæans who colonised the province were probably loyal to him, or were employed by him. By their aid he was able to levy contributions from the Arabs, or Nabatæans, of the provinces of Hesbon and Medaba, as ruthlessly as his father Joseph had once done in Cœlesyria. In this way he accumulated vast wealth. He erected a wonderful citadel of white marble, upon a rock near Hesbon, to all intents and purposes a fortress, but of surpassing beauty. He called this magnificent palace Tyrus; he surrounded it with a wide moat of great depth, and constructed the gates of the outer wall of such narrow dimensions that they admitted only one person at a time. Hyrcanus spent several years, probably from 181 to 175, in this mountain retreat. The surplus of the wealth accumulated by Hyrcanus was sent from time to time, for safe-keeping, to the Temple in Jerusalem, which enjoyed the privilege of inviolability.

Simon, the Benjamite, held some kind of an office in the Temple, whereby he came into conflict with the high-priest. Onias banished Simon from Jerusalem, and in order to stem the ever-growing anarchy in the city, he passed a similar sentence of exile upon the Tobiades. But by doing this he only added fresh fuel to the flames. Simon devised a diabolical scheme for wreaking vengeance upon his enemy. He repaired to the military commander of Cœlesyria and Phœnicia, Apollonius, son of Thraseius, and betrayed to him the fact that great treasures, not belonging to the Sanctuary, and consequently royal property, were hidden in the Temple of Jerusalem. Apollonius lost no time in giving the king, Seleucus II. (187–175), information on this subject. Seleucus thereupon sent his treasurer Heliodorus to Jerusalem with orders to confiscate the treasures concealed in the Temple. Onias naturally resisted this unjust demand. Heliodorus then showed his royal warrant, and prepared to force his way into the Sanctuary. Great was the consternation in Jerusalem at the thought of a heathen's entering the Temple and robbing it of its treasures. However, by some means or other, this sacrilege was not perpetrated. We are not told what means were employed for preventing it, but tradition, born of pious reverence for the Temple of God, has given the colouring of the miraculous to the whole proceeding.

But Simon could not desist from his attempts to bring about the downfall of the hated high-priest. He even had recourse to the aid of hired assassins. Fortunately, he was unsuccessful; but Onias was now thoroughly alarmed. He determined to lay the real state of affairs before King Seleucus, with an account of the conflicting parties and of the motives that induced Simon and the Tobiades to conspire against him, imploring the king's protection and aid.

He appointed his brother Joshua, or Jason, as his delegate, and repaired to Antioch. During his absence the Hellenists, eager to obtain the office of high-priest for one of their own party, redoubled their intrigues. A high-priest from among their own number would not only be master of the treasures in the Temple, but leader of the nation. He could assist them in the introduction of Greek customs, and, by reason of his spiritual office, add weight to the efforts of the Hellenists, who had become so demoralised that they held nothing sacred.

These secret devices soon became known, and roused the indignation of many who clung to the old customs and traditionary teachings. Amongst these was a poet and writer of proverbs, Jesus Sirach by name, the son of Eleazar (200–176). He was prompted by the wrongdoing he witnessed in Jerusalem to write a book of pithy sayings, applicable to the evils of the age, which might prove salutary to its Judæan readers. He was a successor of the proverb-writers. He was familiar with the Law, the prophets, and other instructive and spiritual works, and he was a close reader of the older Book of Proverbs, imitating the style of that work, though without reaching its graceful simplicity.

Sirach did not belong to the sterner Chasidim who refrained from all harmless pleasures, and who denounced others for enjoying them. On the contrary, he was in favour of the social meal, enlivened by music and wine. To those who made a point of interfering with innocent pleasures, and whose dismal talk put an end to all gaiety, he addressed the following rebuke:—

"Speak, thou elder in council, for it becometh thee, but with sound judgment, and shew not forth wisdom out of time. As a signet of an emerald set in a work of gold, so is the melody of music with pleasant wine." (ECCLUS. xxxii. 3, 4, 6.)

There were some over-pious Judæans who condemned the use of all medical skill and aid; they insisted that as all maladies were sent from God, He alone could cure them. Sirach explained in his proverbs that the skill of the physician and the virtue of medicines were also the gifts of God, created to serve the purpose of healing.

But all his zeal was kindled at sight of the social and religious backsliding of his brethren, and their consequent humiliation in the eyes of the neighbouring peoples. The social depravity of his coreligionists grieved him more than their political oppression. Sirach stung with the lash of sarcasm the arrogance, deceit and lust of the rich Hellenists, who worshipped Mammon. He also denounced lechery, warned them against the companionship of dancers, singers and painted women, and he painted in no flattering colours the portraits of the daughters of Israel.

Sirach declared that the root of all this evil was the indifference of the Judæans to their sacred Law. His aim was to reinstate it in the hearts of the people. He touched upon another subject, a burning question of the day. Many in Jerusalem, particularly among the upper circles, were anxious to substitute for the high-priest Onias one of their own party, even though he were not a descendant or Aaron. Was it necessary to restrict the priestly office to one family? This was the question propounded by the ambitious. Sirach's proverbs are directed against the possibility of a revolution in the sacred order.

By various examples, taken from the history of the Judæan people, he endeavoured to show that obedience to the Law and to established rule would entail happy consequences, but that disobedience must lead to fatal results. He gave a short account of illustrious and notorious personages, dwelling upon their virtuous deeds or nefarious practices, as the case might be. He described the rise of the family of Korah against Aaron, their final destruction by fire, and the heightened glory of the high-priest. This was a hint to his co-religionists that the zealous Hellenists should not be allowed to provoke a repetition of Korah's punishment.   He also dwelt upon the history of Phineas, Aaron's grandson, the third in glory, who was permitted to make atonement for Israel.

He passed rapidly over the division of the two kingdoms and the depravity of the people, lingering upon the activity and energy of the prophets.   He mentioned with loving recollection the names of Zerubbabel, the high-priest Joshua, and Nehemiah, in the days succeeding the Captivity.   And at length he closed with a brilliant description of the high-priest, Simon the Just, of his good deeds and the majesty of his priesthood, hoping that this example of the ancestor of the family of the high-priest and of the Tobiades might instruct and warn the ambitious desecrators of the priestly diadem.   But instead of the unity for which he prayed, at the end of his book, the dissensions increased, and the plots and wickedness of the Hellenists brought the Judæan nation to the brink of destruction.

CHAPTER XXII.

THE TYRANNICAL CONVERSION TO HELLENISM AND THE ELEVATION OF THE MACCABEES.

Antiochus Epiphanes—His Character—His Wars with Rome—He appoints Jason to the High Priesthood—Introduction of the Greek Games—Jason sends Envoys to Tyre to take part in the Olympian Games—Affairs in Jerusalem—Antiochus invades Egypt—Report of his Death in Jerusalem—Antiochus attacks the City and defiles the Temple—His Designs against Judaism —His Second Invasion of Egypt—The Persecution of the Judæans—The Martyrs—Mattathias and his five Sons—Apelles appears in Modin—The Chasidim—Death of Mattathias and Appointment of Judas Maccabæus as Leader—His Virtues— Battles against Apollonius and Heron—Antiochus determines to exterminate the Judæan People—Composition and Object of the Book of Daniel—Victory of Judas over Lysias.

175—166 B. C. E.

THERE now appeared on the scene a royal personage who seemed destined to increase the hopeless disorders in Judæa, and to bring greater misery upon the House of Israel than it had ever known before. This man was Antiochus Epiphanes, whom history has justly branded. He belonged to a class of men who have a double nature. He was a mixture of malice and noble impulses; he was cunning and calculating, yet capricious, petty in great enterprises, and great in trivialities. His contemporaries even could not fathom his character, nor understand whether a naturally crippled intellect or simulation was the cause of the absurdities by which he made himself ridiculous in the eyes of the people. He seemed to covet the name of "Epimanes," or the *Madman*. His early training encouraged him to lead an irregular life. He resided for thirteen years at Rome, whither his father had sent him as hostage for the maintenance of peace and the payment of the costs of the war.

Rome had just become the capital of the world. The Romans had conquered the Carthaginians, the Macedonians and the Syrians, and the Eternal City was passing from the austere morality of the Catos to the wantonness of the Claudii. Debauchery and unnatural lust—the immoral practices of the Greeks—speedily took root there. But what Antiochus learnt principally at Rome was contempt of men and their cherished customs; there also he acquired not only insolence, but a hardness of heart which knew no compassion, and the malice which sports with its victim before it strangles it.

Antiochus succeeded in obtaining permission to leave Rome, and to send his nephew Demetrius, son of the king Seleucus Philopator, as hostage in his place. He returned to Syria, probably with the intention of dethroning his brother, but his design had been anticipated by Heliodorus, one of the court magnates, who had murdered Seleucus (175), and taken possession of the kingdom. It may be questioned whether Antiochus was not implicated in this deed; he was at that time at Athens, on his way home. His father's enemy, Eumenes, king of Pergamus, with his brother Attalus, put the murderer Heliodorus to flight, and proclaimed Antiochus king of Syria and Asia. Thus Antiochus attained to power by craft and usurpation; for Demetrius, now a hostage at Rome, was the rightful sovereign. The Romans favoured the usurper, for they hoped, by increasing the dissensions among the royal families, to bring about the fall of those kingdoms which still resisted their power. Antiochus, however, was determined to foil this stratagem of the Romans. A Judæan seer thus graphically describes his accession to the throne:—

"And in his place shall stand up a contemptible person to whom they had not given the honour of the kingdom ; but he shall come suddenly, and shall obtain the kingdom by flatteries. ... And after the league made with him he shall work deceitfully; for he shall come up and shall become strong, with a small number of people.

Suddenly shall he come even upon the fattest places of the province; and he shall do what his fathers have not done, nor his fathers' fathers; he shall scatter among them prey, and spoil, and substance." (DANIEL xi. 21–24.)

It was in the execution of his designs to deceive the Romans that he introduced in Antioch the Roman gladiatorial combats, in which prisoners of war or slaves were made to fight each other with arms until one succumbed or was killed. Antiochus had entirely banished from his soul the fear of any deity; "he neither reverenced the gods of his ancestors, nor any god whatever, for above all he magnified himself." The Judæans were now in the hands of this monster, who had a heart of stone, and scorned alike man and law, morality and religion. If peace had reigned in Judæa, the country might have escaped his notice, but the discord which the Hellenists had excited there directed his attention towards the Judæan people and their land. The Hellenist party themselves requested his interference in the internal affairs of Judæa, directing his notice to Hyrcanus, whom they hated, and who, residing in his castle near Hesbon, collected the taxes from the Arabian or Nabatæan inhabitants of the land in the name of the king of Egypt. Hyrcanus, dreading an ignominious death, committed suicide, and Antiochus seized all his property.

The Hellenists then carried out their long-cherished plan of divesting their other enemy, the high-priest Onias, of his dignity. The brother of the latter, called Jesus or Jason, promised Antiochus a large sum if he would transfer the high-priesthood to him; and the needy king did not scruple to grant the request. Onias, who journeyed to Antioch, to bring charges against his enemies, was denounced as a partisan of the Ptolemies, and the accuser thus became the accused. The Hellenists, or rather the high-priest, next petitioned Antiochus that those Judæans who were trained for the Greek combats should be registered as Antiochians or Macedonians, and as such be entitled to the privileges of full citizenship, and admitted to all public meetings and games of the Greeks. Games were serious occupations to the Greeks, not mere amusements, but rather the aim and end of life. The Grecian settlers in Palestine and Phœnicia maintained the national tie with their brethren at home by introducing the Olympian games, held every four years, in the land of the barbarians, and such of the latter as were allowed to take part in these games felt themselves greatly honoured by their admission to the Greek nobility.

By introducing gymnasia into Jerusalem, Jason and the Hellenists hoped to obtain the right of Greek citizenship for the Judæans, and thus to diminish the hatred and contempt from which they suffered. As soon as Antiochus had conceded the privilege for which the Hellenists had petitioned, Jason took great interest in superintending the exercises which were to be practised before the Judæans could take part in the Olympian games. The high-priest selected (174) a site for the games in the Birah or Acra (Acropolis), north-west of the Temple. It comprised a gymnasium for youths and an ephebeion for boys. Greek masters were most probably hired to teach the Judæan men and youths their games, which consisted in racing, jumping, wrestling, in throwing discs, and boxing. It soon became evident, however, that these games, which owed their origin to quite a different mode of life, were incompatible with Judaism. According to Greek custom, the men who took part in these contests were naked. The Judæan youths who consented to compete were therefore compelled to overcome their feeling of shame and appear naked in sight of the Temple. Besides, in uncovering their bodies they could immediately be recognised as Judæans. But were they to take part in the Olympian games, and expose

themselves to the mockery of the Greek scoffers?
Even this difficulty they evaded by undergoing a painful operation, so as to disguise the fact that they were
Judæans.   Youths soon crowded to the gymnasium, and the young priests neglected their duties
at the Temple to take part in the exercises of
the palæstra and the stadium.   The pious saw with
terror this adoption of foreign customs, but they
held their peace.   Meanwhile even Jason's confederates were dissatisfied with his leaning to Greek
manners, when it led to the denial of the fundamental
truths of Judaism.   When (June, 172) the Olympian
games were celebrated at Tyre, at which sacrifices
were offered up to the Greek god Hercules, the alleged founder of these combats, Jason sent as ambassadors men who were practiced in these games, and
entitled to take part in them.   According to custom,
they were entrusted with a money contribution to be
devoted to sacrifices to Hercules.   But the ambassadors, although Greek at heart, felt conscience-stricken
at the manner in which this sum was to be employed ;
it seemed to stamp them as idolaters, and to prove
their belief in the divinity of a marble statue.   They
therefore accepted the commission on condition that
the disposal of the money they took with them was to
be left to their own discretion.   The belief in Israel's
God was too deeply rooted even in the hearts of
those men who were partial to the Greek customs,
and attached to the Hellenistic party to admit of this
desecration.   Jason's ambassadors gave the money
as a contribution to the fleet which Antiochus was
fitting out at Tyre.

Meanwhile the dissensions in Jerusalem increased
so greatly that pernicious consequences could not
fail to follow.   The Hellenists were devising intrigues to overthrow Jason, and to have the office
of high-priest placed under their own control.   They
were impelled to this either by feelings of ambition,
or by the fear that the brother of Onias was too partial

to Judaism, and not sufficiently energetic, to overthrow the patriarchal customs. One of their number, Onias Menelaus, an unscrupulous man, and a brother of that Simon who had denounced Onias, and revealed the existence of the treasures in the Temple, was to be made high-priest. Jason sent the annual contributions to the king through Menelaus, who promised to increase them by 300 talents, if he were made high-priest. He boasted of his great credit, which would enable him to further the king's cause more energetically than Jason. Antiochus did not scruple to transfer the dignity of the high-priest to the highest bidder (172–171). He immediately sent Sostrates, one of his officers, with a troop of Cyprian soldiers, to Jerusalem, to subdue any opposition that might be made, and to watch over the punctual delivery of the promised sums. Sostrates placed the soldiers in the fortified Acra to keep down the inhabitants of Jerusalem, and proclaimed the dismissal of Jason according to the king's order. The latter was either banished or he escaped from Jerusalem, whence he crossed over the Jordan into the land of the Ammonites. This district was governed by a Nabatæan prince, named Aretas, by whom he was cordially received. This change only increased the disorders in Jerusalem; the greater part of the people were indignant that Menelaus, who was a Benjamite, and not of the family of the high-priests, and who besides was known to be opposed to the patriarchal customs, had been invested with that holy dignity. Even the admirers of Greek customs and the lovers of innovations condemned the selection of Menelaus.

Both the followers of Jason and those who did not wish to break entirely with Judaism disapproved of his dismissal. But the malcontents were compelled to be silent, because they feared the presence of the Syrian officer and the Cyprian troops which he commanded; but great excitement prevailed in the minds of the people, and threatened to break

forth at the earliest opportunity.   Menelaus brought
matters to a climax.   He had promised the king
more than he could give in payment for the dignity
he had received.   Antiochus was indignant, and
summoned him to come and justify himself.   Compelled to go to Antioch, he left the capital in charge
of his brother Lysimachus, who was as unconscien-
tious as himself, and took holy gifts out of the
Temple, intending to sell them in order to make up
the required sum.   Not finding the king at home,
he bribed his lieutenant Andronicus with part of the
costly vessels.   The worthy high-priest, Onias III.,
who still resided at Antioch, heard of this crime ;
he also learnt that Menelaus had sold utensils from
the Temple in Tyre and other Phœnician towns.
Indignant at such behaviour, he accused Menelaus
of robbing the Temple, a crime which was considered heinous even amongst the Greeks.   This
accusation hastened the death of the deposed high-
priest.   For Menelaus conspired with Andronicus to
remove Onias before the king was informed of the
theft committed in the Temple, and of the use made
of the plunder.   Andronicus, being himself implicated, was anxious to make Onias harmless.   He
enticed him from the temple of Apollo at Daphne,
near Antioch, where he had taken refuge, and slew
him (171).   This was one more crime added to those
of which Menelaus had already been guilty.   The
murder of the high-priest produced a great sensation, even among the Greeks in Syria, and Antiochus,
on his return, was compelled to punish the murderer
Andronicus.

Meanwhile Menelaus, although his accuser had
been silenced, was forced to try to conciliate the king.
In order to do this, he ordered his brother Lysimachus to steal some more of the treasures of the Temple.
These thefts, however, did not remain unnoticed ;
as soon as they were discovered and the perpetrator
found out, there arose a feeling of great bitterness

against him, which culminated in violence. When the shameful conduct of the two brothers became known to the people outside of Jerusalem, they hurried into the city, and joining the inhabitants of the capital, they threatened the violator of the Temple with death. Lysimachus armed his followers, and placed at their head a man named Avran, an old comrade and fellow-sinner. The unarmed people were not frightened by the soldiers, but attacked them with stones and sticks, blinded them with heaps of ashes, killed a great many, and put others to flight. Lysimachus himself was slain in the vicinity of the treasury of the Temple. Menelaus naturally brought an accusation against the rebels of Jerusalem before the king, and the latter organised a judicial court in Tyre to try the cause. Three members of the council, whom the people had selected for the purpose, proved in so convincing a manner the guilt of Lysimachus and his brother in the matter of the desecration of the Temple that the verdict would have turned against him. But the inventive genius of Menelaus managed to secure the interest of a creature of like mould, who succeeded in turning the balance in favour of the culprit. Antiochus, from his seat of justice, exonerated the criminal Menelaus, whilst he condemned to death the three deputies from Jerusalem, who had so clearly proved his guilt. The Tyrian witnesses of this breach of justice evinced their displeasure by taking a sympathetic part in the funeral of the three noble men, but Menelaus and injustice triumphed. He retained his coveted power, and he formed plans to revenge himself upon the people that hated him so fiercely. He calumniated his enemies, that is to say, the whole nation, before the king. On the one hand, he maintained that his enemies were partisans of the Egyptian court, and that they persecuted him only because he opposed their party intrigues; on the other, Menelaus maligned Judaism; he said that the Law of

Moses was replete with hatred of humanity, for it forbade the Jews to take part in the repasts of other nations, or to show any kindness to strangers. As Antiochus was then concentrating all his thoughts on the conquest of Egypt, he believed Menelaus's calumnies, and regarded the Judæans with distrust. If he undertook the hazardous expedition against Egypt, it would be dangerous to leave an enemy in his rear who might become formidable.

At last he carried out his long-cherished plan of attacking Egypt. A pretext for war is easily found, and Antiochus soon discovered one. His sister Cleopatra, married to Ptolemy V., had died, and left two infant sons, Philometor and Physcon, the former of whom was the nominal king, but his two guardians, Eulæus and Lenæus, ruled the country. Antiochus pretended that he was only anticipating the war which would shortly be directed against himself, and assembled his troops to make a descent upon Egypt. He delayed his attack, however, for some time, out of fear of the Romans. But when the latter became involved in a new war with Perseus, king of Macedonia, he ventured at last to cross the Egyptian frontier (170). He defeated the Egyptian army near Pelusium, and penetrated deeper into the country.

The two guardians fled with the young king Philometor. Thereupon Antiochus took possession of the whole of northern Egypt, and advanced to Alexandria to besiege it. The inhabitants meanwhile proclaimed the younger brother Ptolemy Physcon king, and defended the town so valiantly that the Syrian king despaired of conquering it. He therefore entered into negotiations with the elder brother, sent for him, signed a treaty with him, and pretended to continue the war for his benefit. The two kings " at one table spake lies to each other." In Judæa the consequences of the war were watched with eager suspense. If the Egyptians were victorious, the probability was that the sad misfortunes brought about by the hated high-priest would come to an end. The Egyptian court favoured the national Judæan party, and received all the patriots who fled from the tyranny of Antiochus and Menelaus. The report was suddenly spread that Antiochus had fallen, and the intelligence produced great excitement. The deposed high-priest Jason left the Ammonites, with whom he had found refuge, and hurried to Jerusalem, accompanied by a thousand men, by whose aid he hoped to take possession of the town. Menelaus barricaded the gates of Jerusalem, and fought the enemy from the walls. Thus arose a civil war through the ambition of two men, who both sought the high-priesthood as a road to power. But as only a small number of the inhabitants sided with Menelaus, Jason succeeded in entering Jerusalem with his troops. Menelaus took refuge within the walls of the Acra.

Meanwhile Antiochus left Egypt with rich spoils (169), perhaps with the intention of raising new troops. Having heard of the occurrences in Jerusalem, his anger was roused against the Judæans, and the Covenant of Judaism; his wicked, inhuman nature broke forth against the people. He suddenly attacked Jerusalem, and massacred the inhabitants without regard to age or sex, slaughtering friend and foe alike. He forced his way into the Temple, and entered even the Holy of Holies, and as a mark of contempt for the God who was worshipped there, he removed the golden altar, the candlestick, the table, the golden vessels, and all the treasures which still remained. Menelaus acted as guide in this spoliation of the Temple. Antiochus blasphemed the God of Israel, whose omnipotence was sung by His followers, but whom he scorned, because He did not interfere with these sacrilegious actions. To palliate both the massacre of innocent people and the desecration of the Temple, he invented a falsehood which long afterwards continued to bring Judaism into bad repute amongst all civilised nations. Antiochus de-

clared that he had seen in the Holy of Holies the
statue of a man with a long beard, mounted on an
ass, and holding a book in its hand. He believed
it to be the statue of the law-giver Moses, who had
given the Judæans inhuman, horrible laws to separate them from all other peoples. Amongst the
Greeks and Romans the rumour was spread that
Antiochus had found the head of an ass made of gold
in the Temple, which the Judæans venerated, and
that consequently they worshipped asses. Antiochus
was probably the author of another horrible lie invented to blacken the Judæans: it was said that
he had discovered, lying in bed in the Temple, a
Greek, who entreated to be released, as the Judæans
were in the habit of killing a Greek every year, and
feeding on his intestines, meanwhile swearing hatred
against all Greeks, whom they were determined to
destroy. Whether this vile calumny proceeded
directly from Antiochus, or whether these fables were
only attributed to him, there is no doubt that he
blackened the reputation of the Judæans by spreading
the report that Judaism inculcated hatred towards
all other nations. This was the first fruit of the long-
cherished wish to be associated with the Greeks.

A veil of grief was drawn over Jerusalem, and the
house of Jacob was dishonoured.

"The leaders and the elders moaned, youths and maidens hid
themselves, the beauty of the women was disfigured, the bridegroom
lifted up his voice in sorrow instead of joyous song, and the bride
wept in her bridal chamber." (I MACC. i. 26–28.)

But this was by no means the end; more sorrowful
days were in store for Judæa. Antiochus undertook
a second campaign against Egypt, and the Judæans
were destined a second time to suffer from his anger
at the unsuccessful termination of the war. The two
royal brothers Philometor and Physcon were reconciled with each other by the help of their sister and the
Romans; Philometor was proclaimed king in Alexandria. Antiochus was furious at this; for his desire

was to employ the helpless and cowardly Philometor as his tool, and to rule Egypt through him. As the Romans were still involved in a Macedonian war, he thought he might venture to attack Egypt a second time (168). He entered the country without opposition, and pushed on as far as Alexandria; the king of Egypt had meanwhile despatched envoys to Rome to ask for help from the senate. Three Roman deputies, with instructions to tarry on the road until they heard the issue of the Macedonian war, were thereupon sent to Antiochus to bid him desist. After the successful battle of Pydna, the destruction of the Macedonian army, and the flight of King Perseus (June 22, 168), the three Roman deputies hurried to the camp of Antiochus, and brought him the command of the senate to leave Egypt. When the Syrian king asked for time to consider, Popillius Lænas, drawing a circle with his stick, sternly declared that, before stepping out of this circle, Antiochus was to state whether he wished for peace or war with Rome. Antiochus knew how inexorable were Roman commands, and therefore determined to depart immediately (end of June, 168).

Antiochus, "the Illustrious," returned to his capital. The knowledge of his humiliation tormented him the more, as he had to feign friendship and satisfaction before the Romans. He vented his secret anger in unparalleled cruelties upon the Judæans. They had, he said, shown pleasure at his degradation; they had proclaimed aloud that the God they worshipped humbled the haughty, and had therefore prepared this mortification for him. Apollonius, one of his princely subjects, and former governor of Mysia, entered the Judæan capital, accompanied by fierce troops, apparently with peaceful intentions. Suddenly, however, on a Sabbath, when resistance was impossible, the Greek or Macedonian mercenaries threw themselves on the inhabitants, killed men and youths, took women and children prisoners, and sent them to the slave markets. Apollonius also destroyed many houses in the capital, and pulled down the walls of Jerusalem, for he wished it to disappear from the list of important cities. What induced the madman and his wild troops to spare the Sanctuary? They did not destroy it, because Antiochus wanted the Temple for another purpose; but they gave vent to their anger by attacking its surroundings, burning the wooden gates, and destroying the halls "with hammer and axe." Within the Temple there was nothing left to steal. The inhabitants who had not met with death escaped, and only the most rabid Hellenists, the Syrian soldiers, and strangers remained in the deserted places. "Jerusalem became strange to her own children." The Temple was also abandoned, for the faithful priests and Levites had left, and the Hellenists did not trouble themselves about the sacred building; the Acra was their resort. Here was stationed the strong Syrian garrison, and here also dwelt the Hellenists. This place was protected against any attack by high, strong walls and towers overlooking the Temple, and it was filled with arms and provisions.

The desolation soon became unbearable to Menelaus, the instigator of all these horrors. Of what use was it to be high-priest if no worshippers came to the Temple, or to be ruler over the nation if the people turned their backs upon him? Hearing nothing but the echo of his own voice, he became gloomy. To free himself from this painful position he resorted to new infamy. Judaism, with its laws and customs, was to be abolished, and its followers were to be compelled to adopt the Greek faith. Antiochus, full of hatred and anger against both the Judæans and their religion, acceded to Menelaus's plan, and had it carried out with his usual inflexibility. The Judæans were to become Hellenised, and thereby reduced to obedience, or, if they opposed his will, to be put to death. He not only wished to become master of the Judæan people, but to prove to them the impotence of the God they served so faithfully.   He, who disdained the gods of his ancestors, considered it mockery that the Judæans should still hope that their God would destroy him, the proud blasphemer, and he determined to challenge and defeat the God of Israel.   Thereupon Antiochus issued a decree, which was sent forth to all the towns of Judæa, commanding the people to renounce the laws of their God, and to offer sacrifice only to the Greek gods.   Altars and idols were to be erected everywhere for that purpose, and, in order to strike an effectual blow at Judaism, Antiochus ordained that unclean animals, particularly swine, should be used at the sacrifices.   He forbade, under severe penalty, three religious rites which outwardly distinguished the Judæans from the heathen, namely, circumcision, the keeping of the Sabbath and the festivals, and the abstinence from unclean food.   Officials were appointed to see that his orders were carefully carried out, and these officials were hard-hearted men, who punished with death any person infringing the royal commands.   The Temple was first desecrated, and Antiochus himself sent a noble Antiochian thither to dedicate the Sanctuary to Jupiter.   A swine was sacrificed on the altar in the court, and its blood was sprinkled in the Holy of Holies, on the stone which Antiochus had imagined to be the statue of Moses ; the flesh was cooked, and its juice spilt over the leaves of the Holy Scriptures.   The so-called high-priest Menelaus and the other Judæan Hellenists were to partake of the swine's flesh.   The roll of the Law, which was found in the Temple, was not only bespattered, but burnt, because this teacher of purity and love for all humanity,—so Antiochus maintained,—inculcated hatred of mankind.   This was its first baptism of fire.   The statue of Jupiter, "the abomination of destruction," was then placed on the altar, and to him sacrifices were henceforth to be offered (17 Tammuz, July. 168).

Thus the Temple in Jerusalem, the only place of holiness on earth, was thoroughly desecrated, and the God of Israel was apparently unseated by the Hellenic Zeus. How will the people bear this unparalleled violation? Will they submit to the stern edict of the heartless king and his officials, and allow themselves to be deprived of their nationality and their God? It was a severe and momentous ordeal. Death threatened all those who openly confessed Judaism, and they dared not even call themselves Judæans. But the persecuted people came out of their trial victoriously, and the blood of martyrs sealed their union with God and His Law.

The Judæans who were dispersed in Syrian and Phœnician towns, in closest proximity to the Greeks, and were included in this forced conversion, affected submission to the order, sacrificed to the Greek gods, and concealed or denied their religion. But even amongst these some remained faithful, and gave their lives in testimony of the truth of the Law. In Antioch an aged man named Eleazar suffered a martyr's death rather than partake of the idolatrous sacrifices. It was related in Jewish circles outside of Judæa, that a mother and seven sons, defying threats and persuasion, cheerfully went into death for the Law. These heroic martyrs, both young and old, set a noble example to the Judæans, and the number of those who suffered for their faith increased from day to day. The overseers whom Antiochus had appointed to carry out his decrees directed their attention to the smaller towns, whither the inhabitants of Jerusalem had fled. Here they built altars, and summoned the people in the name of the king to offer swine to Jupiter, and then to eat the flesh, and to break the Sabbath by working on the day of rest. They particularly insisted that sacrifices should be offered every month on the date which corresponded to that of Antiochus's birthday. On the bacchanalian festival of Dionysus, the celebration of which consisted in opening barrels of wine, they were compelled to deck themselves with ivy, like the Greeks, to institute processions, and to utter wild cries of joy in honour of the Greek Bacchus. When one of the officials came into a country town, and called the people together to give proofs of their secession from Judaism, he found but few to meet him. Many had fled and sought shelter in the caves and ravines of the Judæan mountains, or in the waste land near the Dead Sea. Antiochus was greatly irritated by this resistance, and he issued command upon command, recommending the utmost cruelty in the punishment of the disobedient people. The officials therefore continued their persecutions with redoubled zeal. They tore and burnt the rolls of the Law whenever they found them, and killed those who were found to seek strength and consolation in their perusal. They destroyed all houses of worship and education, and if they found women in confinement who, in the absence of their husbands, circumcised their sons themselves, these barbarians hanged them with their babes on the walls of the city.

But all such cruelties, instead of intimidating the people, only increased their determined resistance. Death had lost its terrors. Many preferred even death to violating the dietary laws. This noble firmness was particularly encouraged by the strictly religious sect of Chasidim. Some of these emerged from their hiding-places, and entering towns and villages, called the inhabitants together, spoke with warmth and conviction, and incited them to be steadfast and constant. Their preaching was all the more effective as they gave proof of indomitable courage in the face of death.

Before long, however, the Syrian commanders in Jerusalem discovered the leaders of this courageous resistance; some reprobate Hellenists had probably betrayed the hiding-place of the Chasidim. Thereupon the Phrygian Philip, commander of the garrison, went in search of the concealed fugitives. On a Sabbath he and his soldiers surrounded the caves in which thousands of men, women and children had sought refuge, he summoned them to come out in obedience to Antiochus's commands, and promised them safety if they submitted voluntarily to his orders. They answered unanimously, " We will not obey your command to break the Sabbath." Then Philip ordered his troops to commence the attack. The Chasidim looked on with undaunted courage, but did not try to defend themselves, nor to raise a stone to close the entrance to the caves, for fear of desecrating the Sabbath. Thus calling heaven and earth to witness their innocence, all the people perished in the caves by the hands of the murderous followers of Philip. Some were killed by the firebrands thrown into the caves, whilst others were suffocated by the smoke, which had penetrated into the interior.

Great was the grief of the faithful Judæans when they learned the horrible death of the men who had been to them a light and an example. The most courageous lost heart. What was to be the outcome of this unbearable position ? The faithful were bowed down by the thought that Heaven vouchsafed them no visible sign of hope in this, their unparalleled trial; no prophet rose up to foretell when this fearful ordeal was to end.

When the bloody persecution of the Judæan people had reached such a height that either the destruction of the whole nation, or their submission from exhaustion and despair seemed imminent, an open rebellion took the place of passive resistance.

It was brought about by a family whose members combined the purest piety with courage, wisdom and prudence; this was the family of the Hasmonæans or Maccabees. An aged father and five heroic sons brought about a revolution, and kindled a spirit of enthusiasm which secured the existence of Judaism for all time. The aged father, Mattathias, was the son of Johanan, son of Simon Hasmonai, an Aaronide ; he had left Jerusalem in consequence of the desecration of the Temple, and had established himself in the small town of Modin, three miles north of Jerusalem. His five sons, who all helped to raise the people from its deep degradation, and found their death in defending their country, bore Aramaic names : Johanan Gadi, Simon Tharsi, Judas Maccabi, Eleazar Hawran, and Jonathan Haphus. This family of Hasmonæans, who had many followers, on account of the consideration in which they were held, felt the miserable condition of their country with poignant sorrow. " What is life to us, now that the Sanctuary is desecrated and Judæa has become a slave?" Thus spoke Mattathias to his sons, and he determined not to remain quiet and sorrowing in his hiding-place, but either to help the good cause or to die courageously for it.

When Apelles, one of the Syrian overseers, reached Modin, to summon the inhabitants to abandon the Law and to become idolaters, Mattathias and his sons intentionally appeared, and when commanded to set an example of submission, the former answered: " If all the people in the kingdom obey the order of the monarch, to depart from the faith of their fathers, I and my sons will abide by the Covenant of our forefathers." When one of the Judæans approached the altar to sacrifice to Jupiter, Mattathias could no longer restrain his wrath, but rushed upon the apostate, killing him at the altar. His sons, armed with long knives, fell upon Apelles and his troops, killed them, and destroyed the altar. This act proved the turning-point; it set an example of courageous resistance as against inactive despair. Immediately after this attack upon the officers of Antiochus, Mattathias cried out: " Whosoever is zealous for the Law, and whosoever wishes to support the Covenant, follow me." Thereupon the inhabitants of

Modin and the vicinity followed him to a secure hiding-place which he selected for them in the mountains of Ephraim; and there the remainder of the Chasidim, who had escaped death in the caves, and all those who had fled from oppression joined him.

The number of resolute defenders of their country daily increased. Mattathias did not conceal from them that they would have to fight hard battles, but exhorted them to be ready to face death. Warned by the exaggerated piety of the Chasidim, who had scrupled to move a stone on the Sabbath in their own defence, the assembly which surrounded the aged Hasmonæan decided to repulse with arms any attack made upon them even on the day of rest. The Chasidim accepted this decision, and the men of peace, hitherto entirely absorbed in the Holy Scriptures, now prepared to wage war. A commander who inspires confidence creates warriors. There was a recurrence of the hopeless condition which had prevailed at the time of the Judges and at the beginning of Saul's reign. Some of the inhabitants were hiding themselves in caves, others went over to the enemy, and only a small number were willing to sacrifice their lives for their country; they had no arms, and knew nothing of warfare. Victory seemed more hopeless now than in those olden days. Mattathias was careful not to wage open war against the Syrians with his small band. Well acquainted with every inch of the country, he entered the towns unexpectedly with his sons and followers, destroyed the idolatrous temples and altars, punished the inhabitants who sided with the enemy, chastised the Hellenists whenever he came upon them, and admitted into the Covenant the children that had been left uncircumcised. From time to time he routed small troops of Syrian soldiers whom he happened to encounter, but whenever the commander of the garrison of Jerusalem sent a larger detachment to pursue the rebellious Judæans, the latter disappeared as suddenly as they had come.   In short, Mattathias waged a kind of petty warfare against the enemy, such as can be carried on only in mountainous districts, but may wear out the most powerful enemy.

When the death of the aged Mattathias drew nigh (167), his followers had no need to be anxious about his successor; the only difficulty was the choice of one from amongst his five heroic sons.   The dying father designated Simon as a wise counsellor, and Judas as the commander, and exhorted them all to sacrifice their lives for the Covenant of their fore- fathers, and to fight God's battle.   As soon as Judas Maccabæus was in command, matters took a favourable turn.   He was a warrior such as the house of Israel had not known since the time of David and Joab, than whom he was nobler and purer. Invisible strength seemed to emanate from his hero- soul, which imbued all who surrounded him with the same dauntless courage.   He was endowed with the instincts of a general, and this enabled him to fight at the right moment, to take advantage of his enemy's weakness, and to deceive him by means of feigned attacks.   In the hour of battle, "he was like a lion in his rage," and when at rest, like a dove in gentleness and simplicity.   He was as resigned to the will of God as the holiest men of old in Israel, and relied not on his sword, but on God's help, praying to Him before each decisive action.   Judas Maccabæus was a true hero of Israel, who only resorted to bloodshed when compelled by necessity in order to recover lost freedom, and to raise a humbled people.   He gave his name to the whole epoch.

At first he followed the example of his father, and sallied out only secretly or at night to punish the apostates, to win over the wavering, and to harass small bands of Syrian troops.   But as the number of his followers steadily increased, augmented by pretended converts to heathendom, who were glad to throw off their masks, and by those who were cured of their love for the Greeks by the cruelty and despotism of the latter, Judas ventured to confront a Syrian army under Apollonius. The latter had united the garrison at Samaria with other troops which he had collected in order to fight the rebels, for he had deemed it imprudent to withdraw the soldiers from Jerusalem, or rather, from the Acra. This was the first open battle which Judas fought, and success rewarded his valour. Apollonius was killed, and his soldiers were either slain on the battle-field, or sought safety in flight. Though the number of the defeated Syrians was small, still this victory encouraged the Judæans. They had met the cruel foe face to face, and their daring had triumphed; they considered it a proof that God had not abandoned His people, but still watched over and protected them. Judas took the sword which had dropped from the hand of Apollonius, and fought with it until his death.

A Syrian commander named Heron, guided by some treacherous Hellenists, pursued Judas and his followers into the mountains, and hoped to crush them with his overwhelming numbers. When the Judæan soldiers first saw the great numbers of men assembled near Bethhoron, they cried out, "How can we wage war against such an enemy?" But Judas knew how to calm their fears, and reminded them of the precious treasures they were called upon to defend,—their lives, their children, and the Law. A vigorous attack was made on the Syrians, who were totally defeated. Eight hundred men of Heron's army remained dead on the battle-field, and the others fled westward into the land of the Philistines. This first decisive victory of Judas, at Bethhoron, over a much larger army than his own (166), inspired the Judæans with confidence, and filled their enemies with terror; they were amazed both at the bravery and the strategical skill of the Maccabee, and at the endurance of the people.

What was Antiochus, the author of all these calamities, doing meanwhile? At first he troubled himself little about the Judæans, foolishly believing that his decrees would suffice to subdue and convert them. But when he learned of the losses of his army, and when the fame of Judas reached his ear, he at last admitted that he had underrated his enemy's power of resistance. In the first moment of anger he determined to send forth a large army, and make an end of his refractory opponents. But he was unable to carry out his plans immediately; he had few troops left, and would have been compelled to obtain mercenaries. For this purpose he needed money, and his treasury was but scantily supplied; for his extravagant expenditures were greatly in excess of his revenues, and owing to the war with Judas, the taxes were not collected in Judæa. Other embarrassments were added to these, for alarming news reached him from the east and the north. Arsaces, his satrap of Parthia, had revolted against the Syrio-Babylonian Empire, and had freed himself and his people. Artaxias, king of Armenia, totally ignored his fealty to Antiochus, and acted like an independent sovereign. The inhabitants of Aradus, and other Phœnician towns, also refused to obey him, and thus his revenues decreased steadily. In order to replenish his treasury he would have been compelled to wage war against these revolted nations, but to carry on this war he needed money. Thus he fell from one trouble into another; but, somehow, the half-insane Antiochus managed to hire some mercenary troops for a year. Intending to lead half of the troops himself against the rebellious provinces beyond the Euphrates, he placed the other half under the command of Lysias, a man of royal parentage, whom he appointed his lieutenant for the country between the Euphrates and the Egyptian border. To Lysias also he entrusted the education of his son. Antiochus's intentions regarding Judæa were now quite altered. Hellenisation was no longer thought of. His plan of changing the Jews into Greek citizens had been frustrated. They had shown themselves incorrigible, and quite unworthy of the benefit he wished to confer upon them. He therefore determined that they should be exterminated. He commissioned Lysias to march against Judæa with the troops left in his charge, and, after conquering the Judæans, to destroy and uproot every remnant of Israel and every trace of Jerusalem ; and the land was to be colonised by foreign tribes, and divided among them. The Judæan Hellenists were likewise comprised in this plan of destruction. Antiochus gave them up to their fate. He did not care for the small number who slavishly adhered to his commands. As soon as this plan became known, all the Judæans were seized with terror and despair, especially those who lived among other nations, outside of Judæa. Would the small but heroic army, under the guidance of the Maccabees, be able to resist the onslaught of a numerous horde, provided with elephants? " In every town, and in every country, where the king's commands became known, great terror filled the hearts of the Judæans, and they fasted and wept. The Elders dressed themselves in their penitential garb, and lay in ashes." But this unprecedentedly cruel plan of destroying a whole people, men, women and children, roused new champions for the defence of their country. Even the more worldly-minded men among the Judæans, and those who, though anxious for innovation, had not entirely fallen away from Judaism, now joined the Maccabees, for they had no other alternative.

However, the actual state of affairs was dismal enough. A large Syrian army was expected at every moment to crush the Judæan soldiers. It was absolutely necessary, therefore, that the whole nation should be animated with enthusiasm to fight and to endure.   A peculiar book was compiled to further this object, and circulated amongst the more educated of the Judæans; this was the Book of Daniel.   It was undoubtedly written by one of the Chasidim, and intended for his party.   The object of this apocalyptic and artistically compiled work, written partly in Hebrew and partly in Chaldæan, was to give examples of firmness in adhering to religious convictions, to encourage the reader to endurance, and to make him feel that this bloody persecution of the people would not be of long duration.   Even the most pious and faithful were beginning to doubt God's mercy, for no prophet appeared to reveal the object of their cruel sufferings, or to announce when they would cease.   The Book of Daniel offered consolation in this respect, showing that prophecy was not wholly extinct in Israel, for here was a vision, which announced the aim, and predicted the end of their misery.   "There is yet prophecy among us"—this is repeatedly urged as a consolation.

The Book first quotes examples of constancy in religious observances even under great difficulties and danger, and shows that this constancy was rewarded by a miraculous escape from death; the end of the book also contains prophecies for the future. The book further tells how the kings who violated the Sanctuary, or exercised religious despotism were humiliated, and forced to repent of their crimes. The Book of Daniel half conceals and half reveals, in a sort of allegory, the destruction of the wicked Syrian Empire, which was the heir to former kingdoms.   It foretells that the fourth kingdom on earth, following that of the Babylonians, the Medo-Persians and the Macedonians, would utter foolish words against the Almighty, seek to destroy the pious and to turn them away from the festivals and the laws. The pious would fall into its clutches for "a time, two times, and half a time."   Then dominion would pass into the hands of the people of the Holy One for ever, and all knees would bow down to Him. In another vision he saw the fourth Syrian Empire extending far away to the south, to the east and to the north, rising to the heavens, and casting down stars unto the earth, and crushing them. It would exalt itself over the King of the heavenly Hosts, it would abolish the daily sacrifice, and set up an idol in the Sanctuary. To the question:

"How long shall be the vision concerning the continual burnt-offering and the transgression that maketh desolate, to give up both the Sanctuary and the host to be trodden under foot?" (DANIEL viii. 13.)

a voice answered—

"Unto two thousand and three hundred evenings and mornings; when the Sanctuary shall be justified." (verse 14.)

The Book of Daniel, with its mystical revelations, was undoubtedly read with great interest by the Assidæans. The apocalyptic form, which gave each line a peculiar meaning, and reflected the present conditions, lent it a great attraction. Moreover, it solved the problem of the present calamities, and showed the object of the horrible persecutions; these were intended, on the one hand, to destroy sin, and on the other, to ennoble believers. It was evident that the duration of the period of affliction had been determined from the beginning, and that this very duration, too, had a secret meaning. The worldly kingdoms would disappear, and at the end of this time, God's kingdom, the kingdom of the holy ones, would commence, and those who had died or had been slain during the persecutions would awake to eternal life. Thus, though no prophet arose, still there existed a prophecy for the present time.

Meanwhile the danger became daily more threatening for the Judæans. Whilst Antiochus had been marching eastward (166) with a part of his army, his lieutenant Lysias had chosen a general called Ptolemy, son of Dorymenes (the one who had favoured

Menelaus, and who was commander in Cœlesyria and Phœnicia), and had appointed two able and experienced generals under him, Nicanor son of Patroclus, and Gorgias. The latter, having received orders to begin the campaign against the Judæans, led his division, which, it is said, consisted of 40,000, including cavalry, along the coast into the very heart of Judæa. Samaritans and Philistines, both arch-enemies of the Judæans, placed themselves at his disposal. He was so certain of victory that he invited slave-traders to come into his camp, and to bring with them money and chains. The Syrian commander thought that it would be more prudent to sell the captives as slaves than to kill them; but whilst he was thus prematurely disposing of them, the Judæan warriors, numbering 6,000, assembled round Judas Maccabæus. Before leading them into action, the commander, in order to animate them with the spirit of heroic self-sacrifice, organised a solemn assembly in the mountain city of Mizpah. It is a remarkable coincidence that, nine hundred years before, the prophet Samuel had, on a similar occasion, assembled the people in the same place, in order to select a leader against the enemy who was then planning the destruction of Israel. Judas chose Mizpah, because it had been a central meeting-place for those Judæans who had survived the destruction of the Temple under Gedaliah, when there had been a small temple there. The assembly was deeply moved; all its members observed a strict fast during the day, wore mourning garments, and prayed with all the fervour of their sorrowing hearts for help and compassion. A scroll of the Law, which the Judæan army carried with them, was unfolded, and excited great lamentations, for it reminded them that Antiochus wished to force them to abandon the Law and to become heathens.

But Judas endeavoured, not only to awaken emotion, but to arouse courage, and to prepare the people for the difficult and bloody action that awaited them.

He divided his army into four parts, and placed his three elder brothers each in command of a division. In accordance with the Law, he issued a proclamation to the effect that all those who were newly married, who had built a house or planted a new vineyard, or who lacked sufficient courage, were permitted to withdraw from the ranks. Then he marched towards Emmaus, an eight or nine hours' journey from Mizpah, to meet the enemy. Gorgias had encamped, with about 5,000 foot-soldiers and 1,000 cavalry, in the plain near Emmaus, because he thought it easier to penetrate from there into the mountains of Judæa to attack the Maccabæan army. The Syrian leader wished to surprise the Judæans in the night, but was outwitted by Maccabæus. As soon as night set in, Judas left the camp with his followers, marched by well-known roads to the west, and came upon the enemy's rear. When Gorgias found the camp of the Judæans deserted, he imagined that fear had driven them into the mountains, and he pursued them thither. This was the object of Judas's stratagem. He followed the Syrians, reached their camp, set it on fire, and pursued the troops. Gorgias noticed only at dawn that the enemy he was seeking in the mountains was following him from the plain; he had no time to order more than a part of his army to halt, and to confront the Judæans.

Meanwhile Maccabæus had arranged his division in perfect order, and encouraged them to fight for their country, their Law, and their Sanctuary. His younger brother hurriedly read to them a few encouraging verses out of the Law, and gave the warriors the watchword "God's help!" The Judæan army was greater in number than the single division of Syrian troops, and fought with great enthusiasm. Thus the enemy was beaten, and put to flight. Judas forbade his soldiers to seize any booty, as they still had to fight the other division of the enemy's army, which was returning from the mountains. These troops shortly made their appearance, and the Judæans stood ready to resume the battle; but it did not take place, for as soon as the Syrians saw the smoke rising from their camp, they turned and fled southwards into the land of the Philistines. "There was a great rescue on that day." The victory of Emmaus (166), gained by clever strategy and resolute valour, was of vast importance. It crippled the enemy, and inspired the Judæans with confidence in their own power. Neither the cavalry nor the foot-soldiers, with their helmets and shields, alarmed them any longer, and the arms which they needed fell into their hands after the enemy had taken to flight. The booty consisted of gold, silver, and purple, and of the sacks of money belonging to the numerous slave-traders who had come to the Syrian camp. All these things were not to be despised, as they became the means of victory to them in future struggles. The victors returned to their meeting-place at Modin with songs of rejoicing, the refrain of which was, "Praise the Lord, for He is good; for His mercy endureth forever."

But not yet could they lay down their arms; they knew that Lysias, who had received orders to destroy the Judæans, would not let this first defeat pass quietly, but that he would strain every effort to repair the disaster. They therefore remained armed, and had the happiness of seeing their numbers increase to 10,000. If ever a war deserved the name of "holy," the one conducted by the Maccabæans certainly proved worthy of that appellation. In the following year (165), when Lysias attacked Judæa with a powerful, picked army of cavalry and foot-soldiers, he found the Judæans more courageous and determined than ever. He had not ventured to enter their land on the same road as before, but had taken a circuitous route, intending to invade Judæa from the territory occupied by the Idumæans. He encamped near Bethzur, a five hours' march to the south of Jerusalem. Maccabæus marched with his 10,000 men to meet him ; a regular battle ensued, in which the impetuous attacks of the Judæans again secured a victory over the strategy of the Syrian hirelings. Lysias departed, furious at his defeat ; but he flattered himself that by increasing the number of his army he would ultimately master his opponents. Only in the Acra of Jerusalem, the incorrigible Hellenists, with Menelaus and a small Syrian garrison, still held sway.

CHAPTER XXIII.

VICTORIES AND DEATH OF JUDAS MACCABÆUS; JONATHAN THE HASMONÆAN.

Return of Judas to Jerusalem—Reconsecration of the Temple—The Feast of Lights—Fortification of the Capital—The Idumæans and Ammonites defeated by Judas—Ill-treatment of the Galilean Judæans—Measures against Timotheus—Death of Antiochus—Embassy of the Hellenists to Antiochus V.—Battle at Bethzur—Retreat of Judas—Affairs in Jerusalem—Alcimus—Intervention of the Romans—Nicanor's Interview with Judas—Battle of Adarsa—Death of Judas—Results of his Career—Condition of the People after the Death of Judas—The Chasidim, the Hellenists, and the Hasmonæans—Jonathan—His Guerilla Warfare against Bacchides—Death of the High-Priest Alcimus—Truce between Jonathan and Bacchides—Jonathan as High-Priest—His far-sighted Policy—His Captivity and his Death.

165—143 B. C. E.

THE two decisive battles of Emmaus and Bethhoron had entirely altered the position of Judæa. The imminent danger was averted. Three years and a half had passed since the beginning of the religious persecution and the desecration of the Temple (Tammuz, 168—Marheshvan, 165), and, just as the Book of Daniel had prophesied, peace had followed the disastrous excitement of this period. Maccabæus and his followers took advantage of this favourable moment to march into Jerusalem, and put an end to the desecration which had hitherto held sway there. The condition of the holy city was deeply distressing to her faithful sons, who had shed their hearts' blood to save her. The town looked like a desert,—the sporting-place of her desecrators. The Sanctuary was deserted, its gates were burnt, its halls were destroyed; idolatrous altars stood everywhere; the image of Zeus, the desolating abomination, towered on the altar, and statues of Anti-

ochus insulted the Judæans.   But the holy warriors had not time to give vent to their sorrow
at the general desecration, for they were forced
to act quickly for fear of being disturbed in their
work of purification.   Their first duty was to destroy
all statues of Jove, and to remove all unclean objects
from the Temple courts (3rd Kislev, 165).   They
also removed the altar, thinking it unfit for their
sacrifices, as it had been so frequently polluted. A
council of elders determined to place the stones of
the altar in one of the porches of the entrance-court,
and to keep them there until the prophet Elijah
should appear and decree what was to be done with
them.   Meanwhile a new altar was built, new doors
were put up, and new vessels were brought to the
Temple to replace the old ones.   All these preparations were finished in three weeks, and early in the
morning of the 25th Kislev (November), 165, the
Temple was consecrated with sacrifices and thanks-
givings.   The two former consecrations certainly
could not have been held with greater fervour and
devotion.   The purest feelings animated the congregation, and the mortal anguish, which they had
endured for three years and a half, now gave place
to feelings of joy and hope.

The consecration of the Temple not only denoted
the victory of the weak over the strong, the faithful
over the sinner, but also, and especially, the victory
of Judaism over Hellenic paganism, of the God of
Israel over idols.   People from every town of Judæa
took part in the festival, and the inhabitants of
Jerusalem lit bright lamps in front of their houses
as a symbol of the Law, called "Light" by the poets.
The Hasmonæan brothers and the other members of
the Great Council decided that in future the week
beginning on the 25th of Kislev should be held as a
joyous festival, to commemorate the consecration of the
Temple.   Year after year the members of the House
of Israel were to be reminded of the victory of the

few over the many, and of the re-establishment of the Sanctuary. This decree has been conscientiously carried out. For two thousand years these days have been celebrated as the " Days of Consecration " (Hanukkah) by the lighting of lamps in every household in Israel. From this custom the days derived their name of " Feast of Lights." Naturally, the old order of things was restored in the Temple. Priests and Levites were reinstated in their offices; only those Aaronides who had taken part in idolatrous worship were excluded from the Sanctuary. This severity, just as it was, produced bad results, and increased the difficulty of the position of the Judæans. The priests among the Hellenists and followers of Menelaus, despairing of reconciliation with the representatives of the people, became more and more embittered in their hatred against the patriotic, pious party. Maccabæus had placed his soldiers on guard whilst the Temple was being restored, to prevent the Hellenists from hindering the people in their work, and now that the consecration was over, he fortified the Temple Mount by means of a high wall with two strong towers, and placed a garrison in them, to protect it from sudden attacks from the neighbouring Birah or Acra. Foreseeing that the people would have to fight more battles before they could secure their freedom, he took the precaution of protecting the country in different ways, among which was the fortification of Bethzur, the town from which Lysias had sought to penetrate into Judæa with his army. It was to be in particular a stronghold against the Idumæans. The victory of the heroes of Israel over the well-armed Syrian troops increased the burning hatred of the neighbouring nations against the Judæans, and goaded them on to cruel enmity against the members of the people who dwelt amongst them, or who had fled to them for refuge. They either grudged them their victory or feared their superiority. The Philistines, in the south-west;

the Phœnicians, in the north-west; the Ammonites, on the other side of the Jordan; the Syrians and Macedonians everywhere in the neighbourhood, and the Idumæans in the south, were imbued with hatred of the Judæans.

When driven away from their homes by the Nabatæans, the Idumæans had settled in the old Judæan territory, and had even taken possession of Hebron. They showed themselves the bitter enemies of the Judæans in Antiochus's time, just as they had done under Nebuchadnezzar's despotism; they were ever on the watch for the fugitives, whom they ill-treated, and sometimes even killed. It was therefore very important to reduce them to subjection. Judas first undertook an expedition against the sons of Esau in Akrabattine, defeated them, and drove them from their dwelling-places. He then crossed the Jordan with his army, fought the Ammonites, who were led by a Syrian warrior, Timotheus, an implacable and indefatigable enemy of the Judæans. When Judas had defeated him and the Ammonites, and had taken possession of their capital Rabbath-Ammon (Philadelphia), Timotheus sought shelter in the neighbouring fortress Jaazer, commanded by his brother Chaireas. Twenty Judæan youths are reported to have shown wonderful valour, climbing the walls of this difficult fortress, and making a breach for the troops to enter. Judas accomplished his object by taking Jaazer and its "daughter towns"; he obtained peace for the Judæans residing in this part of the country, and inspired the peoples with respect for the name of Israel.

The Judæan troops had hardly returned to Jerusalem before they received intelligence of other cases of ill-treatment of their Judæan brethren at the hands of their heathen neighbours. The Judæans turned in their distress to Maccabæus, as the Israelites had done of old to Saul. The inhabitants of Gilead and Bashan informed him by letter that the heathen tribes had collected, with Timotheus at their head, with the intention of utterly destroying them; that 1,000 Judæans had been slaughtered in the province of Tobiene; that women and children had been dragged into captivity, and that their property had been plundered by the enemy. Messengers, with rent garments, followed upon this missive, bringing letters from the Galilean Judæans, that they also were threatened with death by the inhabitants of Acco, Tyre and Sidon. They implored Judas to come to their aid before it was too late. He had no need, like Saul, to send messengers with threatening words, in order to call together an army to the assistance of the threatened Jabesh-Gileadites, for his devoted followers constituted the whole fighting power of the land. Maccabæus gave the command of one part of his army to his brother Simon, with orders to march to the assistance of the Judæans of Galilee, whilst he and his brother Jonathan, with another division, prepared to rescue his oppressed brethren beyond the Jordan. The rest of the Judæan forces, under the command of two leaders, were to guard the western boundary of Judæa from the inroads of the Philistines. Simon accomplished his task with rapidity and good-fortune. He began by hastening to Acco, whose Judæan inhabitants were the worst sufferers at the hands of the Greeks or Macedonians. His well-trained soldiers, meeting with some hostile forces, defeated them easily, put them to rout, and pursued them to the very walls of their sea-port town. This successful feat of arms relieved him from the necessity of further engagements, for the Macedonians of the neighbouring towns did not venture to encounter the Maccabæan troops. Simon was therefore able to progress unmolested through Galilee, and to persuade the Judæans of that province to migrate to Judæa.

A more laborious contest awaited Judas in the Transjordanic provinces, for on his march he again

met with the obstinate hostility of Timotheus. As
in former ages, the heights were still crowned with
fortresses. However, Judas succeeded in reducing
several of them ; he razed their walls to the ground,
disarmed their defenders, and delivered his imprisoned countrymen. He then assembled the Judæan
population, led them across the Jordan, through the
friendly city of Bethshean (Scythopolis), and shortly
before the celebration of the feast of Pentecost (May,
164) he returned to Jerusalem with a number of
emigrant Judæans from Gilead. From all cities of
Judæa the enthusiastic people streamed to receive
the victors and to celebrate the festival with feelings
of joy and gratitude. New songs of praise resounded
in the Temple.

But Judas soon marched out again, in order to
avenge an injury which had been received during
his absence. His two generals, Joseph, the son of
Zachariah, and Azariah, whom he had left behind
to guard the land in the west, had, contrary to his
orders, attacked Gorgias, who was occupying Jamnia
with a force ; but they had suffered a defeat, and had
been driven back to the Judæan mountains. Judas
therefore embarked on a new campaign. His arms
were again crowned with success, he destroyed several cities on the sea-coast, together with their temples and idols.

Whilst the hero of the Maccabees had been making
fearless warriors out of his miserable and trembling
countrymen who had hidden in caves, whilst he had
been inspiring his people with self-confidence, and
vanquishing the enemy far and near, the court of
Syria had remained wrapped in the most complete
indifference. What could have induced Lysias, who
held the reins of government, to remain passive in
the face of this daring defiance? Had he not the
means of hiring mercenaries ; or did he think the
Judæans invincible? It is said that a distinguished
man at the Syrian court, named Ptolemy Macron,

had advocated the cause of the Judæans, and had declared that the religious restraint imposed upon them was unjust.

Suddenly important news came to Palestine concerning Antiochus Epiphanes. The progress of that monarch through Parthia had not been signalised by any military success ; nor had he been able to refill his treasury. Driven by want of money, he undertook an expedition to the city of Susa, in Elymais, to plunder the temple of the goddess Anaitis; but the inhabitants resisted the invader and forced him to retreat. He fell sick in the Persian city of Tabæ, and while in a state of delirium, expired (164). He who had derided the idea of a Divine Being and Divine justice, who had deliberately assaulted all that men hold sacred, in the end lost confidence in himself in consequence of the frustration of all his plans. It is quite possible that on his deathbed he repented of his desecration of the Temple, or, as another report has it, that his attack of frenzy resulted from the stings of conscience. At all events his last orders savour of madness, for he appointed one of his favourites, Philip, as regent of his kingdom and guardian of his young son Antiochus V., although previous to his departure for Persia he had invested Lysias with absolute power. This, his dying act, of pitting two rival governors against each other, thus dividing his country into factions, proved fatal to the Syrio-Macedonian kingdom, and to the Seleucidæan house.

The death of Antiochus produced no change in the position of the Judæans. Lysias, who was guardian of the young king, Antiochus V. (Eupator, from 164 to 162), undertook no expedition against the Judæans. Judas Maccabæus took advantage of this inactivity to improve the unsatisfactory internal condition of his country. At that time there existed in Jerusalem two neighbouring fortified places that were in daily feud with each other, namely the Sanctuary, and the fortress of the Acra, occupied by the Hellenists, who, with their pretended high-priest Menelaus, continued their hostilities against the patriotic and loyal Judæans by making attacks upon the fortifications of the Temple. Judas Maccabæus took measures to bring this intolerable state of affairs to an end. He undertook the formal siege of the Acra, and raised earthworks on which he placed catapults, to discharge stones against the walls.

In this emergency some of the Hellenists resolved to have recourse to the young king, Antiochus V. (Eupator), and, eluding the besiegers, travelled for that purpose to Antioch. Upon their arrival, they declared that they had been cruelly treated by the Judæan party, on account of their devotion to the royal cause ; that they had been robbed of their property, and threatened with death. They also represented to the king and his guardian that if the Acra were allowed to fall into the hands of the Hasmonæans, the rebellious Judæans would be utterly invincible. A council was thereupon held at the Syrian court, and it was agreed to commence hostile proceedings against the Hasmonæans. Ptolemy Macron, who alone spoke in favour of peaceful measures, could gain no hearing.

The flame of war again blazed up in the spring of 163 B. C. It was an unfortunate time for the Judæans, as this happened to be a Sabbatical year, which was strictly kept by those ready to forfeit their lives for the Law. There was neither sowing nor reaping, and the people had to content themselves with the fruits of the trees, with the spontaneous aftergrowth of the soil, or with what had been planted before the beginning of the Sabbatical year. The garrisons of the fortresses could not be supplied with food.

Lysias, accompanied by the royal child Eupator, and at the head of a large army with elephants, marched towards the south side of Judæa. Iudas could only send a small army into the field, as he required the greater number of his forces for the defence of the Temple and of the fortress of Bethzur. Thus he was compelled to restrict himself to defensive operations. The garrison of Bethzur fought bravely, and attempted to destroy the siege-train of the invaders. Unfortunately, the scarcity of their provisions would not permit the beleaguered to undergo a long siege, and, moreover, they were betrayed by a traitor, Rodocus, who is accused of having revealed to the enemy the secret ways by which food was introduced into the fortress. At length famine and treachery compelled the garrison of Bethzur to surrender; but they were allowed free egress from the fortress. Relieved on this side, the Syrian army was now able to march upon Jerusalem. Nothing was left to Maccabæus but to meet them in the field. He advanced at the head of his troops to Beth-Zachariah, not far from Bethsur, where he awaited the enemy. The Judæans again performed prodigies of valour. Eleazar, one of the Hasmonæan brothers, thinking that the magnificently-attired rider of an elephant was the king himself, crept boldly under the animal, stabbed it to death, and fell crushed by its enormous weight. But in spite of the courage and daring of the Judæans, they were obliged to retreat before the superior numbers of the Syrians. Judas retreated to Jerusalem, and entrenched himself with his army in the Temple fortress. Lysias soon followed, and began a formal siege of the Sanctuary. Judas did not fail to defend himself, and also erected catapults. As the siege continued for a long time, the supplies, which were not plentiful on account of the Sabbatical year, were soon consumed by the garrison. Tortured by hunger, the troops began to desert the fortress by subterranean passages. Only Judas Maccabæus, his three brothers, and a small band of devoted followers remained steadfastly at their post of danger, defying the pangs of hunger.

Jerusalem, or, more properly speaking, its last place of refuge, the Temple, was about to fall, as in the time of Nebuchadnezzar, through want of food; but help came unexpectedly.

Philip, who had been named regent of Syria by the dying king Antiochus Epiphanes, had raised a large army of Medo-Persians, and was marching upon Antioch to deprive Lysias of the rule. As soon as Lysias heard of the advance of his rival, he was forced to withdraw his troops from Jerusalem to lead them against this new enemy. He therefore persuaded the young king to make peace with the Judæans, and thus a treaty was concluded, the chief condition being that the Judæans should enjoy complete religious freedom, and that the fortress of the Temple should remain inviolate. Lysias agreed by oath to these conditions, but as soon as the gates of the fortress were opened, he ordered his soldiers to raze the walls and the towers to the ground. In no other way, however, did he seek to molest the Judæans, for he neither destroyed nor desecrated the Sanctuary, and he soon commenced his march to Syria, where Philip had taken possession of the capital. Thus the numerous battles of the Hasmonæans were crowned after all with success, and the Judæans were once more permitted to enjoy religious liberty, and were no longer compelled to sacrifice to Jupiter.

But these wars had another fortunate result: the Syrian court withdrew its protection from the Hellenists, who were obliged to leave their fortress in the Acra. Menelaus, the usurping high-priest, the author of untold misery, was sacrificed by Lysias. The latter looked upon him as a firebrand, and had him executed in Berœa (Aleppo), after he had, for ten years, degraded his priestly diadem by the most execrable conduct. Jason, who had not, indeed, been so great a criminal as Menelaus, but who had done his best to disturb the peace of his country, had expired somewhat earlier in a foreign land. Persecuted by Antiochus Epiphanes, and driven by the Nabatæan prince, Aretas, out of his country, he had fled to Egypt, but finding no safety there, had wandered from town to town, until at last he had found a grave in Sparta.

The truce between the Syrian court and the Judæan people making a return to the old order of things possible, it was necessary to elect a new high-priest as political chief, and who could be found worthier of that office than Judas Maccabæus? The great Hasmonæan hero was most probably raised to that dignity by Antiochus Eupator, or by his guardian, Lysias.

During these days of peace, the warrior was able to lay aside his arms, the peasant to till his fields, and the scribe to devote himself to the study and the expounding of the Law; the bleeding wounds of the commonwealth began at length to close and to heal. But peace was not to be of long duration.

The excitement, resulting from years of civil warfare, was not so easily allayed that a veil could be thrown over the past. There were still avowed and clandestine Hellenists, who hated Judas Maccabæus and his devoted adherents, especially the Chasidim, on account of the restraint imposed upon them and the frustration of their efforts. They took advantage of a turn in the political tide to gratify their bitter animosity. Prince Demetrius, who had been debarred from the succession to the throne of Syria by his uncle Antiochus Epiphanes, and who had been left by that monarch as hostage in Rome, seized upon a favourable opportunity for quitting that city to depose the son of the usurper and his guardians.

Lysias had foolishly and publicly maintained trained elephants and built ships of war, though the Roman Senate had interdicted both. Hereupon Rome sent one of its severest censors to Syria, the envoy Cneius Octavius, not only to pronounce a severe reproof against the regent, but also to order the slaying of his elephants and the burning of his fleet. The orders were carried out without opposition; but Octavius met with his death, at the hand of a patriot, in a bath at Laodicea. Thus the authorities in Rome, displeased with the court of Antiochus, overlooked the escape of Demetrius. When this prince appeared as an invader in Syria, he gained over the people and the army to his cause, and put the king and the regent to death (162). The discontented Judæan party made use of this change of rulers to lodge their complaints against the Hasmonæans. They were led by a priest of the name of Jakim, or in Greek Alcimus, the nephew of one of the teachers of the Law, Josê, son of Joëzer, but himself an adherent of the innovators. Alcimus and his adherents, embittered at having been excluded from the Temple and the altar, repaired to the king of Syria—it is said, with a golden introduction—to whom they gave a gloomy picture of the state of Judæa, ascribing the misfortunes of the country to Judas and his followers. The accusation was levelled chiefly against Maccabæus. So long as he lived, they said, the land would not obtain the blessings of peace. This accusation was pleasing to Demetrius, as it gave him an opportunity of asserting his power over a small, semi-independent province. Though he did not mean to walk in the footsteps of his kinsman, Antiochus Epiphanes, in the matter of religious persecutions, still, the fact of his being able to name Alcimus high-priest and political head of the Judæan commonwealth, would be a sign that he was master of the people. In order to prevent any opposition to his wishes, he sent Bacchides, a rude, inexorable warrior, with a large troop of Syrians, to Jerusalem. He came with peaceful assurances on his lips. But Judas and his brethren were not deceived. Convinced that their freedom and their lives were at stake, they quitted their beloved city, and retreated to the mountains

The unsuspicious Chasidim, however, allowed themselves to be deceived; they trusted Alcimus, because he was of the house of Aaron. A large assembly of distinguished scribes, possibly the whole body of the Synhedrin, repaired to Bacchides and Alcimus, assuring them of their friendliness and devotion, and begged them to take measures for restoring the quiet of their country. Alcimus, the new high-priest, solemnly swore that this was his intention; but as soon as he had taken possession of the city, he ordered sixty of the Chasidim to be slain, his uncle Josê being probably one of the victims. This outrage, coupled with his perjury, spread terror and mourning through the whole country. Again all hearts turned towards the Maccabees, and many of those who had joined the faction of Alcimus left him, and sought the Hasmonæan brothers at Modin.

It hardly required a new outrage, perpetrated by Bacchides, to light the torch of civil war. The Syrian army had intercepted the march of a number of Judæans who were leaving Alcimus in a body, had surrounded them near Jerusalem, at Beth Zachariah, and after slaying them, had thrown their dead bodies into a cistern. All who loved their freedom and their country now gathered round the Hasmonæans. But Alcimus succeeded in attracting the ambitious, luxurious and law-breaking Judæans. The nation was once more divided into two rival factions. At first the Hellenists were the stronger, as they were under the protection of foreign troops. Alcimus lost no time in marching through the land, in order to force the inhabitants to pay submission to Demetrius, and obedience to himself as high-priest. Meanwhile the army of the Maccabees was growing in strength and numbers. Judas was once more able to take the field against the Hellenists, and to punish the deserters, and he spread such terror that the adherents of Alcimus did not dare show themselves outside of Jerusalem.

Alcimus founded his hopes of ultimate success on the devotion he showed to the Syrian court, more than on his popularity among the people.   Therefore he hurried to Antiochia with fresh accusations against the Hasmonæans.   Demetrius thought he could easily cope with the rebellion of his Judæan subjects.   He sent Nicanor, one of the warriors who had escaped with him from Rome, to Judæa, commanding him to treat the insurgents with the utmost harshness.   This leader, too, considered it necessary to proceed gently at first, if only to gain time until the troops placed at his disposal arrived.   It is said that having heard of the valour and heroism of the great Judæan commander, he desired to effect a reconciliation between Judas and the king, and to this end offered to send three confidential envoys to confer with Maccabæus. The proposals of Posidonius, Theodotus, and Mattathias being acceptable to Judas and his adherents, an interview took place between him and Nicanor.   The latter was so enchanted with the Judæan hero, that he advised him after the conclusion of peace to take a wife, and bring an heroic race into the world. Alcimus, however, put an end to this good understanding by informing the king that Nicanor was playing a false part, that he favoured his enemy Judas, and contemplated raising him to the office of high-priest.   Hereupon the king sent strict orders to Nicanor to cease all negotiations, and to send Judas in chains to Antiochia.

Meanwhile Judas, who had been cautioned not to trust Nicanor, had retreated to his mountain fastnesses, whither he was followed by Nicanor and his army.   A battle ensued at Caphar-Salama, on the confines of Samaria, where Nicanor's army suffered defeat, and was driven back to the fortress of the Acra.   Enraged at this repulse, the Syrian renewed hostilities with untiring energy, his chief object being to make Judas prisoner.

He repaired to the Mount of the Sanctuary, there

to make known his orders that the hero should be delivered up to him.   In vain did the Council come forth to meet him, assuring him of their devotion to the king, for whose welfare they offered up daily sacrifices; he treated them all with rough contempt, and swore that he would burn the Temple down, if Judas were not delivered into his hands.

In order to induce the Judæans to surrender him, Nicanor ordered that the most respected man in Jerusalem, Ragesh, or Razis, called by general consent "Father of the Judæans," should be seized and kept as a hostage, but Ragesh, it is said, committed suicide upon the approach of his intended gaoler.   Nicanor was now determined to vanquish the Maccabees.   He marched out from Jerusalem at the head of an immense army, pitching his camp at Bethhoron, whilst Judas, surrounded by 3,000 of his bravest followers, took up his post at Adarsa.   Judæan valour was once more triumphant over the superior numbers of the Syrians.   Nicanor fell on the battle-field, and his army fled in utter confusion. The inhabitants of the towns and villages poured forth in pursuit of the fugitive Syrians, and cut off their retreat to Gazara, so that not a single man reached that town.   The battle of Adarsa (160) was of so decisive a character that its anniversary was afterwards celebrated under the name of the day of Nicanor.   The head and one of the arms of the Syrian commander were severed from the body, and hung as trophies on the walls of Jerusalem. Judas and the Hasmonæans were once more masters of Jerusalem, since Alcimus had withdrawn even before the battle.

At this juncture, Judas, foreseeing that Demetrius would avenge the destruction of his army, and feeling the insecurity of his position, took a step of doubtful wisdom—that of making overtures to the all-powerful State of Rome.   He entrusted two of his countrymen with the important mission—Eupolemus, the son of

Johanan, of priestly family, and Jason, the son of Eleazar. They were both proficient in the Greek tongue. But hardly had they reached the end of their journey before Judas was obliged once more to draw his sword.

Demetrius, upon hearing of Nicanor's defeat, had sent an immense army, commanded by the merciless Bacchides, to Judæa. This general marched through Galilee, killed all the Judæans whom he met on his way, and in the spring-time of the year encamped before Jerusalem. Judas had again been obliged to leave the capital, because, stripped as she was of her walls, she afforded no shelter. He issued a proclamation to the men and youths of Judæa to come forward and fight for their fatherland, their Law, and their freedom, but only 3,000 responded to the call. Led by Judas, these troops marched southward, encamping near Eleasa, because the mountains in the north were no longer safe. Bacchides followed the Judæan army with 20,000 foot and 2,000 mounted soldiers, taking up his position at Birath, near Beth-lehem. Confronted with this vast host, the Judæan warriors lost heart. They declined to give battle for the moment, but insisted upon dispersing to await reinforcements. In vain did Judas employ all his eloquence to urge steadfastness upon them. The greater number deserted, leaving only eight hundred men to support Judas. Selecting the most valiant of this little band, he successfully attacked the right wing of Bacchides, and drove the enemy to the confines of Ashdod. But the small troop of Judæan soldiers left behind, unable to withstand the desperate onslaught of the left wing of the Syrian army, was routed, and when Judas returned from the pursuit he was obliged to resume battle with the latter. He and his band of picked men performed wonders of bravery. On both sides fell the dead and wounded, and the battle lasted from morning till evening. But the Judæan army became smaller and smaller, and its survivors were entirely surrounded by the enemy. At last even Judas Maccabæus fell, sword in hand. The few remaining soldiers fled from the battle-field, the Maccabæan brothers being fortunate enough to save the body of their heroic commander from disgrace.

The defeat at Eleasa or Birath (160) seemed to have rendered ineffectual all the previous Jewish victories. The lion-hearted troop of Hasmonæans were dispersed. Alcimus once more took possession of the Temple and the Holy City, and could gloat over his antagonists.

But the long years of Maccabæan warfare had not been in vain. They had roused the nation from its torpor, and had rejuvenated it. The blood of martyrs, it is said, heals wounds. In truth, all old wounds were healed by this free-will sacrifice of so many lives. So far as the world at large was concerned, the stigma that had been fastened upon the Judæan name had vanished. The contemptuous Greeks, who had felt the force of Judas's arm, no longer derided the Judæan soldiers, and the Judæans were no longer required to prove their equality with the Greeks by joining in the Olympian games. The Judæans themselves had learnt to know their own prowess and their mission; they had proved themselves to be God's people, destined to guard His law and His teaching, and capable of defending those precious gifts. Self-devotion, taught by the prophet Elijah to a few disciples, and inculcated by the second Isaiah with fiery eloquence, had become, through the action of the Maccabæan warriors and martyrs, the recognised duty of the whole nation.

Judas Maccabæus had breathed out his heroic soul on the battle-field of Eleasa. The whole nation mourned for him, and justly, for it had become orphaned by his loss.

The sublime enthusiasm that had led to the valiant deeds of the Maccabees, that had moved singers to extol the Lord "in new songs," could not be of lasting duration. It was the result of a noble excitement, and a reaction had to follow. An entire nation, bred to farming and cattle-breeding, cannot continue in arms from year's end to year's end. Besides, the principal cause which had prompted a warlike rising had ceased to exist. It was no longer demanded of them to deny the God of Israel, or to sacrifice to Jupiter. One of the terms of the truce that Judas Maccabæus had concluded with the young king Antiochus Eupator, or with his general-guardian Lysias, was the religious freedom of the Judæans. Demetrius I. did not interfere with this concession; in the Temple at Jerusalem, the sacrifices were offered up according to law, and although the high-priest, Jakim or Alcimus, was not a favourite of the people, yet, unlike his predecessor Menelaus, he came of priestly descent.

It is true, the party of the Hellenists still held the fortress Acra in Jerusalem, whence they menaced the faithful with the destruction of their city and the violation of their Temple. The conqueror, Bacchides, after the death of Judas, had made them masters of the land, and they were resolved to use their authority in order to bring about the downfall of the pious Judæans. But such proceedings, well as they may be adapted to rouse noble natures to active measures, do not seem important enough to warrant a shortsighted, and, above all things, peace-loving people to take any decided steps against their enemy, and to hazard their own safety and that of their families, unless a voice of authority calls upon them to act.

But after the death of Judas Maccabæus there was no one left to claim such authority.

Although the Hasmonæan brothers were beloved by the people, they had not the power to summon the whole nation to their standard, and they were looked upon only as leaders of a faction.

In fact, after the death of Judas one could discern

the beginnings of three distinct parties amongst the people; party spirit, always a symptom of national vitality, had, as far as Judæa was concerned, its origin in the Maccabæan wars. First, there were the pious Chasidim, or Assidæans, as they are more generally called. These obeyed not only the Law, but the additional enactments promulgated by Ezra and the Supreme Council. Then came their persistent antagonists, the Hellenists, who, in violent contrast to the former, scorned the earnest Judæan life, and sought to introduce Greek customs. These were despised of the people, who called them "Traitors to the Covenant." In spite of this they numbered among their adherents Temple officials, priests, and the old and distinguished family of Odura, and the sons of Phasiron. Lastly, there were the Hasmonæans, who had raised themselves to great power in a short time, and whose leaders were the three remaining sons of Mattathias, Jonathan, Simeon and Johanan. The Hasmonæans resembled the Assidæans in their love for Judaism and the Sanctuary, but they differed from them in their wider view, in their practical judgment, and in their manly energy, which could not be deterred from its purpose by any adverse circumstances. They were not content with having averted the violation of the Sanctuary, or with having obtained the recognition of their religious liberty; but they longed to rid themselves of the causes which had brought misfortune on their country. A Psalmist describes them most accurately in these words: "The praise of God is in their mouth, and a two-edged sword in their hands." They could not bear to have the Judæans remain under the hateful yoke of the Greeks, or to know that Judaism depended for its very existence upon the whim of a Syrian despot, or the intrigues of a treacherous party. They were not content with mere religious freedom; they wished to establish political independence. But the Hasmonæans feared that they lacked the strength to effect this purpose.   They therefore determined to rely upon extraneous aid, and for this purpose they desired to connect themselves with the Roman government and, it appears, also with the Parthians, who had freed themselves from Syrian rule.   But it was this worldly policy that incensed the Assidæans. They put their trust in God alone, and could imagine warfare possible only if conducted according to Biblical precedent; they believed that God would confound the enemy in a miraculous way, and, in their opinion, to seek foreign help was to cast a doubt upon the omnipotence of God.   "It is better to trust in the Lord than to confide in man," they quoted, "it is better to trust in the Lord than to confide in princes." This discontent, it may be surmised, was the cause of the separation of the Assidæans from the Hasmonæans, thereby reducing the number of the Maccabæan warriors.   This circumstance may have brought about the death of Judas.

Of these three parties, the Hasmonæans alone had a chance of being ultimately the leaders of the nation. The Hellenists had destroyed their prospects by disregarding entirely the observances or prejudices of the people; whilst the Assidæans entertained views of an intensely narrow character, and were too fond of repose to disturb it by seeking to remedy the state of anarchy in which Judæa was plunged.

Confusion was indeed rampant at that time.   Wherever Hellenists and Hasmonæans met, a disgraceful conflict was the result; no voice of authority forbade such practices; there was not even a court of justice. Famine did but aggravate this miserable state of things.   "There was great affliction in Israel, the like whereof had not been seen since a prophet had been among them."

In their anguish the unfortunate people turned to Jonathan Haphus, hoping that he would humiliate the Hellenists, and restore peace to the country.   But Jonathan did not possess the warlike energy of his brother Judas, nor was he supported by the whole nation. He was more of a politician than a general. Too weak to attack the army that Bacchides had quartered in Judæa, he was merely able to take measures of defence. Threatened by the Syrian host, the Hasmonæans entrenched themselves in the woodland country on the shores of the Jordan; but, conscious of their weakness, they sent their wives and children to join the friendly Nabatæans. On the way, however, this peaceful troop was suddenly attacked by a warlike tribe, that of Bene Amri, from the city of Madaba, and with their leader, the Hasmonæan Johanan, was put to the sword—a deed of infamy that was subsequently avenged by Jonathan.

But even in their hiding-places, in the valley of the Jordan, the Hasmonæans found no rest. Bacchides sought them out, attacked them on the Sabbath-day, when indeed they were not forbidden to defend themselves, but when they were too much hampered by legal minutiæ to join battle with full force, and compelled them to swim the river, and find safety on the opposite side. The whole country was now at the mercy of the enemy. Bacchides restored the fortresses, reinforced the strong places, the Acra, Bethzur and Gazara, storing them with provisions and weapons, He enforced the loyalty of the people by seizing the children of the most distinguished families, and placing them as hostages in the Acra. Thus, in the space of one year (160–159), Bacchides succeeded in entirely putting down all armed opposition to the Syrian rule, a feat which the previous Syrian commanders had not been able to accomplish in six years.

The strong arm of the Maccabæan hero was sorely missed. Had King Demetrius wished to make any important changes in the religious condition of the Judæans, he could not have chosen a more opportune moment; the strength of the people was broken, and their leaders were banished from the scene of action. But the successor of Antiochus Epiphanes, sunk in a life of debauchery, was content with having assured himself of the sovereignty over Judæa, and of the annual payment of the tribute-money. The Syrian court, even after the death of Alcimus, troubled itself but little, if at all, about the religion of the Judæans. Although disliked by the people, the high-priest Alcimus had not belonged to the extreme Hellenists. He was merely an ambitious man who always worshipped the rising power. An offence with which he was reproached appears, on careful examination, hardly to have been a sin against the religion of the Judæans. It appears that between the inner and outer courts of the Temple there was a sort of wooden screen, of lattice-work, called "Soreg." This screen, the work of the prophets, as it was called, was the boundary, beyond which no heathen, nor any one who had become unclean by contact with a corpse might pass. But Alcimus gave orders for the destruction of this partition, probably with the intention of admitting the heathen within the sacred precincts. The pious Judæans were so highly incensed at this, that when Alcimus was seized, directly after this command, with paralysis of speech and of limbs, from which he never recovered, they attributed his fatal illness to the wrath of Heaven.

After the death of Alcimus, the Syrian court left the office of high-priest unfilled, evidently with the intention of removing even this semblance of Judæan independence. For seven years the Temple had no high-priest, and the country, no political head. Probably the priestly functions were carried on by a substitute for the high-priest, under the name of Sagan. We hear nothing of further Syrian interference. Bacchides left the country, and Judæa was at peace for two years (159–157).

Jonathan and Simon, the leaders of the Hasmonæans, made use of this pause to strengthen themselves, and to arm their followers. They fortified the oasis of Bethhagla, in the desert of Jericho, within the grateful shade of a wood and near a spring with an ample supply of sweet and limpid water. The river Jordan protected their rear.

In the conduct of this war Jonathan enjoyed no other authority than that of a Bedouin chief who extorts an armistice from the governing power; but as the sympathy of the people went with him, and as he carried his sword in a holy cause, he attained greater power Without doubt the harm he did the Hellenists was considerable, for we hear of their carrying fresh complaints to the Syrian court. But as Demetrius was hopelessly indifferent, and as Bacchides was weary of carrying on a guerilla warfare at a great disadvantage, they remained inactive, whilst the Hellenists proposed to fall treacherously upon Jonathan and Simon, and to deliver them as prisoners to the Syrians. An ambush was laid for the two commanders, but the conspiracy was revealed, and the Maccabæans were able to take measures of defence upon this occasion. Fifty Hellenists were seized and executed. Bacchides, who had counted upon the rapid success of the conspiracy, felt himself involved in a new war, and proceeded to besiege the Hasmonæans in their fortress of Bethhagla. But the latter had attracted a number of followers, large enough to enable them to divide their forces. Jonathan and his followers defended the fortress, whilst Simon with his division, sallying out by an unguarded road, attacked the Syrians in the rear, and after defeating the Hellenists, burnt the siege-machines of the enemy. Threatened on both sides, Bacchides was forced, not without a considerable loss of soldiers, to raise the siege of Bethhagla, and as an outlet for his rage executed many of the Hellenists in his army. This was an appropriate moment for Jonathan to demand a truce, which was granted. The condition agreed upon was that Jonathan, after giving hostages as pledges of peace, might return to Judæa unmolested, but should not be permitted to dwell in Jerusalem. Prisoners were exchanged, and Bacchides marched out of the land, leaving his allies, the Hellenists, unprotected.

Jonathan took up his position in the fortress of Michmash, where Saul had once fixed his headquarters. He was tacitly acknowledged as the head of the Judæan people, and treated its enemies with relentless severity. For nearly four years "the sword rested in Israel." How this undecided state of things would finally have ended it is difficult to say, but it is certain that, without the aid of an unexpected piece of good fortune, the dream of the Hasmonæans could never have been realised.

A revolution in the Syrian kingdom effected a happy change in the fate of Judæa, and increased the power of Jonathan and the nation.

An obscure youth of Smyrna, Alexander Balas, was the cause of this revolution. He happened to bear an extraordinary likeness to the late king of Syria, Antiochus Eupator. This resemblance prompted Attalus, king of Pergamum, to induce Alexander to play the part of pretender to the Syrian throne. Alexander, richly supplied by Attalus with money and troops, was recognised by the Roman Senate as heir to the kingdom of Syria. Demetrius, roused from his indolence, began to look about him for allies. Above all he was anxious to win Jonathan over to his side. This led him to write a flattering epistle to the Hasmonæan commander, in which he called him his ally, and authorised him to raise troops and procure weapons. The Judæan hostages were at once to be set free.

Jonathan did not neglect so favourable an opportunity. He hurried to Jerusalem, repaired the walls, and fortified the city. The Hellenists sought refuge in the fortress of Bethzur. But Alexander, who was also in want of help, was equally eager for Jonathan's alliance, and succeeded in gaining it. He nominated Jonathan high-priest, sent him a robe of purple and a crown of gold, thus declaring him tributary prince of the Syrian kingdom and friend of its monarch.

Jonathan donned his priestly garment, and officiated for the first time as high-priest in the Temple upon the Feast of Tabernacles (152); he was the first of the Hasmonæans to gain so great a distinction.

Thus Judæa, thanks to the valour and self-sacrifice of a handful of warriors, was raised, after a war of nearly twenty years, from the brink of destruction to an influential position. The sufferer's part which she had played for so long was now to be exchanged for one active and heroic.

Jonathan greatly contributed to the growing power of the nation during his rule (152–144). He justly divined which side he should espouse in the struggle for the Syrian crown. He allied himself to Alexander, although Demetrius, like all who have nothing left to lose, was profuse in the most liberal offers. Ignoring the high-priest, Demetrius wrote " to the Judæan people," promising to relieve them from most of their taxes and imposts, to restore to their jurisdiction three districts that had been added to Samaria, to recognise Jerusalem as an asylum, and even to give up the important Acra. He declared that he would defray the expenses for conducting divine service in the Temple out of the royal treasury, reserving for that purpose the revenues of the town of Ptolemais. The Judæan army was to be levied at Syrian cost, promotions and rewards were to be given according to Syrian custom, and the forces consisting of 30,000 men were naturally to serve as his allies. Even the Judæans settled in the Syrian provinces were, in consideration of this alliance, to be protected from the oppression of their neighbours, and were to be exempt, on all Sabbaths and festivals, and for three days before and after the festivals, from duties in any court of justice.

But nothing could bribe the Judæan people to desert Jonathan; they were not blinded by these brilliant prospects, and their leader was too well acquainted with the character of Demetrius to give heed to his promises.   He allied himself with Alexander, aided him in crushing his rival, and never had cause to regret the step that he had taken.   The usurper loaded Jonathan with marks of favour, and plainly showed his gratitude to the Maccabæan leader.   When he entered the city of Ptolemais, to receive the daughter of the Egyptian monarch, Ptolemy VI. Philopator, as his bride, he invited Jonathan to meet him, and the two kings entertained the Judæan warrior as their equal.

During the reign of Alexander Balas (152–146) Judæa recovered from the cruel blows which despotism and treachery had dealt her, and was soon able to call 10,000 men into the field.   Jonathan, on his side, repaid Alexander with unalterable loyalty.   For when Demetrius II., the son of Demetrius I., contested, as rightful heir to the throne, the sovereignty of Syria, Jonathan upheld Alexander's cause most strenuously, although that monarch was deserted by Egypt and Rome.

The Maccabæan chieftain began by opposing the advance of Demetrius's general Apollonius on the shores of the Mediterranean.   He besieged and took the fortress of the seaport town of Joppa, destroyed the old Philistine city of Ashdod, which had declared for Apollonius, and burnt the Temple of the god Dagon.   As a reward for his services, Jonathan received from Alexander the city of Ekron, with the surrounding country, which from that time was incorporated with Judæa (147).

The Syrian people were now divided in their allegiance, some of them acknowledging the rightful king Demetrius II., others clinging to the house of the usurper Alexander, even after the latter had been treacherously slain.   In this general confusion Jonathan was able to besiege the Acra, the stronghold of the Hellenists.

The besieged turned for help to the Syrian king, and Demetrius II., eager to overthrow the powerful Maccabæan, listened to their appeal, marched to their rescue, and commanded Jonathan to meet him at Ptolemais. But when Jonathan obeyed and came with rich presents, Demetrius thought that his alliance might be of use to himself, and not only did he abandon his march upon the Acra, but he confirmed Jonathan in his priestly office.

Jonathan, well aware that the king was in sore need of money, offered him 300 talents in exchange for a few districts of land, and for the promise of exempting the Judæans from all taxation. The compact was made, written, and placed for security in the Temple; but Demetrius, in spite of his solemn protestation, soon regretted having freed the Judæans from their imposts. No Syrian monarch was ever known to be loyal to his word, or to refrain from recalling favours granted in some pressing moment of danger. The Judæan army meanwhile was soon to enjoy the unexpected triumph of inflicting the same degradation upon the Syrian capital which the Syrians had so often inflicted upon Jerusalem. Demetrius had excited the discontent of his people to such a degree that they actually besieged him in his own palace at Antioch, and his troops, who were clamouring for pay, refused to aid in his deliverance. Thus he felt himself in the unpleasant position of being compelled to seek the help of Jonathan's Judæan troops. The 3000 men sent by the high-priest destroyed a portion of the Syrian capital by fire, and forced the inhabitants and the rebellious soldiers to release their king and sue for pardon. But no sooner was Demetrius at liberty than he treated his deliverer with the basest ingratitude. Jonathan, therefore, refused to come to his rescue, when a general of Alexander Balas, Diodotus Tryphon by name, conspired against him, attempting to place Antiochus VI., the young son of Alexander Balas, on the throne of Syria.

Demetrius was forced to flee from his capital. Embittered at the faithlessness of the Syrian monarch, and grateful to the memory of Alexander, Jonathan espoused the cause of the young king and his regent Tryphon. The latter confirmed him in his priestly office, and permitted him to wear the gold clasp, the distinguishing mark of an independent prince. Simon, his brother, was made commander of the Syrian forces on the shores of the Mediterranean, from the ladder of Tyre to the Egyptian confines.

Bravely did the Hasmonæan brothers fight for Antiochus, upon the triumph of whose cause the freedom of the Judæans depended. Victory and defeat succeeded each other; but at last the Hasmonæans remained victorious; they besieged and took several towns on the coast, and finally entered Damascus. They drove the Hellenists out of Bethzur, and garrisoned it. But their greatest desire was to make Jerusalem impregnable. They increased the height of the walls, extending them eastward to the vale of Kidron, thus creating a defence for the Holy Mount; they erected a rampart in the middle of the city, facing the Acra, to keep out the Hellenists, and they filled up the moat " Chaphenatha," which divided the Holy Mount from the city, and which was but partially bridged over, thus practically bringing the Temple closer to the town.

Jonathan would not attempt the siege of the Acra, partly because he might have given umbrage to his Syrian allies, and partly because he did not dare concentrate all his forces at one point so long as the generals of the fallen Demetrius maintained a threatening attitude. At that time Judæa could boast of an army 40,000 strong (144–143).

Subsequent events showed only too plainly that the prudence evinced by the Hasmonæans in fortifying the country, and maintaining a powerful army at the outset of this campaign had not been superfluous. As soon as the rebellious general, Diodotus Tryphon,

had possessed himself of the supreme power in
Syria, he determined to overthrow the puppet king
Antiochus, and to place the crown upon his own
head. But the greatest hindrance to the attainment of these ends was Jonathan himself, who,
true to the memory of Alexander, was the devoted
champion of the rights of Antiochus, and who,
moreover, was in possession of a great part of the
sea-coast. Tryphon was well aware that Jonathan
would not become party to his treachery, so he
determined to rid himself of the high-priest, and thus
weaken the followers of the young king. But a
course of open violence being impossible, he resorted
to craft, and actually succeeded in outwitting the
wariest of all the Hasmonæans, and getting him into
his power. Upon the news of Tryphon's entry into
Scythopolis, at the head of a powerful army, Jonathan hurried to oppose him with 40,000 picked warriors. To his amazement he was most courteously
received by the Syrian commander, and loaded with
presents. Entirely duped by so flattering a reception,
he was persuaded by Tryphon to dismiss the greater
number of his troops, and to follow his host into the
fortified seaport city of Acco (Ptolemais), which Tryphon promised to surrender to him. Of the 3,000
soldiers remaining with Jonathan, 2,000 were now sent
to Galilee, 1,000 alone following their chief. But
hardly had they passed the gates of the fortress before Jonathan was seized, and made prisoner by the
treacherous Tryphon, whilst the Syrian garrison fell
upon his men, and massacred them. After the accomplishment of this infamous deed, the troops rushed
out in pursuit of the Judæan soldiers, who were stationed in the plain of Jezreël and in Galilee. But the
Judæans had already heard of the fate that had befallen their brethren, and they turned, and gave battle
to the Syrians, putting them to flight. With the report of Jonathan's death they entered Jerusalem, and
great was the consternation of their sorrow-stricken

brethren. They believed that their beloved Jonathan
had fallen, like his thousand followers at Acco, a victim to the faithless commander. Syrian domination,
with its usual terrible consequences, seemed impending.
The Hellenists were suspected of being implicated in
these disastrous events, and, in fact, there was a secret
understanding between Tryphon and the remnant of
the Hellenists; the Syrian commander appears to
have promised them aid from without, while they were
to assist him from within, should the Judæan capital
be besieged. But Simon Tharsi, the last of the Hasmonæans, successfully averted this twofold danger.
In spite of his advanced age, he was a man of
lofty enthusiasm and singular heroism, so that he
was able to rouse the people from despair to hope.
When he exclaimed to the multitude assembled in
the outer court of the Temple, "I am no better than
my brothers who died for the Sanctuary and liberty,"
the Judæans replied with one voice : "Be our leader,
like Judas and Jonathan, your brothers." Placed at
the head of the nation by the people themselves,
Simon was determined to secure Jerusalem from a
sudden attack on the part of the Hellenists, and at the
same time to block Tryphon's entry into Judæa. He
sent a Judæan contingent, under the leadership of
Jonathan ben Absalom, to Joppa, in order to prevent
the landing of the Syrian army, whilst he assembled
his forces at Adida.

Tryphon, accompanied by his prisoner Jonathan,
had already passed out of Acco with the intention of
falling upon Judæa, which, he thought, would be paralysed by his act of treachery. He was determined,
moreover, to frighten the Judæans into subjection
by threatening to assassinate their high-priest. But
upon hearing, to his amazement, that all Judæa was
in arms, and that Simon was the leader of the people,
he began artfully to enter into negotiations with the
enemy. He pretended to have made Jonathan prisoner only for the purpose of securing one hundred

talents of tribute-money which the Judæans had formerly paid to Syria, and promised that if this indemnity
were forthcoming, and Jonathan's two sons were
delivered up as hostages, he would release his prisoner.   Simon was in no way deceived by this artifice
of Tryphon, but trembling to incur the reproach of
having caused his brother's death, he paid the tribute-
money, and delivered up the hostages.   Tryphon,
however, had no intention of making peace with the
Judæans ; on the contrary, he was at that very moment
taking a circuitous road to Jerusalem, not daring to
run the risk of meeting the Judæan forces in the open
field.   He might have reached the capital in safety,
had not a heavy snowfall, most unusual in that hot
climate, made the mountain roads of Judæa impass-
able, and forced him into the trans-Jordanic country.

Enraged at this defeat of his plans, he caused
Jonathan to be executed at Bascama (143).   The
remains of the great Maccabæan high-priest and
commander were ultimately recovered, and buried by
Simon and the whole people at Modin, in the tomb
of the Hasmonæans.   Thus ended the fourth of the
Hasmonæan brothers.   He achieved more than his
predecessors had done, and more than his successors
could do; for he raised the Judæan republic from the
very lowest depths to an eminence whence, if not
entirely abandoned by fortune, it could easily rise
higher.   It is true that Judas Maccabæus had performed more numerous deeds of valour, and had
gained a more brilliant military renown than Jonathan, but the younger brother had given his people
power and importance, and by virtue of his priestly
office had conferred lasting distinction upon his family.

After the death of Judas, the Judæan nation was
as near dissolution as it had been in the days of the
sanguinary reign of Antiochus; but after Jonathan's
death, there existed the fundamental conditions upon
which a State can be based.

If we may compare Judas Maccabæus to the Judges

of the Biblical age, then we may liken Jonathan to King Saul, who was able to avert ruin and attain safety. As Saul, through the kingly crown, united the dispersed tribes, and moulded them into a powerful people, so Jonathan, by his mitre, united the divided factions, and made of them a strong and self-reliant nation. And although both were deeply mourned by the people, neither King Saul's death nor that of the high-priest Jonathan put an end to the nation's unity, because in neither of these parallel cases did the unity of Judæa rest upon one individual, but upon the whole nation, conscious of its resources. As Saul found a worthy successor in his son-in-law David, so did Jonathan in his brother Simon.

Of Jonathan's descendants, only one daughter is mentioned. She was married to Mattathias ben Simon Psellus, and became the ancestress of the historian Flavius Josephus.

During the period in which the Judæan State was developing through political trials, the Jewish religion was attaining, on another theatre, the sovereign position whence it influenced the civilisation of the whole world. Politically, Judaism was being matured in Judæa, intellectually, in Egypt.

CHAPTER XXIV.

THE JUDÆANS IN ALEXANDRIA AND THE GOVERNMENT OF SIMON.

The Judæan Colonies in Egypt and Cyrene—Internal Affairs of the Alexandrian Community—King Philometor favours the Judæans—Onias and Dositheus—The Temple of Onias—Translation of the Pentateuch into Greek—Struggle between the Judæans and Samaritans in Alexandria—Affairs in Judæa—Independence of Judæa—Simon's League with the Romans—Overthrow of the Acra and of the Hellenists—Simon's Coinage—Quarrel between Simon and the Syrian King—Invasion by Cendebæus—Assassination of Simon.

160—135 B. C. E.

THE magic land of the Nile, once the school of suffering of the children of Israel and the cradle of Israel's religion, became at this period the school of wisdom for the Judæan nation.

The settlement of the Judæans in Egypt was as much encouraged by the Greek rulers of that country as it had been in former ages by the Pharaohs. They spread over the entire district between the Lybian desert in the north and the confines of Ethiopia in the south. They increased as rapidly as they had done in the days of their forefathers, and they numbered one million of souls at the expiration of a century from their first arrival in their adopted country.

In Egypt and Cyrene the Judæans enjoyed rights similar to those of the Greek colonists. They were so proud of this equality that they watched over their privileges with a jealous eye. It is impossible to say from whom they originally held them, whether from Alexander or his successors. The Judæan colony in Egypt began to play an active part at the time when the Egyptian and Syrian courts were hostile to each other, when both were eager for the possession of Judæa, and each was, therefore, anxious to secure the alliance of the Judæans. But the Egyptian Judæans had always been faithful adherents of the Ptolemaic royal house, and Philometor, the sixth prince of that dynasty, had cordially received the numerous fugitives who had fled from Judæa during the persecutions of Antiochus.

Conspicuous amongst those emigrants were several Judæans of distinguished families, as well as the son of the high-priest Onias. They were treated with respect by the Egyptian rulers, and were able, at a later date, to give proof of their intelligence and their learning. Political prudence demanded the friendliest reception of the Judæan malcontents, in order to make sure of their undivided support in the re-conquest of Judæa from Syria. Neither Egypt nor Syria, however, could possibly have divined that the opposition of the Judæan patriots to the Syrian armies would lead to the independence of Judæa.

The Judæans were principally concentrated in Alexandria, second only to Rome in political importance and commerce, and to Athens in love of art and knowledge. Of the five divisions or districts of Alexandria, which were designated by the first letters of the Greek alphabet, the Judæans occupied nearly the whole of two; the district of the Delta, lying upon the sea-coast, had indeed become an exclusively Judæan colony, and its commanding position determined the occupation of its inhabitants. The cargoes of grain that Rome imported for her legions from the rich plains of Egypt were undoubtedly laden upon Judæan ships, and taken into the market by Judæan merchants. They carried the wealth of Egyptian harvests to less fertile countries, as Joseph, their ancestor, had done before them. Prosperity and refinement were the fruits of their enterprise. But commerce was not monopolised by the Judæans, nor was it their only pursuit. Their eagerness to learn and their aptitude enabled them to acquire the skill

of the Greeks, and to succeed in the manufacture of
delicate fabrics. Judæan artisans and skilled workmen were leagued in a kind of guild, and when labour
was required in the Temple of Jerusalem, the Alexandrian-Judæan community supplied the master-hands.
Moreover, the Alexandrian Judæans applied themselves to the Grecian arts of war and of statecraft.
They acquired the melodious Greek tongue, and made
a profound study of Greek learning, many of them
reading and understanding Homer and Plato as easily
as the books of Moses and the writings of King
Solomon.

Prosperity, worthy pursuits, and culture inspired
the Alexandrian Judæans with dignity and self-respect,
and in this they may be compared with their descendants in Spain of a much later date.

The Alexandrian community was looked upon as
the centre of the Judæan colony in Egypt, and other
Judæan colonies, and even Judæa herself, were glad
to lean at times upon this firm pillar of Judaism.
Houses of prayer, bearing the name Proseuche, were
established in all parts of the city. Amongst them
was the principal synagogue, distinguished by its
graceful architecture and its magnificent interior.
These houses of prayer were at the same time schools
of learning, where the most accomplished student of
the Law would stand up on Sabbaths and festival days
to expound that portion of the Pentateuch that had
just been read to the congregation.

But the most brilliant ornaments of the Alexandrian-
Judæan world were the distinguished fugitives who
arrived in Alexandria during the Syrian persecutions.
The most illustrious of these was Onias IV., the
youngest son of the last legitimate high-priest of
the line of Joshua ben Jozadak.

After his father had been treacherously murdered,
on account of his determined antagonism to the Hellenists and his support of Hyrcanus, young Onias
fled for safety to Egypt. There he was kindly

received by the gentle King Philometor, because he represented a party which looked upon him as the rightful successor to the priestly dignity, and the sixth Ptolemy, hoping ultimately to wrest Cœlesyria and Judæa from Syrian rule, believed that he might eventually rely upon the support of this party.

As soon as Onias, who had now reached man's estate, heard that the wicked high-priest, Menelaus, had been slain by order of the Syrian court, and that Prince Demetrius had escaped from Rome, and had conquered Syria, he flattered himself that he would be allowed to return as high-priest to Judæa. His protector, the king Philometor, had meanwhile become an ally of Demetrius, and had probably put in a good word for his favourite. But when Alcimus was chosen high-priest, and was supported by an armed force, even against the Hasmonæans, Onias gave up all hope of receiving the priestly inheritance of his father, and took up his permanent abode in Egypt.

Onias seems to have been accompanied by a man of great distinction, Dositheus by name, and the two men played an influential part during the reign of Philometor. They were given the opportunity of distinguishing themselves during the disorders arising from the rivalry of the two royal brothers, the gentle Philometor and the violent Euergetes, who was a monster in body and in mind, and who was called, on account of his enormous size, "*Fat-paunch*" (Physcon), and on account of his diabolical wickedness, "Kakergetes."

The two brothers, with their sister Cleopatra, who was the wife of her elder brother, claimed the throne at a period when Egypt and Syria happened to be at war with each other. But Physcon, the younger brother, had seized the throne for himself, supplanting the elder one, who fled as a supplicant to Rome. The Roman Senate acknowledged the rights of Philometor, but always greedy for an extension of power, resolved to make use of this opportunity to weaken Egypt. It decreed, therefore, that the north-western province of Cyrene should be separated from the Egyptian kingdom, and placed under the rule of Physcon. But this prince, dissatisfied with his small territory, repeatedly conspired against Philometor, and the two brothers were soon openly at variance. Philometor dared defy Rome, which had taken Physcon's part; but unfortunately his soldiers were unreliable; for the Alexandrian-Greek population, besides having the usual faults of the Greeks, were remarkable for faithlessness and caprice. Still more did Philometor lack commanders. In this hour of emergency he entrusted the Judæan emigrants, Onias and Dositheus, with the command of the campaign against his brother. The entire Jewish-Egyptian population stood by Philometor. The ability of the two Judæan leaders enabled him to weaken Physcon effectually. From that day Onias and Dositheus were held in great favour by Philometor, and they remained commanders of the entire army.

Onias was recognised by the Judæans as head, or prince of the race (Ethnarch). He may have been unanimously elected to that office by his countrymen, and confirmed in it out of gratitude by the king, or Philometor may have taken the initiative, and raised him to this dignity.

In time this office became a very important one. It was the duty of the ethnarch to control all the affairs of the community, to exercise the duties of a judge, and to protect the integrity of contracts. He represented his people at court. The office of ethnarch, which Onias was the first to hold, offered too many privileges to the Egyptian Judæans for them to have objected to it.

As a result, they were now in the fortunate position of having a leader of royal dignity who was able to mould them into one strong body. Their strength was to be enhanced by a new creation amongst them.

In spite of the distinction which Onias enjoyed at the court of Philometor, and amongst his own race, he could not forget that, on account of the events that had taken place in Judæa, he had lost his rightful office of high-priest.

During the uncertain state of things in his own country, when Alcimus was raised above the rightful incumbents of the priesthood, and after his death, when this dignity seemed extinct, Onias conceived the idea of building a Temple in Egypt that should take the place of the violated sanctuary in Jerusalem, and of which he would be the rightful high-priest.

Was he prompted to such an undertaking by piety or ambition?   The innermost workings of the heart are not revealed in history.   To secure the approval of the Judæans, Onias referred to a prophecy of Isaiah xix. 19, " On that day there will be an altar to the Lord in Egypt."   Philometor, to whom he expressed his wish, out of gratitude for his military services, presented him with a tract of land in the region of Heliopolis, four and a-half geographical miles north-east of Memphis, in the land of Goshen, where the descendants of Jacob had once lived until the exodus from Egypt.   In the small town of Leontopolis, on the ruins of a heathen temple, where animals had formerly been worshipped, Onias built the Judæan sanctuary (154–152).   Outwardly, it did not exactly resemble the Temple of Jerusalem, for it was made of brick, and it rose in the shape of a tower. But all the necessary appliances in the interior were on the exact model of those in Jerusalem, except that the seven-armed candlestick was replaced by a golden lamp hanging from a golden chain.   Priests and Levites who had fled from the persecutions in Judæa, officiated in this Temple of Onias.   The king generously decreed that the revenues of the whole district of Heliopolis should be devoted to the needs of the Temple and the priests.   This small province was formed into a little priestly state, and was called Onion

Although the community looked upon the Temple of Onias as their religious centre, visiting it during the festivals, and sacrificing in its courts, still, unlike the Samaritans, they did not withdraw their allegiance from the sanctuary of Jerusalem, or in any way depreciate it; on the contrary, they venerated Jerusalem as their sacred metropolis, and the Temple as a divine residence. But the wonderful fulfilment of the prophetic words, that "in Egypt a temple of the Lord should arise," was a source of great pride to them. They called Heliopolis the "City of Justice" (Irhazedek), applying to it this verse from the prophets, "Five Egyptian cities will at that day recognise the God of Israel, and one of them will be called the City of Heres," but they read Ir-ha-Zedek.

Had Judæa been enjoying a state of peace and prosperity, she would have resented this innovation, and laid an interdict upon the Temple of Onias, as she had done upon that of Gerizim, and the Egyptian-Judæan congregation would have been excluded from the community, as had been the case with the Samaritans. But the desolation of the Temple in Jerusalem was so great, the dismemberment of the commonwealth so complete, that there could have been no valid reason for preventing the accomplishment of a design springing from the purest of intentions. The founder of the Temple was descended from a long line of high-priests, which had its origin in the days of David and Solomon. His forefathers had been instrumental in rebuilding the Temple after the Babylonian exile he could claim Simon the Just as his ancestor, and his father was the pious Onias III. Later, when the Hasmonæan high-priest had restored the divine service in Jerusalem, in all its purity, the Judæans of the mother-country looked with regret upon the Temple that existed in a foreign land, and the uncompromisingly pious party never could forget that its existence was in violation of the Law. But by that time the Temple of Onias had become firmly established.

Philometor gave Onias permission to build a fortress for the protection of the Temple, in the province of Onion, and placed the stronghold and its garrison under his command. Onias was at the same time military commander of the district of Heliopolis, called the Arabian province ; hence his title Arabarch. In Alexandria, Onias was the communal and judicial head of the Jewish population resident there, while in the province of Onion and Arabian Egypt he was commander of the Judaic soldiery settled there.

The complete confidence that this king reposed in Onias and his co-religionists induced him to raise the high-priest to another post of importance. The seaports and the mouths of the Nile were of the greatest moment for the collection of the royal revenues. The taxes here levied on all incoming and outgoing raw materials and manufactured goods made Egypt the richest country during the rule of the Ptolemies, and later, under that of the Romans. Onias was entrusted with the custody of the ports, and the Alexandrian Judæans living upon the sea-coast had, no doubt, the privilege of selecting the officials for the custom-houses.

At this period, Egypt was the scene of an event of the utmost importance in the history of the world, though giving rise at the time to views diametrically opposed to each other. The devotion of the Judæan fugitives to the Law, for whose sake they had fled from their homes in Palestine, may have awakened in the cultivated King Philometor the desire to become acquainted with the time-honored Torah of Moses; or perhaps those Judæans, who were allowed access to the person of the king, so stimulated his interest in their laws, so shamefully reviled by Antiochus Epiphanes, that Philometor was at last eager to read them for himself in a translation.

It is also possible that the insulting libel on the

Judæans and their origin, written in the Greek tongue, apparently by an Egyptian priest, Manetho, (who describes the Israelites as being a noted shepherd race in Egypt (Hyksos), expelled as leprous under a leader called Moyses), may have made the king anxious to learn the history of that people from its own sources. Whatever was the nature of the inducement, it was a matter of great importance to the Alexandrian Jews that the sublime Pentateuch was translated into the polished Greek tongue.

We have no particulars of the way in which this work was brought about. Apparently, with a view to lightening the task, it was divided among five intrepreters, so that each book of the Pentateuch had its own translator. The existing translation, though through various corruptions it has lost much of its original character, shows by its very lack of uniformity that it could not have issued from one pen.

The Greek translation of the Torah was, so to say, another sanctuary erected to the glory of God in a foreign land. The accomplishment of this task filled the Alexandrian and Egyptian Judæans with intense delight; and they thought, with no little pride, that now the vainglorious Greeks would at last be obliged to concede that the wisdom taught by Judaism was at once more elevating and of more ancient date than the philosophy of Greece. Their satisfaction was doubtless enhanced by the fact that the noble work owed in part its successful termination to the warm sympathy of the friendly king, and that a path was thus opened for a true appreciation of Judaism among the Greeks. It was natural, therefore, that great rejoicings should take place among the Egyptian Judæans on the day of presentation of the version to the king, and that its anniversary should be observed as a holiday. On that day it was customary for the Judæans to repair to the Island of Pharos, where they offered up prayers of joyful thanksgiving. After the religious ceremony they partook of a festive repast, either in tents or under the free vault of heaven, each according to his means. Later on this anniversary became a national holiday, in which even the heathen Alexandrians took part.

But far different was the effect produced by the translation of the Torah into Greek upon the pious inhabitants of Judæa. Not only was Greece the object of their hatred, on account of the sufferings they had endured at her hands, and the indignities she had offered to their religion; but they feared, not unnaturally, that the Law, translated into another language, might be exposed to disfigurement and misapprehension. The Hebrew language, in which God had revealed Himself upon Mount Sinai, alone appeared to them a worthy medium of the Divine thought. Presented in a new garb, Judaism itself appeared to the pious Judæans estranged and profaned. Consequently the day that was celebrated as a festival by the Judæans in Egypt was considered by their brethren in Judæa as a day of national calamity, similar to that upon which the golden calf had been worshipped in the desert, and it is even said that this day was numbered amongst their fasts.

Different as were the points of view from which the work was regarded, judged by the results produced by the Greek translation, there was reason both for the joy of the Alexandrian and the sorrow of the Palestinean Judæans. Thanks to its Grecian garb, Judaism became known to the Greeks, who were the civilisers of the world; and before five centuries had elapsed, the principal nations had become acquainted with its teachings. The Greek translation was the first apostle Judaism sent forth to the heathen world to heal it of its perversity and godlessness. Through its means the two opposing systems—the Judæan and the Greek—were drawn nearer together. Owing to their subsequent circulation through the world by means of the second apostle, Christianity, the tenets of Judaism were fused into the thought and language of the various nations, and at present there is no civilised language which has not, by means of this Greek translation, taken words and ideas from Judæan literature. Thus Judaism was introduced into the literature of the world, and its doctrines were popularised.

On the other hand, however, it innocently led to a mistaken view of the Judæan Law, becoming in a measure a false prophet, promulgating errors in the name of God. The difficulty of translating from Hebrew into Greek, a radically different language, at no time an easy task, was greatly increased at that period by the want of exact knowledge of Hebrew, and of the true nature of Judaism, which made it impossible for the translator always to render correctly the sense of the original. Moreover, the Greek text was not so carefully guarded but that, from time to time, arbitrary emendations might have been introduced. Added to this, the translation was probably used as a guide for the interpreter on the Sabbaths and Holy Days, and it depended upon his taste, learning, and discretion to make what changes he pleased. And, in fact, the Greek text is full of additions and so-called emendations, which later on, in the time of the conflicts between Judaism and Christianity, became still more numerous, so that the original form of the translation cannot always be recognised in its present altered state. Nevertheless the Alexandrian Judæans of later generations be lieved so firmly in the perfection of this translation, that by degrees they deemed that the original could be dispensed with, and depended entirely upon the translation. Thus they came to look upon the mistakes which had crept into the Greek Bible either through ignorance, inability to cope with grammatical difficulties, or arbitrary additions, as the word of God, and things were taught in the name of Judaism which were entirely foreign or even contrary to it. In a word, all the victories which Judaism gained during the lapse of years over civilised heathendom as well as all the misconstructions which it suffered, were the effects of this translation.

The great estimation in which this work was held by the Greek-speaking Judæans, and in time also by the heathens, gave rise to legendary glorifications, which were finally, about a century later, crystallised in a story which relates that the origin of the translation was due to the steps taken by Ptolemy Philadelphus, whose attention had been attracted to the value of the Book of the Law by his librarian Demetrius. Demetrius declared it worthy of a place in the Royal Library, provided it were translated into Greek. Thereupon the king sent his ambassadors to the high-priest Eleazar with costly presents, requesting him to choose several wise men, equally versed in Hebrew and in Greek, and to bid them repair to his court. The high-priest selected seventy-two learned men, taking representatives from the twelve tribes, six from each, and sent them to Alexandria, where they were received with great pomp by the king. The seventy-two delegates finished the translation of the Torah in seventy-two days, and read it aloud before the king and all the assembled Judæans. It was from this legend, looked upon till recently as an historical fact, that the translation received the name of the Seventy-two, or more briefly, of the *Seventy*, Septuagint.

A beginning having been made, it was natural that a desire should arise to render the other literature of Judaism accessible to Greek readers, and so, by degrees, the historical books of the Jews also appeared in a Grecian garb. On account of the greater difficulties they offered, the poetical and prophetical books were the last ones to find their way to the Greek world. These translations gave birth to a new art in the Egyptian community—that of pulpit oratory Was it, perhaps, customary in Judæa, when the Law was read, not only to translate the portion into the language then in use among the people (the Chaldæan or Aramæan), but also to explain it for the benefit of the ignorant, and was this practice also introduced into the houses of prayer of the Egyptian Judæans? Or was it adopted by the latter because the Hebrew language had become foreign to them? However, whether it was an imitation or whether it originated with the Egyptian Judæans, this custom of translating and explaining obscure verses and portions not easily understood created a new art. The interpreters, with the fluency of speech derived from their work, were not satisfied with merely rendering the original text, but expanded it, adding reflections thereon, and drawing from it applications to contemporary events, and notes of admonition and warning. Thus out of the explanation of Scripture arose the sermon, which, in the Greek spirit of giving to all things an attractive and beautiful form, came by degrees artistically to be developed Pulpit oratory is the child of the Alexandrian-Judæan community. It was born in its midst, it grew up and was perfected, becoming later a model for other nations.

The charm which the Hellenistic Judæans found in the Biblical writings, now made accessible to them, awoke among the learned the desire to treat of those writings themselves, to bring to light the doctrines contained in them, or to clear up their apparent crudities and contradictions. Thus arose a Judæo-Greek literature, which spread and bore fruit, influencing an ever-widening circle. But little is known of the infancy of this peculiar literature which held, as it were, two such repellent nationalities in close embrace. That literature appears also to verify past experience, that rhythmic and measured sentences are more pleasing than simple prose. There are still some fragments of these writings extant which relate, in Greek verse, the old Hebrew history. This literary activity reawakened in Egypt the old anger of the Samaritans against the Judæans. These two peoples

agreeing in their adherence to the Law, in their recognition of one God, and in their condemnation of
idolatry, still retained their old hatred against each
other.   Although the Samaritans, like the Jews, were
forced by the officers of Antiochus to renounce the
worship of the God of Israel, yet they did not assist
the Judæans to fight their common enemy, but rather
sided with the latter against their own co-religionists.

During the religious persecutions many Samaritans appear to have emigrated into Egypt, and to
have joined the descendants of their own tribe who
had been established there since the time of Alexander.   These Egyptian Samaritans had, like the
Judæans, adopted the customs and the language of
the Greeks which prevailed in Egypt, and now the
enmity which had existed between the adherents of
Jerusalem and of Gerizim was transferred to a foreign
land, where they opposed each other with that furious
zeal which co-religionists in a strange country are wont
to exhibit in support of cherished traditions.   The
translation of the Torah into Greek, under the
patronage of the king Philometor, appears to have
cast the firebrand into their midst.   How fiercely
must the anger of the Samaritans have been pro-
voked by the omission in the text of the Septuagint
of that verse which they looked upon as a proof of
the sanctity of their Temple, "Thou shalt build an
altar in Gerizim"!   The Samaritans in Alexandria
desired to make a protest against the translation, or
rather against the alleged falsification, of the text,
and as some of their number were in favour at court,
they induced the mild Philometor to appoint a conference between the two religious sects, at which the
question of the superior sanctity of the Samaritan or
of the Judæan Temple should be decided.   This was
the first religious dispute held before a temporal
ruler.   The two parties chose the most learned men
among them as their advocates.   On the side of the
Judæans appeared a certain Andronicus, the son of

Messalam, whilst the Samaritans had two champions, Sabbai and Theodosius. In what manner the religious conference was carried on, and what its consequences were, cannot now be ascertained, the accounts that have come down to us having assumed a legendary form; each party claimed the victory, and both exaggerated its effects. Religious disputations have never yet achieved any real results. The Judæan historians pretend that an arrangement had been made to the effect that it should be the right and the duty of the king to put to death those who were defeated in argument—a statement for which there is no foundation. When the Jewish advocates pointed out the long roll of high-priests from Aaron down to their own time who had officiated in the Temple at Jerusalem, and how that Temple had been enriched by holy gifts from the kings of Asia,—advantages and distinctions which the Temple at Gerizim could not boast, the Samaritans were publicly declared to be vanquished, and according to agreement they were put to death. The Samaritan accounts, which are of a much later date and more confused, ascribe the victory to their side.

This controversy respecting the superior sanctity of Jerusalem or Shechem was, it appears, carried on in Greek verse. A Samaritan poet, Theodotus, praised the fertility of the country round Shechem, and in order to magnify the importance of that city he related the story of Jacob, describing how he rested there; also the ill-usage which his daughter Dinah received from the young nobles of Shechem, and the revenge taken upon them by her brothers, Simeon and Levi. In opposition to Theodotus, a Judæan poet, Philo the Elder, exalted the greatness of Jerusalem in a poem. He extolled the fertility of the Judæan capital, and spoke of its ever-flowing subterranean waters, which were conducted through channels from the spring of the

High Priest.   The poet endeavoured to enhance the
sanctity of the Temple in Jerusalem, which stood on
Mount Moriah, on the summit of which Abraham
had been about to offer up his son Isaac—an act
which shed everlasting glory upon all his descendants.

Meanwhile, the sky which, during the reign of
Philometor, had shone so brightly over the Judæans
in Alexandria, became dark and threatening.   It
seemed as if the parent state and its offshoot were
linked together for good or evil.   Prosperous and
adverse days appeared to visit the two communities
almost in the same alternation.   Through the misfortune of Jonathan, Judæa had fallen into adversity, and a new reign in Egypt had brought trouble
and sorrow to the Judæans in Alexandria.   That
same Ptolemy VII. (Physcon), who had reigned
many years with Philometor and had conspired to
destroy him, sought, after his death, to obtain the
crown in spite of the existence of a rightful heir.
The novelty-loving, fickle and foolish populace of
Alexandria was inclined to recognise as king the
deformed and wicked Physcon.   The widowed
queen, Cleopatra, who had governed during her
son's minority, had likewise many adherents, and in
particular Onias was devoted to her cause.   When
war broke out between Cleopatra and her hostile
brother, Onias with his Judæan army received as their
share of the spoil one district or province.   At last a
compromise was effected, in virtue of which Physcon
was to marry his sister, and both were to reign together.   This doubly incestuous marriage was most
unhappy.   No sooner had the inhuman Physcon entered Alexandria than he put to death, not only the followers of the rightful heir, but also the youth himself,
who was slain on the very day on which Physcon married Cleopatra.   Bitter enmity between king and
queen, brother and sister, was the consequence of this
cruel deed   The sensual and barbarous monster vio-

lated his wife's daughter, and filled Alexandria with
terror and bloodshed, causing the greater part of the
inhabitants to flee from the city.   Was it likely that he
would spare the Judæans who, as he well knew, were
the supporters of his hated sister and wife?   Having
heard that Onias was bringing an army to her assistance, he ordered his soldiers to seize all the Judæans
in Alexandria, with their wives and their children,
and to cast them bound and naked upon a public
place, to be trampled to death by elephants.   The
animals were intoxicated with wine in order to irritate
and excite them against their helpless victims.   But
the latter were rescued from impending death in a
manner which seemed miraculous to the trembling,
unhappy Judæans.   The enraged beasts rushed to
the side where the king's people were seated awaiting
the cruel spectacle, and many of them were killed,
while the Judæans were unhurt.   The Alexandrian
Judæans kept the day of their heaven-sent deliverance as a perpetual memorial.   From this time,
indeed, Physcon appears to have left the Judæans unmolested.   Indeed, during the remainder of his reign
their literary ardour and their zeal for the acquisition
of knowledge increased greatly, and their writers
appear to have applied themselves undisturbed to
their works.   Physcon himself was an author, and
wrote memoirs and memorabilia, dealing with historical events and facts in natural history.   A Judæan
called Judah Aristobulus is said to have been his or
his brother's master.

Whilst the Alexandrian-Judæan community was
occupying a high intellectual position, the Judæan
people in their own land attained a lofty political
eminence, from which they could look proudly back
on their former abject state.   What progress they
had made during the reign of Jonathan is clearly
shown by the simple comparison of their condition
after his death, with that in which they found themselves at the fall of Judas.   Judas's successor at first

had been able to draw around him only a handful of faithful followers; a leader without right or title, he possessed neither fortresses, nor means of defence or attack, and was hard pressed by enemies at home and abroad. Jonathan's successor, on the contrary, Simon Tharsi, the last of the heroic sons of Mattathias, inheriting a recognised title, and being invested with the dignity of high-priest, became at once the ruler of a powerful people. He found strong fortresses in the land, and but one enemy in his path, who had already been much weakened by his predecessor. Jonathan's death, therefore, was followed by no disastrous results to the nation, but served to inflame the whole people to avenge the noble Hasmonæan high-priest upon his crafty murderer. Simon had simply to step into the vacant leadership. Although approaching old age at the time when he became the leader of his people, he still possessed the freshness of youth and the fiery courage which marked him when his dying father directed him to be the wise counsellor in the then impending war against Syrian despotism. So vigorous was the Hasmonæan race that few indeed of their members could be accused of cowardice or weakness, and the greater number of them evinced till their last breath the strength and courage of youth. By the side of Simon stood his four sons, Jonathan, Judah, Mattathias, and one whose name is unknown, who had all been moulded into warriors by the constant fighting in which they had been engaged. Simon, following the policy of his brothers, took advantage of the weakness of the enemy to increase the defences and strength of his country, and to extend the dominion of Judæa; but he achieved even more, for he delivered his people completely from Syrian rule and raised Judæa to the rank of an independent nation. Simon's government, which lasted almost nine years, was therefore rightly described as glorious. The aged were allowed to enjoy their closing days in peace; while the young rejoiced in the exercise of their activity and strength; "they sat every one under his vine and fig tree, with none to make them afraid."

Simon's first step was an act of independence. Without waiting, as had been the custom hitherto, for the confirmation of the Syrian princes, he accepted at once the office of high-priest offered him by the people. To provide against the war which this step of his might bring on, he hastened to provision and place in a state of defence the fortresses of Judæa. He also opened negotiations with the dethroned king Demetrius II., although the latter had repaid Jonathan's assistance with base ingratitude. Simon sent him, through a solemn embassy, a golden crown as an acknowledgment of his regal power, and promised him aid against Tryphon on condition that the independence of Judæa should be fully recognised by a complete release from payment of taxes and services. The result justified his calculations. Demetrius willingly accepted Simon's offer, hoping to assure himself of a faithful ally, who would assist him in a possible war against Tryphon. He wrote "to the high-priest and Friend of the King, to the elders and the people of Judæa," as follows : " We have received the golden crown which you have sent us, and we are ready to make a lasting treaty of peace with you, and to write to our administrators that we remit your taxes. What we have granted you shall remain yours. The fortresses that you have erected shall be yours. We give you absolution for all the offences, intentional as well as unintentional, that you have committed against us up to this day ; we release you from the crown which you owe us, and we remit the taxes that were laid on Jerusalem. If there be any among you anxious and fit to enter our army, they may be enlisted, and let there be peace between us." The day on which this immunity had been granted was considered by the Judæans so important and valued an era, that its date, the 27th of Iyar (May), was recorded among the half-holidays commemorative of victory.

The people looked upon these concessions of Demetrius as the inauguration of their independence, and from that epoch the customary manner of counting time according to the years of the reigning Syrian king was discontinued. They now reckoned from the date of Simon's accession to the government. All legal documents of the year 142 were dated "In the first year of Simon, the High-Priest, Commander of the Army and Prince of the Nation." Confident of their strength, the people anticipated this royal prerogative for their leader, who was not at that time entitled to it, for he had as yet been recognised as the legitimate prince neither by Syria nor by the nation. Simon himself does not appear to have looked upon the concessions received as sufficient to bestow complete independence upon his country, but dated his reign from a later year, when he obtained the right of coining money. The joy experienced by the inhabitants of Jerusalem at the recovery of their freedom, the loss of which they had bitterly bewailed since the destruction of the Judæan kingdom under their last king Zedekiah, was so great that the elders or members of the Great Council felt impelled to communicate the all-important event to the Judæans in Egypt. In doing so however, they had to overcome a serious difficulty: so to word their communication as not to offend Onias, the founder of the Onias Temple, the descendant of the family of high-priests which, by the acts of the Hasmonæans in Judæa, had been completely and hopelessly supplanted. Even supposing that Onias or his sons had entirely relinquished the prospect of ever possessing the office of high-priest, it must have been painful to remind them, and their followers in Egypt, that their family had been thrust aside by the people in Judæa.

The representatives of the nation managed to pass lightly over this difficult subject, and descanted upon the fact that, after their long sufferings and persecutions, God had heard their prayer, and had once more given them the power of offering sacrifices, of re-kindling the holy lights, and of placing the shew-bread in the Temple, which had been spoiled by the enemy and polluted by the shedding of innocent blood. This delicate statement, which carefully avoided giving any offence to the Judæans in Egypt, appears to have produced a very favourable impres-sion upon them. They likewise rejoiced at the recovered independence of Judæa, and ascribed great importance to the year in which it was obtained.

The second noteworthy act of Simon consisted in driving out the remaining Hellenists from their various hiding-places in the Acra at Jerusalem, and in the fortresses of Gazara and Bethsur, and in completely destroying any influence they may have possessed. Gazara surrendered unconditionally. Simon allowed · the Hellenists to leave the place, and ordered their dwellings to be cleared of their idolatrous images. The Hellenists in the Acra, how-ever, had fortified their position so well that Simon was obliged to lay siege to it, and to reduce its defenders by famine. At last they were overcome, and the victors entered the Acra to the sound of music and with solemn hymns of praise. In com-memoration of the taking of the Acra, the 23rd Iyar (May 17) was ordered thenceforth to be kept as a day of rejoicing. The taking of Bethsur appears to have caused little difficulty. Of the expelled Hel-lenists, some, it seems, found refuge in Egypt, others renounced their idolatrous practices, and were again received into the community, whilst those who re-mained unchanged fell victims to the religious zeal of the conquerors. It is related that the 22nd Elul (Sep-tember) was set apart among the days of victory, because it saw the death of those idolators who had allowed the respite of three days to elapse without returning to their faith. Thus at length disappeared the last vestiges of that party which, during nearly

forty years, had shaken the foundations of Judaism
and which, in its apostate zeal, had called down upon
the people the calamities of civil contests and cruel
religious persecution, and brought a country to the
verge of ruin.   The fortresses which Simon had
taken from the Hellenists, Bethsur and Gazara, were
remodelled, so as to serve as places of defence.
Of great importance, likewise, was the capture of
Joppa (Jaffa), by the acquisition of which seaport the
State received a large revenue ; the export and import duties, which the Syrian kings had introduced,
now fell to the share of Judæa.

The Acra underwent a peculiar change at the
hands of the last of the Hasmonæan brothers.   The
wrath of the people against this fortress was too
intense to allow of its standing intact.   Apart from
political considerations, there was also a religious
sentiment adverse to its continuing unaltered.   The
fortress, with its lofty towers, which the Syrians had
erected to keep the city in check, overtopped the
Temple-capped mount itself, and this was not to be.
According to the prophecies of Isaiah, "in the last
days the Mountain of the House of the Lord was to
be established on the top of the mountains, and be
exalted above the hills."   This was literally explained
to mean that no mount or building was to overtop
the Temple, and Simon, even if unconvinced himself,
was obliged to bow to that belief.   On the other
hand, however, it seemed imprudent to destroy a fortress which, like the Acra, was so conveniently situated for the accommodation of troops, and so well
fitted to serve as a storehouse for arms.   Simon and
his counsellors hit upon a middle course in dealing
with it.   The towers and bastions of the fortress were
taken down—a work of destruction which, it is said,
it cost the people three years to accomplish; the walls,
courts and halls, on the contrary, were left standing
but the hated name of Acra or Acrapolis was no
longer used, but changed for that of Birah (Baris),

which had first been introduced by Nehemiah. In this transformed edifice the Judæan soldiers were quartered, and there they kept their weapons. Simon himself dwelt in the Birah in the midst of his soldiers, while his son Johanan (John), as governor of the sea-coast, resided at Gazara.

In spite of the favourable position in which he found himself, Simon was obliged to remain armed and prepared for war. At present the two pretenders to the throne, whilst they weakened each other, left him in peace. Demetrius II. (Nicator), who had granted independence to Judæa, was now engaged in an adventurous expedition in the east against Persia. His brother, Antiochus Sidetes, governed in his place, and was at strife with Diodotus Tryphon, who, having treacherously killed Jonathan and the young Antiochus, the son of Alexander Balas, had made himself ruler over Syria. Simon, urged by political motives to weaken this cunning, evil-minded enemy, assisted Antiochus Sidetes, and received from him the confirmation of the privileges granted to Judæa by his brother in the hour of his need. In addition thereto, Antiochus gave Simon the right of coining money, which was the especial mark of independence.

Unfortunately, as is but too often the case, the hand that planted the tree of liberty, also placed the gnawing worm in the noble blossom. Wanting as he was in that far-sightedness which belonged to the genius of the prophets of old, and guided only by present emergencies, Simon believed that he would ensure the hard-won independence of his country if he obtained for it the protection of that people which, never tired of making conquests and aggrandising itself, was constantly and everywhere the foe of liberty. In order to put an end to the ceaseless provocations given by the petty Syrian tyrants, Simon entrusted the welfare of his country to the mighty tyrant, Rome, in whose close embraces the nations that sought protection were unfailingly suffocated. Simon despatched as delegates Numenius, the son of Antiochus, and Antipater, the son of Jason. They carried with them a heavy golden shield and a golden chain, which, in the hope of gaining for the Judæans the favour of being received as allies of Rome, they were to present as a mark of homage.

The Roman Senate was not indisposed to enroll the most insignificant nation among their allies, being well aware that in granting the favour of their protection they had taken the first step towards reducing it to vassalage. Rome resembles an unfaithful guardian, who takes infinite care of the property of his ward, only to gather riches for himself. The Roman Senate made known to their friends and vassals that they had accepted Judæa as their ally, and the Syrian rulers were forbidden to attack it (140). Scarcely two hundred years later, a shameless, bloodthirsty Roman Emperor will insist upon being worshipped in the Temple at Jerusalem, and after another thirty years will have passed, Rome will break the strength of the Judæan nation, kill its heroes, and hunt its sons like wild beasts. But these dire results of the Roman alliance were unsuspected by Simon or his contemporaries, who rejoiced at being called friends, brothers and allies of the great Roman nation. In order to show their gratitude to their leader for the boon he had procured for them, the Jewish people conferred upon him, with great solemnity, supreme and permanent sovereignty over themselves.

One can hardly find, in all antiquity, a similar example of absolute power thus bestowed upon a prince, and of a quiet, peaceful transformation of a republic into a monarchy like that carried into effect by the people of Judæa at that time. The deed which endorsed this gift of the monarchy to Simon is preserved in a record, which places strikingly before us the gratitude felt towards the Hasmonæans by the newly-constituted nation.

On the 28th Elul (September) of the year 140, the third year of Simon's tenure of the high-priesthood, the priests, the elders and representatives of the nation, and all the people of Jerusalem were assembled, probably upon the Temple Mount, and there agreed, in recognition of the great services rendered by Simon and the Hasmonæans to the people and the Sanctuary, to consider him and his descendants as their leader (Nassi) and High-Priest, "until such time as a prophet should arise." As the outward sign of his dignity, Simon was to wear a purple mantle with a golden clasp. All public acts were to be in his name; peace and war were to be decided upon by him; he was to have sole power to appoint the commanders of the army and the fortresses, as well as the managers of the Temple and all its sacred trusts. Whoever opposed him was liable to punishment.

This decree of the people, a copy of which was deposited in the Temple archives, was engraven on brass tablets, which were placed in a conspicuous position in the Temple court; and besides, memorial columns in its honor were erected on Mount Zion. In spite of their antipathy to the customs of the neighbouring Greeks, the Judæans had learned from them the art of immortalising their deeds in stone and metal. Unlike the Greeks, however, they were not capricious in the honours and favours they granted. Those to whom monuments were erected one day were not bespattered with mud the next, but, on the contrary, lived forever in the grateful hearts of their countrymen. Israel had now again a prince lawfully chosen by the people, having been deprived of a ruler for the space of nine jubilees, ever since the captivity of Zedekiah. If the nation did not give Simon the title of king, but only that of prince, it was not done in order to lessen his power in any way, but that they might remain faithful to the house of David. According to the views held at that time in Judæa, it was only a descendant of David who could be king, he being also the expected Messiah. The deed which gave the sovereign power to Simon contained the proviso that he should, therefore, retain it until the appearance of the true prophet Elijah, who was expected to be the precursor of the Messiah.

It was not until Simon had been formally recognised as ruler, that he made use of the right to coin money granted him by Antiochus Sidetes. This was the first time that Judæan coins were struck. On one side was stamped the value of the coin with the inscription " Shekel of Israel "; on the other, the words " Jerusalem the Holy " (Jerushalaim Hakkedosha), the date being indicated by an abbreviation. Emblems of the high-priesthood of Israel were used as devices for the coins; upon one side was engraven a blossoming branch (Aaron's staff); upon the other a sort of cup, probably representing a vessel for incense. But Simon's name or dignity, his title of prince or high-priest, did not appear on them. The letters used in the inscriptions were old Hebrew or Samaritan, probably because these characters were familiar to the nations around, whilst they would have been unable to decipher the new ones. The earliest date we find on the coins of Simon is that of the fourth year of his reign, from which we may infer that it was not till some years after he had assumed the regal powers (about 139) that he commenced coining money.

Friendly as Antiochus Sidetes had shown himself towards Simon whilst he had but little hope of defeating the usurper Tryphon, his demeanour completely changed as soon as, by the help of the Judæans, he had nearly attained his aim, and he became as cold as he had previously been gracious and well disposed. To avoid the appearance of ingratitude in his subsequent conduct, Antiochus sent back the two thousand troops, as well as the money with which Simon had supplied him for the siege of the town of Dora (139)

The Syrian king despatched his general Cendebæus to Simon to reproach him for having overstepped the limits of independence granted to him, and with having taken the Syrian possessions, Joppa, Gazara and the Acra in Jerusalem, without offering any compensation. He therefore called upon Simon to restore those places or to pay a thousand talents of silver. Simon replied that he had only recovered the former inheritance of his fathers, but was ready to give a hundred talents for Joppa and Gazara. The dispute, however, could not be settled by friendly means, but was left to the arbitrament of the sword.

Whilst Antiochus himself pursued Tryphon, who had escaped from the fortress of Dora, he sent troops of infantry and cavalry under the general Cendebæus, the Hyrcanian, to invade Judæa, and bring the whole country again under the Syrian rule. Simon prepared for a hard struggle. Fortunately he could assemble a considerable army, 20,000 men, and he was able to raise troops of cavalry, the want of which on former occasions had been so disastrous to Judæa. Simon, being too old to take an active part in the war, named as his generals his two sons, Johanan (John) and Judah, who marched out of Gazara against the enemy. In the meantime Cendebæus had penetrated into the country as far as Ekron, plundering the inhabitants and carrying away captive those who dwelt in the lowlands. On a plain situated between Ekron (which Cendebæus fortified) and Modin, a battle was fought and gained by the Judæans. Cendebæus and his army were defeated and pursued to Azotus, which town, having offered resistance, was destroyed by fire. Johanan, to whom the success of the campaign was chiefly due, received in commemoration of his victory over the Hyrcanian, the name Hyrcanus. This was the last war which took place in Simon's time (137–136), and it inspired him with confidence in the capacity of his sons to uphold the aspiring power of

Judæa. Antiochus was still more embittered against Simon by the defeat his arms had suffered, but, too weak to attempt a new attack, he now had recourse to stratagem, and hoped by a cunning plot to sweep from his path the whole family of the Hasmonæans, the obstinate and successful foes of his house. To accomplish this aim he strove to awaken the ambition and avarice of one who, being Simon's son-in-law, might easily find opportunities for committing the wished-for crime. This shameless man, Ptolemy ben Habub, was not held in check, either by gratitude or the ties of family affection, nor did feelings of reverence for one grown old in deeds of heroism or the love of his country restrain him. With his daughter's hand Simon had given him riches, and had made him governor of Jericho and the surrounding district, but the ambitious spirit of his son-in-law remained unsatisfied, and he was eager to seize upon the inheritance of Judæa, and with the help of the foreigner to rule in the kingdom. It was easy for Ptolemy to carry out the villainous design he had conceived, for the most vigilant and farseeing mind could hardly have suspected so base an act. In spite of Simon's great age it was his custom to visit all parts of the country, in order to make himself acquainted with the wants of the people and the manner in which the laws were administered. During one of these journeys he came to the fortress of Dok, near Jericho, where his son-in-law resided. He was accompanied by his wife and his two younger sons, Judah and Mattathias, but the elder one, John, had remained at his post at Gazara.

Ptolemy proffered friendly hospitality to the victims he meant to sacrifice; he prepared a splendid banquet for them, and whilst they were enjoying themselves at the feast, Ptolemy and his satellites fell upon and massacred Simon and his sons (Shebat, February, 135).

As soon as the crime had been committed, the

murderer sent messengers to the Syrian king, asking for troops to assist him in his ambitious designs. He also despatched soldiers to Gazara to assassinate John, and to Jerusalem to take possession of the city and the Temple. But Ptolemy was not to reap the expected reward of his treachery. A friend, who had managed to escape from the fortress of Dok, hurried to Gazara, and warned John of the impending danger, and as soon as the assassins reached the city they received the due punishment of their crime. John was likewise successful in reaching Jerusalem before Ptolemy, and had little difficulty in persuading the people to stand by him. The expected help from Antiochus also failed, doubtless because that king was engaged in warlike operations elsewhere, so that Ptolemy was obliged to shut himself up in his own fortress. Here he kept his mother-in-law imprisoned as a hostage, and prepared to defend himself against the attacks which would probably be made upon him.

Thus perished Simon, the last of the Hasmonæan brothers, not one of whom had died a natural death, one and all having lost their lives in the service of their country and their faith. Judah and Eleazar were killed upon the field of battle, whilst John, Jonathan, and Simon less fortunate than their brothers, succumbed to the cruel treachery of the enemies of their people.

END OF VOL. I

INDEX.

Aaron, 12.
  called to join Moses, 15.
Aaronides. See Priests.
Abdon, the judge, 66.
Abiathar, advises Adonijah, 152.
  deposed, 168.
  high priest in Jerusalem, 120.
  priest of Nob, flees to David, 100.
  sides with David against Absalom, 141.
Abigail, wife of David, 134.
Abijah, son of Samuel, 79-80, 107.
Abijam, son of Rehoboam, 189.
Abimelech, son of Gideon, 63.
Abir = Apis, 11.
Abishai, brother of Joab, 126.
  defeats the Aramæans and Idumæans, 128.
Abner, Saul's cousin and general, 84-111.
  defeats the Philistines, 108.
  founder of the kingdom of the ten tribes, 108 f.
  murdered by Joab and Abishai, 111.
  negotiates secretly with David, 110.
Abraham and his descendants, 4-6.
Absalom, avenging Tamar, kills Amnon, his half-brother, 134.
  defeated and killed by Joab, 144.
  intrigues against David, 136.
  rebellion of, 138.
Achish, the Philistine, and David, 100.
Achitub, grandson of Eli, at Nob, 79.
Acra, fortress of, 433, 470, 477, 495, 496 and 498.
  Hellenists expelled from, 523.
  in the hands of Simon and called Birah, 524.
Adarsa, battle of, 485.
Adonai Zebaoth = Lord of hosts, 130.
Adonijah, acknowledges Solomon, 154.
  declared king by his friends, 151.
  fourth son of David, 135.
  killed by Solomon through Benaiah, 160.

Adoniram, chief superintendent of Solomon, 163, 172.
  killed by the Shechemites, 182.
Agag, the Amalekite, defeated by Saul, 91.
  killed by Samuel at Gilgal, 93.
Ahab, Omri's son and successor marries Jezebel, 194.
  and Elijah, 202 ff.
  character of, 196.
  death of, 206.
  takes Naboth's vineyard, 202.
  war with Benhadad II., 205.
Ahaz, king of Judah, 257.
  calls Tiglath-Pileser to assist him, 258.
Ahaziah, Ahab's son, king of Israel, 206-7.
  Jehoram's son, king of Judah killed by Jehu's followers, 211.
Ahijah, of Shiloh, the prophet, 175
  rebukes Jeroboam for his idolatry, 187 f.
Ahikam, son of Shaphan, 303.
Ahishar, major-domo of Solomon, 172.
Ahithophel, David's adviser, 122.
  grandfather of Bathsheba, 133.
  hangs himself, 143.
  intrigues against David, 138.
Ai, Israelites defeated at, 33.
  taken by the Israelites, 33 f.
Akko, 3.
Alcimus = Jakim, the high priest, 482-508.
  returns to Jerusalem, 487.
Alexander Balas, king of Syria, 494-6,
  the Great, and the Judæans, 412-15.
  's successors, struggles between, 416.
Alexandria, importance of, 504.
  and the Judæans, 418, 503.
Alexandrian Judæans influence those in Jerusalem, 427.
Allegorical poems of Solomon, 158.
  poetry long before Solomon, 159.
Allotment of land to the tribes, 36 f.

Idolatry introduced by Jeroboam I. and II., 186, 233.
Israelites influenced by, 57.
of the nations surrounding Israel, 54 ff.
of the Phœnicians in Israel under Omri and Ahab, 195 ff.
of the wealthy exiles, 340.
permitted by Solomon, 175.
to be spurned, 41.

Idumæans, assisted by Egypt, defeat Judah, 226 f.
defeated by Abishai, 128.
defeated by Uzziah (Azariah), 230.
fight the Israelites, 27.
intercourse of the Israelites with, 55.
kill fugitive Judæans, 318.
make settlements in Southern Judæa, 325.
remain enemies of Judæa, 435, 474.
subdued by Amaziah, 222.

Impurity, laws concerning purity and, 401.

Indian trade of Solomon, 169.
renewed by Uzziah (Azariah), 130.

Inhabitants of Canaan, original, 1.

Intermarriages between Israelites and their neighbours, 56.
between Judæans and their neighbours, 361.
dissolved and forbidden by Ezra, 367–9, 386.
practised again, 383.

Internal affairs of the Alexandrian community, 504.
conflicts in Judæa after the death of Maccabæus, 491.
government of Israel under David, 121, 154.
government of Israel under Saul, 90.
government of Israel under Solomon, 162, 172.

Ipsus, battle at, 417.

"Iron sea" of Solomon's temple, 165.

Isaiah, Amoz's son, of Jerusalem, 251–4.
disciples of, 253.
's efforts to restrain Hezekiah from war with Assyria, 270.
immediate and permanent effect of the speeches of, 252–3.
opposes Ahaz's seeking Assyrian help, 258.

iah, predicts Jerusalem's deliverance, 272.
sons of, 251, 258–9.

Isaiah, the Babylonian, 344 ff.
Isaiah i. 11–14, 253; ii. 2–4, 243; vi. and vii., 252, 258; viii. 5–8, 259; x. 5–xi. 10, 272; xxii. 1–14, 16–25, 271; xxviii. 1–4, 266; xxix. 13, 253; xl., 345; xlii. 1–4, 347; liii. 3–7, 344; lv. 12, 355; lvi. 7, 347; lxiv. 9, 325; lxvi. 1, 5, 348, 349.

Ishbosheth and David, 106–124.

Ishmael, son of Nethaniah, 317, 321.
flees to Egypt, 323.
murders Gedaliah, 322.

Isolation of the tribes, 36.

Israel = Jacob, 7.

Israel and Judah, kingdoms of, 182 ff.
at Goshen, 7.
claim of, to Canaan, 4.
distinctions of the land of, 42.
end of kingdom of, 265.
remnant of = kingdom of Judah, 266.

Israel under Eli and Samuel, 68–81.
under the judges, 60–67.
"   King David and Ishbosheth, 106–24.
under David, 125–55.
"   Saul, 82–105.
"   Solomon, 156–78.
"   Ahab, 196–206.
"   Ahaziah, 206.
"   Ba'asha, 189–91.
"   Elah, 191.
"   Hoshea 263.
"   Jehoahaz, 221.
"   Jehoash, 221 f.
"   Jehoram, 207.
"   Jehu, 211.
"   Jeroboam I., 182–9.
"   Jeroboam II., 225–43.
"   Menahem, 244–7.
"   Nadab, 189.
"   Omri, 192–6.
"   Pekah, 248.
"   Pekahiah, 248.
"   Shallum, 244.
"   Tibni, 192.
"   Zechariah, 243.
"   Zimri, 192.

Israelites and Egyptians, 7.
and the neighbouring nations, 53.
crossing the Jordan, 29.
exodus of, from Egypt, 17.
influenced by their pagan surroundings, 51 f.

Shechem, 4, 36.
capital of Jeroboam, 180.
Shechemites' feud with Abimelech, 63.
Shefelah = low country, 45.
Shemaiah, the prophet, prevents a civil war between Judæans and Benjamites, 184.
Shiloh (Salem), ark of the covenant at, 41, 57.
at the time of the Judges, 69.
destroyed by the Philistines, 71.
Shimei executed by Solomon, 160 f.
of Bahurim reviles David, 142.
pretends enthusiasm for the returning king, 147.
Shir-ha-shirim = song of songs, 431.
Shishak of Egypt inimical to Israel, 176.
assists Jeroboam against Rehoboam, 184.
Shobi, Hanun's brother, assists David against Absalom, 144.
becomes king of the Ammonites, 129.
Shofetim = judges, 59.
Sidon, 3.
Sihon slain by the Israelites at Jahaz, 27–29.
Simeon and Judah assist the other tribes under Samuel, 76.
tribe of, merged in the tribe of Judah, 39.
Simon I. the Just and his descendants, 420.
improvements of, 421.
's children, 423.
Simon II., the high priest, 432.
Simon, the Benjamite, 437 f.
Simon, brother of Judas Maccabæus, 459, 461, 475, 489, 498.
and Demetrius II., 521.
at the head of the nation, 500–31.
becomes high priest, 521.
defeats the Syrians, 493.
expels the Hellenists, 523.
killed by his son-in-law, 530.
quarrels with the Syrian king, 528.
Simon's coinage, 525, 528.
league with the Romans, 525.
sons defeat Cendebæus, 529.
Sinai, Mount, 20.
Sirach, Jesus, 439.
Sisera defeated by Barak and slain by Jael, 61.
Sochen = superintendent of the palace, 249, 268.
Solomon, 133–77.

Solomon, and queen of Sheba, 173–4.
anointed king during David's life time, 153.
author of allegorical poems, 158.
causes the murder of Adonijah and Joab, 160.
David's successor, 153.
discontent of tribes against, 174.
king over Israel, 156–78.
Solomon's buildings, 162.
children, 177.
choice of wisdom, 158.
court, 161.
death, 177.
fleet, 170.
greatness, 156.
temple, 162.
weaknesses, 157.
Song of Deborah, 61.
Moses, 293.
Song of songs, 430 f.
Songs of praise, an element in worships, 78, 120.
Songs of praise by David, 120 f.
Songs of war, the earliest Hebrew poetry, 29.
Songs of the prophets, 200, 205, 234, 253.
Sopheric age, the, 389 ff.
regulations, 395.
Sopherim and schools, 396.
Spirit, prophetic, and its meaning, 14.
Successors of Alexander the Great, 416.
Supreme Council of the Judæans, 394.
Symmetry in Hebrew poetry, 29.
Synagogues, 401.
Syrians. See Seleucidæ.

Tabernacles, Feast of, 380.
Tabor, Mount, 44.
Talmide Chachamim, 396.
Tamar seduced by her half-brother Amnon, 134.
Tax-collector, Joseph appointed as, 425.
Tekoa, Amos of, 235.
Tekoah, wise woman of, 136.
Temple at Jerusalem planned by David, 150.
built by Solomon, 162 ff.
cleansed and repaired by Josiah, 288, 294.
consecrated (1007 B. C.), 166.
defiled by Antiochus Epiphanes 451, 454. See also Sacrilege.